Empire and Islam

COMPARATIVE STUDIES ON MUSLIM SOCIETIES

General Editor, Barbara D. Metcalf

1. William R. Roff, ed., *Islam and the Political Economy of Meaning*
2. John Davis, *Libyan Politics: Tribe and Revolution*
3. Yohanan Friedmann, *Prophecy Continuous: Aspects of Aḥmadī Religious Thought and Its Medieval Background*
4. Katherine P. Ewing, ed., *Sharīʿat and Ambiguity in South Asian Islam*
5. Edmund Burke, III, and Ira M. Lapidus, eds., *Islam, Politics, and Social Movements*
6. J. R. I. Cole, *Roots of North Indian Shīʿism in Iran and Iraq: Religion and State in Awadh, 1722–1859*
7. David Gilmartin, *Empire and Islam: Punjab and the Making of Pakistan*

common political status in British Indian society, inculcated by the press and popular electoral politics, communalism produced that sense of "deep, horizontal comradeship," which Benedict Anderson argues has defined the modern national community.[9] This development was encouraged by the British themselves, who defined Muslim identity in the census and in politics as an ethnic category, encompassing all Muslims equally and defining their common relationship to the political system.[10] Nothing symbolized this status more clearly than the existence of separate electorates for Muslims, introduced by the British into the twentieth-century political system. With the increasing importance of popular electoral politics, Muslim leaders appealed to this communal Muslim identity, using Islamic symbols (and a common Islamic terminology) to mobilize popular support. The appeal to Islamic symbols thus fixed the political existence of a "community" of equal and like-minded Muslims in the minds of many Indian Muslims. Communal rhetoric paved the way for the definition of an "imagined" political community—a nation—whose presence justified the emergence of an independent state.

But however important the emergence of such an "imagined" community, communalism cannot explain the full history of the movement for Pakistan. The power of communalism lay in the fact that it linked the religious identity of the individual directly to the larger cultural identity of the state. But the "communal" image of Muslim India nevertheless remained a product of politics within a limited segment of Muslim Indian society. The concept of a "community" of equal and like-minded Muslims, however deep its symbolic roots in the pristine history of early Islam, gained force and believability in the nineteenth and twentieth centuries largely through the growing power of the press and the pamphlet in India's cities. For the great majority of India's Muslims, the concept of Muslim community had long carried a very different meaning. For most rural Muslims the concept of Islamic "community" was one constructed not from ideas drawn from the press or from the public rhetoric of colonial politics, but from local organization and ritual. The structures of kin-based organization that defined the contours of local life shaped also the broader concept of Islamic community. Hardly a community of equal and like-minded believers, the religious community of rural Islam was rooted in ideas of spiritual inequality, mediation, and hierarchy.

9. Benedict Anderson, *Imagined Communities: Reflections on the Origin and Spread of Nationalism* (London: Verso, 1983), 16.

10. Kenneth Jones, "Religious Identity and the Indian Census," in N. Gerald Barrier, ed., *The Census in British India: New Perspectives* (New Delhi: Manohar, 1981), 83–85.

Munir seven years after Pakistan's creation. Jinnah's idea, he wrote, was of a "nation," in which religion was "to have nothing to do with the business of the State and to be merely a matter of personal faith for the individual."[6] For many, this was a contradiction in terms. As Munir well realized, Pakistanis had sharply differing ideas about the religious meaning of Pakistan.

Recent debate on the nature of the Pakistani state in fact has focused attention on Islam's political role in the movement. Many historians ascribe the origins of the movement's particular combination of Islamic symbolism and practical politics to *communalism,* a political style emphasizing the importance of religious "community" in politics and combining an appeal to religious symbols with an attempt to mobilize support within the structure of colonial politics. In describing communalism's causes and contours, some historians have emphasized the normative role of the Islamic religious tradition itself—with its strong emphasis on "community"—in predisposing Muslim political leaders in India to a twentieth-century "communal" political style.[7] Others stress the ready availability of various Islamic symbols for manipulation by Muslim political leaders developing their constituencies within the contexts of colonial politics.[8] But nearly all historians see communalism's development as a critical backdrop to the coming of Pakistan.

Most have assumed, in fact, a direct line of development from Muslim "communalism" to Muslim "separatism" to Pakistan's creation. Few accept Jinnah's "two-nation theory," with its implication of a Muslim "nation," stretching backward in time, as anything more than a historical justification for a claim to twentieth-century nationhood. But most historians have seen the emergence of a sense of nationality among many twentieth-century Muslims as rooted deeply in the communal political style that was a product of the colonial era. Based on a sense of

6. Punjab, *Report of the Court of Inquiry Constituted Under Punjab Act II of 1954 to Enquire into the Punjab Disturbances of 1953* (Lahore: Government Printing, 1954), 201.

7. Francis Robinson, "Islam and Muslim Separatism," in David Taylor and Malcolm Yapp, eds., *Political Identity in South Asia* (London: Curzon Press, 1979), 78. Mushirul Hasan develops similar ideas in *Nationalism and Communal Politics in India* (Columbia, Mo.: South Asia Books, 1979), 306.

8. See, for this view, Paul Brass, *Language, Religion, and Politics in North India* (London: Cambridge University Press, 1974); and Brass's defense of his position against Robinson: "Elite Groups, Symbol Manipulation, and Ethnic Identity among the Muslims of South Asia," in Taylor and Yapp, *Political Identity in South Asia.* Brass stresses the manipulation of symbols by elites protecting their political power, an argument used earlier by nationalists such as Nehru. Following W. C. Smith, many have seen the development of communalism as a product of the political strategies of an emerging Muslim middle class, competing with a more powerful Hindu middle class. See Wilfred Cantwell Smith, *Modern Islam in India* (Lahore: Sh. Muhammad Ashraf, 1969).

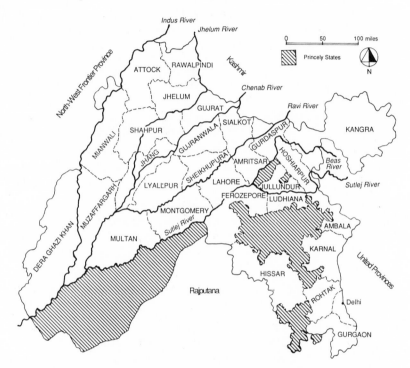

Map 1. *Districts of British Punjab (1931)*

the west; the history of Muslim empires had deeply influenced the urban Muslim presence in central and eastern Punjab, which in the twentieth century contained numerous cities and towns with predominantly Muslim populations. In most of the districts west of Lahore the Muslim population was overwhelmingly rural.[16] In the districts along the base of the Himalayas, where rainfall was greatest, this rural population had largely settled in nucleated villages. Of the Muslim-majority districts of Punjab, population density was greatest here.[17] In areas of less rainfall, south and west, the population had been far more sparse, settled primarily in the major river valleys. As late as the middle of the nineteenth century, the population of much of southern and western Punjab had been pastoralist, migrating between the river valleys and the *barr,* the flat upland tracts between the rivers. But in the late nineteenth and early twentieth centuries much of southwestern Punjab had come under canal irrigation—leading both to the settling of pastoralists and to the migration of settlers from central Punjab. This led to the implantation of an important rural Sikh minority in some areas, and to the growth of Hindu-dominated market towns. But in the canal colonies, as elsewhere in western Punjab, the great majority of the population remained Muslim and rural. From urban populations, with ties to the Mughal past, to only recently settled pastoral populations, the confession of Islam linked together peoples of wide diversity.

In the face of this diversity, Islam had historically served as a symbol of participation in a larger world. With the establishment of British rule, Islam continued to play this role, strongly influenced by the colonial state. The first three chapters of this book outline the imperial system of authority established by the British in Punjab, and the relationship of Islamic ideas and institutions to that system. The political role of Islam in British Punjab was embedded in the distinctive cultural relationship established by the British between the state and Punjabi society. The

16. Muslims also constituted an important part of the rural population in parts of eastern and central Punjab; and there were several Muslim towns of importance in the west. Overall, the percentage of Muslims in the urban population of Punjab varied little between the major geographical zones defined by the census, ranging between 50 and 56 percent in all regions except the heavily Hindu Himalayan zone. But in the western part of the province the proportion of Muslims in the rural population was as high as 80 percent (in the North-West Dry Area), whereas in the census zone including most of eastern and central Punjab (the Indo-Gangetic Plain West) the rural Muslim population was only 38 percent (Ibid., 321).

17. Ibid., 106. Compare rural density figures for Gurdaspur, Sialkot, and Gujrat districts with those for Shahpur, Mianwali, Jhang, or Multan. Though Lyallpur and Montgomery districts in southwestern Punjab also showed relatively high rural density in 1931, these figures reflected canal colony settlement.

first chapter examines the structure and ideology of British rule in Punjab, showing how the British attempted to build an indigenous, hierarchical ideology of state authority by appealing directly to the political primacy of local Punjabi identities. The second chapter details the impact of this system on the province's Islamic institutions. Although it nurtured the mediatory Islamic institutions of the countryside, which were often rooted in local organization and hierarchy, the British system offered to Islamic authority no central symbolic focus. The tensions created by this system crystallized most clearly in Punjab's cities, examined in chapter three, where "communalism" emerged as a powerful force.

The crucial political conflicts of the decade after 1936—which led directly to Pakistan's creation—occupy the second half of this study. While a series of predominantly urban Muslim political parties challenged the colonial structure, which lacked central Islamic symbols, rural Muslim interests dominated Punjabi politics under the banner of the Unionist party, controlling the votes of the overwhelming majority of rural Muslims. But the increasing "democratization" of the political system threw into sharp focus the growing tension between the communalism of the cities and the Islamic structure of the Punjabi countryside. Faced with increasing conflict within the structure of British imperial power, Muslim leaders sought in the concept of Pakistan a new symbolic Islamic foundation for the political order. The demand for Pakistan reflected both an ideology of Muslim "national" solidarity rooted in the new institutions of urban, public life and a response to long-standing tensions in Muslim politics. As the British prepared to leave, the movement defined new cultural foundations for the state. But it also inherited a system of state authority developed under British imperial rule. As Pakistan emerged in 1947, its legacies were, equally, empire and Islam.

University of California Press
Berkeley and Los Angeles, California

University of California Press, Ltd.
London, England

© 1988 by
The Regents of the University of California

Library of Congress Cataloging-in-Publication Data
Gilmartin, David.
  Empire and Islam.
  (Comparative studies on Muslim societies ; 7)
  Bibliography: p.
  Includes index.
  1. Punjab (India)—Politics and government.
2. Pakistan movement. 3. Muslims—India—Punjab—
Politics and government. 4. Islam and politics—
India—Punjab. I. Title. II. Series.
DS485.P2G54 1988   954'.5   88-8592
ISBN 0-520-06249-3 (alk. paper)

Printed in the United States of America
1 2 3 4 5 6 7 8 9

Empire and Islam

Punjab and the Making of Pakistan

David Gilmartin

UNIVERSITY OF CALIFORNIA PRESS
Berkeley · Los Angeles · London

CHAPTER I

The British Imperial State

Will you be governed by the sword or the pen?
—*Inscription on Lawrence Statue, Lahore*

From its pedestal outside the Lahore High Court, John Lawrence's statue demanded that Punjabis choose how they would be governed. "Head thrown back and legs astride," a sword in one hand and a pen in the other, Lawrence's statue confronted Punjabis in the heyday of British rule with what seemed a simple choice.[1] But the choice, as Lawrence and other administrators knew, was no choice at all. Physical force underlay British colonial rule from the beginning. And yet British rule could not have survived without legitimizing principles.

To understand British rule in Punjab requires an examination of the structures of power through which the British controlled the Punjab and of the ideology of authority that defined the relationship of the colonial state to society. Punjabi administrators gained notoriety in the mid-nineteenth century for the direct, paternalistic style of administration known as "the Punjab school." But in the following decades, as Punjab officials evolved a bureaucratic style similar to that of the rest of India, they also began to articulate principles of authority that defined their relationship to Punjabi society and justified their control.

Punjabi administrators shared such principles, in their basic outlines, with British rulers in much of the rest of India. As Bernard Cohn argues, the period after the suppression of the Mutiny proved critical in the ideological constitution of British authority in India. With the direct as-

---

1. Erected in Lahore in the 1880s, the Lawrence statue was a focus of nationalist protest in the 1920s. "The pose," as one official noted, "has been not infelicitously described as that of a foreman haranguing a gang of coolies" (National Archives of India [NAI], Home Political; file 53, 1923).

sumption of authority by the British crown in 1858, the British became, in a sense, "insiders" in India for the first time. "A theory of authority became codified," Cohn argues, "based on ideas and assumptions about the proper ordering of groups in Indian society, and their relationship to their British rulers."[2] For the British, notions of hierarchy lay at the center of this imperial structure. "A social order was established with the British crown seen as the centre of authority, and capable of ordering into a single hierarchy all its subjects, Indian and English."[3] This theory of hierarchy underscored the colonial state's claim to exclusive authority.

But the British linked this theory to careful analysis of the structure and organization of the society they ruled. As Cohn describes it, "The period from 1860 to 1877 saw a rapid expansion of what might be thought of as the definition and expropriation of Indian civilization by the imperial rulers."[4] "Knowledge" of India in all its aspects—"its life, thought, sociology, and history"—preoccupied the British. Like colonial rulers virtually everywhere, the British appealed to the newly developing "sciences" of social and historical study to order the society they ruled.[5] Relying on a detailed study of the indigenous social order, British administrators developed in the late nineteenth century the classifications and categories that defined and justified the hierarchies on which the imperial edifice rested.

In practice, clear statements of a British "ideology" of imperial rule are elusive at best—in the Punjab as elsewhere. Not all British administrators in Punjab agreed on the principles that legitimized their position as imperial rulers. Some stressed the opening of Punjab to "civilisation" and to the laws of political economy, to justify imperial authority.[6] But in seeking to rationalize their rule and to legitimize it in the eyes of the population, most Punjabi officials defined principles

    2. Bernard S. Cohn, "Representing Authority in Victorian India," in Eric Hobsbawm and Terence Ranger, eds., *The Invention of Tradition* (Cambridge: Cambridge University Press, 1983), 165.
    3. Ibid., 180.
    4. Ibid., 182.
    5. On the role of the new "sciences of man" in colonialism, see T. O. Ranger, "From Humanism to the Science of Man: Colonialism in Africa and the Understanding of Alien Societies," *Transactions of the Royal Historical Society* 26 (1976): 116–17. See also Roger Owen, "Anthropology and Imperial Administration: Sir Alfred Lyall and the Official Use of Theories of Social Change Developed in India after 1857," in Talal Asad, ed., *Anthropology and the Colonial Encounter* (London: Ithaca Press, 1973).
    6. For a discussion of British ideas about "political economy" in the Punjab, see P. H. M. van den Dungen, *The Punjab Tradition: Influence and Authority in Nineteenth-Century India* (London: George Allen & Unwin, 1972).

that tied the new hierarchies of the imperial order to Punjabi society. Though these principles reflected commonalities in the Indian colonial situation, they nevertheless shaped a distinctive Punjabi tradition. And in so doing, they created the ideological structures within which the politics of Punjab developed in the twentieth century.

THE BRITISH AND THE CUSTOMARY LAW

Nothing more clearly dramatized the nature of these principles than the system of colonial law developed in Punjab by the British. Although the law was but one element in the structure of imperial authority, it provided a critical arena for the enunciation of the principles defining the state's relationship to society. Most pre-British states in India drew such principles in important measure from religion. The Mughals, for example, for all their compromises with custom, based their legal system symbolically on principles of Islamic law. However often in practice they ignored the *shari'at* for political expediency or reasons of state, the Mughals, like other Indian Muslim states, maintained a symbolic commitment to *shari'at* as an important source of legitimation for their authority.[7]

By contrast, as an alien power that shared its religion with no significant portion of the population, the British found in religion little ideological foundation for the exercise of imperial power. The law in British India as a whole reflected paradoxes that were inherent in the nature of the colonial state. As David Washbrook argues, "The Anglo-Indian legal system was distinctly Janus-faced and rested on two contradictory principles with different social implications." Whereas the "public" side of the law encouraged the emergence of free market relations, personal law under the British encouraged the preservation of ascribed, "traditional" status.[8] In this regard, the law was an indicator of the conflicting purposes of colonial rule itself. On one level, the colonial state was the agent of an expanding commercial society, which had tied India into the world economy. But on another level, the state depended, for purposes of political control, on the maintenance of an indigenous political base. Even as the British bureaucratized the administration of the law, there-

7. Although the practical requirements of governing a largely non-Muslim population dictated many allowances for local custom, Mughal jurisprudence was grounded in principle on the *shari'at* (Muhammad Basheer Ahmad, *The Judicial System of the Mughal Empire* [Karachi: Pakistan Historical Society, 1978] 46, 52–54).
8. David Washbrook, "Law, State, and Agrarian Society in Colonial India," *Modern Asian Studies* 15, no. 3 (1981): 653–54.

fore, they elaborated British principles of commercial and criminal law
and drew on European scientific and bureaucratic technology to define
a legal system that underscored the state's power in Indian society. But
at the same time, they articulated indigenous principles of personal law,
some religious and some not, that linked the state to the organization of
Indian society.

Nowhere was this process more evident than in the system of "customary law" developed in the Punjab in the late nineteenth century. The
roots of this system lay in Lord Dalhousie's annexation dispatch of
1849, which called for upholding "Native Institutions and practices as
far as they are consistent with the distribution of justice." The Punjab
Laws Act of 1872, which established the primacy of "customary" over
religious law in the Punjabi legal system, made this principle official.[9] In
using "custom" as the foundation for a system of personal law that was
the equivalent of religious law, the British sought to order and classify
it so that it might be incorporated into a system of law enforced by
the state. The development of customary law thus required both an
effective bureaucratic apparatus and an effective analysis of indigenous
society—not only of "custom," but also of the "principles" of local social organization from which custom grew. The state's ability to analyze
indigenous customs even as it bureaucratically appropriated them for
its own use thus underscored both its legitimacy and its claim to imperial power.

The foundations of customary law were elaborated by a series of late
nineteenth-century colonial administrators. Most important among
these was C. L. Tupper, who prepared the first official compendium of
customary law in 1881. In analyzing Punjabi customs, Tupper argued
that one "native institution" was at the center of rural Punjabi social
organization: the "tribe." As the foundation of the rural social order,
the concept of *tribe* proved central to the definition of customary law.
Nevertheless, the term remained, for most British analysts, extremely
vague. For some, "tribes" differed little from the "castes" found in other
provinces of India. But in a Muslim-majority area, with a strong influence from the northwestern frontier, most found the term *caste*, with its
Hindu associations, inadequate to explain Punjabi kin-based communities. "Tribes" varied, as Tupper described them, from the "local tribe
of the frontier, with its known leader or council" to the "village clans of

9. Quoted in C. L. Tupper, *Punjab Customary Law* (Calcutta: Government Printing,
1881), 1:2. Ibid., 7–8.

the central Punjab, still acknowledging a common tribal name." [10] In southwestern Punjab, many tribes were pastoralist, ranging over large areas of grazing land. In northwestern Punjab, many were composed of hill settlers or groups of related warrior families. In eastern and central Punjab, many lived in "village communities."

However varied, tribes were nevertheless alike, as the British saw them, in deriving their social organization from a belief in patrilineal descent from a common ancestor. Whatever their political structure, "tribal" communities in Punjab preserved this memory of a common ancestor in their customs. A prime example lay in the common Punjabi prohibition against the inheritance of land by daughters. Punjabis generally contracted marriages, as Tupper observed, "outside the closely drawn limits of the clan, but within the looser, but still remembered, circle of the tribe or race of origin," the largest group for which a common ancestor could be asserted. [11] To pass land on to daughters thus meant to pass it outside the clan. Since control of land determined the distribution of status and authority in most Punjabi villages, the structure of "tribal" kinship dictated that inheritance by daughters had to be strictly controlled. Indeed, as such examples demonstrated, Punjabi custom itself rested on principles derived from the structure of Punjabi kinship. Whether for villagers or pastoralists, the presumption underlying custom throughout Punjab remained that "the rule, whatever it be, that tends to preserve tribal cohesion, community of interest in the village, and the integrity of the family must . . . always have the weight of past practice in its favour." [12]

Such common patterns of Punjabi custom were not, Tupper emphasized, simply a product of religious law but derived from the internal logic of the kinship system itself. Although customs such as the exclusion of daughters from inheritance bore a resemblance to those sanctioned by Hindu law, they were sharply distinguished from Hindu law in Punjab by the lack of appeal to sacred justifications. "The Hindu law extravagantly exalts the Brahman," Tupper said, "it gives sacerdotal reasons for secular rules." According to custom, however, it was not the religious requirement of caste but "clanship" that "determines

10. Ibid., 2:69.
11. Ibid., 70. Tupper was aware that not all Punjabis followed the same marriage patterns, and that some Muslim groups in particular married close relatives (a preferred parallel cousin pattern). But he saw marriage outside the clan as the dominant pattern, defining "tribal" kinship.
12. Ibid., 78.

the choice of a bride."[13] The requirements of kinship separated custom even more strikingly from the Muslim law. *Shari'at* dictated that a share of inheritance must go to the daughters, and this clashed sharply with common village usage. This provision of the *shari'at*, Tupper believed, suited a pastoral rather than an agricultural community. But the vast majority of the Muslim agricultural population ignored the *shari'at* in matters of inheritance in favor of custom.[14]

Punjabi custom, in such a view, thus represented an independent, tribally based "system" of rules and principles that structured the personal relations of rural Punjabis. Its independence from religion, in fact, heightened its political significance for the British. As an autonomous, indigenous system, which had been delineated and systematized by the British themselves, it offered an alternative to religion as a system of principles tying the state to the organization of society. "If you weaken the sense of tribal fellowship," Tupper thus noted, "the only thing that could be put in its room would be religion, not a polytheistic indifferentism or a contemplative philosophy, but a religion like that of the Sikhs or Mohammadans, that by inspiring enthusiasm would generate a sense of brotherhood: and here," he added pointedly, "the British Government could take no part."[15] In basing the law on Punjab's "tribal" structure, however, the British forestalled such a danger. They tied their authority to a structure of social organization central to Punjabi life, but one defined and systematized, through British social analysis, by the state itself. The protection of Punjab's "tribal" structure became, in effect, a central principle of and a justification for imperial rule.

The development of the customary law thus dramatized a set of principles that linked the British to Punjabi society and at the same time justified the authority of the imperial state. This association of the state with Punjab's "tribal system" was completely in keeping, as Tupper saw it, with the requirements of colonial empire—political stability (including army recruiting) and social progress. He admitted that in one sense social progress meant "the break-up of primitive groups" and that the erosion of "tribal" bonds might be inevitable. But the attempt of the British to preserve those bonds as long as possible would give them the leverage to control and direct change. "The maintenance of the tribe, the village, and the clan would not impede, but further the sort of progress that is most wanted in this part of India. . . . A tribe in the chains of

13. Ibid., 87.
14. Ibid., 87–89.
15. Ibid., 1:19.

its own customs, unrelaxed and unrefined, may stand still for centuries, but a tribe recognised and lifted into the system of British administration has, in the guardianship of the governing body, the best possible chance of disusing savagery and learning the wisdom of civilised men." [16] Tupper pointed out that these groups could figure in British plans to irrigate and settle the Punjab's wastes, foreshadowing later canal colony settlement. "If we succeed in peopling the extensive tracts still unredeemed in the Bari and Rechna Doabs, it will probably be by a repetition of the process of tribal immigration that brought the Jats and Beloches along the Indus banks. By maintaining the tribal system the colonisation of the Punjab wastes would be rendered easier." [17] His analysis outlined, in other words, a theory of Punjabi society that served the purposes of British rule generally. It justified British power, but at the same time bound the authority of the state to the structure of indigenous society itself.

Not all British officials, of course, accorded to the law the same ideological importance that Tupper did. But in his efforts to define the structural foundations of customary law, Tupper relied heavily on "scientific" methods of argument, which exerted an increasing influence on late-nineteenth-century British colonial thinking. Tupper's work, and that of other administrators, foreshadowed the work of anthropologists who have more recently analyzed the "ideologies" embodied in Indian kinship patterns. In describing state-clan relations in northern India, for example, Richard Fox shows the persistent political and economic importance of "tribal" kinship in northern Indian society, in spite of cyclically changing patterns of kinship organization. [18] Fox, in fact, points to the persistence of an "ideology of extended kinship" in northern India, embodied in marriage patterns, as the key to this phenomenon. [19] Tupper's concern with marriage patterns lay at the heart of his efforts to define principles of Punjabi kinship as well. Though Tupper did not explicitly identify an "ideology" of tribal kinship, he was concerned in his analysis of customary law to define a set of principles based on kinship,

16. Ibid., 19–20.
17. Ibid., 20. The Bari and Rechna Doabs are the lands between the Sutlej and Ravi rivers and the Ravi and Chenab rivers respectively.
18. Though the political character of tribal bonds varied with the relations between kinship units and the state, nevertheless, "even after numerous state developments," Fox writes, "tribal bases of politics remained as an integral aspect of the political order" (Richard G. Fox, *Kin, Clan, Raja, and Rule* [Berkeley: University of California Press, 1971], 170–71).
19. This extended kinship encouraged the persistence of widespread "tribal" or status categories that integrated regions independently of the state's political authority and of the tribes' political organization (Richard G. Fox, "*Varna* Schemes and Ideological Integration in Indian Society," *Comparative Studies in Society and History* 11 [1969]).

independently underlying the organization of all the dominant land-holding tribes of the Punjab. His theorizing thus aimed, in effect, at linking the British state to an "ideology" of tribal organization. Such analysis provided the foundations for an ideology that justified the power of the imperial state through an appeal to the structure of the society it ruled. Though these arguments were not immediately adopted by all British administrators, their long-term influence proved central to the development of Punjabi politics.

THE ADMINISTRATION AND THE TRIBES

Arguments and analysis were important in crystallizing an ideology of imperial authority, but the practical construction of a hierarchy of administrative authority based on this view proved to be another matter. The construction of an administration tied to indigenous social divisions raised substantial problems, suggested by the extremely fuzzy efforts of British administrators to define indigenous Punjabi kinship categories.[20] Terms such as *zat, qaum,* and *biradari* all were used by the British as equivalents of "clan" and "tribe," but with little clear agreement on their definitions or on the precise political character of the groups they described. Evidence suggests that these terms possessed vague and widely variant meanings even in indigenous usage.[21] How, then, were the "tribal" foundations of the administration to be practically defined? Tupper suggested that two questions were central for the British in assessing the political character of Punjabi "tribes." "In measuring the degree of tribal organisation," he wrote, "perhaps the most important points to keep in view are local contiguity and political leadership. How far is the tribe still a local one? How far has it become merged in the general population? Are there still any headmen, or traces of former leadership?"[22]

The question of tribal leadership, in fact, lay at the heart of British efforts to adapt the "tribe" to their own hierarchical political purposes. The British found few established "tribal" leaders in Punjab as they began to construct their rural administration. In central and eastern Punjab particularly, the policies of the Mughals and the Sikhs had reduced

20. Tupper, *Punjab Customary Law,* 3:4.
21. The vagueness of the term *biradari* in rural Punjab is suggested in Hamza Alavi, "Kinship in West Punjab Villages," *Contributions to Indian Sociology,* new ser., 6 (December 1972): 1–4. Alavi notes how the term is used in Punjab, in different contexts, to signify groups of varying sizes and political structures.
22. Tupper, *Punjab Customary Law,* 3:5.

the power of former tribal leaders to insignificance. As B. H. Baden-Powell wrote, "Neither the Muhammadan empire nor the Pathan conquerors, nor the later Sikh rulers, ever allowed the local chiefs such power as belonged to the Taluqdar of Oudh or the Zamindar of Bengal." The Sikhs exercised a strong leveling influence on central Punjab.[23] In western Punjab, this was considerably less true. In the far western districts, never fully subdued by the Mughals or Sikhs, many nomadic tribes had preserved an important degree of independence from state authority. The Sikhs had given *jagirs* (land assignments) to several western Punjabi families, whose heads the British recognized at annexation as important "tribal" leaders. But taking the province as a whole, the "traces of former leadership" provided little foundation for structuring the rural administration.

The British thus found little evidence of a clearly demarcated system of "tribal" leadership or political organization in most of the Punjab. But this in no way suggests that the idea of "tribe" was a wholly British creation. The idiom of "tribe" drew its significance from the prevalence in rural Punjab of forms of social organization tied to reckonings of descent. However varied the forms of local social organization that the British found as they established their rule, local organization drew widely in rural Punjab on idioms of *biradari* solidarity—idioms that suggested the importance of genealogy in the construction of local systems of organization and authority. Though variations in the legacies of previous states and in local power relations had produced different patterns of local influence, the potential political power of notions of *qaum* and *biradari* nevertheless provided important foundations for British efforts to tie their administration to "tribal" categories.

Indeed, British efforts to adapt their administration to Punjab's "tribes" were facilitated by an administrative recognition of Tupper's second criterion for the assessment of tribal organization, patterns of contiguous "tribal" settlement. If existing leaders were few, patterns of local "tribal" contiguity nevertheless provided a critical foundation for British efforts to link the administration to a "tribal" structure. As Tupper argued in his analysis of customary law, the pattern of "tribal" village settlement in Punjab—of families branching off old villages to colonize new ones—had left groups claiming common descent in con-

---

23. B. H. Baden-Powell, *Land Systems of British India* (London: Oxford University Press, 1892), 2:617. See also Tom G. Kessinger, *Vilyatpur, 1848–1968: Social and Economic Change in a North Indian Village* (Berkeley: University of California Press, 1974), 29–32.

trol of contiguous areas throughout much of Punjab. British administrators took note of these settlement patterns all over the province. As Baden-Powell observed, "if we look at any tribal map of a Central Punjab district, though time and the effect of wars, feuds and subsequent conquests, have much 'honey-combed' and broken up the original areas, it is impossible not to see what large territories 'Jats,' 'Gujars' and other great tribes have occupied." [24] As Tupper noted, though no "tribe" or "clan" was within a "ring-fence," many had "recognized headquarters" and "large tracts where they congregate in strength." [25] District settlement reports and gazetteers echoed such observations: in Hoshiarpur district, "clans" held "clusters of villages situated close together"; in Gujranwala, different "clans" dominated different sections of the district; in Gujrat district, the 1892–93 *Gazetteer* reported, "the principal tribes occupy large unbroken tracts." [26] Parts of western Punjab revealed patterns of local tribal contiguity even more clearly, and blocks of tribal settlement distinguished much of northwest Punjab. In Attock district, the settlement officer reported that "throughout the district ownership is in blocks of tribes, the present boundaries being the tribal limits as the result of internecine strife before annexation." [27] The 1883–84 *Gazetteer* of Jhelum district noted that "all the more important tribes, and many of their sub-divisions also, occupy fairly defined areas, of which they are the sole or the predominant population." [28]

This contiguity provided a framework for British administrative divisions, though the precise political meaning of "tribal" bonds remained ambiguous and congruence between settlement patterns and district or tehsil boundaries proved difficult to attain.[29] The key unit in this was the *zail*, an administrative division unique to the Punjab, usually comprising from five to forty villages. Between the 1860s and the opening of the twentieth century, British officials delineated *zail*s in most of the Punjab, drawing them to reflect the tribal distribution of the population. "In ar-

24. Baden-Powell, *Land Systems*, 2:611.

25. Tupper, *Punjab Customary Law*, 2:64–65.

26. *Hoshiarpur District Gazetteer*, 1904, 45. *Gujranwala District Gazetteer*, 1925, 79. *Gujrat District Gazetteer*, 1892–93, 56.

27. A. J. W. Kitchin, *Final Report of the Revision of the Settlement of the Attock District* (Lahore: Government Printing, 1909), 3.

28. *Jhelum District Gazetteer*, 1883–84, 67.

29. McKim Marriott, "Village Structure and the Punjab Government: A Restatement," *American Anthropologist* 55 (1953): 141. Marriott cites Baden-Powell's description of the large "tribal" blocks of settlement in Gujrat, which corresponded roughly with tehsil boundaries, but notes that this degree of congruence was impossible in most districts.

ranging the zails or circles," the government instructed in 1873, "care should be taken to include in one circle as far as possible the people of one tribe—or having some sort of affinity so that discordant elements can be reduced to a minimum."[30] Though zails rarely corresponded exactly with "tribal" blocks, the ultimate aim was, as one administrator put it, to "strengthen our administration by connecting it more intimately to the people."[31]

Perhaps most important, however, the delineation of zails according to patterns of "tribal" settlement gave the British an administrative framework within which the problem of local leadership could be confronted. In every zail the government appointed a zaildar, who was intended to be "the leading [man] of a particular tribe or section of the country,"[32] and "the representative of Government in his circle."[33] Though his duties were not clearly defined, he was to provide aid to the administration, supervise village officials, and, at the same time, represent the interests of his zail to the government. These zaildars were, ideally, the leaders of the local "tribes" and "clans." Where possible, the British designated as zaildar the "leading zamindar" of the dominant "tribe" in the zail.[34] Where no influential leaders appeared, however, the agency of the zaildari became a vehicle by which the British created them. In Ludhiana district, for example, the settlement officer found that, as "the Jat society of the district has no natural heads," the granting of the zaildari represented a means by which the British could "ennoble a family" to give them status as local leaders. In 1890, an official noted that where local leaders were few, the zaildari system was "perhaps the most hopeful means available of gradually creating them."[35]

Such new leaders were tied from the start to the British administration.[36] But through the procedures for their selection, the British tried to preserve an indigenous "tribal" idiom for their authority. The early practice in the selection of zaildars called for elections among the zail's

30. Government letter to settlement commissioner, Delhi division, 30 June 1873 (Punjab Board of Revenue [Board of Revenue], file 61/142).
31. E. A. Prinsep, settlement commissioner, Punjab, to secretary to financial commissioner, 27 June 1871 (ibid.).
32. Ibid.
33. Proceedings of the lieutenant-governor, 29 February 1872 (ibid.).
34. For example, F. W. R. Fryer (settlement officer, Jhang) to settlement commissioner, Multan and Derajat, 4 March 1875 (Punjab Archives, Revenue, Agriculture, and Commerce, proc. 564, April 1875).
35. Report by J. M. Dunnett (settlement officer, Ludhiana) on zaildars in Ludhiana, 18 April 1911; P. J. Fagan, Jr. (secretary to financial commissioner to revenue secretary), 25 October 1890 (Board of Revenue, file 61/134).
36. This had been predicted by Tupper Punjab Customary Law, 1:18.

*lambardar*s (village headmen), whose vote, though not binding, was intended to guide the choice. "It is impossible to obtain men of influence," wrote the settlement secretary in 1875, "without an election of some kind." In fact, intense local factionalism frequently made such elections impractical.[37] But selection of *zaildar*s nevertheless produced families of considerable local influence, who used their position to claim the leadership of the *zail*'s dominant "tribes." The administrative influence of *zaildar*s guaranteed that the positions, though not initially hereditary, usually passed from father to son. As one deputy commissioner wrote in 1909, "when a zaildar has to be appointed I have always found that the man with most influence is the son of the deceased zaildar, and the reason of this is that the father has acquired influence from the mere fact of his being a zaildar and carrying out Government duties."[38] Naturally, the local influence of these *zaildari* families varied considerably within the province. But by and large, by the opening of the twentieth century British policy had produced a class of rural leaders, tied closely to the administration, exercising its authority largely in a "tribal" idiom.

Equally important, the development of this class helped to define, in a broader sense, the combination of attitudes necessary for the exercise of legitimate rural authority within the British imperial system. The influence of *zaildar*s depended on their relationship to the administration, and their status depended on their claims to tribal leadership. But frequently, within the structure of the administration, the appeal to "tribal" authority provided an idiom of legitimation rather than an effective political foundation for a class of rural intermediaries within the imperial system. In practice, as the system of imperial control developed in the late-nineteenth century, land came to be a central element in supporting the position of tribal leaders within the administration. "Tribal" leadership and land control came to be closely related, defining the legitimate position of a politically effective intermediary elite in rural Punjab.

There was considerable irony in this relationship. In the early years of British rule, many British administrators had distrusted the existing

37. W. M. Young (settlement secretary) to financial commissioner, 22 April 1875 (Punjab Archives, Revenue, Agriculture, and Commerce, proc. 690, May 1875). Elections for *zaildar*s were largely abandoned by the end of the century. These elections are discussed in correspondence of J. W. Macnabb (commissioner, Ambala) to senior secretary to financial commissioner; and J. Wilson (settlement officer, Sirsa) to settlement commissioner, Punjab, 25 April 1882 (India Office Library and Records [IOL], Punjab Revenue and Agriculture, proc. 178, July 1882).

38. R. Humphries (deputy commissioner, Delhi) to commissioner, Delhi division, 26 June 1906 (Board of Revenue, file 61/134).

To My Parents

Contents

List of Maps   ix

Acknowledgments   xi

Note on Transliteration   xiii

Introduction   1

1. The British Imperial State   11
2. Islam and the Colonial State   39
3. Urban Politics and the Communal Ideal   73
4. Elections, Ideology, and the Unionist Party   108
5. The Cultural Definition of Power, 1937–1944   146
6. *Din* and *Dunya:* The Campaign for Pakistan   189

Conclusion   225

Glossary   235

Bibliography   239

Index   251

Maps

Map 1. Districts of British Punjab (1931)   7
Map 2. Selected Cities and Shrines of Punjab   44

Acknowledgments

In writing this book I was fortunate to have the help and support of many guides and friends. In Pakistan and India, during my research funded by a Fulbright grant, I enjoyed the help and hospitality of many people. I especially thank the many Pakistanis who generously allowed me access to papers and books in their possession: Mian Abdul Moied and the family of the late Mian Abdul Aziz of Lahore, who allowed me to use the excellent collection of twentieth-century political pamphlets and correspondence in their possession; Nawabzada Naushad Ali Khan, who gave access to papers of his father, Nawabzada Khurshid Ali Khan; Sardar Shaukat Hyat Khan, who showed me some of Sir Sikander Hyat Khan's papers in Islamabad; Ali Raza Khan Qasuri, who let me see important letters of his father, Nawab Muhammad Ahmad Khan Qasuri; and Khalid Shamsul Hasan, owner of the Shamsul Hasan collection of Jinnah papers in Karachi. To Nazar Hyat Khan Tiwana I owe a special debt of gratitude for allowing me access to the trunks filled with papers of the Unionist party at his family estate at Kalra, Sargodha district, and for showing me, at his home in Chicago, other papers of his father, Malik Khizr Hyat Khan Tiwana. Many other Indians and Pakistanis helped me in my research. Saiyid Hur Gardezi and his family, of Multan, showed me unusual hospitality. In both India and Pakistan, the staffs of the archives and libraries I used were always helpful and cooperative. I want to thank, in particular, the staff of the Punjab Archives and of the Board of Revenue at Lahore; of the Freedom Movement archives at Karachi University; of the Quaid-i-Azam papers at Islamabad; and of the National Archives of India, New Delhi.

I owe a debt of gratitude also to many friends and colleagues who helped me with discussion and criticism while I was working on this book. I profited greatly from discussions with many people—Katherine Ewing, Richard Eaton, Pamela Price, Kathleen Dickson, Emily Hodges, Keith Luria, and Eugene Irschick. Special thanks go to my dissertation adviser at Berkeley, Thomas Metcalf, and to Barabara Metcalf, who were always generous and sure intellectual guides. Moazzam Siddiqi helped me in learning Urdu. I owe thanks also to my colleagues at North Carolina State University who gave me much encouragement and advice—particularly Jonathan Ocko, Risa Ellovich, and John David Smith. Above all, I thank Sandy Freitag for special friendship and for willingness to argue.

A final word of thanks goes to Catherine Alguire, who drew the maps, and to Gerald Barrier, Renee Anspach, David Beer, Gregory Kozlowski, Steven Gilmartin, Michael and Gail Gonzales, Gerald M. Horan, Nancy and Vince Blasi, David Pfeifer, Lynne Withey, Kirby, William M. Gilmartin, and Marcia Gilmartin, who read all, part, or none of the book and who offered valuable suggestions.

Note on Transliteration

The system of transliteration roughly follows that used by John Platts, *Dictionary of Urdu, Classical Hindi, and English*. Exceptions are as follows: the letter *chim*, as in *chaudhri*, is transliterated as "ch," and the letter *ghain*, as in *tabligh*, as "gh"; the *izafat* is transliterated as "-i" following a consonant and "-yi" following a vowel; the Arabic definite article is "al-." Other hyphens that Platts uses between words, as in *sajjada-nishin*, are generally omitted. An apostrophe is used to signify both *hamza* and *'ain*, except in the glossary. Diacritical marks above and below the letters are also used only in the glossary. A few words common in Anglo-Indian usage, such as bania, maulvi, and zamindar, are not put in italics. Personal and place names are not rigorously transliterated but spelled according to the conventions most common at the time. As these were not wholly consistent, names may appear in variant forms in quotations or titles.

Introduction

As the movement for the creation of Pakistan gained momentum in the mid-1940s, Mumtaz Daultana, the Oxford-educated son of one of the Punjab's most influential landlords, told a gathering of Muslim students to "arm" themselves "with the mighty armour of your faith, bedeck yourself with the simple virtue of your past, and once again bring back on earth the Kingdom of the religion of God."[1] Following this, Muhammad Ali Jinnah, the leader of the All-India Muslim League, told the students that their primary responsibility was to succeed in their schooling. Urging them strongly to support Pakistan, but warning them against slogans and catchwords, Jinnah told them that their main object was to equip themselves with the education necessary to handle the political and economic problems of the practical world. Politics, economics, and the kingdom of God—these concerns combined to produce the movement for Pakistan.[2]

The movement for the creation of Pakistan was the first and perhaps the most successful of those twentieth-century Islamic movements that sought to bring about an Islamic transformation of the postcolonial state. Organized under the leadership of Jinnah, the movement succeeded in 1947 in forcing the partition of the Indian subcontinent and

1. Address by Mumtaz Muhammad Daultana, chairman of the reception committee, Punjab Muslim Students Federation, to the fourth annual session, Lahore, 18 March 1944 (Pamphlet in Mian Abdul Aziz collection, Lahore).
2. Speech to the Punjab Muslim Students Federation, Lahore, 18 March 1944 (Jamil-ud-din Ahmad, ed., *Speeches and Writings of Mr. Jinnah* [Lahore: Sh. Muhammad Ashraf, 1964] 2:22).

founding a new Muslim state. But the movement remains in many ways a paradox. Like movements elsewhere that have aimed toward the establishment of an "Islamic state," it drew on the concept of a return to the pure time of the Prophet's early community. Much of the political literature of the mid-1940s equated the struggle for the creation of Pakistan with the paradigmatic religious struggles of early Islamic history. Indian Muslims were urged to identify with the Prophet and the *Qor'an* in a struggle between right and wrong (*haqq o batil*), a struggle in which Muslims, like the supporters of Husain at Karbala, were "forming their ranks under the flag of Islam."[3] But despite the movement's millenarian tendencies, its political objectives were shaped by the institutional structures of the British colonial state.[4] The language of Islamic revivalism and the language of British imperial politics were inextricably joined.

This seemingly paradoxical combination of elements in the Pakistan movement was not unique. Historians have noted the importance of such a combination of ideas in Islamic political movements throughout the Muslim world. Many Islamic reformers of the nineteenth and twentieth centuries attempted at the same time to recover the first principles of Islam and to adapt Muslim political organization to European and colonial models for the modern state. Indeed, as many historians and anthropologists have noted, the Islamic tradition has provided a repertoire of concepts that have been employed to validate and explain a wide variety of political movements.[5] But the relationship of Islamic ideas to the practical goals of the Pakistan movement remains a topic of considerable debate and confusion, indicated most clearly in the debate on the Islamic definition of the state. "What is then the Islamic State of which everybody talks but nobody thinks?" asked Justice Muhammad

3. This depiction of the Pakistan movement as a conflict of "haqq o batil," a common one, occurs in a Punjab Muslim League election poster, "'Ashura-yi Muharram aur Musalmanon ka farz" (The tenth of Muharram and the duty of Muslims) (collection of Muslim League election posters, 24, in Abdul Aziz collection).

4. Jinnah moved the Pakistan movement outside strict constitutional limits when he appealed for "direct action" in August 1946, after the Cabinet Mission plan failed. The threat of widespread violence subsequently played an important role in the evolution of the partition proposal, but the shape of Muslim League organization throughout was determined largely by the colonial political system. The best account of the negotiations preceding partition is probably still that of V. P. Menon, *The Transfer of Power in India* (Princeton: Princeton University Press, 1957). For a good, though controversial, account of Jinnah's role, see Ayesha Jalal, *The Sole Spokesman: Jinnah, the Muslim League, and the Demand for Pakistan* (Cambridge: Cambridge University Press, 1985).

5. Numerous recent works suggest the adaptations of Islamic ideas to differing social and political contexts: see Michael Gilsenan, *Recognizing Islam* (New York: Pantheon Books, 1982); introduction to Barbara Daly Metcalf, ed., *Moral Conduct and Authority: The Place of Adab in South Asian Islam* (Berkeley: University of California Press, 1984), 15.

landed elites, particularly the old Sikh *jagirdars* of central Punjab, whose power they saw as a legacy of the rule of Ranjit Singh and as the antithesis of tribal authority. When the British were considering giving magisterial powers to landed notables in 1860, for example, the commissioner at Amritsar pointed out that the *jagirdars* left by Ranjit Singh had no links of "old association" with the villages, being solely the "creatures" of Ranjit Singh.[39] To many British administrators, developing a tribally based local administration thus represented an alternative to relying on this old Sikh aristocracy.[40] But after the 1857 Mutiny, as the British consolidated their authority in Punjab, British views toward landlord influence shifted. In the aftermath of the Mutiny, the British confirmed the titles to substantial landed estates for many of the Muslim "tribal" *maliks* of western Punjab who had supported them. Many of these landowning families began to play central roles in the British administration. The influence conferred by landed estates was seen increasingly as an important, and natural, concomitant of "tribal" leadership.

Yet the power of the landed magnates of western Punjab did not fit easily or immediately into the *zaildari* system. British administrators recognized that the influence of these families, with their warrior heritage and large estates, often transcended the boundaries of tribally defined *zails*. Rather than create *zails* in accord with "tribal" settlement patterns, the British tried initially to incorporate local leaders into the administration through the granting of a certain number of hereditary *in'ams*, or revenue-free grants, in each district.[41] But when they introduced a regular system of *zails*, the British tried to adapt it for these influential "tribal" magnates. One settlement officer wrote of *zails* in the Pindigheb tehsil of Attock district that it was "not sufficient to regard only tribal limits; the limits of family influence must be no less carefully

---

39. R. Cust (commissioner, Amritsar) to judicial commissioner, 18 February 1860 (Punjab Archives, Political/Judicial, procs. 11–22, May 1860).

40. This policy grew in part from the policy John Lawrence developed immediately following annexation. Lawrence's mistrust of the old Sikh aristocracy led in the short run to a British bias against aristocrats and, in central Punjab in particular, to an emphasis on peasant proprietors. But in many cases British recognition of local leaders with "tribal" associations rather than ties to the old Sikh court led simply to a recognition of new intermediaries between government and cultivators.

41. Some *in'ams* were tied to old fiscal divisions called *'ilaqas*, forerunners of *zails* (*Jhelum District Gazetteer*, 1883–84, 148–50; Meredith [commissioner, Rawalpindi] to senior secretary to financial commissioner, 28 August 1905 [Board of Revenue, file 61/134]).

regarded. . . . The system I am proposing is to make the zaildari arrangements fit in with the families, and not to attempt to squeeze the
families into the harsh limits of a preconceived system."[42] *Zails* were
thus specially drawn in parts of Attock to respect these families' authority. In Shahpur district, British administrators similarly named the
leading Tiwanas and Noons, former warrior clans who controlled large
estates, as honorary *zaildars* "within the estates owned by themselves or
their near relations."[43] Though the power of such landlord families did
not always fit easily into the *zaildari* system, extending often beyond the
limits of clearly defined "tribal" blocks of settlement, their increasing
importance to the British nevertheless cemented the association of tribal
and landed influence.

In fact these western Punjabi magnates came to play a pivotal role
within the imperial system. Through their authority as the most powerful rural leaders, they served the administration in the late nineteenth
and early twentieth centuries as models for the effective exercise of power
by rural intermediaries. Though landed estates had not initially been
prerequisites for the authority of *zaildars*, the British realized that grants
of land not only cemented the loyalties of *zaildari* families to the government but also increased their local influence within the *zail* system. One
deputy commissioner remarked in the 1890s that in the revision of *zail*
boundaries at the settlement, preference should be given to *zaildars*
with landed wealth because the more wealthy *zaildars* could afford to
keep horses and could exercise more effective influence for the government.[44] After 1890 the British made widescale use of grants of land to
bolster the position of many Punjabi *zaildars*—a practice greatly facilitated by the opening up of large quantities of land in the canal colonies.
Few *zaildars* became landlords as influential as the magnates of western
Punjab. But the distribution of land tended to redefine the meaning of
tribal authority within the British system generally. To be a "tribal"
leader meant increasingly to be a landlord, who asserted his claim to
leadership in a "tribal" idiom. The idiom of "tribal" influence thus
helped to define landed patrons as legitimate links between the imperial
state and the populace. It defined, in other words, a certain class of intermediaries, and a certain style of authority, as central to the political
structure of British Punjab.

42. Report by A. J. W. Kitchin (settlement officer, Attock) on introduction of *zaildari*
system in tehsils Fatehjang and Pindigheb of Attock district, 27 July 1906 (ibid.).
43. *Shahpur District Gazetteer,* 1917, 243.
44. Deputy commissioner, Gujrat, to commissioner, Rawalpindi, 5 September 1905
(ibid.).

This class emerged in the twentieth century as vital to the structure of
the imperial hierarchy in Punjab. Wide variations in agrarian structure
existed in Punjab in the first half-century of British rule, in commercialization, in systems of credit, and in landlord-tenant relations. British rule
itself heightened many of these variations.[45] But in defining principles of
legitimate rural authority the British laid the foundations for a dominant ideology of rural authority in the province. This ideology did not
operate equally effectively in all parts of the province. But in defining a
pervasive idiom for the exercise of rural influence by such a dominant
rural class, the British offered an ideological foundation for the political
integration of the imperial political system as a whole.

The increasing importance of this rural class in the early twentieth
century emerged in Sir Michael O'Dwyer's scheme for grants to the
"landed gentry," which was first developed in 1914 in connection with
the distribution of land in the Lower Bari Doab colony. O'Dwyer initially envisioned the scheme as a plan, in part, to raise a declining Punjabi aristocracy, who had at one time held large ancestral estates.[46] But
as the British distributed the grants, they broadened the definition of
landed gentry. In fact, the distribution affirmed a class of "hereditary
landed gentry" in Punjab, whose influence was defined by "tribal" standing as much as by landholding. *Zaildars* were an important portion
of those receiving grants, yet many of their ancestral estates were extremely limited. In Sialkot district, for example, one Jat *zaildar* with
only five acres of ancestral land received a landed gentry grant. British
administrators admitted that his grant stretched the definition. But as
one officer noted, "this zaildar is one of the few" in Sialkot "who has
not got a grant already,"[47] and that alone, with its implication of "tribal"
leadership, qualified him for landed gentry status. In Muzaffargarh district in southwestern Punjab, British administrators sanctioned grants
for seven *zaildari* families who, the deputy commissioner admitted,
could be accurately described as "successful farmers who have risen to
their present position in recent times." But the government nevertheless
agreed to recognize them "on the score of influence."[48] The biggest win-

45. On economic change and British rule in Punjab, see Himadri Banerjee, *Agrarian
Society of the Punjab, 1849–1901* (New Delhi: Manohar, 1982). The impact of British
economic policy on different regions of Punjab is also discussed by Richard G. Fox, "British Colonialism and Punjabi Labor," in Charles Bergquist, ed., *Labor in the Capitalist
World-Economy* (Beverly Hills: Sage Publications, 1984).

46. Note by Sir Michael O'Dwyer, lieutenant governor, on the Lower Bari Doab colonisation scheme, 8 August 1913 (Board of Revenue, file 301/1176).

47. Register of Landed Gentry grants, Lahore division, 21 (ibid., file 301/1176KW).

48. Note by C. P. Thompson (officiating commissioner, Multan), n.d., Register of
Landed Gentry grants, Multan division, 13 (ibid.).

ners in the landed gentry distribution were those powerful western Punjabi families who could claim convincingly that they had combined tribal leadership with large landholdings. The Tiwanas and Noons of Shahpur and the *tumandars*, or Biloch chiefs, of Dera Ghazi Khan received numerous grants.[49] The scheme of landed gentry grants thus helped to consolidate a key landed elite in Punjab.

Most important, however, the elite was one whose influence was also tied to the "ideology" of imperial authority on which the British had built their regime. Structuring their administration in large part around Punjab's "tribal" settlement patterns, the British had defined an indigenous ideological framework that would facilitate and legitimize the inclusion of rural intermediaries in an imperial administration. Such an effort would not have worked had not the idiom of kin-based solidarity carried real significance in rural Punjab. *Qaum* and *biradari* identity were important elements in rural social organization, although the local meanings of these terms varied widely. The British were not concerned with all their meanings; they were concerned with constructing a system in which leadership could be defined both with relation to the state and with relation to rural society. Through grants of land (and other honors), they sought to bind this class of rural patrons to their regime. Naturally, the character of the authority of these rural leaders varied considerably from place to place; few *zaildars* in eastern and central Punjab, for example, could claim the wide political influence of families like the Tiwanas and Noons in the western part of the province. The power of these local patrons varied sharply with the resources they could command. But the overall pattern of the administration was significant. In creating a class of landed and administrative leaders in rural Punjab, the British created an administrative structure mirroring the developing ideological structure of imperial rule.

THE LAND ALIENATION ACT
AND PROVINCIAL POLITICS

Not all forms of twentieth-century popular politics can be explained with reference to the structure and ideology of British control. But the system of imperial authority devised by the British strongly influenced the general course of twentieth-century politics. Throughout India it shaped the responses of local elites, as emerging institutions of "self-

49. Register of Landed Gentry grants, Rawalpindi division, 15 (for grants to the Tiwanas); Multan division, 14–19 (for grants to the Dera Ghazi Khan Biloch) (ibid.).

government" created new opportunities for power.[50] Rural leaders
played increasingly important political roles on district boards and provincial legislatures. But politics were also shaped by the ideology of integration on which the imperial system had been built. For rural patrons,
the structuring of the British administration around "tribal" identities
guaranteed the practical power of this idiom in local politics. The structure of "representative" political institutions in fact encouraged this.
The political significance of "tribal" identities emerged most clearly in
the case of district boards. In the 1880s, the boards were the first organs
of rural self-government introduced in Punjab. As the *zail* was the normal district board constituency, representation on these boards tended
to take on from the beginning a "tribal" cast. Though initially most
district board members were nominated, the maintenance of *zail*s as
constituencies, even as elections were gradually introduced, encouraged
the emergence of a "tribal" idiom in district board elections. And this
pattern, though not universal, dominated local politics right up until
partition.

"Tribal" representation was not the only idiom of political significance in Punjabi politics. The idiom of religious solidarity was incorporated into the structure of the representative system when separate
communal electorates were introduced—first in the 1880s in municipal committees, and later in elections for the provincial Legislative Council and Assembly.[51] Separate council electorates, first introduced in the
United Provinces and Bengal in 1909, became the norm in Punjab after
1919. But the pattern of rural political association derived primarily
from the central integrative ideology of local solidarity. In rejecting
communal electorates for the district boards, the British affirmed this
pattern.[52] And nothing demonstrated this more clearly than the central
symbolic role in provincial politics assumed after 1900 by the Punjab
Alienation of Land Act. More than any other piece of legislation, this

50. The clearest statement of this view is in Anil Seal, "Nationalism and Imperialism
in India," in John Gallagher, Gordon Johnson, and Anil Seal, eds., *Locality, Province, and
Nation* (Cambridge: Cambridge University Press, 1973).
51. N. Gerald Barrier, "The Punjab Government and Communal Politics, 1870–
1908," *Journal of Asian Studies* 27, no. 3 (May 1968): 537.
52. Introducing communal electorates into the district boards in the 1920s was considered but rejected by the British, who argued that it would threaten this parochial,
largely tribal, political pattern. The governor, Sir Edward Maclagan, argued that, in contrast to people living in cities, "the people interested in the proceedings of the Boards are
more scattered, less liable to association, and less under the influence of communal enthu-
siasts and newspapers." He allowed, however, for electoral circles to be constructed "subject to . . . the maintenance of Zail boundaries" to approximate communal balance (Punjab Archives, Local Self-Government/Boards, B. procs., file 499, July 1923).

act crystallized the assumptions underlying the British imperial administration and translated those assumptions into popular politics.

A late-nineteenth-century crisis of indebtedness among Punjabi landholders precipitated the passage of the Alienation of Land Act in 1900.
To many British officials, the large-scale expropriation by moneylenders
of peasants' land struck close to the heart of British rule, undermining
rural stability. Widespread land alienations, many feared, would lead to
rural revolt. At its core, however, the issue hinged on the conflict they
perceived between a stable agrarian society on the one hand, and the
free working of natural economic laws on the other. Official correspondence on this issue reveals the difficulties British officials had in reconciling the contradictions that lay at the center of British colonial rule. In
the end, however, political stability took precedence. The British affirmed
in the Land Alienation Act the significance of the tribal structure of society for the stability of imperial authority.[53]

The provisions of the Land Alienation Act did not bar transfers
of land altogether, but they restricted transfers of land from peasants
to moneylenders. Moneylenders were, in the eyes of the British, "outsiders"—men without connections to the tribal political fabric of rural
society. "Tribes" themselves were not, of course, landholding units, as
the British realized well. But in preventing the transfer of land to men
outside the tribes, the British intended to preserve an idiom that defined
and legitimized the power of rural leaders. At the heart of the Land
Alienation Act lay a defense of a structure of rural power based on landed
patronage and the "tribal" structure of the British administration.

The character of the act was set by the adoption of the "agricultural
tribe" as its critical unit. It barred sales of agricultural land from members of "agricultural tribes" to individuals who were not members of
these groups.[54] "Agricultural tribes" were gazetted by name in each district. Compromises leading to the passage of the act resulted in initial
exceptions to the strict use of tribal categories to restrict sales. Land
transfers were allowed, for example, to landowners who, whatever their
tribe, had held land in a village since the first regular British settlement;
these men were known under the act's definitions as "statutory agriculturalists." Whatever the political objects of the act, it would be unfair,

53. The most complete account of the administrative debates that produced the Alienation of Land Act is van den Dungen, *The Punjab Tradition*.
54. Significantly, designation of these tribes was to be determined both by their agricultural character and by their political importance to the British (N. G. Barrier, *The Punjab Alienation of Land Bill of 1900* [Durham: Duke University, 1966], 112).

the lieutenant governor, Sir Mackworth Young, argued, "to degrade the class hitherto regarded as old agriculturalists to the level of the money-lender" simply because they might not be members of an "agricultural tribe." [55] But equity, ultimately, proved far less important than political principle. "If a bania has held land for thirty or forty years in a village," the financial commissioner wrote in 1904, "he does not thereby cease to be a bania; and if he is a landowner, it does not follow that he is not also a moneylender. There is nothing in the structure of rural society in the Punjab to separate banias who have held land since the first regular settlement from others." [56] After all, if "tribe" was the operative basis of the act, then a bania was a bania; whether he happened to be a land-owner was irrelevant. In the end, such exceptions were therefore abol-ished. With the elimination of the "statutory agriculturalist" in 1907, the overriding "tribal" principle of the act was firmly established.

But the practical adaptation of the act to the structure of rural Pun-jabi society proved to be no easy undertaking. The confusion in the "tribal" structure of the province had been clarified for administrative purposes by the demarcation of *zails*; but for other purposes these divi-sions remained largely artificial. "Tribal" names and identities included those such as Jat, embracing millions of Punjabis, and others of the most localized significance. The Land Alienation Act initially provided for the grouping of tribes solely for purposes of land alienations. The grouping was to be based on characteristics that linked similar tribes—common origin, social position, religion—creating reasonable markets for land exchange. The Punjab government soon discovered, however, that vagueness in the definition of "tribe" made workable principles for tribal grouping extremely elusive. Some deputy commissioners suggested sep-arating the market gardening "tribes" (Arains, Kambohs, and Malis) from the dominant Jats and Rajputs; [57] but most local officials found few meaningful principles on which to differentiate and group agricultural tribes. Religion provided perhaps the clearest distinction, transcending "tribal" divisions in rural Punjab. But significantly, many deputy com-missioners were wary of its use.

Reasons for the reluctance to use religious distinctions varied. Reli-gious identity provided the foundation for much in the structure of Brit-

55. Sir Mackworth Young quoted by Humphries (financial commissioner) to commis-sioners, 30 June 1904 (Board of Revenue, file 441/100).
56. Humphries to commissioners, 30 June 1904 (ibid.).
57. For example, note by C. L. Tupper (financial commissioner), 11 February 1901 (ibid., file 442/1/00/7).

ish authority, including seats on elected bodies and reserved places in
the government services. But Punjabi administrators were hesitant, in a
system built on distinctions of "tribe," to apply a category far different
in its ideological implications from those on which the Land Alienation
Act had been based. As the commissioner of Rawalpindi division reported, "Our agricultural tribes are all zamindars proper, whether Muhammadan, Hindu or Sikh, and distinctions by religion are neither necessary nor advisable."[58] Other deputy commissioners agreed that to
introduce religious distinctions could only be counterproductive.[59] Some
deputy commissioners even tried to justify this with the argument that
where "tribal" identities were strong, religious identities were often of
little account. The deputy commissioner of Ambala, for example, wrote
that "religion, in the rural parts of this district, is by no means a potent
divider of hearts."[60] As the deputy commissioner of Gurdaspur observed, "the Jat peasant here is still a farmer first, and a Sikh or Muslim,
as the case may be, in the second place only."[61] It was "tribe," these officials suggested, that was at the heart of rural identity.

This is not to suggest that religion did not also hold an important
place in the construction of rural identities. But only in two areas of the
province did administrators seriously suggest that distinctions of religion warranted recognition in this system. In heavily Muslim southwestern Punjab, several deputy commissioners suggested that religion
was a convenient guide to the division between agriculturalist and nonagriculturalist, as few non-Muslims of the "agricultural tribes" lived in
the area. In parts of central Punjab, British officials advanced the more
substantive suggestion that religion provided a basis for separating Sikh
from Muslim Jats. As the settlement officer of Fazilka wrote, the Sikh
Jat, unlike the Muslim, was "willing and able to undertake small moneylending transactions" and "just as eager to exact his pound of flesh as
any bania or Arora." To group Muslim and Sikh Jats together meant
delivering "the thriftless Muhammadan from the bania to hand him
over to the Jat Sikh."[62] Religious distinctions were thus linked, as some
officials saw it, to differences in customs and in attitudes that were of

58. Lt.-Col. J. A. L. Montgomery (commissioner, Rawalpindi) to junior secretary to
financial commissioner, 14 January 1901 (ibid.).
59. For example, Capt. P. S. M. Burton (deputy commissioner, Rohtak) to commissioner, Delhi division, 27 December 1900 (ibid.).
60. Note by H. J. Maynard (deputy commissioner, Ambala), 16 December 1900
(ibid.).
61. Note by J. R. Drummond (deputy commissioner, Gurdaspur), 21 December 1900
(ibid.).
62. Note by C. M. King (settlement officer, Fazilka), 15 January 1901 (ibid.).

vital importance in matters of land alienation. But the reactions to this suggestion indicated the political and ideological importance for the British in maintaining a system defined primarily by "tribal" terms: though religious distinctions might be very real, the use of broad religious categories could not be effectively reconciled with the premises of the act. The only division of significance for the act, the lieutenant governor concluded after examining the correspondence on grouping, was that between "agricultural tribes" and nonagriculturalists. "The distinction between a man who is a member of an agricultural tribe and one who is not appeals to the innate ideas of the peasantry, but distinctions between real agriculturalists, such as it is necessary to make in forming groups of tribes, do not, and such distinctions must be more or less artificial and irritating."[63]

This attempt at grouping thus placed all the "agricultural tribes" in each district into a single unit. It lessened the possibility of keeping land within each individual "tribe." It had the effect of making the more general designation of membership in the "agricultural tribes" the central foundation of the act. In fact, it highlighted the degree to which the term referred not to preexisting political divisions in Punjabi society but to categories the British used to define who would have the right to own land and wield power within their system. Control of land had increasingly come to dictate social and political status in British Punjab. In the Land Alienation Act, the British implied that, in the eyes of the government, only in certain hands was landholding politically legitimate. Though the act did not bar nonagriculturalists from owning land, it made landholding with its political power a legitimate prerogative of those whose roots were, in the terms of the act, "agricultural" and "tribal."

The act thus strengthened the control of land by one category of individuals and restricted its control by another. Those who did not fall into the proper category, whether they were the moneylenders against whom the act was originally aimed or urban merchants, artisans, *kamins* (village menials), or religious specialists, were now defined politically not by whether they in fact owned land, but by whether they claimed landholding status as measured by membership in the "agricultural tribes." It was this which defined the political legitimacy of rural intermediaries within the British imperial system. Though many British administrators denied that the act was intended to have such a sweeping effect (technically it restricted only alienations), others soon realized that its pri-

---

63. Note by A. H. Diack (financial secretary) to secretary, Revenue and Agriculture, Government of India, 16 April 1901 (ibid.).

mary political significance lay in defining a dominant social category with which the British had in large part identified their rule.

After the passage of the act, one high British official with long Punjab experience provided the most trenchant critique of what the British had done. H. J. Maynard argued that the British had identified the fortunes of their regime with those of the agricultural tribes as defined in the act. The government had "conveyed the impression," Maynard wrote, "that it regards itself as the patron of the zamindar, and that it identifies political advantage with his contentment and well-being, not with the contentment and well-being of the whole mass of its subjects."[64] The British, in other words, had linked the state to a class of intermediary patrons, who in turn linked it to the population. That the ideological presumptions on which the British based the colonial state led directly to their definition of this class Maynard did not explicitly state. But he noticed that the effect of British policy had been to exclude important segments of the population from the political hierarchy that grounded the power of the regime.

In fact, the most pointed criticism of the act came from those who had been excluded from the agricultural tribes and implicitly relegated to secondary status within the colonial political community. For some groups, the Land Alienation Act thus defined the terms in which their struggles for political status in the ensuing decades would be couched.[65] But for others, the act's most significant burden lay in its definition of a touchstone of political status that ignored the language in which their own claims to political status and position had been asserted. Prominent among these groups were those who had attempted to define an idiom of political solidarity based on religion. Though religious identity had been recognized officially in the structure of Punjabi municipal electorates, the Land Alienation Act had defined an idiom for the exercise of provincial power in which religious identity played a secondary role. The Punjab Hindu Sabha, a largely nonagriculturalist and urban body, thus attempted to deny altogether the significance of the act's definitions, suggesting that, despite its language, the act itself was based on an only thinly veiled policy of religious favoritism. "The practical working of the Act has been extremely detrimental to the Hindus," the Sabha declared in 1909, "in as much as, while almost all Muhammadan castes have been notified as agricultural tribes, the high caste Hindus have

64. Quoted in van den Dungen, *The Punjab Tradition*, 291.
65. See chapter 3 for a discussion of the Land Alienation Act in the politics of Kashmiris.

been scrupulously kept out, even where they have held land and followed agriculture as a profession for several generations. . . . The con-
cessions granted to Syeds and mujawars (persons receiving offerings of a
shrine) have been refused to the Brahmans; the privileges conferred on
Pathans and Mughals have been denied to Khatris."[66] Many urban Hindus saw the act itself as a "communal" measure; their reaction reached
its most impassioned climax in the declaration by a Brahman in the
Punjab Legislative Council in 1926 that the Land Alienation Act, and
the government policy it represented, embodied "an attack on the Hindu
religion."[67] It was true that prominent urban Hindus had largely been
excluded from the "agricultural tribes," whereas their most serious
rivals for provincial power, the leading Muslim landholders of Punjab,
had been brought in. But their characterization of the act in communal
terms reflected also the degree to which the act challenged the categories
on which their own status was based. Though leading Punjabi Muslims
supported it, many Muslims came eventually to feel uneasiness with the
act's definitions as well.

Criticisms of the act came also from those who objected to its manipulation of indigenous "tribal" terminology. Many leaders of the
Congress considered the appeal to tribal identity little more than an "artificial" appeal to indigenous kinship categories to legitimize the authority of the British administration. These critics tried to strip away the
act's rationale of protection for the peasantry, arguing that its definitions delivered the peasants into the hands of the rich and powerful
among the agricultural tribes, who were now given a free field to expro-
priate the peasants' land. Sir Harnam Singh warned at the time the act
was passed, "There will be monster fishes in the agricultural community
who will be encouraged by law to swallow smaller fishes." In the ensuing decades critics repeated this argument.[68] These criticisms were intended to highlight the differentiation within the agricultural tribes,
which was itself, in part, a product of British administrative policy and
imperial ideology. Nonagriculturalists persistently demanded official in-
quiries into the act to show that the dominant status given to the "agri-

66. Memorial to Lord Minto from Punjab Hindu Sabha, 24 June 1909 (Board of
Revenue, file 441/212A).
67. Statement of Pandit Nanak Chand (Punjab, *Legislative Council Debates*, vol. 9A
[1926]: 842).
68. Quoted in Barrier, *The Punjab Alienation of Land Bill*, 74. These repeated criticisms, which came to a head in the 1920s, are assessed in Board of Revenue, file 442/1/
00/3 (August 1931), "Enquiry into the alleged expropriation of small land-owners by big
landlords as a result of the Punjab Alienation of Land Act."

cultural tribes" had little to do with protecting the land of the peasantry
and was in fact intended to bolster the local intermediaries who supported the administration. The Lahore *Tribune* stated in 1915 that the
government had as yet done little to submit the working of the act to
serious scrutiny and had yet to answer to "the more or less specific alle-
gation that the big fish among the *State-made* agricultural 'tribes' which
are now swallowing the smaller fry are themselves playing the role of
the bania against whom the legislative safeguard was devised." [69] This
was an attack on the concept as a purely artificial creation of the British
colonial system.

Such arguments arising out of the political implications of the Land
Alienation Act set the stage for provincial politics in the ensuing era of
political reform. The leaders of the agricultural tribes dominated politics in the provincial council after 1920. Constituencies for the council
were demarcated on a communal and territorial basis, with separate
constituencies for Hindus, Muslims, and Sikhs, and for the rural and
urban areas. But for rural Muslim leaders, who formed the strongest
bloc in the council, the Land Alienation Act laid down the terms in
which they defined their interests. The typical member of the Legislative
Council was, as H. J. Maynard described him, the "middling" landowner, "who is probably both a headman in his village and also a zaildar, or tribal head of a group of villages." [70] As a group, the power of
these rural leaders rested at the local level on land and position in the
rural administration. But at the provincial level their claim to influence
was based on membership in a dominant province-wide status group;
as Muslims, most of them responded to communal issues and supported
Sir Fazli Husain, the leader of the rural party in the council in the early
1920s, in efforts to increase Muslim representation in the services and
on local bodies. But Muslim identity in the council was defined largely
within the context of the political oppositions established by the Land
Alienation Act. "In practice," Maynard wrote, "the tendency has been
for Muhammadans to speak of themselves as 'zamindars' and to view
Hindus as representing the urban, shopkeeping and moneylending
classes." This was the language which provided the foundation for the
integration of these local leaders in a province-wide political system,
linking the foundations of their local authority to their claims to politi-

69. The *Tribune*, Lahore, 6 January 1915 (*Report on Newspapers and Periodicals in
the Punjab*, 1915); emphasis added.
70. Sir John Maynard's note on certain aspects of the reforms in the Punjab, May
1923 (Punjab Archives, Home General, B procs., file 176, 1925).

cal influence at the provincial level. Although communal issues were often raised in the council, "a very strong and obvious material interest," Maynard noted, "particularly if it appeals to the substantial zamindar majority in the Council, will transcend the communal bond."[71] In fact, Muslims, Hindus, and Sikhs of the "agricultural tribes" in the council combined on a number of issues of common concern. This tendency gained organized expression in the council in 1923 with the formation of the Punjab National Unionist party, combining the Muslim agriculturalist followers of Sir Fazli Husain with the Ambala division Hindu agriculturalist group of Chaudhri Chhotu Ram.[72]

By the 1920s support of the Land Alienation Act had thus become a symbolic political issue of first importance in Punjab. The issue of "zamindar" status—membership in the "agricultural tribes"—even shaped the Unionist party's support for a policy of preferential categories in recruiting zamindars to government services. The use of communal categories in government recruitment began in the nineteenth century, but after World War I the Unionists pressed to change recruitment policy to use the categories of the Land Alienation Act. These concerns were powerfully expressed in the council, even in the face of official British reluctance to apply the categories to this purpose. Unionist preoccupation with the issue in fact indicated how close these categories had come to defining the Unionist party's identity.

The issue first prompted attention in 1919 when the government, in response to rural concerns, adopted a resolution calling for greater employment of "zamindars" in government services. Although general British policy supported preferential zamindar recruitment, some government officials balked when the council attempted to equate zamindars with members of the "agricultural tribes." These officials argued that the attempt to use the Land Alienation Act in government recruiting stretched the definitions of the Land Alienation Act far beyond the areas to which they originally had applied. "The Alienation of Land Act," P. J. Fagan somewhat disingenuously wrote, "was never intended to be used for the purpose of defining or constituting privileged classes."[73] Though supporting the resolution on zamindar recruitment, these officials convinced the lieutenant governor in 1919 to adopt a definition of "zamin-

71. Ibid.
72. *Muslim Outlook*, Lahore, 30 July 1924 (cutting in Abdul Aziz collection). In a note on the formation of the Unionist party, Malik Firoz Khan Noon declared that the party and its supporters would "stand by the Alienation of Land Act."
73. Note by P. J. Fagan, 31 January 1919 (Punjab Archives, Home General, B procs., file 534, June 1922).

dar" that initially included all "hereditary proprietors" of agricultural land residing in the rural areas—irrespective of "tribe."

But the British themselves had largely guaranteed, by their structuring of political authority in Punjab, that no other interpretation of the term "zamindar" would carry the same political significance as one derived from the Land Alienation Act. Despite the official British position, Unionist leaders such as Sir Fazli Husain and Sir Chhotu Ram pressed strongly to include only "agricultural tribes" in the zamindar category. "The reason for their recommendation," H. D. Craik wrote, "was that the point which interests the members of the Legislative Council and the public generally is the employment of members of the agricultural tribes." [74] The symbolic significance of the issue was clear in a petition of zamindars in Ludhiana district to limit the definition of zamindar to the "agricultural tribes." "To recognize others as such," it said, "would mean to offend their social susceptibilities and to injure their rights." [75] Besides, as Chhotu Ram pointed out, the "agricultural tribes" presented a clear, popularly recognized definition that avoided the administrative difficulties of the 1919 definition. [76] In 1926 the government yielded. It instructed that the census of government servants, used to measure both communal and zamindar employment in the services, should classify government servants only according to religious community and "membership in agricultural and non-agricultural tribes under the Land Alienation Act." Concern in the council for the position of zamindars in government employment was subsequently demonstrated by the introduction of at least ten resolutions on this subject from 1925 to 1933. [77] The government's performance on the subject was, as one government officer noted, generally "judged by the number of members of agricultural tribes they recruit." [78]

The identification of the dominant majority in the Legislative Council by its association with the "agricultural tribes" thus became a central feature of provincial politics in the Punjab after the formation of the Unionist party. This was not lost on the Unionists' opponents in the council. They focused their attacks on the Unionists' claims to pro-

74. Note by H. D. Craik, 10 December 1926 (ibid., file 288, 1927).
75. Address by Ludhiana district Zamindara League, 1926 (ibid.).
76. Note by Chhotu Ram, 13 December 1926 (ibid.).
77. Note by F. H. Puckle, 10 February 1934 (ibid., file 11, 1937). For discussion of "zamindar" recruitment controversy in the early 1930s, see Satya M. Rai, *Legislative Politics and the Freedom Struggle in the Punjab, 1897–1947* (New Delhi: Indian Council of Historical Research, 1984), 191–92.
78. Note by Miles Irving, 29 June 1934 (Punjab Archives, Home General, B procs., file 11, 1937).

vincial leadership and often followed the long-standing pattern of attacks on the Land Alienation Act itself, on the concept of "agricultural tribes," and on the claims of these "tribes" to superior social and political status. These assaults on the Unionists in the 1920s came from several sides. Sikhs active in the movement for gurdwara reform, Hindu Sabha leaders, and urban Muslims of the Khilafat committees and the Ahrar, all of whom sought a greater religious identification in politics, strongly attacked the political dominance of the "agricultural tribes." In addition, supporters of the Congress criticized the links of the agricultural tribes to the British and attacked the administrative framework that allowed "tribal" leaders to "pose as champions of the rural population while pleading for the continuance of the old order of things." [79] For all these groups, despite their differing perspectives, the concept of the "agricultural tribes" as the basis of political power was an artificial one. For them, claims to political leadership were determined not by patronage—justified by principles of "tribal" kinship—but by religion or political principle.

Continuing criticisms of the Land Alienation Act in the 1920s led the government to reaffirm the act's political significance. British officials were aware, as they had been from the start, of the act's inequities, which were the target of much of the criticism. As the governor, Sir Malcolm Hailey, wrote of the act in 1928, "the broad definitions which we are obliged to adopt necessarily involve our including in the notified category large numbers of men whom it is unnecessary to protect, and excluding others who have, on any logical ground, a perfectly good claim to protection." [80] But such considerations seemed of minor import when measured against the act's political and symbolic significance: The British could not change the basic operation of the act without changing their political base in the country and the ideological justification for their regime. The act tied British authority to the structure of Punjabi society. It justified a whole system of authority based on *biradari*, patronage, hierarchy, and mediation. To a large degree, the British imperial state legitimized its authority not by casting itself as the symbolic upholder of a religious order but by acting as the central systematizer and protector of an indigenous structure of local, kin-based social organization.

The act thus came to occupy a central, symbolic place in the thinking of a wide range of Punjabi political leaders. As Sir Chhotu Ram noted,

79. The *Tribune,* Lahore, 17 April 1925.
80. Note by Sir Malcolm Hailey, 18 December 1928 (Board of Revenue, file 442/1/00/3).

even inquiry into the working of the act would "engender unnecessary and avoidable alarm and concern in the minds of the zamindars."[81] Sir Jogendra Singh observed that "even if in the strict economic working it was found inoperative I don't think for many years to come it need be touched. We must respect the wishes of the majority."[82] The government's answer to the growing criticism of the Land Alienation Act in the 1920s was to declare to the council in 1929 that it stood by the act and had no intention of either expanding or restricting its scope. The rural leaders' response to the increasing criticism of the act, as Sir Fazli Husain noted, was to stiffen the resolve of the "agricultural classes" to stand by the act. With the act continually under attack, he said, the rural people had come to see it as "the Magna Carta of their political and economic life."[83]

81. Note by Chhotu Ram, 13 December 1926 (ibid.).
82. Note by Jogendra Singh, 13 December 1926 (ibid.).
83. Punjab, *Legislative Council Debates*, vol. 12 (1928–29): 709.

CHAPTER II

Islam and the Colonial State

Twentieth-century Punjabi politics were substantially shaped by the principles that had defined the British imperial state. British administration and ideology encouraged the emergence in the twentieth century of an intermediary rural elite, defined largely in an indigenous, "tribal" idiom. Though the politics of Punjab reflected tensions and contradictions within the colonial order, the integrative ideology of imperial rule helped to center provincial politics on the "agricultural tribes" and the Unionist party.

But religion also had shaped many aspects of Punjabi political life. In spite of the dominant ideological structure of the imperial system, religion was excluded neither from the British administrative system nor from colonial politics. The development of separate electorates and communal recruiting to government services reflected this clearly. But the political place of religious identities within the colonial order was also shaped by the principles on which the British had grounded the colonial state. Of critical importance was the British refusal to set the state's authority on a symbolic religious foundation. This profoundly affected the development of Islamic thinking and political organization in twentieth-century Punjab. But it did not limit the impact of the British imperial system on the development of Punjabi Islam. Changes in political and economic organization in Punjab exerted important influences on the nature of Islamic organization. But perhaps most important of all, the articulation of an ideology of political integration based on the state's relationship with the "tribes" served itself, ironically, to bring many religious institutions into important places within the British imperial system. But it did so within the context of a system that had no symbolic religious foundation.

The relationship between religious organization and political structure of the state is, analytically, a close one. Clifford Geertz writes of religion as a "cultural system," a system of symbols which synthesizes a people's "ethos" and explains their world.[1] To explain Punjabi Islam in these terms would be far more ambitious than anything that could be attempted here. But the concept of a "cultural system" is useful in pointing toward the systematic relationship between religious institutions and ideas, on the one hand, and the political context in which they develop and operate, on the other. In Punjab, structures of political power and religious organization had developed in close relationship and remained so within the British imperial system. Understanding the place of Islam within the local structure of Punjabi society is thus central to understanding the development of the imperial system and the emerging role of religion in twentieth-century politics.

THE STRUCTURE OF RURAL ISLAM

To understand the place of Islamic institutions in rural Punjab, it is important to step back to view their development in historical perspective. Though highly speculative, a look at the origins of Islamic institutions in rural Punjab provides insight into the ways local, tribal identities and local forms of religious organization developed in close association. Though the early history of Punjabi Islam awaits detailed research, western Punjab's conversion to Islam is usually credited to the great sufi mystics of the Delhi sultanate period—Baba Fariduddin Ganj-i Shakar of Pakpattan, Shaikh Bahawal Haq Zakariyya of Multan, Saiyid Jalaluddin Bokhari of Uch, and others. Many rural Punjabi "tribes" have traced their conversion to these medieval saints.

But despite these traditions, the process of conversion was also deeply influenced by the position of early Muslim states. There is in fact relatively little hard evidence to suggest that active proselytization by saints played a direct role in mass conversions.[2] Instead, the role of the saints

1. Clifford Geertz, "Religion as a Cultural System," in *The Interpretation of Cultures* (New York: Basic Books, 1973), 89.
2. See, for example, Khaliq Ahmad Nizami, *The Life and Times of Shaikh Farid-u'd-din Ganj-i-Shakar* (Lahore: Universal Books, 1976), 107. Several tribal traditions of con-

in conversions should probably be seen as symbolic, reflecting the early interaction between local cultures and the culture of newly powerful Muslim states—an interaction that gave rise to rural Punjab's early Islamic institutions. As Richard Eaton argues, the pattern of conversion in rural Punjab was a product of simultaneous ecological and political change, as pastoralists in western Punjab adapted both to a spreading agricultural way of life and to the political and cultural hegemony of imperial Muslim states. In this context the great medieval *sufis* were symbolically important. The construction of *sufi khanaqah*s (hospices), and later *sufi* tombs, produced symbolic cultural outposts of the power of Islam and of the Muslim state in a world where local, tribal identities continued to be of vital importance. Imposing *sufi* tombs, constructed by Muslim sultans, underscored the importance of Islamic shrines as sites of access to transcendent spiritual authority. Equally important, they drew the tribes gradually, and perhaps insensibly, into the state's political—and religious—orbit.[3]

From the beginning, western Punjab's Islamic institutions thus reflected an interaction between the often "tribal" organization of the localities and the Islamic tradition embodied in the culture of an imperial state. The religious devotions and the historical development at these institutions varied widely, but nearly all the major shrines that emerged in the centuries after the arrival of Islam served in some degree as links in the larger "cultural system" of Punjabi Islam—or as hinges that flexed in two directions. In one sense, the shrines served as symbols of the distant, yet transcendent, cultural authority of the Muslim state; in another sense, the shrines embodied diverse local cultural identities, whose variety reflected both the diversity of ecological, social, and kinship organization in Punjab and the diversity in the spiritual needs of the people. Though some shrines, like those of Bahawal Haq and Baba Farid, had wide renown, those of many lesser saints had only the most localized significance, associated with particular villages or tribes or with particular instrumental needs, such as curing snake bite or driving

version at the hands of medieval *sufi* saints are noted in H. A. Rose, *A Glossary of the Tribes and Castes of the Punjab and North-West Frontier Province* (Patiala: Punjab Languages Department, 1970), 2:302, 412, 496, 535; 3:417–18, 491.

3. This argument is highly speculative. The Tughluqs patronized many important *sufi* shrines of Punjab, constructing important tombs at the shrine of Baba Farid and of Shah Rukn-i Alam in Multan. But the pattern of relations between the Delhi sultanate and the shrines of the Punjab has not, to my knowledge, been carefully studied. See Richard M. Eaton, "The Political and Religious Authority of the Shrine of Baba Farid," in Barbara Daly Metcalf, ed., *Moral Conduct and Authority: The Place of Adab in South Asian Islam,* 341–48.

jinn (spirits) from possessed women. Such shrines varied widely not only in importance but in religious ritual as well.[4]

Whatever the variation in religious practices, however, most of these Islamic shrines drew on a common conception of God's transcendence and of his distant relationship to man—a conception that mirrored the rural Punjabi's distant relationship with the imperial Muslim state. For pastoralist and villager alike, the power of the saints derived from the popular belief that the saints, through their spiritual excellence, had secured after death places close to God and were thus in a position to intercede for others. The tombs of the saints became sites of special access to religious power—power that was transmitted through spiritual charisma, or *barakat,* both to the saints' tombs and, perhaps even more important, to their living descendants. The exercise of mediation by these descendants of saints came to define the dominant style of mediatory religious leadership in rural Punjab—a style epitomized by the hereditary custodians of the *sufi* shrines, men known usually as *sajjada nishin*s (literally, those who "sit on the prayer carpet"). These men, who were also generally *pir*s, or religious guides for wide circles of disciples (*murid*s), provided not only occasional religious instruction but also, far more important, mediation with higher spiritual authorities.[5] Their religious leadership, based on possession of *barakat,* reflected a worldview that derived in large part from the political structure in which Punjab's rural Islamic structure had arisen. As one early-twentieth-century observer remarked, in western Punjab God, like any imperial sovereign, was "a busy person," whose "hall of audience is of limited capacity." For all who sought divine intervention in their everyday lives, a spiritual patron or agent was a necessity: "an intervener between them and God."[6] Though religious leaders in rural Punjab might gain respect

---

4. Innumerable examples of the different local cults occur in accounts of shrines even within a single district: in Muzaffargarh, for example, the shrine of Daud Jahanian had "a celebrity for curing leprosy"; the shrine of Dera Din Panah was known for the large order of beggars it supported; and the shrine of Shahr Sultan was noted for the frenzied ceremonies in which *jinn* were expelled from women (*Muzaffargarh District Gazetteer,* 1908, 71–75).

5. The evolution of inherited saintliness among *sufi*s is discussed by J. Spencer Trimingham, *The Sufi Orders in Islam* (Oxford: Oxford University Press, 1971), 102–4. The role of the *pir* is described by Adrian C. Mayer, "*Pir* and *Murshid*: An Aspect of Religious Leadership in West Pakistan," *Middle Eastern Studies* 3, no. 2 (January 1967): 160–63. For a comprehensive study of the *pir* in modern Pakistani society, see also Katherine Pratt Ewing, "The Pir or Sufi Saint in Pakistani Islam" (Ph.D. diss., University of Chicago, 1980). A *pir* was not always *sajjada nishin* of a shrine, but a *gaddi* (throne) greatly increased a *pir*'s prestige; note the complaint of a *pir* without a shrine in Peter Mayne, *Saints of Sind* (London: John Murray, 1956), 177–78.

6. Aubrey O'Brien, "The Mohammadan Saints of the Western Punjab," *Journal of the Royal Anthropological Institute* 41 (1911): 511.

through piety, learning, or other spiritual excellences, the most important religious specialists were interveners, like the *sajjada nishin*s, who were able as the descendants of saints and inheritors of *barakat*, to offer effective access to religious power to others. The saints, as Peter Brown says of the saints of late Roman times, were the model patrons—men who, with their spiritual excellences and the ear of God, embodied the ideal of what a good patron ought to be.[7] If their *sajjada nishin*s were not always men of the same saintly piety, they were nevertheless accessible—men whose connections and whose ancestry made access to these patrons possible.[8]

In the centuries before the British arrived, networks of shrines loosely linked within the *sufi* orders spread through much of the province as the descendants and successors (*khalifa*s) of many of the major saints established their own *khanaqah*s, which in turn developed into new *sufi* shrines. The networks became particularly dense in parts of the Indus valley; in southwestern Punjab the shrines of the descendants of Saiyid Jalaluddin Bokhari of Uch dotted the countryside when the British arrived.[9] Though loosely linked, each of these shrines maintained its distinctive identity. Each shrine (or at least the more important) had its own annual *'urs* (literally, "wedding") festival, commemorating the death anniversary, the joining to God of the original saint—a ritual that defined the shrine's particular identity and its power as a gate of access to transcendent authority.[10] Such festivals also marked many shrines as important centers of rural economic and political power, where offerings—land, livestock, and produce—were collected and partially redistributed to pilgrims.[11] Most shrines maintained a free kitchen, or *langar*. A *sajjada nishin* who kept a *langar* was considered, in the words of one twentieth-century *pir*, like a great patron, "greater than one who

---

7. Peter Brown, *The Cult of the Saints* (Chicago: University of Chicago Press, 1981), 41. See also Peter Brown, "The Rise and Function of the Holy Man in Late Antiquity," *Journal of Roman Studies* 61 (1971).

8. Trimingham describes the increasing dissociation of saintliness from personal piety in the intercession by descendants of saints, certainly the case for Punjab's *sajjada nishin*s. See Trimingham, *The Sufi Orders in Islam*, 141.

9. At the turn of the twentieth century, the British counted at least thirty separate branches of the Bokhari Saiyid family, descendants of Saiyid Jalaluddin Bokhari of Uch and most connected with important shrines (*Jhang District Gazetteer*, 1908, 58).

10. For a British account of the *'urs* at the shrine of Baba Farid, see Miles Irving, "The Shrine of Baba Farid Shakarganj at Pakpattan," *Journal of the Panjab Historical Society* 1 (1911–12).

11. Eaton discusses redistribution at the shrine of Baba Farid as an exchange of *futuh* (gifts to the shrine) for *ta'wiz* (amulets for good fortune or protection against evil or illness) (Eaton, "Shrine of Baba Farid," in Metcalf, *Moral Conduct and Authority*, 336–37).

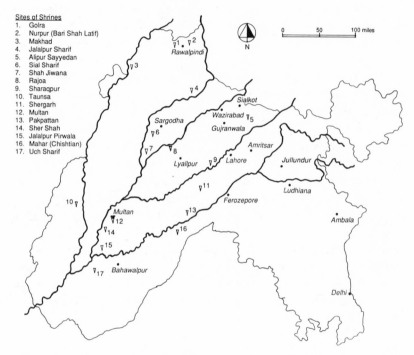

Sites of Shrines
1. Golra
2. Nurpur (Bari Shah Latif)
3. Makhad
4. Jalalpur Sharif
5. Alipur Sayyedan
6. Sial Sharif
7. Shah Jiwana
8. Rajoa
9. Sharaqpur
10. Taunsa
11. Shergarh
12. Multan
13. Pakpattan
14. Sher Shah
15. Jalalpur Pirwala
16. Mahar (Chishtian)
17. Uch Sharif

Map 2.   *Selected Cities and Shrines of Punjab*

does not."[12] Maintaining a *langar* and organizing a large *'urs* in fact signaled a shrine's prestige and authority—as a gate of mediation and, equally important, as a local redistributional center, a focus of economic and political influence.

It was the local political influence of the shrines that most clearly explained their direct connections with imperial political systems of pre-British times. Because of this considerable local influence, Muslim governments were quick to try to tie these shrines to the power of the state. For their part, the *sajjada nishins*, whose influence was grounded in heredity rather than personal piety, were often susceptible to state offers of honors, offices, and lands. In some cases the Mughals made land grants to shrines merely on condition that the *sajjada nishin* pray "for the prosperity of the government," as in a late-Mughal land grant to the shrine of Bahawal Haq at Multan.[13] In others, *sajjada nishins* were incorporated directly into the Mughal administration. The descendants of the sixteenth-century saint Pir Musa Pak Shahid, for example (himself a descendant of the great Qadri saint, Saiyid Muhammad Ghaus Gilani of Uch), served as governors of Multan in the time of Jahangir and Shah Jahan.[14] Though a detailed study of relations between the shrines and the Mughal state has not been undertaken, the Mughals apparently used the support of *sajjada nishins* to extend their hegemony and to dramatize the religious foundations of their regime. Irfan Habib suggests that the Mughal emperors, by offering land grants to *sajjada nishins*, sought to include "descendants of saints or religious divines" along with other *'ulama* in a class whose religious support would legitimize the foundations of their state.[15]

The *sufi* shrines of rural Punjab thus served as critical links between the Punjab countryside and the power of imperial Muslim states. Equally important, their ubiquitousness in rural Punjab dramatized the centrality of *sufi* idioms in rural religious life. If the saints served as mediators, they also embodied a pervasive ideal of religious authority. The

12. Deposition of Mian Mahmud of Taunsa. Privy Council Appeal No. 118 of 1921; Khwaja Muhammad Hamid vs. Mian Mahmud and others (Record of Proceedings, vol. 2 [evidence], 31–41 [Lincoln's Inn Library, case no. 88 of 1922]).

13. The grant was from the time of the Emperor Muhammad Shah; abstract translation of a copy of a Chak Nama dated 25th Rabi al-sani, 1141 A.H. (Board of Revenue, file 131/1575). For a discussion of land grants elsewhere, see Richard M. Eaton, *The Sufis of Bijapur* (Princeton: Princeton University Press, 1978), 203–42.

14. Lepel Griffin and Charles Massy, *Chiefs and Families of Note in the Punjab* (Lahore: Civil and Military Gazette Press, 1910), 2:324.

15. Irfan Habib, *The Agrarian System of Mughal India* (Bombay: Asia Publishing House, 1963), 309.

saints buried at the shrines were not just mediators but exemplars as
well, their lives dramatized in the innumerable hagiographic stories and
tales that inhabited the world of rural Punjabi folklore. Exemplary patrons and intermediaries, they helped to shape a distinctive style of rural
Islam.

THE BRITISH AND THE *SAJJADA NISHINS*

In linking their rule to ideas of local "tribal" authority, the British
also established a special relationship with this system of religious authority. On the level of official policy, the British had rejected religion as
a cultural foundation for the state's authority: in the second half of the
nineteenth century they had tried to dissociate the state from all official
connections with religious institutions and prohibited any direct state
support of mosques, temples, or shrines.[16] But in linking the power of
the state to rural hierarchies of mediation, the British had developed a
structure for incorporating local authorities and cultures into their empire. Despite their rejection of official religious foundations for the state,
British imperial ideology laid the foundations for a close relationship
with many of the rural shrines.

Initially, British relations with many shrines grew from the local political pressures the British faced in establishing their rural administration. At annexation, many of Punjab's *sajjada nishin*s wielded considerable local political power. This power had survived in many cases the
collapse of the Mughals and had been exercised actively in local politics before the arrival of the British.[17] The case of the *sajjada nishin* of
Baba Farid's shrine at Pakpattan provides a good example. The mid-
eighteenth-century *sajjada nishin* had asserted his autonomy from the
Mughals and had fought against other local tribal and Sikh chieftains,

---

16. The most important act in developing the government's religious policy was Act
XX of 1863, which set up legal procedures for the management of local religious institutions but barred the government from direct financial support of or control over them. For
a general discussion of the state's ambivalent role in religious institutions, see Arjun Appadurai, *Worship and Conflict under Colonial Rule: A South Indian Case* (Cambridge:
Cambridge University Press, 1981). In the Punjab, government sought after Act XX to
disconnect itself "from the direct pecuniary support of Native Religious Institutions"
(Punjab Archives, Revenue procs. 21–23, 4 February 1865). But the general difficulties of
the government in such matters, even before the act, are discussed by Ian Kerr, "The British and the Administration of the Golden Temple in 1859," *The Panjab Past and Present*
10, no. 2 (October 1976).
17. For the influence of Muslim shrines in the Sikh period, see W. Murray, "On the
Manners, Rules, and Customs of the Sikhs," in H. T. Prinsep, *Origin of the Sikh Power in
the Punjab* (Patiala: Punjab Languages Department, 1970), 166–67.

gaining political control of a substantial area.[18] A similar pattern involved the Bokhari Saiyids of Rajoa in Jhang district, whose sixteenth-
century ancestor had won from Akbar the grant of a tract around
Rajoa, but whose independence after the collapse of the Mughals "was
probably as much due to their quality as warriors as to the sacred character of the family"[19] Though the Sikhs subdued both these families,
they maintained at the time of annexation substantial independence.
With both religious influence and military power, such families possessed local influence that the British could not ignore.

But official British policy made administrators wary as they sought to
tap the local influence that the shrines supplied. Given the ideological
structure of British rule, officials found little room for shrines—as religious institutions—within the framework of the administration. After
annexation problems emerged clearly in a case involving the shrines of
Bahawal Haq and his grandson, Shah Rukn-i Alam, in Multan fort.
Though the *sajjada nishin* of these shrines had assisted the British during the siege of Multan in 1848–1849, the government of India had refused to sanction a proposed reward grant for repair of the shrines,
which had been damaged during the siege, on the grounds that such
a grant would violate the government's religious policy. The impact of
the *sajjada nishin*'s political influence could not be so easily dismissed
after the 1857 Mutiny when, as one high British official noted, his mere
"presence in our Court convinced the people that the most influential
man of their own faith was on the side of order." In spite of the difficulties, the lieutenant governor thus decided that the local political authority wielded by such *sajjada nishin*s was vital to the government. "In
no division are there so few Chiefs as in that of Mooltan. There is
scarcely an individual of territorial influence between the government
officials and a population almost exclusively pastoral and agricultural,
and as shown by recent experience very liable to be moved to insurrec-
tion by sudden and inadequate causes." Support of local men of influence was, the lieutenant governor thought, "in our obvious interest."
And "in the Mooltan District," he continued, "the foremost and most
influential man is Mukhdoom Shah Muhmood, the Head of the Shrine
of Bahawal Huq."[20]

Whatever their ideological consequences, such links to powerful

18. *Montgomery District Gazetteer*, 1933, 38.
19. *Jhang District Gazetteer*, 1908, 58.
20. Secretary, Board of Administration, Punjab to secretary, Government of India,
Foreign department, 13 September 1860 (Board of Revenue, file 131/1575).

local religious leaders drew the British into local religious affairs. When Makhdum Shah Mahmud died in 1869, for example, the deputy commissioner intervened at the shrine to perform the *dastarbandi* (turban-tying) ceremony signifying official recognition of the heir, a ceremony that local British officers performed for leading local families and "tribal" chiefs within their administration.[21] Intervention in disputes over *jagir* income and over succession soon followed and drew the British even closer to the administration of many shrines. Their involvement became explicit in the cases of shrines taken over by the Court of Wards. An institution established to give economic stability to the local intermediaries who were the backbone of the British administration, the Court of Wards preserved the estates of families facing crises as a result of indebtedness or succession problems. It was, however, a measure of the local political importance the British attached to the shrines that the estates of *sajjada nishin*s were among the earliest targets for Court of Wards takeover. The estate of the Qureshi family, *sajjada nishin*s of the shrine of Bahawal Haq, fell under the court in the 1890s as a result of heavy indebtedness. Estates of several other important southwest Punjab *sajjada nishin*s were also at various times under the court's control.[22] The political concerns prompting the court to assume these estates emerge clearly in the comments of the deputy commissioner of Multan on the case of the *sajjada nishin* of the shrine at Jalalpur Pirwala, whose lands were taken over in 1919. "It seems to me to be of political importance to prevent the disappearance of this family," the deputy commissioner wrote. "The southern part of the Shujabad Tehsil contains a large, rather sullen, very backward and somewhat unreliable population made up chiefly of Biloches. There are no big families and practically no men of outstanding position and influence." In these circumstances, the local influence of the *sajjada nishin* and his family, who were held "in considerable respect in the neighbourhood on account of their saintly descent," could not for political reasons be allowed to deteriorate.[23]

To be sure, Court of Wards control did not automatically bring the religious functions of a shrine under government supervision. On the contrary, the court usually avoided the administration of the religious ceremonies connected with the shrines, concentrating its attention in-

21. Griffin and Massy, *Chiefs and Families of Note*, 2:307.
22. Among the estates under control of the Court of Wards at various times were those at Sher Shah, Shah Jiwana, Jahanian Shah, Jalalpur Pirwala, and Pakpattan, and the estate of the Qureshi family of Multan.
23. J. M. Dunnett (deputy commissioner, Multan) to Lt.-Col. C. Thompson (commissioner, Multan), 11 April 1919 (Board of Revenue, file 601/1/27/23).

stead on the management of the estate. Thus, in the case of the Jalalpur Pirwala estate, the court initially excluded from the estate the shrine's religious income and expenditure, leaving them to the personal management of the *sajjada nishin*. His position, however, as simultaneously a religious leader and a local landed patron, made such distinctions hard to maintain. As the *sajjada nishin* of Jalalpur Pirwala implied in a petition to the government, the attempt to separate management of the estate's income from the *sajjada nishin*'s ritual religious duties only undermined the *sajjada nishin*'s position. Popular association fused the political with the religious influence of the *sajjada nishin*.[24] In the case of the shrine of Baba Farid at Pakpattan, the British themselves came to the same conclusion after that shrine was taken over by the court in the 1930s. Following the succession of a minor and a heated family inheritance dispute, the British decided in the Pakpattan case to include the management of the shrine with the management of the estate. This no doubt simplified the overall administration of the shrine and minimized internal conflict. But it also put the government in the touchy position of supervising the shrine's *'urs*. One annual Court of Wards administration report for the estate declared, "The management of this estate presents peculiar difficulties, and great tact is needed on the part of the manager, as the elder ward, Diwan Qutabud Din is the Gaddi nishin of an important shrine at Pakpattan. The Court of Wards has to see that those religious ceremonies which the sajjada nishin has to perform are properly done."[25]

In spite of official government policy, therefore, the British came to participate in the religious functioning of many rural shrines. The position of the shrines in rural society dictated the practical character of British policy. Though undoubtedly religious institutions, the shrines were also centers of local political influence whose attachment to the administration was critical in establishing local British control. Perhaps most important, as intermediary structures the shrines fit neatly into the ideological structure of the British imperial system. Many shrines served, much as "tribes" did, as foci for local identities, which the state had set itself to protect.

British recognition of this role was strikingly demonstrated in one in-

24. Petition of Makhdum Diwan Mohammad Ghaus (*sajjada nishin* at Jalalpur Pirwala) to Sir Sikander Hyat Khan (revenue member, Government of Punjab) 19 November 1933 (ibid., file 601/1/27/23A).

25. Review of the administration of the Pakpattan estate for the year ending 30 September 1938 (ibid., file 601/10/24/88).

cident in 1915 involving a shrine in Rawalpindi district. Local British officials recommended a small land grant for the shrine of Bari Shah Latif at Nurpur after local villagers had united to thwart an attempted dacoity, or armed robbery, in the area. The villagers credited the shrine itself with having jammed the dacoits' guns. Though perhaps doubting the shrine's instrumentality in the affair, the British recognized the shrine as a symbol of the collective spirit manifested by the villagers in the action.[26] Such direct recognition of a shrine as the embodiment of local solidarity indicated the general tendency of many British officials to treat the heads of shrines like local patrons or "tribal" leaders as cultural embodiments of local identities. Indeed, the British selected many *sajjada nishin*s to serve as local representatives in the rural administration as *zaildar*s, honorary magistrates, and district board members.[27]

Perhaps most significant, many *sajjada nishin*s were in the twentieth century incorporated directly into the framework of the British administration under the terms laid down by the Alienation of Land Act. The "tribes" to which the great majority of *sajjada nishin*s belonged, Saiyids and Qureshis, were gazetted under the act in nearly all districts as "agricultural tribes," whose lands were thus to be protected for political reasons from expropriation. In explaining this inclusion, the Punjab settlement commissioner, James Wilson, noted the political importance of these Muslim religious leaders and stressed the protection of their lands if their position were to be maintained. The Muslim religious "tribes," he said, referring primarily to those associated with the shrines,

> are generally poor managers and very ready to part with the lands, which in most instances their ancestors have acquired by gift in recognition of their sacred character. If it is desirable to maintain their possession of their land, they require protection almost more than any other class. They are generally very poor agriculturalists, but they often own large areas, they do not lend money on interest, and for political reasons they should be protected.[28]

26. The proposal to award the shrine a canal colony grant was ultimately rejected. "I don't think that the shrine promises to make a good colonist," the senior secretary to the financial commissioners wrote. But the shrine was awarded an increased *mu'afi* (revenue-free holding) in the village and a cash reward for the actions of the villagers (ibid., file 131/1742).
27. In Jhang, Muzaffargarh, and Multan districts *sajjada nishin*s played leading roles as *zaildar*s, honorary magistrates, and district board members (*Jhang District Gazetteer*, 1908, 58–60; *Muzaffargarh District Gazetteer*, 1929, 75–77; *Multan District Gazetteer*, 1923–24, 106–10).
28. Note by J. Wilson (Punjab settlement commissioner), 1 February 1901 (Board of Revenue, file 442/1/00/4).

This identification with the "agricultural tribes" emerged even more clearly when the British distributed "landed gentry" grants several years later. Though official policy had initially barred the distribution of land grants to religious institutions, the political logic of British administrators finally overrode these technical considerations. As the lieutenant governor, Sir Denzil Ibbetson, argued in 1907 with regard to a proposed canal colony grant for the *sajjada nishin* of the shrine at Makhad on the Indus, it was quite wrong to associate such grants primarily with religious purposes. "On the contrary," E. D. Maclagan wrote of Ibbetson's attitude, such a grant "appears to him to be in essence a political grant, and the numerous petitions which have been presented to the Deputy Commissioner [of Attock district] praying for such a grant show the popular feeling on the subject." [29]

This logic carried the day when the "landed gentry" grants were distributed in 1914. Although H. J. Maynard noted in the case of Makhad that "it would be a straining of language to call the pir one of the hereditary landed gentry of the province," [30] the lieutenant governor, Sir Michael O'Dwyer, answered that whatever the technical objections, the influence of such local religious heads with the "tribes" could not be ignored. "Besides being the spiritual head of the important Awan tribe," O'Dwyer wrote of the Pir of Makhad, "his influence over the Pathan tribes on both sides of the Indus—notably the Khattaks—and the fact that he is regarded with veneration by many of the leading Frontier and western Punjab chiefs should be taken into account." If other *sajjada nishin*s could show similar influence, then their claims were also to be considered: "If a man has political influence and uses it well," O'Dwyer argued, "the fact that he is connected with a religious institution and even to a certain extent derives his influence from that connection should not in my opinion stand in the way of his obtaining a grant." [31] Subsequently, the Pir of Makhad and a number of other *sajjada nishin*s did receive official "landed gentry" recognition. In Montgomery, Muzaffargarh, and Multan districts of southwestern Punjab, Muslim families of religious influence composed fully one third of the locally influential families who received "landed gentry" grants. [32] By the early

29. E. D. Maclagan (chief secretary, Punjab) to secretary to Government of India, Revenue and Agriculture, 29 April 1907 (ibid., file 131/1479).
30. Note by H. J. Maynard, 17 April 1914 (ibid., file 301/3/00/164A).
31. Note by Sir Michael O'Dwyer, 19 May 1914 (ibid.).
32. Register of Landed Gentry grants, Multan division (ibid., file 301/1176KW).

twentieth century, the *sajjada nishin*s of many important shrines of Punjab were thus incorporated into that class of landed, "tribally" based leaders who formed the backbone of the British administration.

REFORM AND REVIVAL:
THE ISLAMIC SYSTEM

Rural religious leaders thus took their places within the categories designated for Punjab's landed and "tribal" leaders, adding local religious influence and religious legitimacy to the larger British regime. But their incorporation did not eliminate the underlying cultural ambiguities that were a product of colonial rule. As Clifford Geertz writes of the Dutch in Java: the colonial regime, whatever else it might be, could never be Muslim.[33] Although the British established an authority structure that effectively incorporated local patrons of many types—religious and "tribal"—into an imperial system, it was a system from which the central symbolism of Muslim power was entirely missing. Though the shrines, by the very structure of their influence, found a place within the British system, their relationship to the state had undergone a critical change from the days of the Mughals, when state support for the shrines had helped to underscore the state's *religious* foundations. And the result was profound tension in the overall structure of Punjab's Islamic "cultural system" and in the position of the shrines within it.

THE 'ULAMA

The nature of this tension can perhaps best be understood by turning from the Punjabi shrines to another important religious class in Muslim India—the *'ulama*. As a class defined not primarily by heredity or local position but by learning in Islam's classical, normative texts, the *'ulama* provide an entirely different structural perspective on colonial rule. Indeed, although the precise definition of the *'ulama* as a class is problematic, the position of the *'ulama* within the structure of Indian Islam had traditionally been far different from that of the *sajjada nishin*s.[34] The *'ulama* had not historically served as mediators in the countryside, either between man and the saints or between local cultures and the

33. Geertz, *Islam Observed*, 64.
34. Historical problems in the definition of the *'ulama* as a clearly defined "class" are highlighted in Wilfred Cantwell Smith, "The 'Ulama' in Indian Politics," in C. H. Philips, ed., *Politics and Society in India* (London: George Allen & Unwin, 1963), 42.

Islamic tradition; they had served rather, under the Mughals, as learned interpreters of Islam—as *muftis*, or legal scholars; as *imams*, or prayer leaders; as *qazis*, or judges within the state administration. Although their relationship to the court was often ambiguous, the role of the *'ulama* in preserving and interpreting Islamic law and Islam's classical texts had helped to define the Islamic legitimacy of Muslim states themselves. Their relationship with the state was thus very different from that of the *sajjada nishins*.

The reactions of the *'ulama* at Delhi to the collapse of Muslim political power and the rise of colonial rule also greatly differed from those of Punjab's *sajjada nishins*. The history of the leading *'ulama* at Delhi in the years of Mughal decline has been much discussed.[35] Though many *sajjada nishins* kept their political influence in the localities even after the Mughal collapse, the decline of the Mughals seemed for the *'ulama* at Delhi nothing less than a catastrophe. It signaled the disappearance of the cultural axis around which the entire Indian Islamic system had developed. As W. C. Smith argues, the Indian *'ulama* had long perceived themselves to be "the custodians of the conscience of the community." But in the days of the Mughals the "community" had depended on the state for its organized form. With the collapse of central Muslim political authority, the *'ulama* thus faced a new dilemma in defining the practical meaning of Islamic community in India. Not only "had the meaning of the Islamic system as a whole seriously shifted," Smith writes, "but also the responsibility for its maintenance now fell on the ulama class" directly.[36] To suggest that the Indian *'ulama* as a whole self-consciously responded to this crisis with a new style of leadership would overstate the case. But it is no exaggeration to suggest that the decline of the Mughal state prompted a serious reorientation among many of Delhi's leading *'ulama*. Beginning with Shah Waliullah in the eighteenth century, the leading Delhi *'ulama* spearheaded a movement of reform that ultimately effected the entire structure of Indian Islamic leadership, redefining the role of religious leaders in general within Indian Islam's "cultural system."

At the heart of this movement lay an attempt to define a new style of leadership. Reform-minded *'ulama* attempted in the nineteenth century to chalk out for themselves new roles as popular religious teachers,

35. See, for example, Ishtiaq Husain Qureshi, *Ulema in Politics* (Karachi: Ma'aref, 1972), 99–152; Barbara Daly Metcalf, *Islamic Revival in British India: Deoband, 1860–1900* (Princeton: Princeton University Press, 1982), 16–86.
36. Smith, "The 'Ulama' in Indian Politics," 42–43.

whose "leadership rested neither on political position nor on attempts
to influence political leaders," but on their ability to instill in individual
Muslims the basic principles of Islam.[37] By the nineteenth century many
of the leading religious scholars of north India had been dispersed into
the small towns of the northern heartland where the old Muslim service
gentry still held local political sway.[38] But with the disappearance of a
central Islamic state, the definition of the Muslim community had come
to depend for many of these 'ulama not on the state, but on the personal
adherence of individual Muslims to Islamic norms. Such concerns were
only heightened with the establishment of British rule. With no symbolic focal point for Muslim identity, many 'ulama concentrated their
energies under the colonial regime on developing through public debate,
popular preaching, and the extensive dissemination of religious literature in Urdu, a conception of the Islamic community that depended primarily on the popular acceptance by Muslims of the fundamentals of
personal Islamic practice.[39]

The 'ulama predicated their efforts on the spread in the nineteenth
century of a type of popular religious organization far different from
that centered on the shrines. Rather than focusing on institutions of mediation, the 'ulama organized schools to disseminate the knowledge of
correct Islamic thought and practice. The organizational model for the
reformist 'ulama was the dar al-'ulum founded in 1867 at Deoband in
the United Provinces, a religious school organized independent of state
support to train a class of activist, reform-minded 'ulama.[40] Though the
influence of the school at Deoband was greatest in the heartland of the
old Mughal empire, it provided a model to spread the influence of these
reformers to much of the rest of India—including the Punjab. As Barbara
Metcalf points out, the school at Deoband attracted contributions from
numerous Punjabis, particularly those living in cities and towns. Perhaps more important, it ultimately spawned several schools in Punjab
patterned on the Deobandi model.[41]

37. Barbara Daly Metcalf, "The Reformist 'Ulama: Muslim Religious Leadership in
India, 1860–1900" (Ph.D. diss., University of California, Berkeley, 1974), 19.
38. For a discussion of the qasba towns of northern India, see C. A. Bayly, Rulers,
Townsmen, and Bazaars: North Indian Society in the Age of British Expansion, 1770–
1870 (Cambridge: Cambridge University Press, 1983), 189–93. For the significance of the
qasbas for the 'ulama, see also Metcalf, Islamic Revival, 63, 85.
39. Metcalf, Islamic Revival, 198–234.
40. Barbara Daly Metcalf, "The Madrasa at Deoband: A Model for Religious Education in Modern India," Modern Asian Studies 12, no. 1 (1978): 111–34.
41. Metcalf, Islamic Revival, 133–37, 252, 263. For a review indicating the spread of
madrasas of the Deobandi maslak (perspective) in twentieth-century Punjab, see Hafiz

Indeed, the new Deobandi model served as the foundation for a network of religious schools in Punjab that transformed twentieth-century Islamic education in the province. Although Islamic religious schools were nothing new in Punjab, they gained a new independence and importance as popular subscription challenged state and local patronage as a basis for religious education. And the model served as a foundation for schools developed by *'ulama* of differing religious perspectives as well. The Ahl-i Hadis, for example, reformers even more thoroughgoing than the Deobandis in their reformist outlook, founded a number of influential Punjabi schools.[42] By the late nineteenth and early twentieth centuries such schools had come to play an increasingly important part in the religious life of the province.

But the spread of reformist organization was most important perhaps because it called into question the concepts on which the dominant system of religious authority and the power of the rural *sajjada nishin*s were based. In stressing religious solidarity and personal transformation independent of political mediation, the *'ulama* strongly challenged the mediatory concept underlying the entire system of religious authority based on shrines—a concept that many of the *'ulama* saw as increasingly irrelevant in a society under non-Muslim, colonial rule. The attacks of the *'ulama* focused not solely on the relationship that had developed between *sajjada nishin*s and the British administration but on the basic religious foundations of the *sajjada nishin*s' authority. This attack was made most forcefully by the *'ulama* of the Ahl-i Hadis perspective, who emphasized the primary importance of the *Qor'an* and *hadis* as guides for religious practice and who criticized the allegiance to hereditary *pir*s within the *sufi* orders and the worship at tombs as fundamentally un-Islamic. Other reformists, such as the *'ulama* of Deoband, were not so categorical in rejecting sufism or the *sufi* orders; they recognized the continuing importance in religious experience of allegiance to *pir*s. But like the Ahl-i Hadis, they rejected the mediatory organizational forms that had adapted Islam to local culture and had dominated popu-

---

Nazar Ahmad, *Ja'iza-yi Madaris-i 'Arabiya Maghribi Pakistan*, 2 (Lahore: Muslim Akademi, 1972), 17–367.

42. According to a survey published by the All-India Ahl-i Hadis Conference in the 1930s, the Ahl-i Hadis operated twenty-six religious schools in Punjab, a number surpassed in India only by the region including eastern U.P. and Bihar (Maulana Abu Yahya Imam Khan Naushervi, *Hindustan men Ahl-i Hadis ki 'Ilmi Khidmat* [Chichawatni: Maktaba-yi Naziriya, 1970], 172–88). Popular influence of these Punjabi religious schools is difficult to judge, but in 1931 the census recorded 180,000 Ahl-i Hadis adherents in the province (*Census of India*, 1931, vol. 17 [Punjab], pt. 1, 313).

lar religion in the Punjab. The Deobandis did not approve, for example, of the centrality of the worship at tombs in religious organization or believe in the *'urs*.[43] They also attacked the adherence to local customs common in rural Punjabi religion, seeing the power of local custom as a compromise in commitment to the *sunnat,* the way of the Prophet.[44] For the reformist *'ulama* the central duty of a religious leader was not to provide mediation with higher spiritual authority but guidance and example to the common people in the religious duties of Islam. By attacking the religious practice associated with the shrines, therefore, and by emphasizing personal adherence to the basic duties of Islam in defining Islamic identity, the reformists were attacking the very foundation of the conceptual system of rural Islam.

Implicit in this attack was one on the British system of hierarchical imperial authority as well. But of more fundamental significance was a challenge to the structure underlying the "cultural system" of Punjabi Islam. The social model of the reformists was one taken from the time of the Prophet, but the historical inspiration for their reformist outlook was the change after the fall of the Mughals in the character of the state. Without an Islamic state, the *'ulama* saw that a fundamental reordering of Muslim life was required. Structures of mediation could no longer effectively define a Muslim community's presence in colonial India. The cultural meaning of mediation itself had thus undergone a critical change. Though the direct impact of the reformist *'ulama* on rural Punjabi life was limited, the cultural tensions that their work dramatized were reflected not only in the religious schools challenging Punjab's mediational forms of Islam, but also in the development of important currents of reform even within the mediational structure of rural Islamic society itself.

THE MOVEMENT OF *SUFI* REVIVAL

The cultural ambiguities within the British imperial system in fact found their most telling resonance in an important movement of reform within the structure of the rural *sufi* orders. This movement of *sufi* revival suggested, perhaps most clearly of all, the ambivalent impact of the state on the overall development of Islamic religious organization. Though it found its clearest expression in rural Punjab in the eighteenth

43. Metcalf, *Islamic Revival,* 273–74, 181–83.
44. See, for example, Barbara Daly Metcalf, "Islam and Custom in Nineteenth-Century India," *Contributions to Asian Studies* 17 (1982).

and nineteenth centuries, this *sufi* revival movement originated, like that of the reformist *'ulama,* in Delhi in the declining years of the Mughal empire. The original impetus to revive the Chishti order came from Shah Kalimullah of Delhi (1650–1729). To revitalize the Muslim community in India in the face of declining central power, he reorganized the Chishti order and emphasized the central importance of *tabligh,* or the active propagation of Islam, as its fundamental mission. More important for the Punjab was the work of one of Shah Kalimullah's spiritual descendants, Shah Fakhruddin of Delhi (1717–1785). Like his contemporary, Shah Waliullah, he was concerned in a time of declining political authority to make Muslims more aware of participating in the larger Islamic community. Unlike Shah Waliullah, Shah Fakhruddin's influence developed not, ultimately, in new forms of organization, but within the existing institutional structure of the *sufi* orders.[45]

Shah Fakhruddin's influence spread primarily through the establishment by his *khalifa*s of a network of Chishti *khanaqah*s in the eighteenth and nineteenth centuries, whose influence developed most fully in western Punjab. Shah Fakhruddin's most important *khalifa,* Khwaja Nur Muhammad Maharvi (1730–1791), established his own *khanaqah* at Mahar, in Bahawalpur, gathering around him a large group of disciples.[46] The most characteristic of these new *pir*s was Khwaja Nur Muhammad's *khalifa,* Khwaja Suleman of Taunsa (1770–1850), whose work typified the distinctive character of this nineteenth-century rural *sufi* revival. Khwaja Suleman established his *khanaqah* in the north of Dera Ghazi Khan district, along the Indus, at a time when, as K. A. Nizami writes in his history of the Chishti order, Muslims in Punjab were particularly demoralized under Sikh rule. In these circumstances, like the reformist *'ulama,* he was particularly concerned with directing Muslims to internal spiritual regeneration.[47] But at the same time, having established himself among Biloch and Pathan tribesmen, he operated within the context of existing structures of local tribal authority. Though he established a school at his *khanaqah* for teaching the fundamentals of *shari'at,* his *khanaqah,* and later his shrine, became popu-

45. On the work and influence of Shah Kalimullah and Shah Fakhruddin, see Khaliq Ahmad Nizami, *Tarikh-i Masha'ikh-i Chisht* (Karachi: Maktaba-yi Arifin, 1975), 366–426, 460–529.

46. On the influence of Khwaja Nur Muhammad, see Nizami, *Tarikh,* 530–60. See also M. Zameeruddin Siddiqi, "The Resurgence of the Chishti Silsilah in the Punjab During the Eighteenth Century," *Proceedings of the Indian History Congress, 1970* (New Delhi: Indian History Congress, 1971): 1:408–12.

47. Nizami, *Tarikh,* 608–9.

lar largely as a mediatory center, in the tradition of many of the older shrines. Though Khwaja Suleman sometimes criticized the blind faith in *pirs* common among the people, he himself nevertheless became a *pir* of considerable standing and numbered important local leaders among his *murids*.[48] Khwaja Suleman's *khanaqah* in fact received the protection of tribal leaders as a local spiritual center.[49] After Khwaja Suleman's death this mediatory center became a shrine; construction of an imposing tomb over the saint's grave was financed largely by the Nawab of Bahawalpur.[50]

Under the subsequent tenure of Khwaja Suleman's grandson and successor, Khwaja Allah Bakhsh, the shrine prospered, rivaling the influence of many older shrines in the area. Disciples flocked to the shrine for Khwaja Suleman's *'urs*, seeking the instrumental aid and mediation with higher spiritual authority that was promised at any great *sufi*'s tomb.[51] At the same time, as *sajjada nishin*, Khwaja Allah Bakhsh continued the work of spiritual reform and education begun by his grandfather, maintaining the shrine not only as a center of mediation but, in response to the cultural pressures accompanying the establishment of British rule, as a center for personal religious instruction as well.

With the firm establishment of British control in Punjab, such concerns were thrown into even sharper relief. The important religious role of these *pirs* under the British was demonstrated most strikingly by the career of one of Khwaja Suleman's most influential spiritual descendants, Saiyid Mehr Ali Shah of Golra (1856–1937). Saiyid Mehr Ali Shah was the son of the *sajjada nishin* of a Qadri shrine in Rawalpindi district, a man who traced his ancestry to Saiyid Muhammad Ghaus Gilani of Uch. Like many Punjabis who sought an advanced religious education in British India, Mehr Ali Shah traveled to the United Provinces, where he studied *hadis* and *tafsir* (Qor'anic exegesis) with leading *'ulama* in the reformist tradition.[52] Returning to Punjab with a concern for reform, he became the disciple of an important *khalifa* of Khwaja

48. Ibid., 620–22, 638.
49. Griffin and Massy, *Chiefs and Families of Note*, 2:388.
50. *Indian Appeals*, vol. 50 (1922), 97. Privy Council Appeal No. 118 of 1921; Khwaja Mohammad Hamid vs. Mian Mahmud and others.
51. As one early-twentieth-century witness put it, the *'urs* of Shah Suleman attracted so many worshippers that "the town cannot contain them." Deposition of Mahmud, Sadr Qanungo, Dera Ghazi Khan. Privy Council Appeal No. 118 of 1921; Khwaja Mohammad Hamid vs. Mian Mahmud and others (Record of Proceedings, vol. 1 [evidence], 55–59 [Lincoln's Inn Library, case no. 88 of 1922]).
52. Maulana Faiz Ahmad Faiz, *Mihr-i Munir* (Golra: Saiyid Ghulam Mohyuddin, 1973?), 73–84.

Suleman, Khwaja Shamsuddin of Sial Sharif; under his influence Mehr
Ali Shah transformed Golra into a major Chishti center. Subsequently,
as *sajjada nishin* of the shrine at Golra and a leading Chishti *pir*, Mehr
Ali Shah extended his religious influence among many western Punjab
families, "tribal" leaders of growing importance in the British administration. Claiming Unionist party leaders such as Sir Umar Hyat Khan
Tiwana and Sir Sikander Hyat Khan among his supporters and followers, Mehr Ali Shah became, despite his reformist leanings, one of the
most influential *sajjada nishin*s of British Punjab.[53]

Nevertheless, Mehr Ali Shah's religious views set him off from many
*sajjada nishin*s who had come to terms with the British government. He
refused to be drawn into direct association with the British government,
however much it supported a mediational religious style. He maintained
his deep reformist concern with the personal instruction of his disciples
in the individual obligations of Islam, issuing numerous *fatwa*s (rulings)
on points of religious law and gaining a reputation for religious learning among a section of *'ulama*. His position exemplified the two major
aspects of the Chishti revival. With a continuing emphasis on the *sufi*
order, the *piri-muridi* bond, the shrine, and the *'urs*, his influence was
well adapted to the diffuse structure of rural society under the "tribally"
based British administration. But he combined this emphasis with a
deep concern for personal adherence to the obligations of the *shari'at*;
he stressed the need in colonial society for the direct, personal expression of each individual's Muslim identity.

Such views and concerns were not confined to the Chishti order. In
the nineteenth century the Naqshbandi order, with its own reforming
traditions, produced several important rural *pir*s who, like the reform-
minded Chishtis, emphasized the reforming mission of the Naqshbandi
order within the rural organization of *khanaqah* and shrine. The history
of the Naqshbandi order in Punjab remains to be written.[54] But one
Naqshbandi *sajjada nishin* deserves special mention here for his important political role in British Punjab. Pir Jamaat Ali Shah of Alipur
Sayyedan (1841?–1951) came from an old family of Qadri *sajjada nishin*s
in Sialkot district, but like Mehr Ali Shah, he found his religious mission
in one of the more active, reforming orders in Punjab—in this case, the
Naqshbandi. Though Jamaat Ali Shah, like Mehr Ali Shah, was edu-

53. Ibid., 297–98.
54. For a general outline of the history of the Naqshbandi order, see Hamid Algar,
"The Naqshbandi Order: A Preliminary Survey of its History and Significance," *Studia
Islamica* 44 (1977).

cated among the leading reformist *'ulama,* he maintained a deep belief
in *sufi* organization and in mediation. So great was his ideological commitment to these forms that he attempted to organize Indian *sufis* in a
body to meet the attacks of their scripturalist opponents, the Anjuman
Khuddam al-Sufiya. Like the early Chishti revivalists, Pir Jamaat Ali
Shah's most burning religious concern was work in *tabligh,* or the active
propagation of Islam. He made extensive tours of Punjab and much of
India, stressing the importance of the performance of religious duties
according to *shari'at* and establishing mosques in towns and villages.
This work greatly expanded his influence and led to contacts with
powerful Muslims whose wealth he tapped for religious causes. By the
opening of the twentieth century, Pir Jamaat Ali Shah could claim an
extensive following, both in rural northern Punjab and among powerful
Muslims elsewhere, which made his political influence comparable to
that of any Chishti revival *pirs.* Like other *sufi* leaders, he was sensitive
to new responsibilities facing Islamic religious leaders in British India.
But he based his influence squarely within the hierarchical structure underlying the British imperial system.[55]

With such influence, Jamaat Ali Shah and many other revival *pirs*
defined for themselves a distinctive position within the structure of
Punjabi Islam. Their general influence was heightened by the gradual
emergence in the late nineteenth century of a group of sympathetic
'ulama, whose work gave religious coherence to the *sufi* revival movement as a whole. This group of *'ulama,* who called themselves Ahl-i
Sunnat o Jama'at, and who in the twentieth century came increasingly
to be known as Barelvi,[56] defined themselves in the late nineteenth and
early twentieth centuries as distinct from the main body of reformist
'ulama influenced by Deoband. Though they drew on the Deobandi
model for the creation of their own networks of schools, they championed a religious outlook in which religious mediation and custom had
a continuing and central place. Their most important schools in Punjab—the Dar al-'Ulum Naumaniya, founded at Lahore in 1887; and the
Dar al-'Ulum Hizb al-Ahnaf, opened in the 1920s—thus provided a religious and organizational focus for the rural *sufi* revival as a whole.[57]

55. This account of Pir Jamaat Ali Shah's life is based primarily on Saiyid Akhtar Husain Shah, *Sirat-i Amir-i Millat* (Alipur Sayyedan: author, 1974).
56. The Barelvi perspective, similar to that of the self-styled Ahl-i Sunnat o Jama'at of
the Punjab, was defined by the prolific work of Maulana Ahmad Raza Khan of Bareilly
(1855–1921) in the United Provinces. On the Barelvi *maslak,* see Metcalf, *Islamic Revival,* 296–314.
57. On the founding of these schools, see Nazar Ahmad, *Ja'iza,* 2:28–29; and Iqbal

Their schools in fact received direct financial support from many revival
pirs. Pir Jamaat Ali Shah, for example, donated "hundreds of rupees to
the *madrasa* Naumaniya and the *anjuman* Hizb al-Ahnaf, so that," as
one of his followers put it, "these pure religious institutions might ex-
pand, prosper and serve Islam." [58]

Perhaps most important, however, the schools also provided a base
for the definition of a distinct theological perspective supporting the
religious reforms associated with the shrines—a perspective which
crystallized in active debate with the Ahl-i Hadis and the Deobandis: In
theological terms, the disputation of these *'ulama* centered on such
issues as whether the Prophet Muhammad was to be attributed semi-
divine qualities or whether he was to be viewed, in reformist terms, pre-
eminently as a human exemplar, a dispute reflected also in conflict
over the importance to be attached to such ritual celebrations as the
milad al-nabi, the Prophet's birthday. [59] Other disputes centered on the
general meaning of religious leadership: Were religious leaders meant to
serve primarily as teachers and exemplars? as the reformists seemed to
argue, or as spiritual mediators as well, like the reform-minded rural
pirs? Such arguments had important implications for the structure of
Punjab's Islamic "cultural system" as a whole. The arguments of the
Barelvi *'ulama* aimed at legitimizing the religious authority of all the
sufi revival *pirs,* but according to the standards of religious education
and debate developed by the reformers. To an important degree, the
presence of these *'ulama* thus helped to justify the entire movement of
rural *sufi* revival.

By the twentieth century this reform movement thus produced a critical new element within the colonial religious structure. Like the reformist *'ulama,* the *pirs* of the *sufi* revival and the *'ulama* who supported
them increasingly emphasized adherence to scriptural Islamic norms in
defining Islamic identity; in a society without the symbol of a Muslim
state, personal adherence was essential. But unlike the reformist *'ulama*
of Deoband and the even more strident reformers of the Ahl-i Hadis, the
reformers of the *sufi* revival had not abandoned the mediatory organiza-

---

Ahmad Faruqi, *Tazkira-yi 'Ulama-yi Ahl-i Sunnat o Jama'at, Lahore* (Lahore: Maktaba-
yi Nabviya, 1975), 320–21.

58. Haider Husain Shah, *Shah-yi Jama'at* (Lahore: Maktaba-yi Shah-yi Jama'at,
1973), 116. Pir Mehr Ali Shah of Golra spoke at several annual *majlis* (meetings) of the
Dar al-'Ulum Naumaniya (Muhammad Din Kalim, *Lahore ke Auliya-yi Chisht* [Lahore:
Maktaba-yi Nabviya, 1967], 143–44).

59. Such controversy is discussed in Faruqi, *Tazkira,* 207–11.

tional structure of rural Punjabi Islam. The shrines, as hinges within an imperial "cultural system," continued to serve for these reformers, as for the *sajjada nishin*s of the older shrines, as foci for a popular rural Punjabi worldview in which the need for mediation was central. Such a worldview had, in fact, become all the more pervasive within the ideological context of British imperial rule. Just as their concern with religious reform reflected a search in British India for a new definition of Islamic community, their continuing emphasis on mediation reflected the hierarchical structure of local "tribal" authority on which the British had built their administration.

RELIGION AND RURAL POLITICS

How then did the structure of British rule shape the role of Islam in Punjabi politics? The political positions of Islamic religious leaders reflected their places within the larger political and ideological structure of British rule. The most straightforward response to the British came from the *sajjada nishin*s of the older shrines, whose local interests bound them closely to the British administration and to the Unionist party. The position of Saiyid Muhammad Husain, *sajjada nishin* of the Qadri shrine at Shergarh (Montgomery district), epitomized the political roles of these *sajjada nishin*s. Pir Muhammad Husain was elected to the provincial council in the 1920s and became one of the Unionist party's most important spokesmen. As an influential local landowner with ties to the rural administration, he defined no special religious interests in the council apart from his support of the Land Alienation Act and the Unionist party. Though supporting the general Unionist position on the advancement of Muslims in the services, Muhammad Husain tied this to the advance of the "agricultural tribes." [60] The ideological structure of British authority nurtured the religious influence of these local leaders and integrated them into the structure of imperial power. With a secure religious base in the countryside, they saw little reason to advance a distinctively Islamic political position.

But their position clashed with that of many reformist *'ulama*. The universal definition of Muslim identity was far more important to them than a place within the imperial administration. Having focused their attention primarily on the spread of popular religious education in the

60. "The root cause of all the Hindu-Muhammadan disunion in the province," Muhammad Husain said, "is the indebtedness of the masses" (Punjab, *Legislative Council Debates*, vol. 6 [1924]: 229).

late nineteenth century, many of the *'ulama* of Deoband had at that time deemphasized politics.[61] But as popular political institutions gradually emerged in the twentieth century, many began to recognize politics as an important instrument for the public expression of religious concerns. Unlike the rural *pirs*, however, they moved into politics largely outside the structure of the imperial administration. In the Punjab, many reformist *'ulama* participated first in the Khilafat movement, which focused public attention on the Turkish Khalifa as a symbol of Muslim unity transcending the colonial state. But the emerging political ideals of the Deobandi *'ulama* were most clearly embodied in the launching of the Jami'at-i 'Ulama-yi Hind at Amritsar in 1919.[62] Through the Jami'at, the reformist *'ulama* sought to provide political leadership grounded in the universal values of the *shari'at* and entirely independent of the authority of the colonial state. As a blueprint for Islamic authority in India, the Jami'at's founding was punctuated by the passage of a resolution at its 1921 Lahore session calling for the election by the *'ulama* of a learned Amir-i Hind, or leader of the Indian Muslim community, who could implement the "mandates of the *shari'a*" within colonial India.[63] These *'ulama* were searching for a new and independent structure of political organization consistent with their concern for individual Islamic reforms.

It was, however, the *pirs* of the rural *sufi* revival whose political position dramatized perhaps most clearly of all the conflicting cultural and political pressures that had been created for religious leaders by the establishment of the British imperial system. Unlike the reformist *'ulama,* whose practical political influence outside Punjab's cities was limited, the political influence of these *pirs* was firmly embedded in rural society. Their authority was grounded in a world in which local kin-based organization remained vital and in which local "tribal" leaders served as mediators with the imperial government. Many were closely linked to rural, "tribal" magnates by ties of economic and social dependence and by bonds of marriage.[64] But the *pirs* of the *sufi* revival tradition were

61. Metcalf, "The Madrasa at Deoband," 111.
62. Peter Hardy, *The Muslims of British India* (Cambridge: Cambridge University Press, 1972), 189. On the political concerns of the *'ulama,* see also Hardy, *Partners in Freedom—and True Muslims: The Political Thought of Some Muslim Scholars in British India* (Lund: Scandinavian Institute of Asian Studies, 1971).
63. Hardy, *The Muslims of British India,* 193–94; Mushir U. Haq, *Muslim Politics in Modern India, 1857–1947* (Meerut: Meenakshi Prakashan, 1970), 98–99.
64. Marriages to *sajjada nishins* conferred high status in rural Punjab, particularly when the *sajjada nishins* claimed Saiyid or Qureshi ancestry, as most did. Even when they did not, however, religious families were prime marriage alliances for wealthy families of

also attracted strongly to the politics of Islamic symbols. Their associations with many *'ulama* had long sensitized them to symbolic religious issues, and they often sought to remind rural Muslims that, even without a Muslim state, they were all part of a wider Islamic world. They thus repeatedly joined the *'ulama* in defense of Islamic symbols and, at times, in religious attacks on the colonial system. But with fundamentally different ideas about the structure of the Muslim community, and about the proper roles of religious leaders within it, their relations with the *'ulama* were marked by considerable tension.

Such tension emerged, for example, during the Khilafat movement after World War I. Many *pirs* joined reformist *'ulama* in strong support for the Khilafat, which was a symbol of communal unity and a focus for religious organization independent of the colonial government. But many shied away from the structural implications of a reformist attack on the British system, which seemed to threaten the foundations of their mediational authority. Though some revival *pirs*, such as Pir Ziauddin of Sial Sharif, joined the Jami'at-i 'Ulama-yi Hind in issuing anti-British *fatwa*s, others proved less willing to join a direct, reformist attack on British rule and rural mediation.[65] Indeed, the tensions inherent in the movement appeared dramatically when Pir Ziauddin allowed a radical *'alim* of strong reformist leanings, Maulana Muhammad Ishaq Manshervi, to issue a public challenge at the Sial *'urs* for a debate with the Pir of Golra, who opposed the radical phase of the Khilafat agitation. For many *murid*s of the Pir of Golra who were present, the challenge represented an attack on rural religious leadership itself. The result was a near riot.[66] Despite their deep sympathy for the Khilafat cause, many reform-minded *pirs* remained understandably wary of close cooperation with the reformist *'ulama*.

The political dilemmas facing the revival *pirs* thus dramatized the more general ambiguities facing rural religious leaders. The British had officially dissociated the colonial state from religion, but the authority

---

the same "tribal" background, who in turn brought wealth to these religious families. For examples, see below.

65. Attitudes varied, but most *pirs* supported the Khilafat movement. The "Address of the eminent sajjada nashins and zamindars of the Punjab" to the governor of the Punjab, in *Paisa Akhbar* (Lahore), 17 March 1920, shows initial support for the Khilafat among *sajjada nishin*s and Muslim landowners. Among the reform-minded *pirs*, Pir Fazl Shah of Jalalpur helped to organize *sajjada nishin*s at the Pakpattan *'urs* to send a pro-Khilafat telegram to the viceroy (Abdul Ghani, *Amir Hizbullah* [Jalalpur Sharif: Idara-yi Hizbullah, 1965], 255).

66. Faiz, *Mihr-i Munir*, 276.

of all religious leaders, even the revival *pir*s, had become entwined in
rural Punjab with the structure of British rule. The histories of two
prominent families of rural *pir*s illustrate well their political dilemmas.

THE CASE OF TAUNSA SHARIF

The shrine at Taunsa, one of the earliest and most influential of the
Chishti revival shrines, provides an outstanding example. Throughout
the twentieth century the family of the Taunsa *sajjada nishin*s was beset
by internal conflicts. Its conflicts, like those of many other families,
highlighted the tensions inherent in the fulfillment of the family's religious mission within the context of the colonial political order.

Like other shrines of the *sufi* revival in western Punjab, the Taunsa
shrine developed in the nineteenth century with roots embedded deeply
in western Punjab's tribal milieu. The Taunsa family's political involve-
ments, like those of other rural religious families, were strongly shaped
by its marriage patterns and its links to other prominent rural families.
Khwaja Allah Bakhsh, the grandson and successor of the original saint,
Khwaja Suleman, took as his third wife the daughter of one of the
largest and most influential Pathan landowners of southwestern Punjab,
Khan Bahadur Ghulam Qadir Khan Khakwani of Multan. "The marriage took place," one official observed, "simply because the Taunsa
family are the Pirs of the Khakwani family and [Ghulam Qadir Khan]
had great faith in them." [67] It was also calculated, however, to bring land
into the Taunsa family, and in this it succeeded admirably, for Khwaja
Allah Bakhsh's son from this marriage, Mian Mahmud, inherited from
the Khakwani family some three hundred squares of land. But the marriage set the scene for protracted conflict within the Taunsa family.
Mian Mahmud's inheritance set him at odds with his elder half-brother,
Mian Muhammad Musa, who possessed few of Mian Mahmud's social
connections but remained committed to the shrine's reformist religious
heritage.

At the death of Khwaja Allah Bakhsh in 1901, this conflict broke into
the open. The eldest son, Mian Muhammad Musa, was installed as the
new *sajjada nishin,* but Mian Mahmud, with prominent social connections, challenged Muhammad Musa's control of the shrine. Though at-

67. Report of the revenue assistant, Multan, 4 June 1943 (Board of Revenue, file
601/20/27/9). An account of the Khakwani family is in Griffin and Massy, *Chiefs and
Families of Note,* 2:310–12. The Taunsa *pir*s were themselves Pathans.

tempts to resolve the dispute, first by a council of Biloch *tumandars*, and then by a local maulvi, produced some progress, the death of Mian Muhammad Musa in 1906 reopened the dispute, now between Mian Mahmud and Mian Muhammad Musa's son, Khwaja Hamid.[68] In 1911, Khwaja Hamid, who had been officially installed as *sajjada nishin*, took Mian Mahmud to court, charging him with infringing his own position and prerogatives as *sajjada nishin* at the shrine. The issues in the case were numerous and complex. Both men were *pirs* and claimed religious authority as inheritors of the family's *barakat*. But underlying the dispute were their contrasting styles as local religious leaders. The contrast reflected the conflicts that pulled all the revival *pirs* toward two different roles: that of the religiously educated *darvesh* on the one hand, concerned, like the reformist *'ulama*, with piety, religious reform, and scripture; or that of the powerful local patron on the other, tied, like the old landed *sajjada nishins*, into the factional networks of rural society. One British official, H. J. Maynard, marked this contrast clearly when he visited the two *pirs* at the shrine in 1911. Khwaja Hamid he found to be a reclusive religious man who avoided contact with British government officers. Mian Mahmud, on the other hand, visited local government offices frequently. "I recollect nothing," Maynard stated, "[except] that this elder gentleman's [Mian Mahmud's] manner and dress differed markedly from those of the younger gentleman [Khwaja Hamid] whom I understand to be the sajjada nishin. The older gentleman appeared to be a man of the world, a rais. I should say the younger had a very retiring and modest appearance."[69]

The conflict in the Taunsa family was protracted. Both sides in fact cultivated their factional connections to gain support.[70] Even a decision by the privy council in 1921 (in Khwaja Hamid's favor), and the death of Mian Mahmud in 1929, did little to still the dispute. Mian Mahmud's tomb itself became a separate shrine at Taunsa; and the leadership of his faction passed to his son, Mian Nizamuddin. In 1930 the conflict led to a "serious riot" at Taunsa "between the supporters of both Pirs over a petty building dispute," and this, at least temporarily, "alarmed the re-

68. Privy Council Appeal No. 118 of 1921; Khwaja Mohammad Hamid vs. Mian Mahmud and others (Record of Proceedings, vol. 3 [documents], 82–85, 109–41).
69. Statement of H. J. Maynard. Privy Council Appeal No. 118 of 1921; Khwaja Mohammad Hamid vs. Mian Mahmud and others (Record of Proceedings, vol. 1 [evidence]).
70. Though Khwaja Hamid first relied on support from several Chishti *pirs*, he himself had married into the influential Mamdot family of Ferozepore district, the wealthiest Pathan landowners in the province. On the Mamdot family, see Griffin and Massy, *Chiefs and Families of Note*, 1:205–9.

sponsible elements on both sides." But with the death of Khwaja Hamid in 1931, the dispute again broke into the open. When the deputy commissioner of Dera Ghazi Khan district arrived at Taunsa at the time of Khwaja Hamid's death, he found Khwaja Hamid's supporters gathered in force at the shrine to secure for his son, Mian Sadiduddin, the succession as *sajjada nishin*. As Mian Nizamuddin had been caught unawares by Khwaja Hamid's death and was attending a wedding in the Khakwani family at Multan, his supporters urged the deputy commissioner to delay the installation of Mian Sadiduddin and to hold an election among the *murid*s of the shrine. "I can only state," the deputy commissioner replied, "that if the Murids of both parties are to be asked to choose the most suitable candidate the election would inevitably be synonymous with a riot."[71]

The deputy commissioner was in fact wary of involving the government in the dispute any further than was necessary. But the degree to which the dispute had already drawn the Taunsa family into a position of deep dependence on the government was indicated by Mian Nizamuddin's petition to the governor of the Punjab, asking that, until the dispute could be settled, government itself "should take over the management of [the] Khanqah."[72] Mian Sadiduddin was in fact accepted by the government as the official *sajjada nishin*, but the Taunsa family remained notorious as the center of political factionalism in the northern Dera Ghazi Khan district. "In Dera Ghazi Khan District the whole family is an unmitigated nuisance," the commissioner at Multan wrote in 1933.[73]

> Their chronic quarrels have set the whole tehsil of Taunsa by the ears and practically every village near Taunsa is divided into factions supporting one or other sides in the quarrel, lambardar is set against sufedposh and sufedposh against zaildar, and murders, cattle thefts and false cases, are the natural crop of this poisonous seed.

Both branches of the Taunsa family were, in effect, trapped in their circumstances by rural politics under the British. With this dispute at the center of their concerns, both had to devote as much attention to local political ties as to religious leadership. Both sides, like the *sajjada*

71. T. B. Creagh Coen (deputy commissioner, Dera Ghazi Khan) to commissioner, Multan, 12 May 1931 (Punjab Archives, Political General, B procs., November 1931, file 475).
72. Telegram of Mian Ghulam Nizamuddin to governor, Punjab, 4 May 1931 (ibid.).
73. Frank Brayne (commissioner, Multan) to deputy secretary, Revenue, 27 June 1933 (Board of Revenue, file 601/1/27/134).

*nishin*s of the older shrines and in spite of their Chishti revival heritage, had tied themselves to the local political factions that provided the district foundations of the Unionist party.[74] Thus, the dispute between the two sides dramatized the conflicting pressures facing revival *pirs* within the context of the British system.

THE CASE OF JALALPUR SHARIF

An even more striking example of the ambiguous religious and political pressures facing these *pirs* is provided by the case of the Chishti shrine at Jalalpur in Jhelum district. Like the shrine at Taunsa, the shrine at Jalalpur was a product of the Chishti revival. In 1920 the *sajjada nishin* of this shrine was Saiyid Muhammad Fazl Shah, the grandson of the original saint, Saiyid Ghulam Haider Ali Shah, himself a *khalifa* of Khwaja Shamsuddin Sialvi.[75] Like the Taunsa family, this family had established marriage connections in the nineteenth century with leading "tribal" families of northern Punjab. Saiyid Fazl Shah's mother was the daughter of Raja Saif Ali Khan Khokhar, one of the leading Rajput chiefs of Jhelum district.[76] But Saiyid Fazl Shah maintained a deep commitment to many religious principles of his grandfather. By the time he succeeded as *sajjada nishin* at the age of twenty-three, he had already undertaken the *hajj* (pilgrimage to Mecca) and had published several articles emphasizing his adherence to the path of his grandfather and to the injunctions of *Qor'an* and *hadis*. He also asserted his cultural independence of the British and remained wary of dealings with the government.[77]

But Pir Fazl Shah had a younger brother, Saiyid Mehr Shah, who was deeply interested in politics and saw the religious influence of the shrine as a base for launching a political career. He realized, as one deputy commissioner of Jhelum wrote in the 1920s, that in Jhelum a *pir* had only to be "intelligent enough to see the enormous hold *pir parasti* [*pir* worship] in this part of the world gives to a Sayyed wishing to stand for the Council and Assembly," in order to start a political career.[78] During

74. On the family's involvement in politics, see Punjab, *Gazette*, pt. 1 (17 December 1937), 1724–28: election petition case, Hazrat Khwaja Hafiz Sadid-ud-din, *sajjada nishin*, Taunsa vs. Khwaja Ghulam Murtaza.

75. Ghani, *Amir Hizbullah*, 5.

76. For an account of this Khokhar family, see Griffin and Massy, *Chiefs and Families of Note*, 2:208–11.

77. Ghani, *Amir Hizbullah*, 203–5, 218–19; Pir Fazl Shah to the governor, Punjab, n.d. (Board of Revenue, file 301/3/C9/186KW [19]).

78. W. R. Wilson (deputy commissioner, Jhelum) to Calvert, 28 August 1926 (ibid.).

World War I, though Pir Fazl Shah was reluctant to become involved with government recruiting efforts, Saiyid Mehr Shah actively used the religious influence of the shrine to encourage army recruiting and was rewarded for his efforts with the title of "Nawab" from the government.[79] Subsequently he capitalized on this position by standing successfully for election to the Punjab Council in 1923, where he cooperated with the Unionist party at its foundation. He extended the political involvement of the Jalalpur family by alliance with Raja Ghazanfar Ali Khan, Khokhar, the maternal uncle of Pir Fazl Shah, who was elected to the Central Assembly in 1923 and who, as one Jhelum deputy commissioner wrote, worked "hand in glove" with Nawab Mehr Shah to develop an influential political faction in Jhelum district and in Punjabi provincial politics.[80]

The most interesting twist to the political influence of the Jalalpur shrine, however, was provided by Pir Fazl Shah himself. In order to maintain the religious independence of the shrine and to give public expression to many of his reformist concerns, Pir Fazl Shah announced, at the annual 'urs in 1927, the formation of an organization called the Hizbullah, or "party of God," whose purpose was to unite, strengthen, and reform the Muslims under his political and spiritual leadership. The Hizbullah was to be organized as a spiritual army, whose soldiers were to pledge themselves to follow the Pir's leadership in an internal jihad aimed at restoring the dominance of the spiritual life among the Muslims, at assuring the performance of religious duties, and at improving economic conditions and uniting the Muslims politically. This organization was designed to provide cultural leadership independent of the colonial state and to give political expression to many religious concerns of the sufi revival. The Pir's appeal, in fact, specifically compared the spiritual benefits of his organization with the material benefits provided by the British army, an important consideration in an area in which the army recruited heavily.[81]

The practical success of this organization, however, is difficult to measure accurately. In theory overseen directly by the Pir himself, the organization rested on panchayats (local committees) intended to direct the local enforcement of the organization's aims. According to the Pir,

79. Ghani, Amir Hizbullah, 219; Saiyid Mehr Shah to H. D. Craik, 28 September 1928 (Board of Revenue, file 301/3/C9/186KW [19]).
80. W. R. Wilson to Calvert, 28 August 1926 (ibid.).
81. Saiyid Muhammad Fazl Shah, Hizbullah (Lahore: author?, 1928–29), 93–100, 84–86.

the organization claimed fifteen *panchayats* and five thousand volunteers after its first year.[82] In the 1930s the Pir increasingly used the annual meetings of the Hizbullah held with the Jalalpur *'urs* to pressure
local politicians like Nawab Mehr Shah to follow a religious policy. At
the time of the communal award in 1932, he challenged Akali efforts to
pressure the government in favor of the Sikhs by pledging to raise two
hundred thousand Muslim volunteers. During the Shahidganj mosque
agitation in 1935, he not only offered to supply volunteers, but also urged
the Punjabi *sufis* and *masha'ikh* to unite in support of the movement.[83]

    But despite his independent religious rhetoric, the Pir was still bound,
in political organizing, by the local factions. The Hizbullah organization carried significant political weight in Jhelum and western Gujrat
districts, but at election time in 1937 Fazl Shah threw its backing not
behind an independent religious candidate, but behind his uncle, Raja
Ghazanfar Ali Khan, who stood for a rural Jhelum district assembly
seat. Ghazanfar Ali Khan, who had responded sympathetically to the
Pir's appeals on Shahidganj, initially stayed aloof from the Unionist
party and ran on the Muslim League ticket, which offered in Jhelum district at this time a political platform independent of the government. But
almost immediately after being elected, he accepted the Unionist party's
offer of a parliamentary secretaryship, with the patronage that entailed.
The Pir's ability to maintain an independent religious critique of the
Unionists was naturally compromised in these circumstances, indicated
by a well-publicized visit of Sir Sikander Hyat Khan, the Unionist premier, to the Jalalpur shrine, at the time of the 1937 *'urs*, a visit apparently arranged by Mehr Shah.[84] In fact, the Unionists indicated what
they thought of the Pir's independence at this point by simply asking
Raja Ghazanfar Ali Khan to keep the Pir in line.[85]

    The case of Pir Fazl Shah demonstrated the difficulty that even a
reform-minded Chishti *pir* faced in escaping the pressures of the rural
social and political milieu. Though intellectually concerned with many
of the same problems of Islamic identity that motivated the reformist

    82. Ibid., 119.
    83. Ghani, *Amir Hizbullah*, 342, 345–51. Issued by the British, the communal award
distributed seats on a communal basis in central and provincial legislatures; for an account of the Shahidganj agitation see chapter 3.
    84. Ibid., 355–56, 357. For further discussion of this visit, see chapter 5.
    85. Note by Saiyid Afzal Ali Hasnie (resident secretary, Unionist party) to Sir Sikander
Hyat, 2 February 1939; and draft letter to Raja Ghazanfar Ali Khan, n.d. (Unionist party
papers, file G-21). After 1939 the Pir made speeches sympathetic to the Congress, but they
seem to have had little practical influence.

'ulama, the *pirs* of Jalalpur, like the *pirs* of Taunsa, found themselves bound into the rural system that provided both the local political foundations of their authority and the political foundations of the Unionist party. The structure of the imperial political system limited their ability to develop an independent religious challenge to the colonial regime. The conceptual foundations of their religious influence, rooted in an ideology of mediation, in fact drew them into the ideological structure of the British imperial system.

Although it lacked religious foundations, the imperial structure thus played a central role in inhibiting any concerted movement of religious opposition to colonial rule in rural Punjab. Indeed, an understanding of the structure of Islamic leadership and its relationship to the British administration is central to an understanding of the Islamic response to British domination. Here, I have described the overall impact of British rule on Islamic organization in terms of its impact on Punjab's Islamic "cultural system." It is, of course, a mistake to suggest that all religious leadership in rural Punjab developed on a single conceptual foundation, or that the structure of shrine-based authority subsumed all the religious urges of rural Punjabis. But a focus on the dominant "cultural system" of Punjabi Islam highlights the historically critical interaction between the state and the structure of Punjab's Islamic organization. It also leads to an emphasis on the internal tensions in Islamic organization that resulted from the collapse of Muslim authority and the establishment of alien, colonial rule.

In fact, long before the British state was established in Punjab, the collapse of central Muslim authority as a pivot for Islamic leadership had triggered important movements of reform in Indian Islam. They aimed toward new forms of organization and new conceptions of community, based on the spread of religious education and personal commitment to Islamic norms among individual Muslims. But the structure of British administration and authority supported the main institutions of religious influence in the rural areas—the Islamic shrines. Indeed, the British came to justify the state's authority as the protector of local idioms of power. Though the *sajjada nishins* of the *sufi* revival continued to assert the importance of personal commitment to *shari'at* even within this context, the political flexibility of these leaders to challenge the British was sharply circumscribed by their place within this structure. In spite of their failure to assert a religious foundation for their authority, the British thus developed through the shrines a critical base of rural religious support for their regime.

But British rule brought conflicting impulses in the nineteenth and twentieth centuries. While the structure of imperial authority encompassed the religious authority of the rural shrines, it spurred many Punjabi Muslims toward a search for the public expression of Muslim community in arenas independent of the state's authority. Such a search was evident in the reforms of the leading *'ulama* in twentieth-century Punjab, who turned increasingly to public, political activity in the years after World War I. But in structural terms, this search found its clearest expression in those political arenas most independent of the hierarchies of the imperial order. Even in parts of rural Punjab, social and economic changes under the British had begun to weaken the influence of the intermediaries on whom the state depended. In some areas of central Punjab and in the canal colonies, changing patterns of production had opened the doors to new forms of political organization. But nowhere else did the popular concern to define the Muslim community find clearer public expression under British colonial rule than in Punjab's cities. Indeed, in the cities—in a political context largely detached from the hierarchies of rural administration—the search for political and ideological definitions for the Muslim community took on a new meaning.

CHAPTER III

Urban Politics and the Communal Ideal

In the past, sociologists and historians of Islam noted the distinctive importance of cities in the development of Qor'anic Islam. They saw the central doctrines of Islam as particularly suited to the urban environment, for the Prophet's vision of a community of believers bound together by piety and outward obedience to the duties of the faith was one developed at Mecca and Medina. As one sociologist wrote, "Most Islamicists would agree with G. E. von Grunebaum's judgment that Muhammad's 'piety is entirely tailored to urban life.'"[1] Central to the urban character of classical Islamic doctrine, some argued, was the relative weakness in the cities of parochial loyalties to "tribe." In theory, in the cities, as in early Islam itself, "the universalism of the new Islamic community (*umma*) based on faith rather than blood cut right across the particularism of the tribal system."[2]

Few historians today would accept the notion that Islam is somehow a particularly "urban" religion or deny the vitality of the Islamic institutions that characterized rural Islam—in the Punjab or elsewhere. It is nevertheless true that the cities of Punjab in the nineteenth and twentieth centuries provided an Islamic milieu that was in some respects strikingly different from that of the Punjabi countryside. In part this resulted from basic differences between urban and rural life. Major cities of the Punjab, like Islamic cities elsewhere, possessed institutions not

---

1. Bryan S. Turner, *Weber and Islam* (London: Routledge & Kegan Paul, 1974), 35.
2. Ibid., 35–36.

always found in the rural areas. Bazaars, mosques, and *madrasa*s had long played critical roles in the social and religious lives of largely Muslim cities such as Lahore and Multan. Even though such institutions were not entirely absent from the rural areas, in the cities they nurtured an Islam like that of the reformist *'ulama*, based on a sense of personal participation in a universal religious community.

But to understand the cities' role in the development of Muslim politics in twentieth-century Punjab we must look first at the cities' peculiar place within the structure of the British imperial system. Cities were the chief centers of colonial administration. It was in the cities that the colonial bureaucracy and the bulk of Punjab's European population were located.[3] But at the same time, the cities' place within the hierarchies of colonial power was ambiguous. Not only were the foundations of the colonial administration based in the rural areas but, perhaps more important, the ideology of imperial rule was grounded in the state's relationship with rural, kin-based "communities." In fact, the cities of Punjab fit only uneasily into the structure of imperial rule; the British perceived them to be often dangerous and difficult to control.[4] The distinctive politics of Punjab's cities in the twentieth century grew largely from the ambiguities in their position. Cities lay at the heart of colonial political power and yet held a peripheral position in its ideological structure. The distinctive patterns of urban politics in the Punjab reflected this fact.

THE BRITISH AND THE CITIES

To control the cities the British focused initially on the same types of structures they used to establish control in the rural areas. In the cities control depended largely on intermediaries. Just as they tried to identify "tribal" leaders in the countryside, the British sought to find "natural leaders" in the cities—leaders with legitimate indigenous claims to leadership within the local urban context.[5] In the nineteenth century the men who most clearly fit this mold were of the sort C. A. Bayly has

3. Ian Kerr, "Urbanization and Colonial Rule in 19th-Century India: Lahore and Amritsar, 1849–1881," *The Panjab Past and Present* 14, no. 1 (April 1980): 213–15.
4. On the post-Mutiny British view of the Indian city as politically dangerous, see a study of Lucknow: Veena Talwar Oldenberg, *The Making of Colonial Lucknow, 1856–1877* (Princeton: Princeton University Press, 1984), 27–61. The growth of such views in a different context is discussed in Barrier, "The Punjab Government and Communal Politics, 1870–1908," 531.
5. On the role of "natural leaders," see Sandria B. Freitag, "'Natural Leaders,' Administrators and Social Control: Communal Riots in the United Provinces," *South Asia* 1, no. 2 (1978).

called "urban magnate" or *ra'is,* a term he also translates as "patron" or "boss." These men usually owned considerable urban residential property, commanded credit, and controlled broad urban factions.[6] Just as the populations of Punjab's cities were religiously heterogeneous, *ra'is* came from all three of Punjab's major religions.[7] Some were of Hindu banking families, like those described by Bayly in U.P.; others were large landowners, who owned considerable property in the cities and estates in the countryside. Some, like the Qureshi family of Multan, *sajjada nashins* of the shrine of Bahawal Haq, commanded religious prestige; others, like the Arain Mians of Lahore, headed leading families of urban *biradaris,* or "tribes."[8] But all owed their position to their abilities as intermediaries. As Bayly argues, the *ra'is* were marked out by their coincident abilities "to mediate with higher political authority and to control webs of patronage beneath."[9] After the Mutiny these men were increasingly incorporated onto municipal committees as key figures in British urban administration.[10]

Yet mediation in the cities differed from that in the countryside. As Bayly argues, urban *ra'is* themselves exercised influence largely through contacts with "neighborhood leadership," local leaders in the *muhalla*s whose influence depended on local caste and religious groupings, on *'ulama,* petty merchants, and "bazaar factions."[11] Such groups were often less stable than their rural counterparts, making control through these urban *ra'is* difficult and often limited, resulting at times in violence precipitated by those only weakly integrated into *ra'is* patronage networks. Cross-cutting alliances marked urban politics, and conflict over religious issues was common even before the British arrived.[12]

Patterns of urban change exacerbated British problems in maintain-

6. C. A. Bayly, "Local Control in Indian Towns—the Case of Allahabad, 1880–1920," *Modern Asian Studies* 5, no. 4 (1971): 292–93.

7. Of Punjab's total urban population in 1931, 38 percent was Hindu, 52 percent Muslim, and 7 percent Sikh. This compares with 30 percent Hindu, 52 percent Muslim, and 14 percent Sikh in Punjab's population as a whole. (For British Punjab, excluding the Punjab states, the figures were Hindu 27 percent, Muslim 56.5 percent, and Sikh 13 percent.) (*Census of India, 1931,* vol. 17 [Punjab], pt. 1, 96, 290–91).

8. For a list of men from the "leading families of Lahore," see Syed Muhammad Latif, *Lahore: Its History, Architectural Remains, and Antiquities,* rev. ed. (Lahore: Syed Muhammad Minhaj-ud-din, 1955?), 326–27.

9. Bayly, "Local Control in Indian Towns," 293.

10. On the development of Punjab's municipalities and committees, see Amar Nath, *The Development of Local Self-Government in the Punjab, 1849–1900* (Lahore: Punjab Government Record Office, 1929), 6–44.

11. Bayly, "Local Control in Indian Towns," 299.

12. "Communal" conflict in northern India in the eighteenth century and the early British period is discussed by C. A. Bayly, "The Pre-History of 'Communalism'? Religious Conflict in India, 1700–1860," *Modern Asian Studies* 19, no. 2 (1985); see also Bayly, *Rulers, Townsmen, and Bazaars,* 303–45. On religious conflict between Muslims and

ing control. While stressing the importance of mediation and patronage, British rule encouraged the rapid expansion of Punjab's urban population, accentuating the diversity of interests represented within Punjab's cities. Growth was greatest in those cities that became administrative centers for the British regime—most notably Lahore, the capital, where population more than tripled between annexation and the 1920s.[13] Much of the growth came in the new parts of the city, outside the old city walls; it transformed the city's character. Few other important cities of Punjab grew as rapidly, but many had significant growth under the British regime, caused by expanding administration, commerce, and agricultural production. While new agricultural market cities such as Lyallpur and Sargodha emerged in the canal colonies, cities such as Multan and Amritsar grew as commercial and small-scale manufacturing centers. There was no urban revolution in Punjab under the British; the population remained overwhelmingly rural. But Punjab's urban population grew substantially.[14]

Growth was important because it led to new urban institutions that significantly changed the character of politics and political control. As the administration grew, Lahore emerged as a center of education, with a growing middle class, trained for positions in the bureaucracy and in the law. The city in fact became a magnet for migrants from all over the province, who sought service with the new imperial administration. As this class grew in significance in the late nineteenth century, its leaders, like urban *ra'is*, took up roles within the existing urban structures, serving as intermediaries on the municipal committee established by the British. These men communicated in the language and the cultural idiom of the British; they also began to identify directly with the power of the colonial state. They began new interest-oriented associations and pioneered forms of communication that transcended local patronage networks. They began, in other words, to assert claims to political influence based not just on their position as urban patrons and intermediaries but also on their mastery of new structures of organization associated directly with the culture of the alien, colonial state.

Perhaps most important, such organizations also began to assert dis-

---

Sikhs in pre-British Punjab, see brief references in Barrier, "The Punjab Government and Communal Politics," 525.

13. Lahore's population rose from 100,000 in the 1860s to 430,000 in 1931 (*Census of India,* 1931, vol. 17 [Punjab], pt. 1, 95).

14. Punjab's urban population was 11.9 percent in 1881 and 12.4 percent in 1931, an increase of over one million. The largest percentage increases came, significantly, in cities with populations exceeding 100,000 (ibid., 89–92).

tinctive religious identities. Since the British state asserted no religious rationale for itself, voluntary associations provided a means for Lahore's new educated classes to reformulate their religious organization and identity consistently with a direct identification with the state. The earliest such association, the Arya Samaj, was Hindu, largely because Hindus predominated among the first educated and bureaucratic classes.[15] But Muslim associations, or *anjumans*, appeared in considerable numbers in the late nineteenth century.[16] Such *anjuman*s reflected the cultural ambiguities of the British colonial state. Voluntary *anjuman*s linked Muslims culturally with the state's power—immersing them in a style of public, voluntary organization associated increasingly in the late nineteenth century with the culture of British rule. But they also provided an organized forum, within the context of state culture, for the public expression of Muslim identity.

The first important Muslim *anjuman* under British rule was organized largely under the auspices of the British themselves. The Anjuman Islamia was formed at Lahore in 1869 to administer the Badshahi mosque, to protect Muslim interests, and to encourage Muslim loyalty to British rule. It combined urban Muslim *ra'is* and *'ulama* in an organization led by educated Muslims—an organization that sought to assert Muslim identity within the context of imperial political structures.[17] But more important and more broadly based, was the Anjuman Himayat-i Islam, formed in 1884 for the "service and support of Islam." Drawing on British models of organization, the Anjuman Himayat-i Islam defended Muslim interests publicly, publishing tracts to defend Islam against Christian missionaries and against attacks from Punjab's other religious communities. Equally important were the schools it established to instill in Muslim youth an awareness of their Islamic heritage and to prepare them for success within the British system. By the turn of the century, it managed an Islamia College at Lahore and several Islamia high schools.[18] It encouraged the public espousal of Muslim interests as a touchstone for the cultural identity of those Muslims whose lives were increasingly tied directly to the state's power.

These new forms of social and political alliance by no means re-

15. Kenneth Jones, *Arya Dharm* (Berkeley: University of California Press, 1976).
16. On *anjuman*s, see Edward D. Churchill, Jr., "Muslim Societies of the Punjab, 1860–1890," *The Panjab Past and Present* 8, no. 1 (April 1974): 69–91.
17. S. M. Ikram, *Modern Muslim India and the Birth of Pakistan* (Lahore: Sh. Muhammad Ashraf, 1970), 195.
18. Ibid., 200. On activities of the Anjuman, see Shaikh Ziauddin, *Anjuman Himayat-i Islam Diamond Jubilee, 1967* (Lahore: Anjuman Himayat-i Islam, 1967).

placed the patronage networks of urban magnates in the structure of politics in Punjab's cities. But they introduced new standards of cultural legitimacy for urban patrons connected to the imperial power; they put increasing pressure on these Muslim ra'is to acknowledge the public standards of Islamic identity shaped by the new voluntary organizations. Competing interests led to increasing conflict in Punjab's cities in the 1880s, even to religious rioting and violence as ra'is faced challenges to their political control. In part, this reflected the influence of the new associations, which attempted to mobilize popular support on issues of immediate concern to the developing educated class, such as communal competition in recruitment to government services and election to municipal committees.[19] It also reflected increasing pressure from below— from neighborhood leaders, 'ulama, popular orators, and journalists, who used new standards of religious identity and new techniques of popular communication to challenge the legitimacy of the leadership of the urban ra'is who were tied to the administration.

This was exemplified in the growing influence in the late nineteenth and early twentieth century of the men who controlled the vernacular press. The Urdu press became a political force among Lahore's Muslims with the launching in the 1880s of the Paisa Akhbar, the first Urdu daily with a mass circulation.[20] But the most outstanding Muslim leader of this type was Maulana Zafar Ali Khan, the son of a post office inspector and a graduate of Aligarh, who rose to prominence in the years after 1911 when he moved his father's newspaper, Zamindar, to Lahore and established it as a daily. Zafar Ali Khan gained a reputation as one of the leading public spokesmen for symbolically defined Muslim "interests." With a highly charged and emotional style, he defended the symbols of Muslim cultural identity against the British and against India's other religious communities, in spite of frequent clashes with the government and repeated forfeitures of the Zamindar's security under the British press laws.[21] Significantly, he was able through these methods to develop a major following among the large population of Muslim laborers, artisans, and merchants in the city. "As soon as copies of this

    19. Barrier, "The Punjab Government and Communal Politics," 531–37.
    20. Its circulation reached about 13,000 in the early 1900s (S. M. A. Feroze, Press in Pakistan [Lahore: National Publications, 1957], 69–72). For circulation figures, see also N. Gerald Barrier and Paul Wallace, The Punjab Press, 1880–1905 (East Lansing: Asian Studies Center, Michigan State University, 1970), 101–2.
    21. "Data on Zafar Ali Khan and Zamindar, corrected up to 1940" (Punjab Archives, Press Branch, file 1918, 14A). On Zafar Ali Khan as a poet and literary figure, see Ghulam Hussain Zulfiqar, Zafar Ali Khan: Adib o Sha'ir (Lahore: Maktaba-yi Khiyaban-i Adab, 1967).

paper are brought into the bazaar," an intelligence report noted of the *Zamindar,* "large crowds of people surround the news-shops and buy the copies."[22] With such a following, Zafar Ali Khan became a strong supporter of the Khilafat movement—and joined in alliance with the reformist *'ulama* of the city to challenge the cultural legitimacy of the British regime.[23] Most important in the long run, this direct popular support, mobilized through a symbolic appeal to Muslim identity, also challenged the intermediary authority on which urban administration was based, defining cultural standards for leadership that were entirely independent of the hierarchical political structure of British rule.

By the 1920s the power of editors and public men like Zafar Ali Khan helped to define a new urban politics in Punjab, one that bypassed structures of mediation and patronage to focus on the direct political identification of Muslims with Islamic symbols. Its increasing importance was noted with apprehension by British officials, who saw it as a threat to their control.[24] Leading newspaper editors such as Maulana Zafar Ali Khan had emerged, one official wrote in the 1920s, as only the most prominent among "a considerable class" of journalists, "of pamphleteers and cartoonists who thrive by the dissemination of . . . matter deliberately designed to increase communal hostility."[25] The new urban market in cheap publications gave rise to a new type of "communal" consciousness in which the commitment to symbols of religious "community" transcended the political bonds of patronage structures.[26] With over sixty publications existing "apparently for the sole object of attacking the rival community," the government blamed rising communalism for a series of religious riots in the 1920s, affecting several of Punjab's most important cities.[27] Multan (1922), Amritsar (1923), Rawalpindi (1926), and Lahore (1927) all experienced severe communal rioting dur-

22. Quoted in Ravinder Kumar, "The Rowlatt Satyagraha in Lahore," in R. Kumar, ed., *Essays on Gandhian Politics* (Oxford: The Clarendon Press, 1971), 270.

23. Zafar Ali Khan was prosecuted and imprisoned in 1920 for seditious speeches. His religious leanings appeared in strong criticism of Punjab's *pirs*; in 1917, he conducted a Punjabi literary paper that was, said the Press Branch, "chiefly remarkable for violent attacks on Sufis and Pirs" (Press Branch, file 1918, 14A).

24. The role of the press in communal antagonism in the 1920s is discussed in Press Branch, file 5950.

25. H. D. Craik (chief secretary, Punjab) to secretary to Government of India, Home Department, 6 August 1927 (ibid.).

26. On "print-capitalism" in the development of community consciousness, see Anderson, *Imagined Communities,* 46–49.

27. The quotation is from H. D. Craik (chief secretary, Punjab) to secretary to the Government of India, Home Dept., 6 August 1927 (Press Branch, file 5950). For discussion of these riots and their causes, see Prem Raman Uprety, *Religion and Politics in Punjab in the 1920's* (New Delhi: Sterling Publishers, 1980), 134–68.

ing this decade. Explaining the breakdown of official influence in the period immediately preceding the 1927 riot at Lahore, an official wrote, "Muslims are under no definite control, and yield easily to the doctrines preached by such fanatical journalists as Syad Habib of the 'Siyasat' and Zafar Ali of the 'Zamindar.'" [28] The religious communities of Punjab's cities, commented Lahore's deputy commissioner, had become like separate nations. Their relations were, he said, "like those of the French and Germans; and this description would apply equally well to the citizens of many other large towns in the Punjab." [29]

But the press, as many British officers well realized, was not completely to blame for either religious riots in Punjab's cities or communalism. As an urban phenomenon, "communalism"—or the direct political identification of the individual with a religious "community"—was largely the peculiar product of the state's ambiguous cultural position within the cities. Cities were centers of imperial administration. But they were also, increasingly, centers for new forms of association and public communication that had developed with colonial rule. Drawing on these resources, leaders like Zafar Ali Khan sought within the cities a new cultural center for Muslim Punjab—a center tied not directly to the structure of the colonial state, with its hierarchies of mediation, but to the public evocation of the symbols of Islam. Removed from a place in official ritual, such symbols were evoked largely in the context of competition between communities—religious communities who found public voice in the new institutions of the colonial era, the urban press, and the voluntary associations. In a political system without an Islamic ritual expression of political power, the cities thus provided, ironically, a central focus for the public and political expression of Islamic identity independent of colonial state power.

But as a direct challenge to state power, the practical political meaning of urban communalism was limited by the role the cities played in the twentieth-century political system. The structure of British rule had relegated the cities to a secondary position, not only in Punjab's politics but also, and most important, in the politics of the Muslim community. The secondary political role of the cities was confirmed after the 1919 reforms when the British separated rural from urban council constituencies and awarded twenty-seven out of thirty-two Muslim territorial seats in Punjab to the rural areas. [30] Although rural political leaders, like

28. Report on the Lahore communal riot, 1927 (IOL, L/P&J/6/1939 file 1100).
29. H. D. Craik (chief secretary, Punjab) to secretary to the Government of India, Home Dept., 6 August 1927 (Press Branch, file 5950).
30. India, *Report of the Committee Appointed in Connection with the Delimitation*

Sir Fazli Husain, sometimes appealed for urban Muslim political support in a "communal" political style, the appeal hardly disguised the weak position of urban communal leaders within provincial Muslim politics.[31] The cities' place at the administrative heart of Punjab counteracted neither the power of the Unionist party nor the strength of Punjab's mediational hierarchies. Indeed, in spite of the development of urban communalism, institutional politics continued to be influenced, even in Punjab's cities, by hierarchies of patronage linking the cities to the structure of the imperial system. In a system dominated by rural intermediaries, attempts to institutionalize communal politics independently of the local authority of urban ra'is produced only limited success.

The Tanzim movement in Punjab's cities in the early 1920s illustrated these problems. The movement grew up in the cities of northern India after the Khilafat movement failed. The idea for a local Tanzim (literally, "organization") movement was developed by leading 'ulama and publicists as a local, organized answer to the hierarchies of power controlled by the colonial state. The scheme, as first outlined by Dr. Saif-ud-din Kitchlew, a leader of communal opinion in Amritsar, had numerous aspects. In addition to a newspaper, Tanzim, the organization was to include local Muslim committees and jathas, or bands of organized volunteers. At the heart of the Tanzim movement, however, lay an attempt to focus communal political organization on important local religious institutions—the neighborhood mosques. Mosques, as local symbols of the universal "community" of Islam, dotted the urban landscape and were natural centers of independent local organization. They were also symbols of the personal commitment by Muslims, not to a mediating hierarchy, but directly to God, to the shari'at, and to Islam. The potential organizational importance of this commitment was indicated by Kitchlew's proposal to establish primary schools in the mosques, to enforce punctuality in prayers, and to issue khutbas (sermons) to be read in mosques—proposals close to the reformist ideas of the 'ulama of the Jami'at-i 'Ulama-yi Hind. Through a focus on the mosques, Muslim leaders sought to create a symbolically based alternative to the local hierarchies of patronage tied to the state.[32]

of Constituencies and Connected Matters, vol. 1 (Report), 55: Parliamentary Papers, Reports, 1935–36, vol. 9.

31. Urban Muslims supported Sir Fazli Husain's appeal for greater Muslim representation in urban municipalities in the early 1920s but not the domination in provincial politics by rural Muslims; see the Zamindar's complaint about the appointment of Sir Firoz Khan Noon as a "representative" Muslim minister (Zamindar, 4 January 1927 [Press Branch, file 4469]).

32. Kitchlew dreamed, one British official wrote, of "a sort of Muhammadan counter-

But within Punjab's political system, such an organization proved problematic. Few could ignore the networks of patronage on which their own prospects depended. But perhaps even more important, there were even in the cities few arenas of local life—including the neighborhood mosques—into which networks of patronage failed to penetrate. In practice, the administrative control of most urban mosques was itself tied closely to urban patronage structures. Many urban mosques were administered by *mutawallis* (custodians of the mosque endowments) who were often important urban patrons.[33] And perhaps equally important, many of these same influences were reflected in the practical local organization of the urban *'ulama* themselves, whose support was critical in bringing the mosques of Punjab's cities into such a scheme. In spite of the independent organization of the reformist Jami'at-i 'Ulama-yi Hind, divisions among the *'ulama* mirrored to an important degree the political divisions among Muslims in Punjab as a whole. Many Barelvi *'ulama* were closely tied to Punjab's *pirs* and thus to shrine-based structures of mediation, even within the cities.[34] To organize a scheme like Kitchlew's, a network of local organization independent of the structure of imperial influence, proved extremely difficult. As the government itself reported after Kitchlew's scheme was launched, many maulvis "apparently discern that that part of the scheme which relates to control of mosques is an encroachment on their own special sphere."[35] Mosques as symbols of the community thus provided little foundation for an alternative urban political structure.

URBAN POLITICS AND THE *BIRADARIS*

Communal consciousness nevertheless strongly influenced the character of urban politics. And this was evident even in structures of urban power shaped by the ideology of the British imperial administration. The degree to which "communal" identity influenced the everyday operation of urban politics was illustrated by the politics of Punjab's urban

part of the Sikh Shiromani Committee," the central Sikh organization given control of Sikh gurdwaras under the Sikh Gurdwaras Act (Note by C. Kaye on the Tanzim and Tabligh movements, 24 September 1924 [NAI, Home Political, file 6/IX/1924]).

33. Perhaps the most noteworthy example was the administrative control of Lahore's Wazir Khan mosque by a hereditary *mutawalli*, Mirza Zafar Ali, an influential Lahore *ra'is*.

34. Some *'ulama* (presumably the Barelvis) feared the Tanzim movement would "foster reformist aspirations" (G. R. Thursby, *Hindu-Muslim Relations in British India* [Leiden: E. J. Brill, 1975], 171).

35. Note by Abdul Majid, 4 October 1924 (NAI, Home Political, file 6/IX/1924).

*biradari*s (brotherhoods), the ethnic divisions of Punjab's urban population. Based on an ideology of descent, like the "tribes" of the countryside, their importance in Punjab's cities indicated the power of the "tribal" idiom to link even urban politics to the larger ideological structure of the British imperial system. But the *biradari*s of the cities were nevertheless far different from the "tribes" of the rural administration. As Hamza Alavi has pointed out, the term *biradari* itself, even in its rural context, implies elements of both vertical hierarchy and horizontal solidarity—both based on common descent.[36] In the rural areas, it was the vertical significance of *biradari*, as a legitimizer of hierarchy and patronage, that predominated within the context of the imperial administration.[37] But in the cities, *biradari* identity served also as a powerful idiom of horizontal political solidarity. Its articulation represented not just a response to the ideological structure of the colonial state, but a response also to the growth of "communalism." It represented a form of Muslim cultural identity that, like "communalism," worked independently of state authority, in the press, and in newly organized *anjuman*s. In fact, for many urban leaders identification with the *biradari* reconciled commitment to an Islamic "communal" identity with the exercise of power within the imperial administration. An examination of *biradari* politics thus suggests the degree to which the Muslim "communal" concerns were capable of adaptation to the structure of imperial politics.

KASHMIRIS

The Kashmiris formed one of Punjab's most important urban *biradari*s. As a group they were not directly defined by common ancestry but by common geographical origin. Their political self-definition as a *biradari*, on the model of blood relationship, illustrated the flexibility of the *biradari* idiom in Punjab in the twentieth century. Colonies of Kashmiri weavers had been long established in Amritsar and Ludhiana; the numbers of Punjab's Kashmiris were considerably augmented in the nineteenth century by migrants, driven from Kashmir largely by famine and by the establishment of Dogar rule.[38] By the early twentieth century Kashmiris were numerous and important in a number of Punjab's cit-

36. Alavi, "Kinship in West Punjab Villages," 2.
37. The term *biradari* was widely used at many levels of Punjabi society in defining kinship and marriage patterns and had other common rural usages. Within rural politics the sense of vertical hierarchy based on descent was common.
38. Denzil Ibbetson, *Punjab Castes* (1916; reprint, Lahore: Sh. Mubarik Ali, 1974), 194.

ies—Amritsar and Ludhiana; Sialkot, near the Kashmir border; and Lahore, where Kashmiris made up an important percentage of the Muslim population of the old walled city. Most were petty merchants, artisans, and laborers. At Ludhiana, many worked in the hosiery industry.[39] At Amritsar, Kashmiris made up a large portion of the city's extensive Muslim population of artisans and small merchants and worked "in various crafts such as carpet-making, shawl work, coolies, woodmen, poultry keepers and so on."[40] Very few owned land. Denzil Ibbetson summed up the general economic condition of the Kashmiris in 1881: "The Kashmiris of our cities are as a rule miserably poor."[41]

In the late nineteenth century, however, a few Kashmiri families built political leadership upon commercial success. Like other urban *ra'is*, such families began to exercise political influence through wealth, control of patronage, and connections with the urban administration. In Lahore, for example, Mian Karim Bakhsh, who prospered under the British as a public works contractor, served for over thirty years on the Lahore Municipal Committee and founded one of Lahore's most influential Kashmiri families.[42] His descendants remained among the most important Kashmiri leaders in the city; the most notable was Mian Amiruddin, a member of the Punjab Legislative Assembly (1941–1946) and later chairman of the Lahore Municipal Committee. At Amritsar as well, families of Kashmiri *ra'is* long dominated Muslim politics on the Municipal Committee.[43]

But these were not the only urban Kashmiris of political importance in the twentieth century. In some cities, Kashmiri professional men and journalists also gained considerable influence—men whose ideas were deeply shaped by the emergence of "communal" thinking. Among the most important was Dr. Saif-ud-din Kitchlew, an English-educated professional and outspoken critic of colonial domination, leader of Tanzim, who first gained a wide following in Amritsar during the Khilafat movement. For Kitchlew, Amritsar proved fertile political territory, as the city

39. Punjab, *Report on the Industrial Survey of the Ludhiana District* (Lahore: Government Printing, 1942), 39.
40. C. G. Parsons, commissioner, Lahore to junior secretary to financial commissioners, 13 September 1909 (Board of Revenue, file 442/14/00/2A).
41. Ibbetson, *Punjab Castes*, 194.
42. Latif, *Lahore*, 343, 345(e).
43. Though Amritsar produced many prominent Kashmiri families, perhaps the most notable Kashmiri family included Shaikh Ahmad Sadiq, a chairman of the Amritsar Municipal Committee; Shaikh Muhammad Sadiq, a longtime member of the Punjab Legislative Council from Amritsar (1924–36); and Shaikh Sadiq Hasan, a member of the central Legislative Assembly and member of the Punjab Legislative Assembly for Amritsar (1939–48).

contained "a considerable number of Kashmiri Muhammadans, who gave a ready ear to the efforts made to arouse Islamic feeling to open sympathy with Turkey and with the propaganda for the protection of the Holy Places."[44] Kitchlew was arrested more than once for publicly rallying these sentiments, and he worked with the reformist *'ulama* of the Jami'at-i 'Ulama-yi Hind to develop a wide political following. Equally noteworthy among Kashmiri leaders was the poet and philosopher, Muhammad Iqbal, who came from a Kashmiri family of Sialkot. Educated in religious schools, at Lahore Government College, and in Europe, Iqbal was a lawyer, and served a term as Lahore's representative in the provincial council (1926–1930). He maintained close personal relations with many of the notables of Lahore. In sharp contrast to many Kashmiri *ra'is,* Iqbal was a poet and a visionary. His poetry, wrote Iqbal Singh, was "recited not only in the company of the select few, but at the street corners and coffee stalls."[45] Iqbal expressed a vision of Muslim political solidarity that captivated large numbers of urban Punjabis with its emotional intensity and stress on the active, personal commitment of each individual to the mission of Islam.

Such leaders were at times immensely popular with urban Muslims— and at times came into conflict with urban Kashmiri *ra'is.* But the interests of both groups were served by the expression of a Kashmiri *biradari* identity that stressed both the common origins of Muslim Kashmiris and their common commitment to Islam. Articulating this identity was important in legitimizing the political networks of urban Kashmiri patrons. The distinctive political visions of leaders like Kitchlew and Iqbal also infused into this identity a commitment to Islam and to Islamic political solidarity that marked out for Kashmiris a distinctive cultural position in Punjabi politics, a cultural identity independent of the state but compatible with the manipulation of the influence and patronage that the state offered.

The most important vehicle to articulate this identity was the Kashmiri *biradari anjuman,* founded in the late nineteenth century. The Anjuman Kashmiri Musalmanan, organized at Lahore in the 1890s, led the way in the public expression of the elements of Kashmiri *biradari* iden-

44. Punjab, *Report on the Punjab Disturbances, April 1919* (Simla: Government Printing, 1919), 33.
45. Iqbal Singh, *The Ardent Pilgrim* (London: Longmans, Green, 1951), 69. Within the voluminous literature on Iqbal, for a good, brief account of his political career, see Hafeez Malik, "The Man of Thought and the Man of Action," in Hafeez Malik, ed., *Iqbal: Poet-Philosopher of Pakistan* (New York: Columbia University Press, 1971), 69–107.

tity. Under the patronage of Kashmiri *ra'is,* the *anjuman* stressed the Kashmiris' common heritage and history and published articles and poems on their social problems.[46] But the *anjuman*—with help from Iqbal and others—also defined a distinctive religious identity: direct commitment to the *shari'at,* which was for the reformist *'ulama* the touchstone of Muslim identity, became, in much of the Anjuman's rhetoric, an inseparable part of being Kashmiri. At the time of a 1915 conference to consider codification of the customary law, the Anjuman voiced strong ideological opposition to customary law—despite its significance in the ideological structure of the British system—on the grounds that it compromised the *shari'at.* "Kashmiri Muhammadans of this province," the *anjuman* declared, "as a body adhere to the provision of the Muhammadan Law."[47] This public commitment distinguished them from the "tribes" inhabiting the rural administration and underscored their claim to a position at the center of Punjab's Islamic "cultural system."

Their claim to a central cultural position, however, did not prevent Kashmiris from trying also to manipulate Kashmiri identity to gain access to the institutional hierarchies of colonial political power. Following the passage of the Land Alienation Act in 1900, the Kashmiri *anjuman* tried to gain political status for the *biradari* as an "agricultural tribe" under the terms of the act. The Anjuman repeatedly petitioned the government, less from concern for the control of land than from concern for the political status that the act conferred.[48] When such requests were rejected, on the grounds that the great majority of Kashmiris were not hereditary agriculturalists, Kashmiri leaders tried to have the word "Kashmiri" replaced in the revenue records by true Kashmiri caste and tribal names, an attempt that Sir Michael O'Dwyer characterized as a back-door effort "to pave the way to ultimate recognition of Kashmiris as an agricultural tribe." Many Kashmiri leaders proved so persistent that one government official admonished them, "The Punjab Alienation of Land Act was not intended to confer social status."[49] But their effort showed how pervasive this perception of the Land Aliena-

46. Hafeez Malik and Lynda P. Malik, "The Life of the Poet-Philosopher," in Malik, *Iqbal,* 12.
47. Proceedings of Anjuman-i-Kashmiri Musalmanan, Amritsar, 3 December 1915 (Board of Revenue, file 441/270).
48. Kashmiri *anjuman* representations appear in government records under a number of different names; one official suggested they were probably "one body which appears to have been changing its name from time to time" (ibid., file 442/14/00/2A).
49. Note by Sir Michael O'Dwyer, 10 June 1914; D. J. Boyd, commissioner, Rawalpindi to senior secretary to financial commissioners, 3 December 1927 (ibid.).

tion Act was. Though in the end the effort to gain recognition as an "agricultural tribe" failed, it indicated the degree to which the leaders of the Anjuman, whatever their cultural concerns, had adapted their politics to the categories and structures that mediated access to the imperial system.

But the nature of urban *biradari* identity nevertheless remained quite distinct from the "tribal" identities of the countryside. And this was demonstrated by the role of *biradari* in the electoral politics of Punjab's cities. Few elections were contested in urban Punjab in which *biradari* identity did not play an important role. At Lahore, Amritsar, Sialkot, and elsewhere, appeals to Kashmiri *biradari* identity were central features of election campaigns. But this did not mean that appeals to *biradari* loyalty always carried the day. Elections involved complex interactions between *biradari* identity and the conflicting pulls of "communalism" and urban patronage networks. A good example is provided by the Central Punjab (Muslim) Central Assembly election of 1934—one in which Kashmiri identity played a pivotal role. The Unionist leaders of Punjab decided to support the candidacy of Haji Rahim Bakhsh, a retired Kashmiri civil servant and judge, whose candidacy they hoped would appeal to *biradari* loyalty and capture the critical Kashmiri vote in Amritsar and Lahore for the Unionist party's leadership.[50] But Rahim Bakhsh was opposed by K. L. Gauba, son of the Hindu financier Lala Harkishen Lal. Gauba had converted to Islam in defiance of his family and had written a popular biography of the Prophet. As a convert and thus a man of no Muslim *biradari,* Gauba was popularly perceived as a man of deep individual commitment to Islam; his candidacy thus symbolized the primary importance of direct, personal commitment to Islamic solidarity. "People are heard saying," one of Rahim Bakhsh's supporters wrote, "that Gauba should win; because his defeat will be the defeat of Islam."[51] Many influential Kashmiris, including Iqbal, supported Haji Rahim Bakhsh as an important *biradari* leader;[52] nonethe-

50. K. L. Gauba, *Friends and Foes* (New Delhi: Indian Book Company, 1974), 116–17. Haji Rahim Bakhsh ran on a combined Muslim Conference-Muslim League ticket, for a central assembly seat. The Muslim Conference, dominated by Sir Fazli Husain, expressed Muslim Unionist concerns in all-India affairs. Gauba describes his career in *Friends and Foes;* his biography of Muhammad, *The Prophet of the Desert,* was published in 1934.

51. Sir Shahabuddin to Sir Fazl-i-Husain, 1 October 1934 (Waheed Ahmad, ed., *Letters of Mian Fazl-i-Husain* [Lahore: Research Society of Pakistan, 1976], 382–83).

52. Gauba later said Iqbal had secretly supported him but could not openly oppose a "brother Kashmiri" (Interview with K. L. Gauba, 1970, Nehru Library oral history transcript, pt. 2, 280–81).

less Gauba, the convert to Islam, won the support of the religious leadership and the religious sympathy of much of the urban population,
including many Kashmiris.[53] In this situation the support of the *biradari*
leaders, even with access to funds and local patronage networks, could
not offset the importance for urban Kashmiris of a symbolic, public assertion of Islamic identity.

But as long as Kashmiri *biradari* leaders could balance symbols of
Muslim identity and ties to the administration, they had a better strategic political position than those leaders who, in the name of Islam, rejected the structure of imperial authority altogether. Though leaders
such as Kitchlew or Iqbal could stir up deep religious enthusiasms in
defense of Islamic symbols, they could not match leaders like the Lahore
ra'is, Mian Amiruddin, in influencing the day-to-day affairs of urban
politics. And leaders like Mian Amiruddin astutely tried to use the appeal to *biradari* identity to draw these various leaders together.

"Why should one vote for Mian Amiruddin?" an election pamphlet
asked during his 1937 contest on the Unionist ticket for the Inner Lahore (old city) Muslim assembly seat. "If one said that one should vote
for Mian Amiruddin because he is a sub-registrar and because he is a
longtime member of the Lahore Municipal Committee and because by
the beneficence of God he is a rich man, then the argument would be
completely empty." On the contrary, the pamphlet continued, "a vote is
a trust of the *qaum,*" the Muslim community, and this trust should be
given to support the man who has served the community. Mian Amiruddin's appeal was that he had done just that; but in reading the pamphlet one was not allowed to forget that this service was rendered by a
leader of the *biradari* who was rich enough and politically well connected enough to make such support count.[54] Though Mian Amiruddin
could not always win elections with such appeals, they nevertheless
summed up the importance of *biradari* in urban Muslim electoral politics.[55] Through the idiom of *biradari* leaders could assert a distinctive
Islamic identity even as they operated in the world of patronage and mediation that tied urban politics to the imperial political system.

53. Gauba, *Friends and Foes,* 120–21. Shahabuddin noted, "All riff-raffs of Lahore
are with Gauba." Though most could not vote in central assembly elections, they put
pressure on municipal election candidates to support Gauba (Sir Shahabuddin to Sir Fazl-i-
Husain, 1 October 1934, quoted in Waheed Ahmad, *Letters,* 381–82).

54. *Mian Amiruddin Sahib ko Vot Kyon Dena Chahiye,* n.d. [1936–37?] (Election
pamphlet in Abdul Aziz collection).

55. Mian Amiruddin was defeated in the 1937 election by K. L. Gauba but later came
into the assembly in a by-election.

Many Muslims thus conceived of a personal relationship to the state, and a "community" identity, far different from those championed by the proponents of communalism. And, paradoxically, the structure of the British colonial state itself encouraged such conceptions. It was one of the central ironies of British rule that even as it fostered the growth of Muslim nationalism among certain groups, it created a system of state authority that was fundamentally hierarchical. The British colonial state rested on an ideology of authority in which mediation and the bonds of local community were central to the construction of the political order. On the one hand urbanization, a changing colonial economy, and elec- toral politics encouraged the emergence of communalism and of a "na- tion" based on individual Muslim identity; on the other hand the ide- ology of colonial rule supported a hierarchical state system in which mediatory conceptions of Islam and Islamic community continued to shape the social order. The Pakistan movement thus developed within a structure in which the relationship between Islam and the political order was highly ambiguous.

The tensions of this process were not, of course, simply a product of colonial rule. On the contrary, tensions between "the folk Islam of shrine and holy lineage" and the moral Islam of individual commitment had characterized Indian Islam long before the colonial period. Such tensions, common to many Islamic societies, reflected the conflict be- tween Islamic social ideals on the one hand and the political pressures that arose from the social organization of Muslim society on the other.[11] Deriving from the time of the Prophet, the ideal society was, in the eyes of many Muslim scholars, one in which the commitment of individual Muslims to Islam defined a "community" that provided the only legiti- mate foundation for the state's authority. But in practice Muslim states had rarely rested on such foundations. Nearly all Muslim states based their practical authority on a range of internal political structures—and local communities—that intervened between the individual and the state.[12] Ibn Khaldun formulated the tensions to which this gave rise in his classic description of the conflicting roles of Islamic and other group loyalties—particularly those of tribal kinship—in shaping the history of Muslim states. Though Islamic institutions in India had adapted to the

11. See, in particular, the works of Ernest Gellner; the quotation is from Gellner, *Na- tions and Nationalism* (Ithaca: Cornell University Press, 1983), 75–76. On the develop- ment of such tensions in colonial societies, see also Clifford Geertz, *Islam Observed* (Chi- cago: University of Chicago Press, 1968).

12. Clive Kessler, *Islam and Politics in a Malay State: Kelantan, 1838–1969* (Ithaca: Cornell University Press, 1978), 208–34.

social and political structure of Indian society, such conflicts had long remained a central part of Indian Muslim political life.

But if the Pakistan movement echoed such long-standing Islamic tensions, the key to the movement's development lay in the relationship of society and the colonial state in twentieth-century India. Indeed, central to the development of Muslim politics was the political and cultural framework provided by the British colonial system, which embodied the imperatives of colonial rule. Like all imperial states, the British in India had sought to control "the lives of individuals without necessarily sharing their values."[13] In controlling Indian society, the British colonial state had thus defined a distinctive and peculiar cultural relationship between the state and society, a relationship that exacerbated tensions among Indian Muslims and exerted a profound effect on Muslim politics. Historians of India have systematically described imperial political structure and its effect on Indian politics.[14] But few have looked at the impact of colonial structure on conceptions of "community" and of the state among Indian Muslims. It is the thesis of this study that only by examining the relationship between Islam and empire can the movement for the creation of a new Muslim state be understood.

The focus of the study is the British Punjab. As one of the two largest and most important Muslim-majority provinces in India, Punjab figures prominently in the history of the Pakistan movement and illustrates also the crosscurrents in twentieth-century Muslim politics. Stretching from Delhi to the Indus, British Punjab was distinguished by religious and geographical diversity. According to the 1931 census, Muslims made up a little over 56 percent of the population, concentrated in the western part of the province. Sikhs were an important minority both within the predominantly Hindu Jullundur division and within the predominantly Muslim Lahore division in the center of the province. In general Hindus predominated in the east and Muslims in the west, with Muslims composing over 80 percent of the population in the far western Punjab districts bordering on the Jhelum and Indus rivers.[15]

Punjab's history and geography combined to create wide diversity within its Muslim population. The Muslim populations in the eastern and central parts of the province were far more urbanized than those in

13. Michael W. Doyle, *Empires* (Ithaca: Cornell University Press, 1986), 45.

14. See, for example, John Gallagher, Gordon Johnson, and Anil Seal, eds., *Locality, Province, and Nation* (Cambridge: Cambridge University Press, 1973), and many other works of the "Cambridge school" of historians of India.

15. *Census of India, 1931*, vol. 17 (Punjab), pt. 1, 319-20.

Is there a parallel w. the Hindu side?

ARAINS

This situation was not unique to the Kashmiris. The situation of the Arain *biradari,* particularly at Lahore, strongly resembled that of the Kashmiris. Among the Muslim *biradari*s of Lahore, the two groups often competed for political influence. Unlike the Kashmiris, however, Arains also possessed considerable influence outside Punjab's cities; they were gazetted practically everywhere in Punjab as an "agricultural tribe." For urban Arains, the politics of *biradari* identity thus carried a special significance. Identification with the *biradari* allowed urban Arains, like Kashmiris, to express an independent Islamic identity, even as they sought to influence the cities' day-to-day political affairs. Most important, the *biradari* idiom also offered Arains a way past the constraints of urban politics as some sought to influence the politics of the Punjabi Muslim community as a whole.

In fact, the structure of the Arain *biradari* offered an important political link between city and country, a link deriving from the traditional hereditary occupation of the Arains as market gardeners. Though largely agriculturalists, many rural Arains were closely tied to the politics and economies of Punjab's cities. "It is a strange coincidence," a Lahore lawyer reflected on the political importance of the Arains at Lahore, "that whenever a momentous incident of some public interest takes place in the Punjab Legislative Assembly, its inevitable reverberations are always felt in the local vegetable and fruit markets."[56] By no means all rural Arains were market gardeners; where they congregated in the rural areas—in Jullundur, Ferozepore, and Lahore districts and, after the turn of the century, in the canal colonies of Lyallpur—most were general cultivators and tenants.[57] In the cities as well, Arains engaged in a wide variety of occupations. But the traditional association of the Arains with market gardening was sufficiently strong that in the nineteenth century in some areas the term *Arain* was synonymous with *mali* or *baghban,* meaning "gardener."[58]

Probably the single most significant element in the emergence of the Arains in the twentieth century as an urban political force was the rapid

56. Hasan Din Sheikh to Associated Press, 3 February 1939 (Abdul Aziz collection).
57. The 1921 census listed the total Arain population in the Punjab as 1,088,697, and the largest districts as Jullundur, 124,364; Lyallpur, 114,997; and Lahore, 110,625. In Jullundur, Arains made up a third of the Muslim population (*Census of India,* 1921, vol. 15 [Punjab and Delhi], pt. 2, 195).
58. Ibbetson, *Punjab Castes,* 143.

expansion of the city of Lahore under the British. The rapid growth of Lahore in the late nineteenth and early twentieth centuries was of particular significance for Arains because many held land in the villages surrounding the city. As Lahore expanded, it drew these Arain villages increasingly into the urban political world, until Lahore in the twentieth century was ringed by a series of suburbs where Arains were numerous and influential—Baghbanpura, Ichhra, Sanda Kalan. Though there are few precise figures for the Arain population of Lahore in the early twentieth century, by 1920 Arains appear to have formed a significant percentage of the population.

The role of the Arain *biradari* in these circumstances as a meeting ground for the conflicting pressures of rural and urban politics, was epitomized by the position of one Arain family, which because of its pivotal place between town and country was inextricably tied to the political development of the *biradari* as a whole. The Mian family of Baghbanpura embodied in sharpened outline almost all the conflicting elements of Arain identity: If the Arains as a group were caught, as hereditary market gardeners, between the countryside and the city, the Mians were surely the most outstanding gardeners of them all, the hereditary custodians of Shah Jahan's Shalimar Bagh in the suburbs of Lahore. Originally raised to prominence and given two revenue-free villages by the Mughals, the Mians retained their villages and custodianship of the gardens under the British, who appointed the head of the family *zaildar* of Baghbanpura. The Mians thus became one of the most influential families of Arain *ra'is* in the city.

In the late nineteenth century, the family was also one of the first Lahori Muslim families to establish itself in the legal profession. After an exceptional career at Government College, Mian Shah Din was the first Punjabi Muslim to go to England for legal studies. On returning to Punjab, Mian Shah Din established himself in the 1890s as one of the leaders of the Lahore bar, and in 1908 was appointed the first Muslim judge on the Chief Court of Punjab.[59] Only slightly behind Mian Shah Din was his cousin, Mian (later Sir) Muhammad Shafi, who also studied law in England and played an even more prominent role in Muslim affairs at Lahore than Shah Din. Like other educated Lahoris, both Mian Shah Din and Mian Muhammad Shafi asserted a distinctly Muslim public identity, even as they associated themselves with the power and cul-

59. Ikram, *Modern Muslim India*, 206–7; Mian Bashir Ahmad, *Justice Shah Din: His Life and Writings* (Lahore: author, 1962), 51–52.

ture of the colonial state. Indeed, as the first Muslim leaders of Lahore professional society who could challenge Hindu dominance at the bar, they both stressed publicly the importance of Muslim education and Muslim political solidarity—and played active roles in the organization of many of Lahore's early Muslim *anjuman*s. Both were active not only in Sir Syed's Aligarh movement, but also in the Anjuman Himayat-i Islam.[60] They also took a leading part in forming the first Punjab branch of the Muslim League in 1907.

As the leading Arain *ra'is* of the city, however, the Baghbanpura Mians were also concerned with Arain identity.[61] As in the case of the Kashmiris, the organization of an Arain *anjuman* in the early twentieth century reflected the combination of religious and "tribal" elements in *biradari* identity that were important generally for such urban leaders. An early petition of the *anjuman*'s leaders shows these elements. In almost all Punjabi districts the British had gazetted Arains as an agricultural tribe, and an army classification of Arains as *kamin*s, or village menials, prompted this appeal. In a petition to the commander-in-chief, Mian Shah Din, Mian Muhammad Shafi, and more than fifty other Arain leaders asserted that Arains were in fact "one of the doment [sic] agricultural tribes of the Punjab," whose status was "in no way inferior to that of the other principal agricultural tribes such as Jats, Rajputs, etc."[62] To bolster this claim they included a list of Arain *zaildar*s and *sufedposh*es (sub-*zaildar*s) in the province (the *zaildar*s alone numbering over forty) and a list of Arains in military service. But the petitioners went beyond this; they claimed to be "more advanced in Western education than the other agricultural tribes of the Punjab" and "to outnumber the other agricultural tribes of the Punjab as regards service in the Civil Department of the State."[63] Their claim to status was thus not limited solely by the rural standards of "tribal" organization and dominance on the land but rested also on a cultural claim to share directly in the state's power.

Underlying this distinctive cultural identity was the strong connection between Arain *biradari* identity and Islam. As the petitioners expressed it, a strong Islamic component lay at the heart of Arain identity.

60. Mian Bashir Ahmad, *Justice Shah Din*, 31–46.
61. See, for example, Jahan Ara Shahnawaz, *Father and Daughter* (Lahore: Nigarishat, 1971), 23.
62. Petition to Viscount Kitchener of Khartoum, Commander-in-Chief in India, n.d., 1–2 (Abdul Aziz collection).
63. Ibid., 3–4.

It rested both on a claim to special Islamic descent and on a popular commitment among Arains to the purest standards of Islamic behavior—standards that justified a place for Arain leaders at the cultural center of Punjab. Indeed, Arain origins, they said, could be traced to the armies of Muhammad bin Qasim: "Although it is nearly 1200 years since the Arains left Arabia," they declared, "they still possess several characteristics which they have in common with Arabs and which distinguish them from other Mohammadan tribes of the Punjab." A most important example was their adherence to simple Muslim customs in the rites of marriage and death.[64] Like Kashmiris, Arain leaders stressed adherence to *shari'at* in defining a central position for Arains among Punjab's Muslims.

The articulation of such an Arain *biradari* identity thus served important purposes for urban Arain leaders such as the Baghbanpura Mians, linking recognition as leaders of a dominant "agricultural tribe" with an assertion of cultural status justifying a position at the center of political power. But identification with the *biradari* was also important for a broad range of urban Arains. Even for those urban Arains influenced more deeply by reformist religious ideas, and drawn into the more radical Islamic politics of the years after World War I,[65] Arain *biradari* identity provided a critical channel for attempts to influence the broader politics of the Punjabi Islamic community. Whether urban *ra'is*, professional men, or journalists, because of their identification with the *biradari* Arain leaders could attempt to stake a claim to influence beyond the urban context that had shaped them—to gain a voice, in other words, in the politics of the province as a whole.

After the Baghbanpura Mians, Mian Abdul Aziz was probably the most important Arain in the prepartition politics of Lahore.[66] Mian Abdul Aziz was a lawyer from Hoshiarpur who moved his practice to Lahore in 1919 and took a prominent part in public affairs in the city. Deeply concerned with Muslim political identity, Mian Abdul Aziz found an independent voice in municipal politics, often opposing both

64. Ibid., 6.
65. Arains prominent among twentieth-century reformist religious leaders included Mian Sher Muhammad of Sharaqpur, a Naqshbandi *pir,* and Maulana Habib-ur-Rahman Ludhianvi of the Ahrar, a politically active Deobandi *'alim.* Measuring *biradari* participation in twentieth-century political movements is difficult. In 1963 one Arain political leader and member of a prominent Arain landlord family of Lahore district claimed Arains played a central role in nearly all the radical, anti-British movements of twentieth-century Muslim Punjab (Sardar Muhammad Shafi, "Pahle edishan par chand tabassure," in Ali Asghar Chaudhri, *Tarikh-i Ara'iyan* [Lahore: 'Ilmi Kutubkhana, 1963], 21).
66. A. R. Tabassum to Sir Chhotu Ram, 1 July 1944 (Abdul Aziz collection).

the British administration and the rural Muslim leadership. During a stint in the 1920s as Muslim representative for Lahore city in the Legislative Council, Mian Abdul Aziz criticized the subservience of rural Muslims to the British administration. He attacked the office of *zaildar,* the hinge of political power in the rural areas, as an office not of true tribal representation at all but of administrative exploitation pure and simple.[67] In the early 1930s Mian Abdul Aziz was elected chairman of the Lahore Municipal Committee and came into sharp conflict with the government over its attempt to establish greater control in municipal affairs.[68] His rhetorical rejection of the ideology of the British imperial system was in fact symbolized by his repeated demands in the 1920s for the removal of the statue of Lord Lawrence that stood, sword in one hand and pen in the other, in front of the Lahore High Court.

But in spite of, or because of, his strong commitment to independent cultural identity, Mian Abdul Aziz found a stress on his Arain identity vital in pressing his interests in provincial politics. He had long been active in organized Arain affairs, for a time president of the Arain *anjuman.*[69] But he began to consider its political potential most seriously in 1936 and 1937, when provincial autonomy was introduced and elections to the new provincial Legislative Assembly approached. Mian Abdul Aziz was reluctant to support the Unionists; he criticized their " 'parochial, pro-rural,' tendencies," which he feared would lead to the triumph of the "Zaildar class" in the election and thus to the perpetuation of official influence in the new Assembly through the elected element.[70] In his concern to stress the political importance of Muslim identity, he first supported the newly reorganized Muslim League of Muhammad Ali Jinnah, which had an independent, anti-Unionist platform—one he felt embodied his political concerns.[71]

As the campaign developed, however, practical considerations made the alliance inadvisable. Whatever its symbolic attractiveness, alliance with the League would exclude him from provincial political influence,

67. Punjab, *Legislative Council Debates,* vol. 9A (1926): 51.
68. See Mian Abdul Aziz, *Reply to the Dobson Committee Report on the Affairs of the Municipal Committee of Lahore* (Lahore: Maclagan Press, 1932).
69. Chaudhri, *Tarikh-i Ara'iyan,* 171.
70. Note to chairman of the Unionist party on attitude of Mian Abdul Aziz, n.d. [Spring 1936?] (Unionist party papers, file marked 'Miscellaneous Party Organization, 1936–1940').
71. When Mian Abdul Aziz accepted a position on Jinnah's Muslim League parliamentary board, the president of the All-India Arain conference, Mian Muhammad Shah Nawaz, warned him to wait for the conference's decision before declaring his political allegiances (Mian Muhammad Shah Nawaz to Mian Abdul Aziz, 6 June 1936 [Abdul Aziz collection]). For discussion of Jinnah and the Muslim League, see chapter four.

isolating him from Punjab's dominant rural Muslim majority. Though
complete identification with the Unionists was for Mian Abdul Aziz impossible, identification with the Arain *biradari* offered him a platform
on which he could press his claim to provincial influence and yet remain
symbolically committed to an independent cultural position. By running
as a political independent, and stressing his identity as an Arain *biradari*
leader, he spoke in an idiom that the Unionists could not readily ignore.
Indeed, for the Unionists support of Mian Abdul Aziz offered an avenue
for extending their influence in Lahore, identifying the party with an
important urban leader.[72]

But after his election, Mian Abdul Aziz was in an awkward position.
He hoped to be appointed minister in the Unionist cabinet, a position
that would allow him to express his views within the colonial structure.
The undertaking proved difficult. To gain the Unionists' attention he
pressed his claim primarily as a political representative of Punjab's
Arain *biradari*. The Arain *anjuman* wired to the new Unionist premier,
Sir Sikander Hyat Khan: "Anjuman Araiyan fully supports Mian Abdul
Aziz Barrister for Ministership. Arain population nearly 13 1/2 lakhs
[1,350,000], third in Punjab, but claim ignored in last reforms. Arain
community feels strongly now and requests you to appoint Arain Minister."[73] But Sir Sikander was wary. Though recognizing the importance
of Arain support, he was also concerned, as Sir Chhotu Ram later
wrote, "with the service of the individual concerned to the Party and his
readiness to stand by the discipline of the Party."[74] In constructing his
government, Sikander thus bypassed Mian Abdul Aziz as an Arain representative, and appointed Begum Shah Nawaz, a daughter of Sir Muhammad Shafi of the Baghbanpura Mians, as a parliamentary secretary. Begum Shah Nawaz was elected from an urban constituency (Lahore city
Muslim women), but her personal service to the Unionist party, and the
rural connections of the Mian family, made her far more acceptable to
Unionist leaders.[75] For Mian Abdul Aziz and more radical urban Arains,

72. In 1936 Unionists carefully followed developments within the Arain *biradari*,
hoping to gain Arain support (See note by Afzal Ali Hasnie, 8 May 1936, on an Arain
parliamentary board, Unionist party papers, file marked 'Mian Nurullah's Case'). Mian
Abdul Aziz's increasing political importance to them is indicated in Sir Fazli Husain's correspondence (Ahmad Yar Khan Daultana to Sir Fazl-i-Husain, 23 June 1936, and Sikander
Hyat to Sir Fazl-i-Husain, 25 June 1936; in Waheed Ahmad, *Letters*, 600, 604).
73. Quoted in Mohammad Yusuf, Ambala city, to Mian Abdul Aziz, 26 February
1937 (Abdul Aziz collection).
74. Sir Chhotu Ram to A. R. Tabassum, 17 July 1944 (ibid.).
75. Sir Chhotu Ram later noted that Begum Shah Nawaz was probably chosen to conciliate Arains. "Personally," he added, "I would have preferred to select Mian Nurullah
because my personal prejudices against women are unduly strong" (ibid.).

her appointment thus closed off easy access to provincial power. But more important, it indicated clearly the limits of *biradari* identity in facilitating the political expression of the cultural concerns that shaped their identity.

In fact, the case of Mian Abdul Aziz illustrates the inherent political dilemma facing many urban leaders in Punjab—Kashmiris and Arains alike. They sought to define an identity that justified a central cultural position for themselves in Punjabi life. In the eyes of most urban Muslims, only an Islamic idiom could provide this. But such an idiom did nothing to tie urban leaders to the hierarchies of administrative authority linking the imperial state to Punjabi society. Many urban leaders thus found in the language of *biradari* a means of publicly articulating an Islamic identity consistent with the descent-based identities that structured imperial power. They thus used the idiom of *biradari* to shape a place for themselves at the heart of Punjabi Muslim culture. But the idiom of *biradari* could not reconcile the political contradictions that hinged on the ambiguous place of the cities themselves within the larger imperial order.

URBAN POLITICS AND
THE SYMBOLS OF ISLAM

The problem facing urban leaders was in fact not the simple redefinition of their own identities but the place of urban politics in the political system. Centers for administration, commerce, education, communication, the press, and the new forms of voluntary organization, cities remained at the heart of Punjabi public life. But urban politics, despite the efforts of its leaders, remained peripheral to the ideological structure of the imperial state. To redefine its position, urban leaders needed more than *anjumans* or urban *biradaris*; they needed to define in the arenas of urban politics a cultural alternative to the state's authority.

The pressure to find an alternative gave rise in the 1920s and 1930s to popular agitations by urban Muslims focused on Islamic symbols conveyed in press and public rhetoric. For brief moments, many of Punjab's Muslims stepped outside the structure of state politics altogether to express a direct commitment to the ideal of a political order defined by Islam. Urban leaders in politics identified themselves with these symbols and established a public presence in Punjabi politics that at times carried over into the countryside. Yet the concrete results of these communal agitations were limited; lacking institutional foundations, they waxed and waned in reaction to the continuing British manipulation of urban patronage and authority. But the agitations did have a substantial impact. They highlighted the cultural contradictions inherent in the imperial system; perhaps more important, they illustrated the power of Islamic symbols to call forth from Muslims a public commitment that defined the existence of a Muslim political community independent of the structure of the colonial state.

THE AHRAR AND THE KASHMIR AGITATION

These agitations took many forms. The most powerful communal agitation of the early 1930s focused on the defense of Muslim interests in Kashmir, a cause that many Punjabi Muslims made a symbol of direct commitment to the defense of Islam. It brought to prominence the Majlis-i Ahrar, organized mainly by urban Muslims and 'ulama in the late 1920s in the wake of the collapse of the Khilafat movement. Its leaders, including the fiery anti-British orator, Saiyid Ataullah Shah Bokhari, and several of Punjab's leading reformist 'ulama, concentrated their political energies on the defense of Islam. Though never organizationally very strong, the Ahrar sought to use Islamic symbols to create an active Muslim community in Punjab, independent of British imperial authority.[76]

The movement to defend Islam in Kashmir burst into prominence in Punjab in 1931. An alleged insult to the Qor'an by a Hindu police constable in Jammu set off a broad popular challenge to Hindu rule in Kashmir. In the Punjab, the Majlis-i Ahrar portrayed the defense of Kashmiri Muslim rights as symbolic of the protection of Islam itself. With little direct connection with Punjabi politics, support for the Muslims of Kashmir symbolized Islamic unity, even as it challenged the legitimacy of the authority of the British, who supported the Maharaja of Kashmir and whose rule had made oppression of Kashmiri Muslims possible. Separation of this issue from issues of local Punjabi politics in fact gave it special power as a symbol of Islamic solidarity.

But the political significance of the issue did not rest only on the defense of Muslim Kashmiri rights. Its importance as a symbolic appeal to Muslim unity was signaled when the Ahrar combined the defense of Is-

76. On the Ahrar, formed after the Lahore Congress session of 1929, see Smith, *Modern Islam in India,* 270–75. For a more extended treatment in Urdu, see Janbaz Mirza, *Karwan-i Ahrar,* 5 vols. (Lahore: Maktaba-yi Tabassura, 1975–81).

lam in Kashmir with an attack on the Ahmadiyah in Punjab, a small, tightly organized Muslim religious sect that had long been active in Muslim organization. Its leaders had initially played an important role in organizing support for Kashmiri Muslims.[77] But for the Ahrar, the very position of the Ahmadiyah signified the degree to which Punjabi Muslims had failed to use their common commitment to Islam to effectively organize. Ahmadiyah theology was anathema to the leaders of the Ahrar— and to most Muslim religious leaders—who accused the Ahmadiyah of denying one of the central principles of Islamic doctrine, the finality of the Prophethood of Muhammad.[78] As one Ahrar leader, Saiyid Ataullah Shah Bokhari, wrote, "We all follow one principle. Our quarrels are based on the love of the Prophet in which each sect tries to excel the others."[79] But, he declared, in this the Ahmadiyah, by denying the finality of the Prophethood, were men apart. By simultaneously opposing the Ahmadiyah and invoking Muslim solidarity in defense of their brethren in Kashmir, the Ahrar attempted to lay a broad symbolic base for their position. They cast themselves as the defenders not only of the broad Islamic community but also of the Prophethood of Muhammad.

In fact, Ahrar leaders soon extended the agitation over Kashmir into a widespread popular movement in Punjab, anchored in the cities but reaching into the rural areas as well. Hundreds of *jatha*s, or bands of Muslim volunteers, organized themselves to cross illegally from Punjab into Kashmir to aid the Kashmiri Muslims. During November 1931, although the government arrested thousands of people, the agitation expanded so rapidly that the sheer number of those arrested embarassed the jail department and forced the opening of special camp jails.[80] Volunteers and funds for the agitation came from practically all parts of the Punjab. Kashmiris in Punjab's cities seem to have played a particularly important part; heavily Kashmiri cities, such as Amritsar and Sialkot, emerged as Ahrar strongholds. But support for the agitation transcended the interests of the Kashmiri *biradari*. The agitation developed as a defense of the Muslim community as a whole.

77. The Khalifa, or head, of the Ahmadiyah community chaired the All-India Kashmir committee. For a study of the Ahmadiyah, see Spencer Lavan, *The Ahmadiyah Movement* (Delhi: Manohar Book Service, 1974).
78. The movement against the Ahmadiyah was lengthy and symbolically important; see Shorish Kashmiri, *Tahrik-i Khatm-i Nubuwat* (Lahore: Matbu'at Chatan, 1980).
79. Translation of speech by Saiyid Ataullah Shah Bokhari at Muslim Tabligh conference, Saharanpur, 19 May 1935 (NAI, Home Political, file 35/5/35).
80. Punjab fortnightly report for the first half of December 1931 (ibid., file 18/12/31).

Perhaps most significant of all, during the agitation Punjab's *'ulama* took an active political role. Since a large number of urban *'ulama* supported the agitation, meetings in mosques to organize support for the Ahrar became a regular feature of the movement. In some cases influential local maulvis, like the Imam of the Jame' Masjid at Gujranwala, asked their followers to give their *zakat,* or compulsory religious charity, to the Ahrar.[81] But support was not confined to these urban religious leaders. Many of the rural *pirs* also initially gave the Ahrar their support. "The Pirs have begun to take a hand," the government declared as the agitation expanded in November 1931, "and declare the efforts of the Ahrar to be actuated by the right spirit of Islamic sympathy."[82] Most prominent were *pirs* associated with the *sufi* revival, such as Pir Fazl Shah of Jalalpur, who praised the spirit of the common Muslims in their willingness to sacrifice for Islam;[83] Pir Jamaat Ali Shah donated five hundred rupees to the cause.[84] Humbler *pirs* also played a role. Near Wazirabad, for example, a *pir* with "a good deal of following in the surrounding villages . . . electrified" the movement by leading a *jatha* into the town and then heading for Kashmir to court arrest.[85]

Its wide base of religious leadership turned the agitation into a serious ideological challenge to the entire British system of authority. It galvanized large groups of Muslims to a personal commitment to Islam, which they expressed through the agitation in public, political activity. But when the immediate enthusiasm of the cause waned, the Ahrar faced severe practical political problems. After Ramazan in early 1932, the leaders of the Ahrar found themselves increasingly "unable to secure the expected flow of funds and volunteers."[86] Despite widespread popular sympathy, the concrete political organization of the Ahrar, hampered by frequent arrests, deteriorated. Support from religious leaders had proved central to the Ahrar's success, but as the agitation waned the Ahrar found itself unable to exert practical control over funds or administration of the mosques and shrines. Casting about for organized

---

81. Gujranwala situation reports on the Kashmir agitation, 7 December 1931 (Lahore Divisional Commissioner's Files, file P/24).
82. Punjab fortnightly report for the first half of November 1931 (NAI, Home Political, file 18/11/31).
83. Ghani, *Amir Hizbullah,* 349.
84. Saiyid Akhtar Husain Shah, *Sirat-i Amir-i Millat,* 403–4.
85. Gujranwala situation reports on Kashmir agitation, 13 December and 14 December 1931 (Lahore Commissioner's Files, file P/24).
86. Punjab fortnightly report for the second half of February 1932 (NAI, Home Political, file 18/4/32).

support, therefore, many Ahrar leaders were increasingly attracted to their old allies in the Jami'at-i 'Ulama-yi Hind who, whatever their limitations, provided, in alliance with the Congress, a clear organizational focus for opposition to the British. But these allies could provide the Ahrar only a limited popular base, and alliance with them underscored the cultural isolation of the cities from the political networks of rural Punjab. As the government noted, many of the "rural elements" in particular, "though they may sympathize with [the Ahrar's] championing [of] Islam," were highly suspicious of such political connections.[87] Though alliance with the Jami'at-i 'Ulama-yi Hind and the Congress thus offered the kind of strong, independent political organization the Ahrar needed to oppose the political domination of Muslim politics by the rural Unionists, it nevertheless undermined the symbolic force of their leaders as spokesmen for a united Muslim community.

The outcome of the Kashmir agitation dramatized the problems faced by such a movement. Mobilizing action based on Muslim commitment to symbols, the Ahrar tried to create a focus for political authority outside the structure of the state. The power of Islamic symbols was substantial, but without a solid organizational base, the Ahrar became captives of their symbolic issues. The gradual waning of the Kashmir issue and the subsequent move of the Ahrar into cooperation with the Congress and the Jami'at-i 'Ulama-yi Hind thus threw Ahrar politics into confusion. Six months after the peak of the Kashmir agitation, the government reported that the Ahrar's "continued failure to find a program to the liking of their community is almost pathetic."[88] Though the Ahrar continued as an important presence in Muslim politics, particularly in the cities, its experience demonstrated in particularly striking fashion the problems involved in constructing political alternatives to the structures of British authority, even in a serendipitous combination of religious and political issues. But it also illustrated equally dramatically the power of Islamic symbols to mobilize Punjab's Muslims.

THE SHAHIDGANJ MOSQUE AGITATION

The most dramatic demonstration of the importance in Punjab's cities of a "communal" definition of political power came in 1935 in the

87. C. C. Garbett to H. W. Emerson, home secretary, Punjab, 4 March 1932 (ibid., file 14/14/32).
88. Fortnightly report for the first half of April 1932 (ibid., file 18/7/32).

agitation over the Shahidganj mosque. As a symbol of Islamic identity, the Shahidganj mosque provided a focus for Muslim politics in 1935 and 1936 that threw the Ahrar into insignificance and galvanized Muslims in urban Punjab. The agitation dramatized, as clearly as any other single episode in twentieth-century Muslim politics, the emotional power and political importance of Islamic symbols in British Punjab.

The focus of the Shahidganj agitation was the preeminent symbol of classical Islamic solidarity, a mosque. The Shahidganj mosque (literally "treasure of martyrs") was located in the Landa bazaar outside the Delhi gate at Lahore. Though apparently dating from Mughal times, the mosque had not been used as a place of Muslim prayer since the eighteenth century, when it had fallen into the hands of the Sikhs. Both Muslims and Sikhs revered it as a holy place; in the 1930s officials placed the site under the control of a local Sikh gurdwaras committee, in recognition of longtime Sikh occupation of the site. Local Muslims, however, objected to the award of the site to the Sikhs in spite of its long history of Sikh control. In June 1935 the issue precipitated public confrontations when Muslim crowds massed in Landa bazaar to protest Sikh plans for demolition of what Muslims considered to be a mosque.[89]

The reactions of most Muslim leaders were initially moderate. A committee formed, the Anjuman-i Tahaffuz-i Masjid Shahidganj (Committee for the protection of the Shahidganj mosque), including a wide spectrum of Unionist Muslims, lawyers, journalists and *biradari* leaders like Mian Abdul Aziz, to find legal means to protect the mosque and press for peaceful settlement of the issue.[90] But the issue's symbolic, explosive potential was pointed out clearly by Maulana Zafar Ali Khan. If no settlement were reached on the issue, he declared, it could only "result in bloodshed." The Muslims would not hesitate, he said, "to make any sacrifice in the path of preserving the emblems of religion and God."[91]

Recognizing the potential danger in the situation, the governor, Sir Herbert Emerson, hurried down from Simla in the July heat to arrange a negotiated settlement of the issue. But even as negotiations were going on, the Sikhs in occupation of the site, responding to political pressures within their own community, demolished the mosque on 7 July under cover of night. The result was a sensation in the city. Mian Abdul Aziz

89. Ganda Singh, *History of the Gurdwara Shahidganj, Lahore* (Lahore?: author?, 1935), 64–65, 66–72.
90. Report on the Shahidganj affair by Mian Abdul Aziz, n.d. (Abdul Aziz collection); F. H. Puckle, chief secretary, Punjab to deputy commissioners, 19 July 1935 (NAI, Home Political, file 5/14/35).
91. *Zamindar*, 2 July 1935 (Press Branch, file 8331A, vol. 1).

reported, "The news spread like wild-fire throughout Lahore." Widespread posting of troops and a tight curfew initially controlled the situation;[92] but political initiative in the matter quickly passed to more radical Muslims. On 14 July at a huge Muslim meeting in Lahore, Maulana Zafar Ali Khan formed a group to fight for the mosque, the Majlis Ittehad-i Millat, whose program was "to recruit volunteers—and dress them in blue shirts—for the purpose of carrying on the agitation."[93]

Alarmed by the turn of events, the government externed four of the more radical leaders, including Maulana Zafar Ali Khan, from Lahore. But more moderate leaders now proved completely unable to control the religious enthusiasm that had been unleashed. On 19 July at a meeting held after Friday prayers at the Badshahi mosque, Muslim speakers urged the worshippers to march directly on the Shahidganj mosque. Throughout the night, as police made repeated attempts to block it, a crowd of several hundred Muslims attempted to cross the old city to reach the mosque. As morning broke, the crowd emerged from Delhi gate, its strength now swelled to almost two thousand.[94] Efforts of Muslim leaders to control it proved entirely useless, while reinforcements "with religious banners and shouting religious slogans" added throughout the day to the throng that massed at the entrance to Landa bazaar in front of the *kotwali* (city police station). One prominent Muslim wrote, "All [are] ready to die. They don't listen to any one."[95] On 20 July, faced with panic, the police fired twice into the crowd but failed to disperse it. On the morning of 21 July, with new crowds forming in the vicinity, the Punjab Chief Secretary found the *kotwali* "practically in a state of siege."[96] Again the authorities opened fire, and by the time the crowds finally dispersed on the evening of 21 July more than a dozen Muslims were dead.

The martyrdom of these Muslims turned the agitation for the mosque into a cause that could not soon be forgotten. From a symbolic point of view the issue of the Shahidganj mosque struck very close to the heart of urban Muslim identity and self-definition. The Muslim case for control of the mosque, though from a legal point of view untenable, was from a

---

92. Report on the Shahidganj affair by Mian Abdul Aziz (Abdul Aziz collection).

93. *Civil and Military Gazette* (Lahore), 16 July 1935, quoted in Ganda Singh, *History of the Gurdwara Shahidganj*, 80. Maulana Zafar Ali Khan had organized "blue shirt" volunteers for other Islamic causes.

94. Fortnightly report for the second half of July 1935 (NAI, Home Political, file 18/7/35).

95. Malik Firoz Khan Noon to Sir Fazl-i-Husain, 20 July 1935 (Waheed Ahmad, *Letters*, 411).

96. Note by H. D. Craik, 21 July 1935 (NAI, Home Political, file 5/14/35).

religious point of view exceptionally strong. The Sikhs had wantonly destroyed the mosque, but their case for control of the site rested on the legal point of over one hundred seventy years of adverse possession—a point of British law that directly contradicted the *shari'at,* according to which a mosque, when dedicated as *waqf* (a pious endowment) to God, remained a mosque forever. The Muslim case therefore rested clearly on an assertion of their commitment to the *shari'at*—on an assertion, in fact, of the sovereignty of the *shari'at,* and thus of the Muslim community itself, over British law. This assertion had already been punctuated by the martyrs who gave their lives for the mosque. To Muslims concerned with the legitimacy of the political system, the issue could not have been more clear-cut. "The Government must remember," warned Saiyid Zainulabedin Shah Gilani of Multan, "that if there occurs a clash between the law of the Government and the Law of God, the Muslims would be prepared to offer every possible sacrifice considering the Law of God and that of the Prophet as the foremost law." [97]

But the question of politically organizing such a "community" remained to be faced. The supremacy of the *shari'at* was the heart of the issue; would the *'ulama* and other Muslim religious leaders take a central role in developing the agitation? Divisions among the religious leaders of the community quickly appeared. In the case of the Ahrar, political considerations proved uppermost. Influenced by the Jami'at-i 'Ulama-yi Hind and the Congress, they were wary of joining an agitation whose immediate target was not the British but the Sikhs, whose support the Congress was then actively seeking. More important, the Ahrar were looking forward to elections under the new constitution, and they did not want to jeopardize a potential alliance with Congress and the Sikhs that they hoped might bring them a ministership. [98] For their part, the *'ulama* associated with the Ahrar tried initially to stay clear of the agitation altogether. Ahrar leaders after the Lahore shootings issued a statement that the Shahidganj agitators had been misled in a hopeless cause and that the Qor'an itself forbade the useless wasting of human lives.

But their statements infuriated those who had been involved in the agitation; they saw the Ahrar attitude as an almost treasonable mockery of the martyrdom of the individuals killed in the police shootings. As one Shahidganj supporter wrote contemptuously, "The loudest cries of the blood of the martyrs could not disengage them from the sacred oc-

97. Report of speech by Saiyid Zainulabedin Shah Gilani in Multan (*Zamindar,* 13 August 1935 [Press Branch, file 8331, vol. 3A]).
98. *Zamindar,* 9 August 1935 (ibid., file 8331, vol. 2A).

cupations of the courting of the seats for the Ministership."[99] Opposing 'ulama at Lahore were not quick to counter the Ahrar, however, since they were wary of action that might bring them into open conflict with prominent urban ra'is or with the government. In the immediate aftermath of the shootings in July, the leaders of the agitation could only bemoan the general failure of the 'ulama to provide the leadership the movement needed. "A prominent but sad feature of the Shahidganj Mosque affair," the Zamindar commented in August, "is that the local 'ulema' have not published any statement from the religious point of view." While the uninstructed "sacrificed themselves like moths on the lamp of Islam and revived the traditions of the 'self-sacrificing' spirit of early times," the paper declared, the 'ulama, at one time fighters for Islam, remained silent.[100]

With the agitation otherwise stalled and with many of the 'ulama and the Ahrar in opposition, the urban leaders of the Ittehad-i Millat decided on a bold stroke to revive the movement. At a special conference at Rawalpindi in September 1935 they turned directly to one of the most prominent rural pirs, Pir Jamaat Ali Shah, to lead the agitation to regain the site of the mosque. Their move was a calculated gamble, for it meant appointing the Pir as Amir-i Millat, leader of the community, or virtual dictator of the agitation. But the potential rewards of this move were considerable; it would link the agitation to a powerful rural base. Many believed, in fact, that the Pir's appointment would galvanize rural support and would "naturally result in other religious leaders falling into line and taking part in the agitation."[101] Indeed, the move almost immediately revitalized Muslim enthusiasm and led to much talk at the Rawalpindi conference about launching civil disobedience in order to force the return of the mosque. Almost immediately after Jamaat Ali Shah's appointment, other pirs offered to support the agitation, particularly pirs of the sufi revival tradition. Pir Fazl Shah of Jalalpur sent a message to the conference expressing his full acceptance of all the Pir's decisions, as did Pir Ghulam Mohyuddin of Golra;[102] from Multan, Saiyid Zainulabedin Shah Gilani offered his full acceptance of Jamaat Ali Shah's leadership.[103] Support came also from the Barelvi 'ulama of the Anjuman Hizb al-Ahnaf at Lahore, who pledged to carry out all the

99. Statement of Saiyid Sarwar Shah Gilani (Zamindar, 10 August 1935 [ibid.]).
100. Zamindar, 24 August 1935 (ibid., file 8331, vol. 4A).
101. Report on the Rawalpindi conference, 4 September 1935 (NAI, Home Political, file 5/21/35).
102. Zamindar, 8 September 1935 (Press Branch, file 8331, vol. 5A).
103. Siyasat (Lahore), 10 September 1935 (ibid.).

Pir's orders in accordance with the *shari'at*.[104] The Pir's appointment
seemed to provide a clear structure of religious leadership for the defense of the community's interests. Pir Jamaat Ali Shah lost no time in
asserting his religious authority as Amir. Less than two weeks after the
Rawalpindi conference, he issued a call for Muslim volunteers, at the
same time requesting all Muslims to refuse to say the funeral prayers
and to deny burial space in Muslim graveyards to those who were unwilling to participate in the agitation.[105]

Pir Jamaat Ali Shah's appointment as Amir-i Millat and the support
of many other rural *pirs* gave the Shahidganj movement a religious and
political base that previous communal agitation had lacked. The alliance of urban leaders with rural *pirs* in the defense of an urban mosque
provided a symbolic Islamic focus and a potentially powerful political
base. It promised to transcend the cleavages between urban and rural
Punjab, rallying Muslims politically around a symbol of Islamic identity
and also defining an organizational structure for the community independent of the imperial political system.

But at the same time, the appeal to the Pir's leadership made clear the
depth of the cleavages the agitation was trying to bridge. The Pir's religious style created immediate misgivings among some urban Muslims,
particularly those influenced by the reformist *'ulama*. They were uneasy
with the blind faith many of the Pir's rural followers displayed, and they
questioned the oath of allegiance to the Pir taken at the Rawalpindi conference, suggesting that it resembled far too closely the traditional religious oath of fealty to a *sufi pir* (*bai'at*).[106] For them the gulf between the
religion of rural Punjab and reformist Islam had grown too wide to be
easily bridged. But perhaps even more important, the Pir's position as a
rural leader, with close ties to the administrative structure of the British
regime, made it difficult for him to lead the agitation in the manner
many urban Muslims desired. Though the Pir's rural connections provided him, on one level, his political strength, on another level they
compromised his ability to operate independently of the British in the
idioms of symbolic Islamic politics. Ironically, the very character of his
political connections disqualified him, in the eyes of many urban Muslims, from leading an Islamic community defined in symbolic terms.
How can a man who calls the government "mai-bap" (mother and father) be entrusted with leading the Muslims? asked Maulana Habib-ur-

104. *Ihsan* (Lahore), 8 September 1935 (ibid.).
105. *Siyasat*, 11 September 1935 (ibid., vol. 6).
106. *Inquilab* (Lahore), 28 November 1935 (ibid., file 4285).

Rahman, of the Ahrar, incredulous.[107] The answer was that he could not. As one Hindu newspaper declared, "Not to speak of Pir Sahib, all the gaddi holders [custodians of the shrines], whether Muslim or Hindu, cannot rise against the Government."[108]

Pir Jamaat Ali Shah was immediately subjected to intense pressure from all sides as he tried to chalk out a program. Under this political pressure he wavered constantly as he tried to assert his political authority. Though the Rawalpindi conference had hinted strongly at civil disobedience, the influence of moderate Muslims and the government soon completely undermined his freedom of action in that direction. "Deeply as he may have appeared to have committed himself," the chief secretary wrote immediately after the Rawalpindi conference, "there is some reason to think that he is not altogether comfortable about his position, and he may retreat from it. Influences," he added pointedly, "are being brought to bear to this end."[109] Pir Jamaat Ali Shah began his efforts by touring much of the Punjab and by traveling to the 'urs at Ajmer and to Bareilly and Budaun in the United Provinces to meet with religious leaders.[110] But he did little after that to organize the agitation effectively. He briefly proposed, then repudiated, a program of economic boycott of the Hindus;[111] in November 1935 he announced a plan to raise a million volunteers and a million rupees for a common fund. But other than the organization of special days of mourning for the mosque he took little action to effect the scheme. He even briefly sought to enlist the organization of the Khaksars, a body of militarized Muslim volunteers in some of Punjab's cities, whose greatest virtue, he declared, was that they "obey their Amir."[112] But he repudiated even this alliance when he discovered that he disagreed with the Khaksar leader's religious views.

By the end of 1935, as a result of the Pir's inconsistencies, the movement neared collapse. Pressured both by the government and by urban agitators, the Pir "has continued," the government reported, "to change

107. *Ihsan*, 23 September 1935 (ibid., file 8331, vol. 7A).
108. *Pratap* (Lahore), 23 September 1935 (ibid.).
109. Appreciation of Shahidganj situation, F. H. Puckle, 6 September 1935 (NAI, Home Political, file 5/21/35).
110. *Inquilab*, 3 October 1935 (Press Branch, file 4285).
111. Punjab fortnightly report for the second half of September 1935 (NAI, Home Political, file 18/9/35); Punjab fortnightly report for the first half of October 1935 (ibid., file 18/10/35).
112. *Inquilab*, 28 November 1935 (Press Branch, file 4285); Punjab fortnightly report for the first half of December 1935 (NAI, Home Political, file 18/12/35). For an account of the Khaksars, see Shan Muhammad, *Khaksar Movement in India* (Meerut: Meenakshi Prakashan, 1973).

his views from day to day." [113] In January 1936 a Lahore newspaper blasted the leadership of the agitation, declaring that while the Pir waffled, "the Musalmans are still in a state of disintegration. . . . Not to speak of 10 lakh volunteers, the Majlis Ittehad-i Millat has not been able to collect even 10 volunteers and its coffers do not contain even 10 rupees today." [114] But efforts to revitalize the agitation by holding a new Shahid-ganj conference produced only squabbling when the Pir first supported and then forbade the conference after the government refused its approval. When the conference was finally held at Amritsar in January 1936, the results seemed only to confirm the Pir's inability to provide independent leadership for the community. After bitter confrontations between radical urban leaders and conference delegates, including wealthy *murid*s like Mir Maqbul Mahmud, brother-in-law of Sir Sikander Hyat Khan, the Pir departed on *hajj,* perhaps to salvage his personal prestige. [115]

The failure of the experiment with Pir Jamaat Ali Shah's leadership in the Shahidganj agitation was caused to a certain extent by the almost pathetically indecisive leadership of the aged Pir. But it was even more the result of the conflicting and largely irreconcilable pressures to which he was subjected. Behind the Shahidganj agitation lay the impulse of Lahore's Muslims to assert the moral sovereignty of the Muslim community, of which the mosque itself was a symbol and of which the principle of the supremacy of the *shari'at* was more than a symbol. The Pir was selected to lead the agitation because its leaders hoped that he could bridge the critical differences among Punjabi Muslims; they hoped that, as a *pir,* he could command a certain following in the rural areas and at the same time sustain the movement's intense commitment to the Muslim community and to the *shari'at* above all else. He was well placed to serve as a bridge between the rural and urban areas, but he could never reconcile the opposing forces. As a rural *pir,* even as a product of the *sufi* revival, he was closely tied into the rural social structure and thus to the rural Muslims who provided a base for the British administration. He could not therefore provide an alternative to the colonial system. Like the Ahrar, who had blunted the force of their moral leadership by moving too close to the Hindu Congress, the Pir blunted his moral authority by moving too close to the British government.

113. Punjab fortnightly report for the second half of December 1935 (NAI, Home Political, file 18/12/35).
114. *Ihsan,* 12 January 1936 (Press Branch, file 8331, vol. 11A).
115. *Ihsan,* 16 January 1936 (ibid.).

The cities thus produced in twentieth-century Punjab new styles of politics, at the heart of which lay a concern to define a symbolic Islamic foundation for the political order. Though the British had built in Punjab a political system that was based on indigenous structures of hierarchy and patronage, it was a system with no Islamic center. As a result, with the emergence of new institutions of popular politics in the cities—*anjumans*, *biradari* organizations, newspapers, and elected committees— Muslims developed new means of defining an Islamic center in Punjabi politics. Using the institutions produced by British rule, Muslim leaders articulated an Islamic community in Punjabi politics through the active and public defense of Islamic symbols. They tried to step outside the hierarchies that supported the imperial state structure. But the politics of Islamic identity were constrained by the structure of urban political authority and by the place of the cities within the imperial order. Though the administrative centers of Punjab's political system, the cities were subordinate politically to the rural areas, where the power and the ideological roots of the colonial state were based. The ability of urban leaders to express effectively the commitment of Muslims to an Islamic political order was thus circumscribed not only by the strength of patronage networks within the cities themselves, but also by the problems of effective political expression and action in rural and provincial politics. In spite of its promise, even the position of a leading *pir* failed in 1935 to provide an effective bridge. But the politics of Punjab's cities, in contrast with those of the rural areas, nevertheless dramatized clearly the importance of the search in the twentieth century for a new Islamic foundation for Punjabi politics. Indeed, the definition of a cultural foundation for the state, rooted not in imperial ideology, but in the political commitments of the people themselves gained increasing importance with the passage of the 1935 Government of India Act, with its prospect of increasingly "democratic" reform in the imperial order.

CHAPTER IV

Elections, Ideology, and the Unionist Party

The beginning of provincial autonomy and the approach of elections under the Government of India Act of 1935 moved Punjabi politics into a new phase. The act transformed Indian politics by widening the franchise in provincial elections and introducing for the first time a system of significant ministerial responsibility in provincial government. Though the British governors retained considerable power, the act established a foundation for "democratic," party government in the provinces.[1]

The rurally based Unionist party continued to dominate provincial Muslim politics, although provincial autonomy changed the Unionist party's character. It had long been the most important party in the Legislative Council but before 1936 had possessed little institutional identity outside the Council. The party had operated primarily as an alliance of factional leaders within the Council, organized by a handful of council leaders—particularly Sir Fazli Husain, and later, Sir Chhotu Ram. Defense of the "zamindars," the "agricultural tribes" as defined in the Land Alienation Act, gave the party a program; its local political foundations were based on the structure of British rural administration. As Sir Fazli Husain realized, the party's cohesion in the Council was limited; in the late 1920s and early 1930s it had been manipulated easily by the colonial government.

But when Sir Fazli Husain reassumed leadership of the Unionist party in 1936, he set about reorganizing it to meet the challenge of the new

---

1. On the provisions of the 1935 act and their Punjabi political implications, see Reginald Coupland, *The Constitutional Problem in India* (London: Oxford University Press, 1944) pt. 1, 133–36, pt. 2, 41–55.

political situation. In April 1936 he opened in Lahore a Unionist party headquarters independent of the Council, to begin provincial political organization.[2] The party issued a manifesto and a set of party rules for a detailed organizational structure in the country, including local branches in *zails*, tehsils, towns, and cities, all to be directed by the provincial headquarters. "For the first time, under the British Rule," the party manifesto stated, "the Government of the Punjab is coming in the hands of Punjabees. Its success or failure will primarily rest with us." New forms of party organization were essential. "The experience of other countries and the verdict of history alike emphasize the importance of running elections on party basis," the manifesto declared. "The logic of this proposition is obvious. Responsible Government means that the party in majority in the legislature will run the government."[3]

But what did "party" organization or "party" government mean within the imperial administrative structure? How did new "democratic" institutions fit into the hierarchical political and ideological structures of imperial control? The launching of provincial autonomy involved two political processes that highlighted the contradictions Muslims faced within the structure of imperial power. One of these processes was the extension of the franchise. While incorporating increasing numbers into the electorate, this also narrowed assembly constituencies to small geographic areas (usually tehsils) as local units for the election of representatives. Paradoxically, the new rural constituencies coincided, even more than the old council constituencies, with the divisions on which the imperial administration had been based. In drawing the tehsils, as Nawab Muzaffar Khan, the Punjab reforms commissioner, wrote in 1934, the British had taken care to observe "tribal, cultural, political and other considerations" that created political conditions marking "them off from other contiguous tracts."[4] In using these constituencies, as in using *zails* for district boards, the British maintained self-consciously not only the separation of rural from urban politics, but also the idioms of authority on which rural politics had been based.[5] Extending the franchise thus involved little immediate break with the structure of colonial administration; it emphasized the con-

2. *Tribune* (Lahore), 21 April 1936.

3. Punjab Unionist Party, *Rules and Regulations* (Lahore: Punjab Unionist Party, 1936), 1–19 (organizational structure), 20–27 (manifesto).

4. Nawab Muzaffar Khan, *Note on the Delimitation of Constituencies* (Lahore: Government Printing, 1934), 10.

5. On the divisions between rural and urban seats under the reforms, see India, *Report of the Committee Appointed in Connection with the Delimitation of Constituencies and Connected Matters*, vol. 1 (Report), 55–66; Parliamentary Papers, Reports, 1935–36, vol. 9.

tinuing significance of "tribal" idioms even as it incorporated larger numbers into the political process. In this sense, the process of "democ- ratization" preserved the ideological structure of the colonial state.

But set off against this process was the gradual transfer of political sovereignty at the provincial level into indigenous hands, a process that involved clearly defining a symbolic justification for ruling independent of the colonial power. In asserting a claim to "party" government, the Unionists had to establish not only their electoral strength in the coun- try, but also an ideological foundation for the assumption of authority at the provincial level. Unlike the British, who had attempted to sys- tematize local loyalties largely in order to justify their authority as an alien power, the Unionists required a new sort of indigenous justifica- tion for central authority, a new symbolic center for power as the reins of government were transferred into Punjabi hands. Urban politics in the 1930s had in fact dramatized as never before the colonial state's lack of a central, symbolic religious justification for its power. Agitations like those over Kashmir and Shahidganj, with all their contradictions, brought these questions to the forefront of politics. In sharp contrast with the process of extending the franchise, defining a symbolic justi- fication for indigenous rule seemed to require a break with the colonial tradition. But how, for the Unionists, were the conflicting imperatives of "party" organization under the new system to be reconciled?

THE IDEOLOGY OF THE UNIONIST PARTY

In practical political terms, only the Unionist party could in 1936 command the structures of rural political influence needed to win the votes of the majority of Punjab's Muslims. As the inheritors of the colo- nial administrative tradition, most Unionist leaders had easily main- tained their local power as the franchise was extended and electoral politics expanded under the new constitution.[6] But their efforts to define an indigenous cultural foundation for state authority were far more am- biguous. The ambivalent Unionist response to the Shahidganj mosque affair indicated the contradictions in the party's position. Though Union- ist leaders like Sir Fazli Husain and Sir Firoz Khan Noon had con- demned the agitational style of the movement's largely urban leader-

6. Though opposed to universal suffrage, the Unionist party did not oppose the wid- ening of the franchise; see, for example, Punjab, *Report of the Punjab Reforms Commit- tee, 1929* (Lahore: Government Printing, 1929), 11–15, 88. Sikander Hyat Khan, repre- senting the Unionist party, chaired the committee and largely wrote the report.

ship—a style that challenged the administrative structure of Unionist influence—they were nevertheless sensitive to the potential power of Islamic symbols as a cultural focus for Punjabi Muslim politics. Indeed, Sir Firoz Khan Noon had suggested, in the wake of the agitation, that if the Unionists were to organize outside the Council they would need to define their authority in terms that would "catch the imagination of the Muslim masses."[7] In the new political system, he recognized, Islamic symbols would undoubtedly have an important role. Nevertheless, playing to the religious sentiments of the "masses" could, as Sir Fazli Husain realized, be extremely dangerous. Whatever the appeal of such symbols in the cities, Unionist ideology had to be consistent with the structure of imperial hierarchy and with the idioms of authority on which the party's local power was based.

SIR FAZLI HUSAIN AND THE ROLE OF ISLAM

Sir Fazli Husain and the Unionists certainly did not ignore the role of Islam in Punjabi politics. But their response to communal politics was ambivalent. Sir Fazli Husain had gained a considerable reputation in the 1920s and 1930s as one of India's most important spokesmen for Muslim interests. In the 1920s he used his powerful Unionist bloc in the Council to press for greater Muslim representation on municipal committees, in educational institutions, and in government services. Perhaps most important, his reputation in all-India politics had grown with his formation in 1929 of the All-India Muslim Conference and his appointment in 1930 as the leading Muslim representative on the Viceroy's executive council.[8] From this position, he played a critical behind-the-scenes role in the early 1930s "as informal strategist and director of Muslim policy during the great constitutional reappraisals of these years."[9] Sir Fazli Husain's major goal was the protection of Muslim interests—interests he identified with those of Punjab's Muslims.

By the mid-1930s Sir Fazli Husain had thus gained a reputation as a strong advocate of Muslim interests, widely known among Hindus and

7. Sir Firoz Khan Noon to Sir Fazli Husain, 9 August 1935 (Waheed Ahmad, *Letters of Mian Fazl-i-Husain*, 425–26).

8. For a good account of Sir Fazli Husain's role in all-India politics, particularly in the All-India Muslim Conference, see David Page, *Prelude to Partition: The Indian Muslims and the Imperial System of Control, 1920–1932* (Delhi: Oxford University Press, 1982), 195–258.

9. Ayesha Jalal and Anil Seal, "Alternative to Partition: Muslim Politics Between the Wars," *Modern Asian Studies* 15, no. 3 (1981): 433.

Sikhs as a "communal" politician.[10] But he considered religious identity to be important in politics only to the degree that it helped to
define Muslim claims to political power within the larger structure of
the British imperial order. Outlining his conception of Punjab politics
in a 1936 pamphlet, Sir Fazli Husain emphasized the demand of the
Muslim community for its rightful share of places in government services and in local bodies, based on the 57 percent of Muslims in Punjab's population. So important was this aspect of religious identity to
Sir Fazli Husain that he described the Muslims' willingness to accept
the 51 percent of the assembly seats that the communal award gave
them as a willingness to forego "for the time being 6 percent of their
heritage."[11]

Such a quantified conception of the political meaning of Muslim
"heritage" differed substantially from that held by many of Punjab's urban Muslims. In fact, Sir Fazli Husain rejected outright the idea of
building a political party on identification with religious symbols. For
all his support of religious definitions in distributing seats in the assembly and places in the services under the British, he sharply criticized
those who excited "religious feelings, religious animosities based on historical and even mythic events."[12] In short, he rejected the symbolic religious movements of the 1930s—such as Kashmir and Shahidganj—that
had sought to define an ideology of political solidarity based on direct
popular identification with religious symbols. If he could prevent "Muslims from making fools of themselves to the extent they have been doing
in the past," he wrote of the Shahidganj agitation, he would "prevent
the recurrence of such incidents."[13] For Sir Fazli Husain, such a purely
symbolic definition of religious solidarity was anathema. By encouraging the individual to direct political identification with a symbolically
defined religious community, it threatened the structure of rural influence on which he had built the Unionist party and challenged the larger
structure of imperial authority.

Sir Fazli Husain nevertheless recognized that the Unionists needed to
maintain a strong political base of religious support. In differing forms,

10. See the editorial, "Political Kite-Flying," in the *Tribune* (Lahore), 5 April 1936.
See also Y. Abbas, "A Tussle for Punjab Leadership," *Proceedings of the Pakistan History
Conference,* 9th session (Karachi: Pakistan Historical Society, 1959).
11. A Punjabee, "Punjab Politics," reprinted in *The Muslim Revival 5,* no. 1 (March
1936): 49. Sir Fazli Husain distributed this anonymous pamphlet in early 1936 as an expression of his views.
12. Ibid., 65.
13. Sir Fazli Husain to Syed Ata Ullah Shah Bokhari, 1 June 1936 (Waheed Ahmad,
Letters, 570).

Islam had served not only as the foundation for urban agitations, but also as a legitimizer for the hierarchical order on which Unionist power was based. As Sir Fazli Husain reorganized the Unionist party in 1936, he thus sought to strengthen the party's links to the mediatory Islamic leadership of the rural localities. Bound to the hierarchical structure of rural administrative power, the influence of Punjab's *pirs* and *sajjada nishins* provided religious legitimacy to the Unionists. In fact, the British themselves had considered organizing the rural *sajjada nishins* in the early 1930s as a political counterweight to the Congress and to urban Muslim agitators.[14] In 1936 the Unionists followed suit. In response to Sir Fazli Husain's suggestion, the party listed fifteen prominent *pirs* whose support was to be solicited before the upcoming 1937 elections—including Pir Jamaat Ali Shah, the Qureshi and Gilani *pirs* of Multan, and the Chishti *pirs* of Pakpattan, Mahar, Taunsa, Sial, Golra, and Jalalpur.[15] Among these were both landed *sajjada nishins* and *pirs* whose roots were in the eighteenth- and nineteenth-century *sufi* revival. Their support was intended to provide a broad political counterweight to the urban communalism of the 1930s.

Not all these *pirs* could be counted on to offer their open support to the Unionists or to take an active part in "party" politics. But many did support the Unionists, and the influence of these and "other Pirs and Sajjada Nashins who have local influence in districts"[16] provided an important rural religious answer to Unionist critics. As one local Unionist organizer observed in 1936, their support was invaluable in countering urban political groups like the Ahrar. "The Ahrar have begun with an awfully vigorous propaganda," this organizer wrote.

> At least they presume to have captured the towns. Still we don't fear if they do not begin with the villages. Villagers, you know, follow these "Pirs" blindly. . . . Take care of the "Pirs." Ask them only to keep silent on the matter of elections. We don't require their help but they should not oppose us.[17]

The support of these *pirs*, even if expressed only tacitly, guaranteed the Unionists a religious following in rural Punjab even as they rejected a central role for Islamic symbols in Muslim politics.

Rural support provided the context when in May 1936 Sir Fazli Hu-

14. Minutes of Publicity Advisory board, 15 December 1932 (Press Branch, Publicity, file 2).
15. Mushtaq Ahmad Gurmani to Sir Fazli Husain, 19 June 1936 (Waheed Ahmad, *Letters*, 592–94).
16. Ibid., 593.
17. Mohammad Bashir, Gurdaspur to Unionist party headquarters, 9 May 1936 (Unionist party papers, file D-17).

sain rejected Muhammad Ali Jinnah's overture to form a united all-India Muslim party before the 1937 elections. Jinnah had returned from England in 1934 and begun his own efforts in 1936 to reorganize the Muslim League as an all-India party in preparation for the new constitution. Though the League was moribund in the early 1930s, Jinnah began at the League's Bombay session in April 1936 an effort to transform that "small fragmented party into a mass movement with district branch volunteers throughout the country." [18] Appealing to Muslims to unite to protect their interests in all-India affairs, Jinnah gained his strongest backing in the Muslim-minority provinces, particularly in Bombay and the United Provinces. But he found far less support in the Muslim-majority provinces—Punjab, Bengal, Sind, and the North-West Frontier—where local Muslim leaders had focused their organization on the arenas of provincial politics. Nowhere was this more evident than in the Punjab. Though Sir Fazli Husain accepted the theoretical importance of all-India Muslim organization, he was extremely wary of Jinnah's leadership. Fazli Husain's past role in the Punjab Muslim League had been substantial, but he saw in Jinnah's efforts to reorganize the League an attack on the provincial foundations of the Unionist party—an attack not only on Unionist autonomy in Punjab, but also on the structure of their local influence.

Jinnah's "communal" appeal, however ill defined, threatened this structure. [19] In 1936, Jinnah's strongest backing in Punjab came from urban Muslims who had challenged Unionist ideology, Ahrar leaders and "miscellaneous Urbanites" (as Sir Fazli Husain put it) who saw religious commitment as a foundation for a direct challenge to the structure of imperial power. [20] Many were deeply involved in the symbolic Islamic agitations of the 1930s. Whatever Jinnah's personal religious views, nothing illustrated his political leanings more clearly than his attempted alliance with the Jami'at-i 'Ulama-yi Hind. [21] Sir Fazli Husain's rejection of the League appeal for Muslim unity was thus based in part on his fear

18. Stanley Wolpert, *Jinnah of Pakistan* (New York: Oxford University Press, 1984), 140.

19. See Ikram, *Modern Muslim India and the Birth of Pakistan*, 230–31. In 1936 Jinnah advocated working closely with the Congress; many established politicians like Sir Fazli Husain viewed him as anti-British.

20. Sir Fazli Husain to Sir Sikander Hyat Khan, 6 May 1936 (Waheed Ahmad, *Letters*, 534).

21. Wolpert, *Jinnah of Pakistan*, 145. The election program of the Central Muslim League parliamentary board declared that "due weight" should be given in religious matters "to the opinions of the Jamiat-ul-Ulema Hind and the Mujtahids" (Syed Rais Ahmad Jafri, ed., *Rare Documents* [Lahore: Muhammad Ali Academy, 1967], 147).

that Jinnah's interference would undermine factional alliances within the Unionist party—including the position of the Hindu group of Sir Chhotu Ram—and thus disrupt the working of provincial autonomy. But it was based also, and equally importantly, on his fear that Jinnah's efforts would undermine the structure of mediation and local influence on which the imperial system, and the provincial authority of the Unionist party, were based.

THE ROLE OF THE LAND ALIENATION ACT

Sir Fazli Husain's rejection of communal appeals did not however obviate the need for a Unionist ideology consistent with dependence on a rural hierarchy. Unionist leaders had long relied on the Land Alienation Act as a symbol of rural solidarity for the local magnates. Provincial autonomy required, however, assigning a new ideological significance to the Land Alienation Act. In organizing to meet the challenges of provincial autonomy and party government, Unionist leaders broadened their meaning of the act from symbol of rural hierarchy to symbol of an indigenous, cultural claim to power. In 1936 one critic captured the act's new symbolic burden for the Unionists by comparing it to the symbols of religion. "The Unionists seem to believe," he declared, "that the Land Alienation Act is to them what the Vedas and the Holy Quran are to the Hindus and the Musalmans." [22]

Central to such a transformation of the Land Alienation Act was the identification of the act with a popular community—with whom the Unionists could identify their claim to authority. And in the 1930s this community came increasingly to be defined in "class" terms. Indeed, the concept of "class" assumed a critical significance for the Unionists as provincial autonomy approached. The Land Alienation Act, as the Unionists viewed it, had divided Punjabis into two distinct "classes." Punjabi "agriculturalists" were arrayed implicitly against "nonagriculturalists"—their conflicting "class" interests deriving from their contrasting places within the structure of the colonial economy. But their differences were not simply economic. "Class" divisions, as Unionists interpreted them, were cultural as well. The "class" divisions between "agriculturalists" and "nonagriculturalists," between "zamindars" and "capitalists," were inextricably tied to the cultural definitions of the

22. Statement of Raja Narendra Nath in address to Non-Agriculturalist conference at Dera Baba Nanak. *Tribune*, 28 April 1936.

Land Alienation Act itself—reflecting not just economic divisions but differing forms of local political organization. When asked about the meaning of the term *zamindar* in the Legislative Council, Sir Chhotu Ram declared that by the term *zamindar* he always meant the "statutory zamindars," the members of the "agricultural tribes" as defined under the Land Alienation Act. "There are," he said, "no other zamindars in existence."[23] "Tribal" idioms of local organization thus loomed as central to the "class" divisions the act defined. And put in these terms, the definitions of the Land Alienation Act shaped a popular cultural foundation for political power that represented an alternative to the popular "communities" defined by religion.

But the "community" defined by the Land Alienation Act was very different from those defined by religious symbols. In linking the party to an "agriculturalist class," the Unionists were not in fact tying themselves to a broad "community" of individuals, but to a collection of local "communities," of "tribes," with common interests. The term "agricultural tribes" was officially translated as the "*zira'at pesha qaum,*" a term perhaps equally well translated as the "agriculturalist communities." To be a part of this "class" was not to identify directly with the broad "class" itself, but to identify with local, kin-based "communities." As shaped by the Land Alienation Act, the roots of "class" identity thus lay in the linking of rural economic interests to the protection of a system of local organization defined by "tribal," kin-based idioms. And in this, the foundations of such an "agriculturalist class" differed sharply from the direct personal commitments that shaped the meaning of religious "community" for many urban Muslims.

But the language of "agriculturalist class" nevertheless allowed the Unionists to define an effective, popular idiom of support, even as they preserved the mediated political structure of the imperial regime. Not all Unionist leaders, of course, defined the symbolic meaning of the act identically. Organizing in 1936 for the upcoming elections, Sir Fazli Husain tried to cast the Unionists' political net as widely as possible. In inaugurating the new Unionist party headquarters in April 1936, Sir Fazli Husain argued that the party stood primarily for the interests of the "backward" classes, a term he used broadly enough to lay claim to most of Punjab's population. But "backward" also took on for Sir Fazli Husain a particular meaning. The position of the Unionist party as a mouthpiece for the "backward" grew, in Fazli Husain's vision, both

23. Punjab, *Legislative Council Debates*, vol. 32 (17 March 1933): 560.

from the economic structure of colonial rule and from the structure of imperial organization and ideology. In general, the colonial economy had benefited Punjab, tying it to world markets. But the key to the protection of the "backward" lay in the maintenance of a rural political structure that could contain the impact of colonial capitalism within the cultural and political idioms of the imperial administrative system. At its worst, Fazli Husain observed, capitalism could be "selfish," "narrow," and "greedy." But the business of the Unionist party was to "persuade the wealthier classes to become alive to their responsibility" in aiding the "backward." [24] Indeed, the ideological definition of the Unionists as the champions of the "backward" classes drew on the party's role as protector of the imperial order—and of local, kin-based organization—which it saw as the foundation for protecting the economic interests of a rural, agricultural "class."

Many Punjabis of course rejected this definition of Unionist "class" interests. In the eyes of Unionist critics, Sir Fazli Husain's involvement with the "backward" classes only thinly concealed the party's real class identification with Punjab's large landholders. Unionist critics argued that no one had profited more from the high land and commodity prices of the first quarter of the twentieth century than the rural leaders who now styled themselves protectors of the "backward." Far from representing the "backward," Unionist leaders had taken advantage of their position to bolster the class interests of Punjabi landlords—and to increase their landholdings at the expense of small landholders. This attack had been repeated since the Land Alienation Act was passed. As Malcolm Darling testified to the Royal Agricultural commission in 1927, the act had conferred "a very valuable privilege upon the strong, for with the great increase in rural prosperity many agriculturalists are now in a position to buy land and as purchasers are placed in a privileged position by the Act." [25] Small wonder then, critics argued, that these individuals rallied around the Land Alienation Act while claiming to protect the peasantry of the Punjab against the dire consequences of "greedy capitalism."

But whatever the truth of such charges (and there is little doubt that they had considerable substance), the structural foundations of Unionist ideology were rooted not in the protection of the class interests of land-

24. *Tribune,* 21 April 1936.
25. Quoted in Punjab, *Report of the Punjab Unemployment Committee, 1937–38* (Lahore: Government Printing, 1938), 139.

lords but in the logic of the British colonial system itself. No doubt most Unionist landlords were, as H. J. Maynard remarked, men "impressed with the necessity of keeping tenants and labourers in their proper places, very jealous of [their] rights of property."[26] When the interests of tenants or untouchables clashed with those of landowners, as they frequently did, there was little question where Unionist sympathies lay;[27] many small cultivators, particularly among central Punjabi Sikhs, thus strongly opposed the Unionists. But the defense of the structure of political control defined in the Land Alienation Act represented a broader defense of the rural power structure. Though the British themselves had in many areas encouraged the expansion of market-oriented agricultural production in Punjab, they had at the same time attempted, through the Land Alienation Act and other legislation, to maintain, even in the face of increasing commercialization, an effective countervailing structure of local political influence.[28] It was the defense of this tradition that the Unionists now attempted to adapt to a more democratic era. By identifying the Unionist party with the interests of a class of agricultural "tribes," they affirmed the supremacy of the idioms of local political solidarity and community over influence derived from the control of capital. That some Unionist leaders themselves controlled considerable capital was beside the point; they were establishing a popular ideology, justifying in indigenous terms the existing structure of hierarchical authority in their bid for "democratic" provincial power.

THE DEPRESSION AND
AGRICULTURALIST IDEOLOGY

The ambiguities in the Unionist position were substantial. The symbolism of the Land Alienation Act offered little to urban Muslims. Most were excluded from the Unionist definition of power as they were from British hierarchies; the Unionists offered no overarching definition of community to bind Muslims directly to the state. But before the 1937

26. Maynard's 1923 statement referred to rural representatives in the Punjab Council. (Note on certain aspects of the reforms in the Punjab, May 1923 [Punjab Archives, Home General, B procs., 1925, file 176].)

27. In her biography of Sir Chhotu Ram, Prem Chowdhry argues that Sir Chhotu Ram followed a populist political line but privately preferred the interests of substantial landowners to tenants, untouchables, or petty cultivators (Prem Chowdhry, *Punjab Politics: The Role of Sir Chhotu Ram* [New Delhi: Vikas, 1984], 216–25).

28. For another view of this apparent contradiction, see Fox, "British Colonialism and Punjabi Labor," 107–34.

elections, as Punjabis responded to the pressures of economic change in the countryside, the Unionists' ideological appeal grew. For rural Muslims these were years of increasing economic crisis. And for many rural Punjabis, support of the Land Alienation Act came to symbolize the right of rural landowners to control politically the economic forces that seemed increasingly to be overwhelming them.

The great depression provided the backdrop to the political process of the 1930s. As scholars of other peasant societies in Asia have argued, the depression had a dramatic impact on structures of colonial rule. In Burma and Vietnam, the depression served in many areas as a catalyst precipitating widespread rural unrest, rendering the already inflexible colonial mechanisms of taxation and rent nearly unbearable for much of the peasant population.[29] In Madras, the depression "threatened to subvert the social and economic equilibrium" of the province, weakening the political and economic control of the rural elite, causing widespread migration to the cities, and setting the stage for the rise of the Congress civil disobedience movement.[30] Punjab experienced similar dislocation. But in Punjab the structure of the political system itself significantly shaped the depression's political impact.

As elsewhere, the depression first manifested itself in Punjab in a catastrophic fall in agricultural prices.[31] Falling incomes naturally led to heightened tensions in much of rural Punjab in the 1930s. In spite of considerable revenue remissions by the government, the burden of the land revenue increased substantially for many Punjabis.[32] A survey by the Board of Economic Inquiry found that sales of accumulated gold and ornaments were widespread, as cultivators struggled to meet revenue obligations that could not be covered by the sale of produce.[33] Economic pressures provoked unrest, particularly in highly assessed areas like the canal colonies, where the impact of falling agricultural prices was most marked. As the settlement officer for Lyallpur discovered, "the

29. James Scott, *The Moral Economy of the Peasant* (New Haven: Yale University Press, 1976), 114–56.

30. Christopher John Baker, *The Politics of South India, 1920–1937* (Cambridge: Cambridge University Press, 1976), 169–84.

31. The impact of falling farm prices on incomes emerges in the Punjab Board of Economic Inquiry farm income samples; between 1928–29 and 1931–32 average net farm income fell by over half. See Labh Singh and Ajaib Singh, *Farm Accounts in the Punjab, 1937–38* (Lahore: Punjab Board of Economic Inquiry, 1940), 18.

32. See Malcolm Darling, *Wisdom and Waste in the Punjab Village* (London: Oxford University Press, 1934), 225.

33. B. K. Madan and E. D. Lucas, *Note on the Sales of Gold and Ornaments in 120 Punjab Villages* (Lahore: Punjab Board of Economic Inquiry, 1936), 19–21.

burden of the Government demand, by no means heavy in normal times, resulted in the upsetting of the domestic economy of many a small cultivator owing to the abnormal fall in the prices of agricultural commodities."[34] Congress and other radical groups criticized the government's revenue administration in the early 1930s. These groups also organized several antigovernment agitations, particularly in the canal colonies and central Punjab. Tensions associated with the dramatic fall in prices threatened to undermine the structure of government influence in many parts of the province.

But for the leaders of the Unionist party, the depression produced mixed political consequences. While growing rural unrest posed a challenge to local Unionist power in some areas, in ideological terms the depression fit neatly into the Unionist party's worldview. Whereas the Congress and other radical groups blamed colonial authority for the hardships the depression had brought, the Unionists saw an answer to the depression in strengthening the local idioms of political power on which the colonial system, and the power of the Unionist party, were based. Unionists ascribed the underlying cause of economic dislocation not to governmental rigidity but to the power of nonagriculturalist capitalists, of moneylenders, whose influence in rural Punjab was undermining local "agriculturalist" organization. The key to the protection of rural Punjabis lay, as the Unionists saw it, in energizing the structure of rural political power to protect the rural landowner's livelihood. With the Land Alienation Act at the heart of their worldview, the Unionists thus saw the answer to the depression in the mobilization of provincial political support to protect the existing structure of local power.

To be sure, the depression had affected the economic position of the intermediaries who formed the backbone of the rural administration. The Muslim landlords of western Punjab, who dominated the Unionist party, found it increasingly difficult to collect their rents. Most suffered severe declines in income; many also found themselves deeply in debt. The deputy commissioner of Montgomery district observed in 1933 that landlords of that district had incurred heavy debts in the 1920s, because of rising prices and of rising expenses from their "increased political and social importance" after the 1919 reforms. When prices collapsed in the early 1930s, many landlords could not meet their debts and were forced to withdraw credit from tenants and dependents as well. "There are very few of the large landlords of this district who are indebted to the

34. S. K. Kirpalani, *Final Settlement Report of the Lyallpur District and the Rakh Branch Colony Circle of Sheikhupura District* (Lahore: Government Printing, 1940), 53.

extent of less than a Lac," the deputy commissioner wrote.[35] In Multan district, Nawab Ahmad Yar Khan Daultana executed in 1934 a note in favor of a Lahore moneylending firm for seven hundred and fifty thousand rupees.[36] Indebtedness affected the general political influence of rural intermediaries; some influential Unionist leaders found their influence critically weakened. In Muzaffargarh district, for example, their own administrative regulations forced the British to deny a *darbar* seat to a prominent Unionist landlord, Mushtaq Ahmad Gurmani, on account of his "present state of indebtedness."[37] An increased number of estates came under the Court of Wards.[38]

But the depression did not undermine the larger political structure of Punjab's rural mediatory system. In many other parts of India, collapsing agricultural price levels made cash rents difficult to collect, caused widespread tension in landlord-tenant relations, and weakened local hierarchies of influence. But in the Punjab, for both economic and political reasons, the impact of the depression on landlord-tenant relations was far less marked. Though the fall in prices undermined landlord incomes, rents in most of Punjab were taken not in cash but as *bata'i*, or a share of the crop. This was itself symptomatic of the power of landlords within Punjab's provincial political system, where tenants had generally been denied occupancy rights.[39] With nearly three-quarters of rented land under the *bata'i* system, rents tended, as Malcolm Darling put it, to adjust "automatically to the fall in price."[40] The adjustments the *bata'i* system brought about were sufficiently widespread in Punjab that "the landlords who receive their rents in cash found themselves obliged almost at once, by sheer force of example, to reduce or remit their dues."[41] Though this certainly diminished landlord incomes, it left the

35. W. F. G. LeBailly, deputy commissioner, Montgomery to divisional commissioner, Multan, 22 and 23 May 1933 (Board of Revenue, file 901/11/0/5).

36. Mumtaz Muhammad Khan Daultana vs. Bulaqi Mal and Sons, Ltd. *The Lahore Law Times*, Revenue Rulings, 1943, 1–2.

37. Punjab Archives, Political General, B Procs., May 1932, file 208; ibid., 1937, file 165.

38. Punjab, Financial Commissioner, *Report on the Administration of Estates under the Court of Wards in the Punjab* (Lahore: Government Printing, 1936), 1.

39. On the tenancy issue in late nineteenth century, see Banerjee, *Agrarian Society of the Punjab*. Western Punjabi tenants were scarce and thus sometimes had considerable economic leverage; but their legal rights were extremely limited.

40. Darling, *Wisdom and Waste*, 316. According to the Punjab Land Revenue committee, three-quarters of the area cultivated by Punjabi tenants-at-will (the great majority of rented land), was leased on the *bata'i* system; cash rents were the exception (Punjab, *Report of the Land Revenue Committee, 1938* [Lahore: Government Printing, 1938], 33).

41. Darling, *Wisdom and Waste*, 316; the commissioner of Lahore division also noticed the abandonment of cash rents in favor of *bata'i* (Note by Alan Mitchell, commissioner, Lahore division, 24 May 1933 [Board of Revenue, file 901/11/0/5]).

basic structure of landlord-tenant relations intact. The Punjab Land Revenue Committee noted in 1938, "It was owing to [*bata'i* rents] that relations between landlord and tenant were much less seriously affected in the Punjab by the catastrophic fall in prices than in the United Provinces, where cash rents are the rule."[42] *Bata'i* rents also underscored the continuing importance of a hierarchical system of rural political control.

More significant in the structure of Unionist power was Punjab's system of rural credit. Rural magnates in much of India were often important creditors as well as debtors—rural bosses, who depended on control of credit and land to maintain their influence. The depression not only undercut their incomes but significantly loosened their control of rural credit networks, and thus of local political influence.[43] But in western Punjab credit played a far less important role in intermediary political control. Though Muslim landlords made loans to tenants, kinsmen, and political allies—and sometimes used credit networks to build factional alliances—studies in the 1920s found little professional moneylending with interest by Muslim agriculturalists in western Punjab.[44] Even in villages with prominent Muslim landlords, the bulk of the rural debt was often owed to non-Muslim, nonagriculturalist moneylenders.[45] Credit supplied by landlords thus remained, even in the 1930s, far less important than credit supplied by these moneylenders—men barred under the terms of the Land Alienation Act from becoming landlords themselves. In western Punjab in particular, where Unionist power was greatest, the disruptions in credit relations brought by the great depression thus had a more limited impact on the relations between landlords and cultivators than on the relations between agriculturalists and nonagriculturalist moneylenders. Rather than undermining the hierarchical structure of rural influence, disruptions in credit relations tended to strengthen the ideological underpinnings of Unionist power.

Not all "agriculturalists" were debtors, of course, nor did all nonagriculturalists loan money. The categories of the Land Alienation Act

42. *Report of the Land Revenue Committee*, 33.

43. Baker, *The Politics of South India*, 180–85.

44. The Punjab Banking Enquiry committee reported that in the late twenties, 19,000 of the Punjab's 55,000 professional moneylenders belonged to the agricultural tribes; as a Cooperative Department study indicated, the great majority were Hindus and Sikhs of eastern and central Punjab. Only 6 percent were Muslims; and even of these, few lived in western Punjab (Note by C. F. Strickland, registrar of Cooperative Societies [Board of Revenue, file 442/1/00/3]. See also Punjab, *Provincial Banking Enquiry Committee Report* [Lahore: Government Printing, 1930], 129).

45. R. K. Seth and Faiz Ilahi, *An Economic Survey of Durrana Langana: A Village in the Multan District of the Punjab* (Lahore: Punjab Board of Economic Inquiry, 1938), 128.

by no means defined the exact structure of credit relations in rural Punjab. In parts of central Punjab and in the canal colonies, the supply of credit by wealthy farmers was substantial, particularly among the Sikhs.[46] But as the depression took its toll in the Punjab, the language of the Land Alienation Act, equating "debtors" with "agriculturalists," came to have important political relevance. The terminology of the Alienation of Land Act had created a political tradition in Punjab identifying the "agricultural tribes" as a basically noncapitalist, debtor "class." In political terms, the leaders of these "tribes" could thus claim to speak as the leaders of Punjab's debtors. Whatever the precise character of credit relations in the province, the terms of the Land Alienation Act provided the Unionists with a "class" foundation for the mobilization of a political response to the economic conditions the depression had created.

Heightened tension between agriculturalists and moneylenders in the 1930s gave this added political force. In western Punjab in particular, where nonagriculturalist moneylenders were most numerous, debt collection occasioned sporadic outbursts of violence. As economic middlemen and cultural "outsiders" in rural Punjab, nonagriculturalist moneylenders were easy to identify as responsible for the depression's economic disruptions. Religious differences between Hindu or Sikh moneylenders on one side and Muslim agriculturalists on the other exacerbated animosities. Attacks on moneylenders increased noticeably in the early 1930s. In a 1933 circular the government noted, "The increase in this type of crime is causing Government serious anxiety."[47] Provincial Unionist leaders were quick to publicize such violence as proof of the fundamental cultural conflict in rural Punjab between "agriculturalists" and nonagriculturalist moneylenders, which the collapse of prices and the rising burden of indebtedness now exposed. In a pamphlet published in the early thirties, for example, the *sajjada nishin* of the shrine of Bahawal Haq attacked the common religious and political threat that moneylenders posed to Punjab's zamindars.[48] "The murder of the creditors by their rural debtors would continue," one member of

46. On the prominence of Sikh agriculturalists in providing credit in central Punjab, see Malcolm Darling, *The Punjab Peasant in Prosperity and Debt* (1947; reprint, Columbia, Mo.: South Asia Books, 1978), 197–99.

47. The government stated that from 1931 to 1933 in Punjab, moneylenders had been the victims of 53 murders and 91 dacoities, many committed by debtors (Circular of C. M. G. Ogilvie [home secretary] to divisional commissioners, 2 September 1933 [Lahore Commissioner's Files, file P44]).

48. Makhdum Murid Husain Qureshi, *Khatra ka Alarm* (Lahore: author?, 1930–31?), 10.

the Legislative Council warned ominously, "if agricultural indebtedness was not drastically reduced."[49]

Leaders of the moneylenders charged that in many areas rural political leaders were behind the violence. In mid-1931, a raid on Hindu moneylenders at the village of Sikandarabad in Multan district brought charges from Hindu political leaders that a Muslim landlord had incited his followers to burn the moneylenders' account books. This was only the opening wedge, one newspaper declared, in an organized movement against moneylenders such as had briefly convulsed some parts of southwestern Punjab during the early years of World War I.[50] Such fears pervaded the moneylenders' press in the early 1930s. Hindu moneylenders would be well advised, some suggested, to give up moneylending altogether: "Those who will continue moneylending business will lose their heads," the *Mahajan Samachar* wrote, "and those who keep their heads will give up moneylending."[51] Officials observed an exodus of moneylenders from the countryside in these years and an increasing tendency for them to invest their capital in Punjab's towns.[52] Whether this resulted from antimoneylender violence is questionable. But in its 1933 circular on crime against moneylenders, the government took note of the moneylenders' charges and asked its local officials to watch carefully to make sure that propaganda of cooperative societies and district boards—institutions controlled by agriculturalist leaders—did not encourage such violence.[53]

Little evidence in fact substantiated these charges. Few rural leaders were interested in provoking widespread violence that might easily pass beyond their control. Most prominent "agriculturalist" leaders depended on moneylenders for credit and were unlikely to encourage indiscriminate violence against them.[54] But in political terms, the increas-

49. Quoted in the *Tribune*, 28 June 1934.
50. The *Hindu Herald* saw "only an organized manifestation of a movement in the making against Hindu sahukars and traders in particular and Hindus in general . . . like that we witnessed in Punjab about 17 years ago" (*Hindu Herald* [Lahore], 8 and 9 July 1931 [Press Branch, file 6077]). Violence against Hindu moneylenders in Jhang, Muzaffargarh, and Multan districts broke out in the winter of 1915 following price increases and a rumored collapse of British authority during the war. The sacking of a large Hindu village in Jhang, evacuated because of plague, began the violence, which spread rapidly; many prominent *zaildars* and other tribal and administrative leaders participated. Other prominent Muslim *zamindars* helped the police and military to suppress the uprising (NAI, Home Political, January 1916, procs. 545–546A).
51. *Mahajan Samachar*, 13 July 1931 (Press Branch, file 4284).
52. For example, Amin-ud-Din (deputy commissioner, Jullundur) to commissioner, Jullundur, 21 May 1933 (Board of Revenue, file 901/11/0/5).
53. In discussing the circular, few officials agreed that these agencies were to blame (Lahore Commissioner's Files, file P44).
54. Nawab Muhammad Hyat Qureshi of Shahpur stated in the Legislative Council:

ing tensions arising out of rural indebtedness provided the foundations for linking Unionist debates in the Legislative Council to a question of rapidly increasing popular concern in the countryside. At the heart of the Unionist position was the desire to establish political control over the forces of the market. The maintenance of local power continued to preoccupy most Unionist leaders in the Council. But given the definitions of the Land Alienation Act, the protection of Punjabi agriculturalists from the depression now seemed to be intimately linked to the maintenance of the imperial power structure in rural Punjab. The spread of popular concerns about indebtedness, and the escalating potential for rural conflict, provided the foundations for the enunciation by the Unionists of an ideological defense of the whole structure of political power in rural Punjab couched in the Land Alienation Act's language.

Sir Chhotu Ram, who emerged in the 1930s as the leading Unionist spokesman in the Punjab Legislative Council, articulated this defense most powerfully. A Hindu Jat from eastern Punjab's Rohtak district, Chhotu Ram had already established in the 1920s a political organization in Rohtak, the Zamindara League, and a newspaper, the *Jat Gazette*. These articulated the interests of Hindu Jats and attacked the influence of Hindu banias, or moneylenders.[55] Building on his political base in Rohtak, Sir Chhotu Ram played an increasingly prominent role in provincial politics in the 1920s and 1930s. As he described it, he began his efforts with only the organization of the Jats in mind. But, he wrote, he "had perceived almost intuitively that to rescue the Punjab as a whole from the domination of vested interests the net would have to be cast sufficiently wide to embrace all agricultural tribes, irrespective of religion."[56] For that purpose, the Unionist party gave Sir Chhotu Ram the critical provincial vehicle. The "agriculturalist classes are the most numerous and yet most ruthlessly exploited section of the Indian community," he declared. "They provided, at least in the Punjab, ready elements for bringing into existence a powerful well-knit unit of political organization."[57]

"We do not want that the money advanced by the *sahukar*s [moneylenders] should be wasted or not recovered. We want to deal with them fairly. If you go to my *ilaqa* you will learn that we help the *sahukar*s to recover their debts even without seeking the help of the courts of law" (Punjab, *Legislative Council Debates*, vol. 27 [21 November 1935]: 1044).

55. On Sir Chhotu Ram's early career, see Chowdhry, *Punjab Politics*. Other accounts include Madan Gopal, *Sir Chhotu Ram: A Political Biography* (Delhi: B. R. Publishing, 1977) and H. L. Agnihotri and Shiva N. Malik, *A Profile in Courage: A Biography of Ch. Chhotu Ram* (New Delhi: Light and Life Publishers, 1978).

56. "A Speech of Sir Chhotu Ram, 1st March 1942," *Panjab Past and Present* 8, no. 1 (April 1974): 221.

57. Ibid., 222.

In practice, Sir Chhotu Ram did not duplicate on a provincial basis his organizational efforts in Rohtak. The Zamindara League developed no well-coordinated provincial organization, though branches were formed in several districts.[58] But the Zamindara League's significance lay not primarily in the extent of its organization but in its popular ideology, in the degree to which its propaganda lent credence to the political existence in Punjab of a distinct "agricultural class," with distinct political and economic interests. As Sir Chhotu Ram saw it, these interests were defined in opposition to nonagriculturalists and to local British officials as well. In fact, the League's attacks on local British officials were at times so pointed that in Rohtak district one deputy commissioner referred to Sir Chhotu Ram's rural propaganda work as "communist" in nature. Some local officials saw little difference between the Zamindara League and the Congress.[59] But the antigovernment tone of the organization only thinly concealed the organization's underlying ideological support for the existing structure of rural political power.[60] Sir Chhotu Ram's stress on Jat solidarity and on local agriculturalist organization only served to underscore his support for the ideological structure of the colonial regime. He chided the government in 1930 for failing to realize the importance of the League as a defender of the British system against more radical groups. "Zamindara League workers," he declared, after one of them was arrested, "are being opposed by Congress, Kirti Kisan and Hindu Sabha workers and are, in some measure, fighting the battles of Government."[61] Indeed, the significance of the Zamindara League lay primarily in its attempt to mobilize support for the rural power structure in the name of the interests of a popularly defined "class" constituency. And in this, it became a vital model for the Unionist party as the process of "democratization" proceeded. Though the Unionists never established a popular rural political organization of the sort established by the Zamindara League in Rohtak, the party used the Zamindara League name after 1936 as a mantle for its own efforts at popular organizing outside the Council. The name, in fact, came to symbolize the party's claim to an independent, "class" base.

Perhaps most important, however, Sir Chhotu Ram translated the goals of the Zamindara League into a program in the Council in the

58. Zamindara League branches were started in Ludhiana, Lahore, Ferozepore and Lyallpur, although the center of its strength remained Rohtak (Chaudhri Tikka Ram, *Sir Chhotu Ram: Apostle of Hindu-Muslim Unity* [n.d.], 8–9).
59. Chowdhry, *Punjab Politics*, 207–12.
60. Ibid., 216–18.
61. Sir Chhotu Ram to H. W. Emerson, 20 January 1930 (Press Branch, file 34-XI).

mid-1930s, which embodied the interests of the "agriculturalist classes," and laid the foundations for the articulation of a powerful symbolic ideology by the Unionists themselves. Responding to Sir Chhotu Ram's pressure and popular concerns about indebtedness, the government appointed a committee in 1932 to inquire into indebtedness.[62] In response to its recommendations, the Council passed a bill in 1934 that underlined the political vitality of the terminology in which the Land Alienation Act had been framed. Though the Relief of Indebtedness Act of 1934 departed in important respects from the principles of the Land Alienation Act, it built on the foundations provided by the act's language. The measure's central provision authorized the government to set up debt conciliation boards, to arrange the "amicable settlement" of debts between debtors and creditors. But the bill defined *debtor* in a way that made the term virtually synonymous with *agriculturalist;* it automatically assumed that members of "agricultural tribes" were debtors unless it was specifically proved that their income was derived from nonagricultural sources.[63] The result was that the establishment of the boards not only provided an avenue for the adjudication of debts but also underlined the leadership of the debtors by rural landlords, the nominal leaders of the "agricultural tribes." Although intended to balance the interests of creditors and debtors, the boards came to be dominated by rural Unionists. As they were gradually introduced in Punjab during the next decade, nonagriculturalists widely criticized the boards as agencies of Unionist political interests.[64]

Such criticism of Unionist-inspired debt legislation grew even more strident following the passage of the Debtors' Protection Act in 1936.[65] Strongly supported by the Unionists, this piece of legislation, introduced in the Council by Sir Chhotu Ram, stretched the underlying principles of the Land Alienation Act even further. The provisions of the Debtors' Protection Bill included the transfer of all execution proceedings against debtors from the courts to the collector (or deputy commissioner). The

62. Chowdhry, *Punjab Politics*, 252.
63. It extended definitions of the Land Alienation Act: "agriculturalists" were to include those whose livelihood was primarily "connected with agriculture," even those technically not members of the "agricultural tribes."
64. For the act's provisions, see Khuda Bakhsh and Abdul Haque, *Relief Legislation in the Punjab* (Lahore: the authors, 1939), sect. 4. The act was brought into effect in 1935 in parts of only five districts. In Jhang district leading lawyers sharply criticized the board's chairman, charging that he incited agriculturalists to ignore their debts. The controversy had political significance: the board's chairman, Mian Ghulam Rasul Khan Tahim of Chiniot, was asked later to be honorary secretary of the Unionist party in the district (Jhang Deputy Commissioner's Files, file 796-16).
65. For its provisions, see Bakhsh and Haque, *Relief Legislation in the Punjab*, sect. 5.

chief aim of the bill, as in the case of the Relief of Indebtedness Act, was to bring the operations of rural credit under political control. As one analyst put it, the collector was assumed to be "in a better position to appreciate the economic condition of the agricultural classes, who form the backbone of the country."[66] Critics claimed that the bill in fact served the interests of "the big zamindars and rich landlords,"[67] which it probably did. But it also reflected in broader terms the political world-view of the Unionist party. It identified the interests of the "agricultural classes," as did the Land Alienation Act itself, with the maintenance of a structure of imperial authority that kept nonagriculturalist capital under firm political control. The depression had simply given this view added significance.

With the advent of the depression, the Land Alienation Act had emerged as a symbol of an ideology that protected the structure of rural power in Punjab from the disastrous effects of falling prices. In fact, Unionist leaders in the Council produced no groundswell of organized rural support for their position, no popular organization comparable to Chhotu Ram's Zamindara League in Rohtak. Their own local support was not predicated on the direct appeal of ideology; it was based on the local loyalties of mediated authority. But in the Council the Unionists now championed a program that protected this system of local influence. Perhaps most important, with Chhotu Ram as their council spokesman, they could claim to support a program that protected a structure of rural power in the name of a popular, agriculturalist "class."

UNIONIST ORGANIZATION:
A WEST PUNJAB ELECTION TOUR

The political and ideological tradition based on the Land Alienation Act thus proved critical to Unionist party efforts in 1936 to meet the contradictory political challenges of provincial autonomy. It provided a political focus consistent with the idioms of local authority and yet gave the Unionists a symbolic focus justifying the assumption of provincial power. But the political organization of the Unionist party was marked by the contradictions inherent in the party's ideological appeal and in the structure of British rule itself. In adapting to the increasing "democratization" of the political system, the Unionists had sought to organize as a "modern" political party—with its own program, propaganda, and

66. Ibid., 4.
67. Punjab, *Legislative Council Debates*, vol. 27 (21 November 1935): 1041–42.

independent "class" base. But the party's ideology grew from a defense of the existing system of local influence centered on rural intermediaries. The logic of the Unionists' own ideology tended to render a party organization that appealed directly to individuals largely superfluous.

This complexity did not slow the Unionist attempts to establish a modern political party's outward trappings, reflected in the organization of their provincial headquarters, their plans for a system of party branches throughout the province, and their selection of a publicity committee to disseminate party propaganda. Pamphlets were commissioned by the headquarters from leading Unionist spokesmen. Sir Chhotu Ram, for example, produced a pamphlet on indebtedness that outlined the agrarian legislation that the party had pushed through the Council, and the party headquarters commissioned other pamphlets dealing with various Unionist concerns.[68] The party even hired paid propaganda "preachers" to work in the districts under the direction of the headquarters. But the significance of this effort lay not primarily in the creation of a direct popular base for the party. Even the resident secretary of the party admitted in December 1936 that these party propagandists accomplished little unless working directly for local leaders.[69] The significance of these efforts lay rather in shaping the party's public image as an independent political entity, capable of participating in Punjab's reformed political system, and thus ruling the Punjab.

In local politics, the structure of Unionist influence came to hinge on the structure of local, districtwide factions, which themselves reflected the contradictory pressures of the changing Punjabi political system. "Factions," as central elements in Indian politics, have been the subject of considerable interest; the term has been used to subsume a wide variety of political phenomena.[70] But in twentieth-century rural Punjabi politics, the faction developed in a distinctive way as the hierarchical system of imperial Punjab responded to accommodate the increasing pressures of "democratic" politics. It is tautological, but nevertheless

68. Chaudhri Chhotu Ram, *Indebtedness in the Punjab* (Lahore: Punjab Unionist Party, 1936); it was published in Urdu as *Punjab aur Qarza*. Other proposed topics included market reforms, corruption, and cooperation (Minutes of meeting at Unionist party headquarters, Lahore, 5 April 1936 [Abdul Aziz collection]).
69. At least 24 such "preachers" were eventually occupied with propaganda work; note by Khurshid Ali Khan, resident secretary of the Unionist party headquarters, 23 December 1936 (Unionist party papers, file E-27).
70. For a discussion of the literature on factions, see David Hardiman, "The Indian 'Faction': A Political Theory Examined," in Ranajit Guha, ed. *Subaltern Studies I: Writings on South Asian History and Society* (Delhi: Oxford University Press, 1982), 198–231.

true, to say that local factions evolved in twentieth-century politics in response to the structure of the political system within which they operated. Factions relied on local patronage structures. At the root of the factional structure of local politics lay the disjunction between the character (and the issues) of local politics and the issues of party politics at the provincial level. "Class" and "religion" provided the political idioms of party formation in provincial politics, defining in ideological terms the relationship between provincial parties and their constituencies. But they did not tie rural voters directly to the political system. In most of western Punjab power was vested in a limited number of rural intermediaries, who competed for support within the hierarchical structure of the colonial administrative system.

This is not to say that ideology played no role in local political alignments. On the contrary, local factional alliances were often constructed in "tribal" idioms. At the local level, "tribal" loyalties often justified the power of administrative intermediaries and legitimized patterns of alliance among them. Further, Unionist ideology served a critical role at the provincial level in validating local structures of factional organization, and thus in stabilizing factional structures as links between local politics and the larger political system. But the power of local factional leaders in rural electoral politics owed little to provincial ideologies or to the direct commitment of rural voters to party. Malcolm Darling asked a group of peasants in Shahpur district how they had voted in an election in the early 1930s; their reply was typical: " 'The zaildar told us to vote for Umar Din and we gave him our vote.' " [71] The meaning of Unionist party loyalty in these circumstances was problematic. Though few local leaders were willing to challenge the Unionists, whose influence in provincial politics protected the structure of local and "tribal" power, few, at the same time, saw political gain for themselves in developing independent, local Unionist party organization. "Since there is no other party in the district the assumption is that we all are Unionists," one local leader remarked, "whatever the damn thing may mean." [72]

Attempts to transform the Unionists into a popular party thus began with contradictions. Though the Unionist headquarters appointed divisional organizing secretaries and sent circulars and propaganda to Unionist supporters in practically every district, almost everywhere they encountered the same organizational difficulties. Provincial Unionist

71. Darling, *Wisdom and Waste*, 28.
72. Sardar Mumtaz Ali Khan, advocate, Campbellpur, to Unionist party headquarters, 23 May 1936 (Unionist party papers, file D-47).

leaders were dependent on the support of local administrative intermediaries—*zaildar*s, honorary magistrates, district board members— who controlled large, sometimes "tribally" defined blocs of votes.[73] When no one individual controlled a dominant bloc in a constituency, provincial Unionist leaders were sometimes able to mediate the formation of alliances among local leaders and gain some direct leverage in the constituencies, or to engineer the election of officials from the local party headquarters. But nowhere was the provincial Unionist party able to command a political following independent of local intermediaries and the administration.[74]

Practical contradictions facing the Unionists in these circumstances were evident as they began their efforts to organize district and tehsil branches of the party in 1936. The case of Sheikhupura district, near Lahore, provides a good example. Unionist efforts to organize the district began auspiciously enough in early 1936, when a local zamindar and district board member, Malik Muzaffar Ali, called a meeting of prominent zamindars at Shahdara tehsil headquarters and arranged to distribute party literature to all the *zaildar*s and *sufedposh*es in the tehsil that outlined the planned structure of Unionist organization and stressed the agrarian bases of party ideology. Following Unionist organizational policy, Muzaffar Ali subsequently announced his intention to form a party tehsil center and serve as honorary secretary. But factional tension developed almost immediately when another leader, Chaudhri Muhammad Amin, a Sheikhupura lawyer with political ambitions, complained that he was being ignored in local organizing efforts in spite of Sir Fazli Husain's direct requests to him to help.[75]

Though Unionist correspondence on this conflict does not indicate the composition of the factions, in Sheikhupura as elsewhere there was ample factional material on the district board to fuel conflict. Unionist leaders could warn the local leaders, as they did in neighboring Montgomery district, to be "cautious and careful," knowing "the party [that

73. Interview, Saiyid Amjad Ali Shah, Lahore, 23 November 1974. Saiyid Amjad Ali Shah was for a time the resident secretary of the Unionist party headquarters and won a Ferozepore district assembly seat in 1937. In organizing a constituency, Unionist headquarters first obtained lists of *zaildar*s and district board members.

74. A possible exception was Rohtak district, where the Zamindara League had an important Hindu Jat following; the Unionist party was "popularly called the Zamindara Party" (Tikka Ram of Sonepat to Unionist headquarters, 4 May 1937 [Unionist party papers, file D-64]).

75. Malik Muzaffar Ali to Unionist headquarters, 8 April [May?] 1936, Urdu note on 2 May meeting of *zaildar*s and zamindars at tehsil headquarters, Shahdara and Chaudhri Mohammad Amin, advocate, Sheikhupura to Unionist headquarters, 20 May 1936 (ibid., file D-21).

is, factional] strife in this part of the world"; but such warnings could hardly be expected to carry weight when the local organizers were themselves enmeshed in factional conflict. Predictably, when Unionist headquarters requested harmony, each organizer in Sheikhupura responded only by charging the other with attempting to organize Unionist branches to serve personal ends. Provincial Unionist leaders stood helpless. If the party chose sides in such disputes it would defeat the purpose of local organization, as Sir Fazli Husain recognized when he wrote of the Montgomery district case: "So far as organizing Zails and Tehsils is concerned . . . it is not right that anyone should be excluded from that work." With few local organizers committed directly to party interests, united party organization in the localities was impossible.[76]

The nature of Unionist support in such a factionalized milieu emerges clearly in a brief political tour of three important districts of western Punjab: Shahpur, Multan, and Lyallpur. All three districts proved in the election of 1937 to be strongholds of Unionist support. Of the fourteen rural Muslim assembly seats in the three districts, the Unionist party in 1937 nominally won all fourteen. But a closer look at the politics of these districts reveals the complicated interaction between Unionist ideology and local factionalism. Unionist ideology legitimized the broad structure of rural politics and local political authority; it thus held a powerful appeal for local factional leaders. But for all the power of the Unionist party in provincial affairs, the locus of power in the districts lay with the families who dominated districtwide factions.

SHAHPUR DISTRICT

Perhaps no district provides a clearer window on the nature of local factionalism and Unionist power than Shahpur in western Punjab. Shahpur was the home of several of the most prominent Unionist leaders in provincial politics. Among these was Sir Firoz Khan Noon, a political protégé of Sir Fazli Husain who had served as a minister in the Punjab government from 1927 to 1936.[77] Also important was General

76. Ahmad Yar Khan Daultana, organizing secretary, Multan division to Nazir Ahmad Khan, Montgomery, 2 June 1936 (ibid., file D-7); Malik Muzaffar Ali to Unionist headquarters, 10 June 1936, and Mohammad Amin to Unionist headquarters, 5 June 1936 (ibid., file D-21); and Sir Fazli Husain to Nazir Ahmad Khan, Montgomery, 9 June 1936 (ibid., file D-7).
77. Sir Firoz Khan Noon's ties to the family of Sir Fazli Husain were strengthened in the mid-1930s when his younger brother married one of Sir Fazli Husain's daughters (Firoz Khan Noon, *From Memory* [Lahore: Ferozsons, 1969], 137).

Sir Umar Hyat Khan Tiwana, Shahpur's largest landlord who, after a distinguished career in the army, had served on both the provincial and imperial Legislative Councils. Though largely retired from active politics in the mid-1930s, Sir Umar Hyat's family contributed sizeable sums to the Unionist party's coffers. Such men made Shahpur a district of central political significance for the Unionist party.

But in Shahpur politics was connected only indirectly to Unionist organization or ideology. Few families demonstrated local factional dominance better than the Noons and Tiwanas. Two small but extensively intermarried Rajput "tribes," the Noons and Tiwanas had built their power in Shahpur on the extraordinarily favorable position they had gained within the British administration. For their support in the British defeat of the Sikhs, leading Noon and Tiwana *malik*s received sizeable wasteland grants, which they converted, with the construction of private inundation canals, into large and profitable estates.[78] Moving into the administration at all levels, these *malik*s developed an unusual degree of power within the colonial structure.[79] For the Noons and Tiwanas, land, water, and access to the administration provided the levers of local dominance.

But such local power was not in itself sufficient for the creation of a powerful, districtwide faction. Though effective factional organization in district politics rested partly on local resource control, it depended also on the establishment of bonds of solidarity tying local magnates together. At the heart of the Noon-Tiwana faction lay a network of dense marriage connections, linking Noons and Tiwanas together and cementing an ideology of "tribal" solidarity. In spite of conflicts among the *malik*s, it was this which provided the core for a powerful alliance in district politics, an alliance cemented in the early twentieth century by Sir Umar Hyat Khan Tiwana, who used his own prosperous estate to loan money to many other, less prosperous, Noon and Tiwana *malik*s.

---

78. The addition of colony lands in the early 1900s strengthened many of these estates. The largest, most prosperous Tiwana estates were in Shahpur tehsil, at Jahanabad, Khwajabad, and Kalra; the largest and most profitable was the Kalra estate of Sir Umar Hyat Khan, which in 1931 comprised 18,204 acres, not all in Shahpur district (Shahpur Deputy Commissioner's Files, Sargodha, file U-I-402).

79. As one British official put it, the Tiwana *malik*s "feel, what is indeed the truth, that Government has made them what they are, and that they have responded by proving themselves to be loyal supporters of Government not with mere passivity but with real activity" (Comments of F. Popham Young [commissioner, Rawalpindi], Register of Landed Gentry grants, Rawalpindi division, 15 [Board of Revenue, file 301/1176KW]). Tiwanas and Noons served as *zaildar*s and honorary magistrates and sent a considerable number of leaders into the army.

According to Sir Umar Hyat's own account, he had spent, by 1919, "about three lakhs of rupees to save many good families from the clutches of moneylenders," including not only other Tiwanas and Noons, but many of the other landed families of the district as well—the Saiyids of Jahanian Shah and Girot, the Biloches of Sahiwal, and others. He had also served as a critical intermediary for many of Shahpur's landed and religious families with the provincial and central governments, organizing, for example, the participation of many in the Delhi Durbar of 1911.[80] By the 1920s and 1930s, Sir Umar Hyat could claim control of a powerful district faction, dominated by Noon and Tiwana *maliks*, but including many of Shahpur's other landlords as well.

Not all Shahpur's landowners were drawn into the Noon-Tiwana orbit although few could challenge its power. An opposing faction emerged; in the twentieth century this coalition centered on Nawab Muhammad Hyat Qureshi, another powerful landlord. With his own unusually prosperous estate at Sabhowal in Shahpur tehsil, Nawab Muhammad Hyat had also benefited considerably from British rule and, like Sir Umar Hyat, loaned money, sometimes without interest or collateral, to other important, yet indebted, Shahpur landlord families.[81] As representative for rural Shahpur in the Legislative Council from 1926 to 1936, he established his own network of provincial political connections and earned a reputation in the Unionist party as a defender of the Alienation of Land Act and a spokesman for agriculturalist "class" interests.[82] On these ties of patronage and obligation he constructed a districtwide faction that rested also on resentment among many Shahpur landowners of Tiwana and Noon power.

This factional rivalry shaped the dynamics of Shahpur politics. In fact, the difficulty in engaging Shahpur's zamindars directly in Unionist organization was indicated by the attempts of a young landowner of Bhalwal tehsil to form a Zamindara association in 1936 on the Zamin-

---

80. "A Brief Account of the Career of Captain the Hon'ble Malik Umar Hyat Khan, Tiwana, C.I.E., M.V.O." (ibid., file 301/1406). Umar Hyat Khan's estate was under Court of Wards administration during his minority and became prosperous in the late nineteenth century. See also Griffin and Massy, *Chiefs and Families of Note*, 2:182.

81. One deputy commissioner of Shahpur referred to Nawab Muhammad Hyat as "a pillar of our local administration" (Register of Landed Gentry grants for Rawalpindi division, 19 [Board of Revenue, file 301/1176KW]). He offered in 1936 to loan money for marriages in the Jahanian Shah family "without interest and without mortgaging any property to him on the condition that his debt should take precedence over other debts of the estate" (Mueenuddin [deputy commissioner, Shahpur] to Board of Revenue, 23 August 1936 [Board of Revenue, file 601/20/19/6]).

82. Nawab Muhammad Hyat published a pamphlet in the early 1930s attacking opponents of the Land Alienation Act (Muhammad Hyat Qureshi, *Zamindaron ki Barbadi ki Taiyariyan! Kangres kya Karna Chahti he?* [Lahore: author?, 1930?]).

dara League model. As a direct embodiment of a commitment to Unionist ideology, it was intended to serve as a local foundation for the party's
power. Launching the association in June 1936, its secretary, Mian Sultan Ali Ranjha, wrote to Unionist headquarters in Lahore offering to
"assist as a body with all its resources in the Ittihad [Unionist] organisation."[83] But as preparations for the 1937 elections accelerated in
Shahpur, this organization—and other local attempts at Unionist organizing—proved largely irrelevant to the workings of local politics. At
the heart of political alignments in Shahpur district lay not Unionist ideology or the loyalty of individual local zamindars to the party but ties of
patronage, hierarchy, and "tribal" connection, binding landowners to
one faction or the other.

As the elections of early 1937 approached, the competition between
these districtwide factions dictated local political developments. At the
provincial level, all were allied to the Unionist party, but in all four of
the district's rural Muslim assembly constituencies, opposing factional
blocs squared off. The precise conflict differed somewhat from tehsil to
tehsil. In Bhalwal tehsil, the leading families of the Ranjha and Gondal
"tribes," who made up the majority of the tehsil's Muslim electorate, set
up an uneasy alliance among themselves, using idioms of "tribal" solidarity in an attempt to defeat the Noon candidate in the constituency,
Malik Sardar Khan Noon.[84] In Shahpur tehsil, the election developed as
a head-to-head clash between Nawab Allah Bakhsh Khan Tiwana of
Khwajabad, a close ally of Sir Umar Hyat Khan, and Nawab Muhammad Hyat Qureshi himself. So bitter did this conflict become that the
district administration was besieged with complaints that local officials
were involved in canvassing for one side or the other. Even the activities
of *patwari*s (village record keepers), as the deputy commissioner saw it,
had to be "carefully watched."[85] Allah Bakhsh attacked the administration's placement of polling stations, arguing that it intimidated the
voters, forcing his voters near Shahpur town, for example, to cast bal-
lots in the stronghold of a family of Saiyids closely allied with the
Qureshi family.[86] As the election approached, factional conflict pervaded district politics.

83. Sultan Ali Ranjha of Bucha Kalan to Unionist headquarters, 12 June 1936 (Unionist party papers, file D-45).
84. Election petition case, Major Malik Sardar Khan Noon vs. Chaudhri Umar Hayat,
Bhalwal (Muhammadan) constituency; Punjab, *Gazette*, pt. 1 (10 June 1938), 747.
85. Note of deputy commissioner, Shahpur, 12 November 1936 (Shahpur Deputy
Commissioner's Files, Sargodha, file B-I-45).
86. Nawab Allah Bakhsh Tiwana to deputy commissioner, Shahpur, 10 December
1936 (ibid., file U-IX-102C).

In the end it was the Tiwanas who triumphed. As the final returns came in, Malik Allah Bakhsh narrowly defeated Nawab Muhammad Hyat in Shahpur tehsil. And in the district as a whole, the Noon-Tiwana faction captured three of the district's four rural Muslim seats. But whatever the factional balance, for the Unionist party the results proved highly ambiguous. On one level, they showed the party's pervasive power in rural politics. All the victorious candidates in Shahpur were Unionist supporters. Unionist ideology swayed few individual voters but legitimized the power of the landed intermediaries who controlled both major factions. It justified the local power of these leaders and also underscored their rightful claim to provincial political influence. It thus provided a focus for landed Muslim loyalty that few ambitious rural politicians could afford to ignore.

But the party's immediate control in Shahpur was nevertheless extremely limited. Though Shahpur remained a solid Unionist district, the election results revealed, as the deputy commissioner put it, a district so "torn by faction" that "there is no person in it of note and influence who is not believed to owe allegiance to one side or the other."[87] On this immediate, local level, Unionist organization carried little political clout. These were the equivocal results that democratic electoral politics introduced to a society still organized around local structures of imperial hierarchy.

MULTAN DISTRICT

Such factionalism was endemic in other districts as well. In Multan district to the south, the position of the Unionist party also hinged on the control exercised by two broad, districtwide factions, led by prominent Muslim families. But in Multan the additional, complicating element was the role of Islam.

In Multan, factional rivalry had for decades centered on the political opposition between the two leading religious families of Multan city, the Qureshis, *sajjada nishin*s of the Suhrawardy shrine of Bahawal Haq, and the Gilanis, *sajjada nishin*s of the Qadri shrine of Musa Pak Shahid. The rivalry probably dated to pre-British times, but twentieth-century factions followed much the same pattern as in Shahpur. Qureshis and Gilanis battled for control of the district board and the Multan Munici-

87. Kenneth Morton (deputy commissioner, Shahpur) to J. D. Anderson (commissioner, Rawalpindi), 22 May 1938 (ibid., file G-II-140).

pal Committee throughout the 1920s and 1930s. The first nonofficial chairmen of both these bodies were Gilanis; the two factions traded control on more than one occasion.[88] Qureshis and Gilanis also dominated contests for the provincial Council and for the central Legislative Assembly.

In provincial politics, both families supported the Unionist party. The Qureshi family typified the landed *pirs* who had profited greatly under British rule and had subsequently aligned themselves with Muslim landlords and "tribal" leaders to protect their position. Though the shrine of Bahawal Haq was located in the fort at Multan city, the Qureshis controlled large rural estates, their possession confirmed as a result of their support of the British during the Sikh wars and the Mutiny. Makhdum Murid Husain Qureshi, who ascended to the *gaddi* as *sajjada nishin* in 1921, closely identified his interests with those of the administration. A leader of Multan's landowners in the 1930s, he strongly supported Unionist ideology and criticized the power of non-agriculturalists, whom he blamed for the rural cultivators' plight during the depression. Equally important, he developed warm personal relations with many provincial Unionist leaders; one such connection was strengthened in the 1930s when his cousin's son, Major Ashiq Husain Qureshi, married a niece of Sir Sikander Hyat Khan.[89] The Qureshi position demonstrated how fully the political interests of many Muslim *pirs* had become linked to the structure of political influence supporting the Unionist party.

The position of these landed religious leaders was nevertheless not identical to that of other rural landlords, like the factional leaders in Shahpur. In spite of the mediatory foundations of their rural influence, the influence of these *pirs* was not wholly uninfluenced by other religious considerations. As hereditary *pirs*, both the Qureshis and Gilanis claimed large numbers of *murids*, who provided them considerable income, through offerings, and who looked to them for religious leadership. On one level, this cemented their hold on factional followers, who were in some cases longtime religious adherents of the Qureshi and Gilani shrines.[90] But for the Gilanis in particular this also created un-

88. Interview, Pir Khurshid Ahmad Qureshi, Multan, 29 January 1975; Saiyid Aulad Ali Gilani, *Muraqqa'-yi Multan* (Multan: the author, 1938), 86, 279, 320.
89. Ashiq Husain Qureshi was married to the daughter of Sir Sikander's brother, Nawab Liaqat Hyat Khan. On the career of Makhdum Murid Husain, see Gilani, *Muraqqa'-yi Multan*, 272–74.
90. Interview, Pir Khurshid Ahmad Qureshi, Multan, 29 January 1975. As an example, Pir Khurshid Ahmad cited the Bosans, whose tradition was of conversion at the

usual political pressures. Like the Qureshis, the Gilanis had played intermediary roles in the administration and had benefited from British rule. Unlike the Qureshis, the Gilanis had not emerged with large rural estates. Because the Gilani *sajjada nishin* depended for income on the offerings of religious devotees, the family was particularly sensitive to political pressure from religious followers.

These pressures acted to tie the Gilanis to the religious crosscurrents of urban politics in Multan city. Their shrine and *langar* were located within the old city, inside Pak gate. The British commissioner at Multan described their situation in 1915: "Makhdum Pir Sadruddin Shah Gilani [the *sajjada nishin*] occupies a position of exceptional influence in Multan." But his influence was not always exercised with British administrative interests in mind. "His income depends upon the offerings of followers who are very largely [*sic*] men of low status and the Pir often finds himself in a difficulty as to the line of action he should follow, for a definite pronouncement in favour of something desired by the authorities might alienate the bringers of offerings."[91] Such pressures led to tensions within the Gilani family itself.[92] The career of Saiyid Zainulabedin Shah Gilani showed these tensions, for he frequently took a political line independent of the senior family members. With largely urban support, in 1930 he formed the Anjuman Fida'iyan-i Islam, which agitated vigorously for Muslim political solidarity and participated in nearly all the important symbolic Islamic agitations of the 1930s, including the one in defense of the Shahidganj mosque at Lahore.[93]

These pressures considerably complicated the politics of Multan. They did not prevent the leaders of the Gilani family from aligning themselves with the Unionist party as the 1937 elections approached. Though Saiyid Zainulabedin Shah offered his support to Maulana Zafar Ali Khan's Ittehad-i Millat, the leading Gilani politicians in Multan openly declared their allegiance to the Unionist party and did

---

hands of Shaikh Bahawal Haq and who were Qureshi supporters in district politics. He admitted that political alliances could outweigh religious ties, as when Muhammad Akram Khan Bosan stood for the Assembly on the Muslim League ticket in 1946 against Major Ashiq Husain Qureshi.

91. C. J. Hallifax (commissioner, Multan) to Miles Irving (senior secretary to financial commissioners), 16 September 1915 (Board of Revenue, file 301/1176).

92. Both the Qureshi and Gilani families had internal conflict. In 1946, one Unionist party worker noted a "darbar" party and a "city" party within the Gilani family (Unionist party papers, file E-96).

93. On the Anjuman Fida'iyan-i Islam, see Munshi Abdurrahman Khan, *A'ina-yi Multan* (Multan: Maktaba-yi Ashraf al-Ma'araf, 1972), 426–27.

their best to establish themselves in provincial Unionist councils as the party reorganized. Provincial identification with the Unionists, as the Gilanis saw it, gave them the provincial connections they needed to maintain their position as effective political intermediaries. Gilanis began their efforts to counter Qureshi influence within the Unionist party in April 1936. When the Qureshis tried to secure open Unionist assistance for their candidate, Makhdum Murid Husain, in a central assembly by-election, the Gilanis responded by pledging their immediate support to the new Unionist headquarters set up by Sir Fazli Husain at Lahore. "Please enlist Unionist," cabled Saiyid Sher Shah Gilani, the Gilani candidate for the central assembly seat, "Will contribute party funds—request your party to help." And Makhdum Sadruddin Shah, the *sajjada nishin,* followed this with a telegram of his own: "Am with Unionist Party," he declared.[94]

Such appeals demonstrated dramatically the pull that the Unionist party headquarters exerted on local factional leaders. In Multan as in Shahpur, Unionist ideology served as the seal on local power, legitimizing the power of local intermediaries and protecting it within the new political system. But if the adherence of both Qureshis and Gilanis demonstrated the Unionist party's appeal in Punjab's politics in 1936, it also highlighted the continuing ambiguities in the party's position. The local Unionist organization in Multan counted for very little. When the Qureshi faction proposed to oust Saiyid Raza Shah Gilani as chairman of the district board, the frustrations of the provincial Unionist leaders flowed into Sir Fazli Husain's anguished plea for harmony in June 1936 to Ashiq Husain Qureshi, then president of the Multan Municipal Committee: "You should desist from in any way making Raza Shah's position as President of the District Board difficult," Fazli Husain wrote, "but accord him your full cooperation, so that your friends may be in a position to ask Raza Shah's friends to accord you their full cooperation in the municipality. This warfare of extinction cannot be permitted and shall certainly not be encouraged."[95] But with local power firmly in Qureshi and Gilani hands, Unionist leaders could do little. The election campaign in fact hinged in Multan not on the ideology or organization of the Unionist party, but on the power of the competing Qureshi and

94. Ashiq Husain Qureshi to Mian Fazli Husain, 30 April 1936; and telegrams, Saiyid Sher Shah Gilani to Fazli Husain, 3 May 1936, and Makhdum Sadruddin Shah Gilani to Fazli Husain, 4 May 1936 (Unionist party papers, file D-51).

95. Fazli Husain to Ashiq Husain Qureshi, 22 June 1936 (Waheed Ahmad, *Letters,* 599).

Gilani factions. The results in Multan, as in Shahpur, were mixed. Although the Unionist party won solid support in the provincial elections, the results only thinly concealed the bitter factional rivalry that divided the district.

The case of Multan demonstrated, once again, the difficulties in the Unionist position, not least with regard to religion. Even with the support of Punjab's *sajjada nishins* and with religious opposition neutralized, the party could not entirely isolate such leaders from symbolic religious politics. Local factionalism intensified the difficulties. Whatever the party's position in provincial politics, local factionalism created the context in Multan in which, even among *sajjada nishins*, religious dissatisfaction with the Unionists could potentially find public, political expression.

LYALLPUR DISTRICT

One last example fills out the picture of the Unionist party in western Punjab and completes the tour: the canal colonies. In Shahpur and Multan, Unionist organizational problems lay in the contradictions between the party's ideological appeal, which promised to preserve the traditional local systems of "tribal" and land-based politics, and the practical difficulties for the party in breaking through those local systems to establish a "modern" party organization. In a canal colony district like Lyallpur, however, the Unionists faced additional political problems.

The depression disrupted life in the canal colonies, the most commercialized agricultural area in the province, more severely than anywhere else. Collapsing incomes and rural unrest challenged the hierarchical rural authority on which Unionist power was based. During settlement operations in the mid-1930s, government revenue demands set off agrarian agitations that weakened administrative control.[96] Lyallpur contained as many large revenue payers as other districts, but few landlords had the degree of political control exercised by those to the west.[97] The district was shaped by government canals; Lyallpur colonists had a history of far more direct relations with the government (and in particular, with the Irrigation department) than had cultivators in many other parts

96. On the unrest during settlement operations, see Kirpalani, *Final Settlement Report of the Lyallpur District*, 53–54.
97. Despite wealth from irrigated land, Lyallpur landlords controlled less land on average than landlords in Shahpur and Multan. For numbers of large revenue payers by districts, see Punjab, *Report of the Land Revenue Committee, 1938*, appendix 1.

of the province.[98] The power of intermediaries was correspondingly limited, and protest was more difficult to control.

The nature of religious conflict further distinguished the district. Whereas in Shahpur and Multan, religious differences between Muslims and Hindus coincided generally with the differences between agriculturalists and nonagriculturalists, in Lyallpur, with a large population of immigrant Sikh and Muslim agriculturalists, this was far less the case. Sikhs made up 16 percent of the district's population in 1931, most belonging to the agricultural tribes.[99] Conflict between moneylenders and landowners often yielded in Lyallpur to competition for power between Sikh and Muslim agriculturalists at the district level. Communal conflict erupted repeatedly in the 1930s on the Lyallpur district board.[100] In terms of ideology and administrative structure, the foundations for Unionist dominance were far less secure in Lyallpur than in the "older" districts of western Punjab.

But in 1936 and 1937 the politics of Lyallpur nevertheless disclosed the underlying Unionist strength illustrated in other western Punjab districts. The Unionists dominated in Muslim politics largely because rural political alliances tended in Lyallpur, as elsewhere, to be articulated in idioms of "tribal" solidarity. In settling immigrant colonists in Lyallpur, the British had deliberately preserved patterns of "tribal" settlement in the district, grouping colonists from common villages or "tribes" in the same or neighboring villages. They followed the same patterns in settling the district's pastoralists, or *janglis* as they were often derisively called. Patterns of "tribal" settlement were thus readily visible in Lyallpur, from the solid blocs of *jangli* villages along the Ravi side of the district to the clusters of immigrant Arain villages in Toba Tek Singh tehsil, dubbed by one settlement officer "Arainistan."[101]

This structure did not, of course, contain rural unrest. But it underlay the development of a pattern of factional politics in Lyallpur elections that replicated in important respects the pattern of factionalism elsewhere in western Punjab. Drawing support from the structure of local "tribal" politics, several of Lyallpur's leading Muslim families at-

98. See, for example, Richard G. Fox, *Lions of the Punjab: Culture in the Making* (Berkeley: University of California Press, 1985), 128.

99. According to the 1931 Lyallpur census, Muslims made up just over 60 percent and Hindus 18 percent (*Census of India*, 1931, vol. 15, pt. 2, 69).

100. In 1931 the government noted "the acute communal tension unfortunately prevailing among the members of this Board." Of the 42 nonofficial members of the board, 26 were Muslim and 16 Hindu or Sikh (Punjab Archives, Local Self-Government/Boards, 1933, file 108).

101. Kirpalani, *Final Settlement Report of the Lyallpur District*, 9.

tempted to forge districtwide factional alliances as the elections of 1937 approached. No single family had sufficient hold on political resources in Lyallpur to dominate as factional magnates did in Shahpur or Multan. But the pattern of Muslim factionalism was nevertheless strengthened in Lyallpur by the special distinction in the district between immigrant colonists, or *abadkars*, and settled pastoralists.

Differential government treatment of *janglis* and *abadkars* had energized this conflict in Lyallpur politics. Whereas *janglis* paid light assessments, *abadkars*—who had often been selected for the colonies largely for their skill as cultivators—generally paid first-class revenue rates.[102] Perhaps more important in the genesis of factional rivalry, the British had favored *jangli* leaders, whose long history of turbulence made the British uneasy, in matters of government appointments and honors. This treatment naturally caused resentment among *abadkar* leaders. As late as 1940 one Lyallpur deputy commissioner noted the feeling among *abadkars* that they had been "almost totally excluded from consideration in the award of Honours and Distinctions and that the Musalman's share of the Sarkar's bounties has almost wholly gone to the Jangli."[103] *Abadkar* political connections with central Punjab and with Punjab's cities exacerbated this cleavage; *abadkar* leaders were far more likely than were *janglis* to have connections with opponents of the administration and with urban religious movements. A few were active in antigovernment agrarian agitation. Lyallpur's most prominent Arain *abadkar* landlord, Mian Nurullah, was active in the Arain *anjuman* at Lahore; he was a business associate and close political ally of Mian Abdul Aziz. Political connections outside the district thus defined for some *abadkar* leaders a cultural and political outlook that was, at times, significantly different from that of Lyallpur's *jangli* chiefs.

But if such divisions shaped a distinctive pattern in Muslim politics, the critical role of "tribal" idioms in Lyallpur also facilitated the linkage of the district's factional rivalries to the politics of the Unionist party. This had little to do with popular Unionist organization, which, in Lyallpur as elsewhere, was limited. But as the elections approached, Lyallpur's leading Muslim families faced factional pressures that pushed

102. Ibid., 28.
103. Sheikh Nur Mohammad (Deputy Commissioner, Lyallpur) to commissioner, Multan, 19 September 1940. Nur Mohammad added, "The partiality for the Jangli was perhaps never intentional and the grievance may not be genuine. But it is certain that it does exist" (Lyallpur Deputy Commissioner's Files, Faisalabad, file S-729-27). *Janglis* had their own grievances, including smaller grants (half-squares) and generally poorer lands than the *abadkars* got. See Kirpalani, *Final Settlement Report of the Lyallpur District*, 9.

them increasingly close to the provincial Unionist party. To protect their local interests and, at the same time, find leverage in provincial politics, they needed the provincial connections that only alliance with the Unionists could provide. Indeed, the election campaign in Lyallpur was shaped in its final weeks by an accommodation between the two most influential factional leaders in the district: Mian Nurullah, a member of the Legislative Council and a leader of the *abadkars*; and Pir Nasiruddin Shah of Kuranga, vice-chairman of the district board and an influential Bokhari Saiyid landlord and *sajjada nishin,* with substantial influence among the settled pastoral tribes. To avoid a damaging fight in the district, the two agreed to split the seats for Lyallpur and Toba Tek Singh tehsils. Whether leaders of the Unionist party played a direct role in mediating this agreement is unclear. But the agreement, which reflected a concern on the part of both leaders to shore up their political positions within the district, created a solid base in Lyallpur for the Unionist party.[104] For both factions, acceptance of Unionist provincial leadership guaranteed a solid foundation for local power. And in the end, in Lyallpur, as in Shahpur and Multan, the Unionist party swept the district's rural Muslim constituencies.

Even in the canal colonies, then, the Unionist party succeeded in winning the provincial allegiance of the leaders who controlled the votes at election time. In spite of problems of agrarian unrest, Lyallpur's politics indicated clearly the strength of the political and ideological structures that bound local political leaders in western Punjab to the provincial Unionist party. Even an *abadkar* leader such as Mian Nurullah, whose connections in Arain politics linked him to both urban politics and rural radicals, saw little alternative in 1937 to Unionist identification if he were to compete successfully in district and provincial politics. But the situation in Lyallpur, as in Multan and Shahpur, also indicated the party's limitations. In Lyallpur, as elsewhere, the party remained a hostage to local political factions. The same political and ideological forces that underwrote the party's position in provincial politics crippled its efforts to enforce discipline on local supporters.

As provincial autonomy approached, the Unionists had thus established a position of unquestioned dominance in Punjabi politics. The

104. Election petition case, Rahmat Ali (petitioner) vs. Nurullah and Nur Mohammad vs. Pir Nasir-ud-Din Shah, Lyallpur (Muhammadan) constituency and Toba Tek Singh (Muhammadan) constituency. For the machinations involved, see Punjab, *Gazette,* pt. 1 (1 October 1937), 1347–52.

provincial ideology of the party linked it to the structure of intermediary power in rural Punjab. But the contradictions in the Unionist position reflected the contradictions inherent in the effort to organize a "modern" party within the framework of the British imperial system. Far from creating a political party with an organizational hierarchy reaching to the local level, the Unionists remained a combination of local, factional leaders—a powerful combination, it is true—but one without an independent, institutional identity in the localities. When the party secretaries met at headquarters to discuss organizational problems in 1936, Chaudhri Shahabuddin, the speaker of the Council and an astute politician, clearly summarized the contradictions in the Unionists' popular organizing efforts. "In zails, tehsils and districts their [sic] were opposite parties," he said, "which could never be reconciled and would not work jointly together." The only solution for the Unionists, he declared, was to give up altogether the effort to form local party centers and to concentrate instead on identifying the party with the interests of those local candidates in each constituency who were most likely to win.[105] Though logical, this was an open admission of the party's weakness.

But in the end, even this degree of organization and discipline proved to be beyond the party's capabilities. A selection board for assembly candidates was appointed in the fall of 1936 by Sir Sikander Hyat Khan, who led the party after Sir Fazli Husain's death in July 1936. The board selected Unionist candidates where local compromises between rival factions could be arranged. But such compromises proved in most cases to be impossible.[106] No full list of Unionist candidates was therefore ever published. Sir Sikander noted clearly before the elections in January 1937 that selections could not be made in most cases without the risk "that those candidates who were standing on the Unionist Party's ticket might go over to some other party."[107] As a result, in many districts several candidates contested the elections, all running on the Unionist ticket.

105. Unionist party headquarters meeting of 15 June 1936 (Unionist party papers, C-5).
106. In November 1936, Unionist Party members who had filed nomination papers in Gujrat district were summoned to Lahore for mediation. "It is learned that you have filed nomination papers for a constituency in which there are two other candidates who want to stand on the Unionist ticket," the resident secretary wrote. "The Unionist Party does not want opposition among those standing on its ticket" (Resident secretary, Unionist headquarters to Gujrat candidates, 28 November 1936 [Unionist party papers, file F-5]). These efforts failed. In four of the five Muslim rural seats for Gujrat district, Unionist candidates competed against each other.
107. Unionist party secretaries' meeting, 3 January 1937 (Unionist party papers, file marked 'Miscellaneous Party Organization, 1936–1940').

The position of the Unionist party thus revealed the contradictions in the colonial situation. To govern the province the Unionists had developed a claim to rule based on the solidarity of the "agricultural tribes," whose common interests had been defined in the Land Alienation Act. This provided the Unionists with a powerful symbolic ideology. It not only provided them a claim to rule in the name of the welfare of the rural population, but it also legitimized the position of local factional leaders and justified the maintenance of a structure of rural, mediatory political leadership. With this ideology at the heart of their provincial organization, the Unionists swept to triumph in the 1937 elections. But the very strength of their position concealed the party's most fundamental weakness. The Unionists asserted their claim to rule in the name of an agriculturalist "class" that could not directly claim the identities or allegiances of individual Punjabis. The organization of the party's power derived from the structure of imperial rule and from the imperial ideology that had linked the British state to Punjabi society. The party was, despite its apparent power, a prisoner in the ensuing years of its own local, factionalized political base.

CHAPTER V

The Cultural Definition of Power, 1937–1944

Kio [kai?] din men yahan phir
Daur-e-Akbar ane wala hai,
Sikandar hai Abul Fazl
Aur Manoharlal, Todarmal.

(Before long will come here again
The regime of Akbar [the Great]
Sikandar is Abul Fazl
And Manoharlal, Todarmal.)
—*Maulana Zafar Ali Khan*[1]

In assuming the premiership in the wake of the 1937 elections, Sir Sikander Hyat Khan epitomized the Unionist party's power and its contradictions. The son of Nawab Muhammad Hyat Khan of Wah (Attock district), Sikander came of a landed family whose fortunes had been made in the service of the British.[2] He was educated at Aligarh and in London and launched his career during World War I in the army. Sikander proved himself in the 1920s one of the most politically skillful and from the British perspective, most reliable leaders of the Unionist party. Appointed in 1929 revenue member of the governor's executive council, he became the first Indian to officiate as governor of the Punjab during the early 1930s. With great respect for the Aligarh tradition, he was sympathetic to Muslim communal aspirations.[3] But as he assumed

1. Quoted in Yusuf Meherally, *A Trip to Pakistan* (Bombay: Padma Publications, 1943), 108. Abul Fazl was Akbar's political confidant and author of the *Ain-i Akbari*. Raja Todarmal was Akbar's revenue minister.
2. On the Hayat family of Wah, see Griffin and Massy, *Chiefs and Families of Note*, 2: 275–77. See also Iftikhar Haider Malik, *Sikandar Hayat Khan (1892–1942): A Political Biography* (Islamabad: National Institute of Historical and Cultural Research, 1985), 7–12.
3. Ikram, *Modern Muslim India*, 236–51. Sikander had no formal academic degree from Aligarh but he kept his close connections there. On Aligarh's role in the development of communal consciousness, see David Lelyveld, *Aligarh's First Generation: Muslim Solidarity in British India* (Princeton: Princeton University Press, 1977).

the leadership of the newly-elected government, he attempted to place himself above Punjab's parochial political conflicts, including in his ministry not only three of his Unionist colleagues, but also Sir Sunder Singh Majithia of the Khalsa National party as a representative of the Sikhs and Sir Manoharlal of the National Progressive party, an urban Hindu.[4] Drawing on the tradition of authority embodied in the language of the Land Alienation Act, Sikander sought to establish for himself a position at the center of power.

His position was in fact a very powerful one. With a strong base in the assembly and a close relation with the British, the Unionist ministry he established in 1937 was as strong as any other under provincial autonomy in India. But as Zafar Ali Khan's satiric verse suggests, Sikander's role as premier was also culturally ambiguous. In the eyes of many, a new "daur-e-Akbar" was indeed on its way in Punjab, as Punjabis increasingly took the reins of government. In 1937, for the first time, an assembly had been elected from a substantial Punjabi franchise, which now wielded significant power. But if Sir Sikander was the new Abul Fazl, a mastermind of the new political order, he was no Akbar. If he had political power, he had little claim to transcendent cultural authority. As leader of Punjab's first popularly elected ministry, Sir Sikander rested his power on his ties to the British administration, his role as the voice of the Unionist party, and his ability to manipulate the Unionist factions. At the heart of Zafar Ali Khan's satire lay a question that remained, for many, central to the new ministry's power—on what cultural foundation did the structure of this new order rest?

"BLOOD AND COMMUNITY OF INTERESTS"

Sir Sikander's most immediate problem after the 1937 elections was how to distribute patronage, the key to balancing the Unionist factions. "Most of the members of the Assembly have spent very considerable sums in securing their election," the governor wrote, "and most of them expect some material advantage for themselves, e.g. an appointment as

4. Apart from Sir Sikander, the ministers in his government included: Sir Sunder Singh Majithia (Khalsa National party), Minister of Revenue; Sir Chhotu Ram (Unionist), Minister of Development; Sir Manoharlal (National Progressive party), Minister of Finance; Malik Khizr Hyat Khan Tiwana (Unionist), Minister of Public Works; Mian Abdul Haye (Unionist), Minister of Education. The ministry was to be "balanced," with one Sikh, one urban and one rural Hindu, and one urban and one rural Muslim (apart from Sir Sikander).

Sub Registrar or Honorary Magistrate or a post in Government service
for a relative."[5] As Mir Maqbul Mahmud, Sikander's brother-in-law
and chief political advisor put it: "There is a certain amount of *legitimate* patronage available to all parties in power. We should not hesitate
to make full and fair use of it."[6] Unionist distribution of patronage was
complicated by the ties linking district-level factions to broad factional
cleavages within the provincial party itself. As the leader of his own faction, Sir Sikander had a particularly difficult position. In the immediate
aftermath of the elections, he moved to close the most dangerous provincial cleavage in the party by offering a ministry to Malik Khizr Hyat
Khan Tiwana, a factional opponent and the son of Sir Umar Hyat Khan
Tiwana of Shahpur. The offer of a ministry to the Tiwana-Noon group
was in fact an effort to pacify the supporters of Sir Firoz Khan Noon,
who had emerged after the death of Sir Fazli Husain as Sir Sikander's
most serious rival for Unionist party leadership.[7] Subsequently, Sir
Sikander used his control of patronage to conciliate other factional
leaders and to cement his leadership of the ministerial party.

But the control of patronage alone, as Sikander realized, was not adequate. Patronage tended in practice to highlight provincial factional divisions.[8] Indeed, to hold the party's own diffuse political following together, Unionist leaders turned their attention once again, after the
elections, to political ideology. In a confidential memorandum on propaganda and constituency organization, Mir Maqbul Mahmud stressed
the political dangers facing the party after the elections—not only from
the Congress and other opposing parties but from internal "jealousies
and personal bickerings." "The immediate necessity of intensive organization and cautious propaganda," he wrote, "is clearly indicated."[9] But

5. H. D. Craik to Lord Linlithgow, 27 January 1939 (Punjab Governor's Situation Reports [IOL, L/P&J/5/241]).

6. Mir Maqbul Mahmud, "Note on Propaganda and Constituency Organisation of
the Party," May 1937, 6; emphasis in original (Nawabzada Khurshid Ali Khan papers,
Lahore; another copy in Unionist party papers).

7. On factions in Punjab's provincial politics, see Craig Baxter, "Union or Partition:
Some Aspects of Politics in the Punjab, 1936–1945," in Lawrence Ziring, Ralph Braibanti
and W. Howard Wriggins, eds., *Pakistan: The Long View* (Durham: Duke University
Press, 1977), 46.

8. "The Premier has endeavored to hold the party together by distributing loaves and
fishes," Nawab Mushtaq Ahmad Gurmani said in a 1939 interview with Penderel Moon.
"This was a fatal policy and has largely contributed to the present discontent in the party.
It has meant in effect that the loaves and fishes have been given to the worst self-seekers,
who resort to threats if their demands are not granted" (Note by E. P. Moon, 22 April
1939, enclosure in H. D. Craik to Lord Linlithgow, 1 May 1939 [IOL, Linlithgow papers,
vol. 88]).

9. Mir Maqbul Mahmud, "Note on Propaganda," May 1937, 3. Mir Maqbul Mahmud suggested the Unionists survey the constituencies to concentrate efforts on "15 or 20
key villages or towns" in each. His survey efforts in 1937 had little result.

such efforts produced little organizational result. Although Unionists held regular party meetings in 1937 and organized a propaganda committee, popular Unionist organization remained very limited.[10] But in ideological terms, the Land Alienation Act continued to underpin the Unionist ministry's position. "The value which agricultural classes attach to the Alienation of Land Act," Sir Chhotu Ram reported after a 1937 tour, "is not fully realised by most people."[11] To shore up the ministry's influence—and to control centrifugal tendencies within the party—Sikander launched a new legislative program of agrarian reform after the elections, using "agriculturalist" ideology to underscore the ministry's position as the central focus of rural political loyalties.

In fact, Unionist efforts to manipulate agriculturalist ideology developed in response to both internal factionalism and escalating antigovernment agitation. The Congress had emerged after the elections as the largest opposition party in the Punjab Legislative Assembly; it showed an increasing interest in direct rural organizing after the all-India Congress adopted a radical agrarian program in 1937. Congress leaders had long criticized Unionist reliance on the Land Alienation Act in Punjab. They saw it as a smokescreen to protect landlord interests. The Unionists had easily deflected such criticism by portraying it as the self-interested-pleading of a largely urban Hindu, nonagriculturalist constituency. But in 1937 the position became more difficult. After the pro-Congress All-India Kisan Committee decided to set up a Punjab provincial committee, regular kisan committees formed in many districts of central Punjab and the canal colonies, maintaining "a steadily increasing volume of correspondence" with the central Punjab Kisan Committee at Amritsar. In 1937 and 1938, these committees undertook widespread antigovernment activity, particularly against settlement operations in Lyallpur, Amritsar, and Lahore districts.[12] Though they could not channel all agrarian discontent in Punjab behind the program of the All-India Kisan Committee or for that matter behind the program of the Punjab Congress, they substantially increased the pace of rural organizing in Punjab, causing the Unionists more political concern.

Such organizing did not directly challenge the local hierarchies of in-

10. Report of the propaganda subcommittee, meeting at Unionist headquarters, 19 August 1937 (Unionist party papers, file marked "Landholders").
11. Report by Sir Chhotu Ram on tour of the Punjab, 6 June 1937, enclosure in H. Emerson to Lord Linlithgow, 21 June 1937 (IOL, L/P&J/5/238).
12. Punjab fortnightly report for the second half of September 1938 (NAI, Home Political, file 18/9/38); see examples of activities in Punjab fortnightly reports for second half of July 1937, of September 1937, and of September 1938 (ibid., files 18/7/37, 18/9/37, and 18/9/38).

fluence supporting Unionist power. In western Punjab, it did not involve tenants on the large estates.[13] Only in the canal colonies did local kisan committees gain significant influence in western Punjab, and even there far less among rural Muslims than among rural Sikhs.[14] There is thus little evidence to suggest that increased agrarian organizing touched the local political roots of Unionist power. But it posed a symbolic challenge to the ideological presuppositions underlying Unionist policies. Facing also internal pressure from simmering factional rivalries, the Unionist party needed to reidentify itself with the interests of Punjab's agricultural classes to maintain the ministry's position. By offering a package of agrarian legislation in the summer of 1938, the Unionists thus sought to deal with both internal conflict and antigovernment organizing.[15] Building on the language of the Land Alienation Act, Sir Sikander and his colleagues introduced a series of bills that reasserted their protection of local, hierarchical rural influence.

Unionist agrarian legislation in 1938 in fact underscored the central symbolic position of the concept of the "agricultural classes" in the reformed political system.[16] The bills, which supporters called "golden bills" and opponents called "black," included three substantive measures: a bill for the registration of moneylenders; a bill for the restitution of mortgaged lands acquired on mortgage before 1901; and an amendment to the Land Alienation Act that prevented the transfer of lands to nonagriculturalists through *benami,* or concealed, transactions.[17] After some nonagriculturalist criticism, these were followed in

13. Echoes of tenant unrest show up in western Punjab records, often from local factional conflicts; see the Attock deputy commissioner's comments on a rent strike on the Tamman estate (E. A. R. Eustace [DC Attock] to commissioner, Rawalpindi, 1 February 1938, enclosure in Emerson to Linlithgow, 17 March 1938 [Linlithgow papers, vol. 86]).

14. Muslim tenants had some limited organization in Montgomery, Multan, and Lyallpur districts (Punjab fortnightly reports for second half of February 1938, first half of October 1938, and first half of November 1938 [NAI, Home Political, files 18/2/38, 18/10/38 and 18/11/38]; also, Punjab, Information Bureau, *Eighteen Months of Provincial Autonomy in the Punjab* [Lahore: Director, Information Bureau, 1939], 47–48).

15. The timing of the legislation, after twelve Unionist MLAs threatened for factional reasons to quit the party, suggests this strategy (H. D. Craik to Linlithgow, 24 June 1938 [IOL, L/P&J/5/239]).

16. Discussion of other agrarian reform measures preceded the 1938 bills. Sir Sikander formed a Land Revenue committee in July 1937 to consider restructuring the land revenue on income tax principles and to propose other measures "by which the land revenue system can be revised so as to give relief to the small holder." The committee, headed by Sir Malcolm Darling, dropped the income tax proposal as a threat to government revenue and suggested a smallholders' development board (later known as the Peasants' Welfare Fund) to undertake public projects for smallholders (Punjab, *Report of the Land Revenue Committee, 1938,* i, 108–22).

17. For provisions of the Registration of Moneylenders Act (1938) and the Restitution of Mortgaged Lands Act (1938), see Bakhsh and Haque, *Relief Legislation in the Punjab,*

late 1938 by another amendment to the Land Alienation Act that pur-
ported to bring agriculturalist moneylenders under the same restrictions
as nonagriculturalists.[18] This in turn was followed in early 1939 by an
Agricultural Markets Act, establishing local committees, composed
largely of agriculturalists, to regulate the operation of agricultural markets. All raised a storm of controversy. Their practical effects were hotly
debated, and remain, even today, open to debate.[19] But in the political
context of 1938 their symbolic significance was unmistakable. They
underscored, once again, the predominance of local political influence
over the power of capital in rural Punjab.

The political results of these bills were immediate. The Punjab Congress, which had cast itself as the champion of the peasantry after the
1937 elections, found its position seriously undermined. Although unwilling to oppose legislation that stood to benefit many Punjabi cultivators, the Congress could not, at the same time, support legislation
that attacked the interests of its nonagriculturalist financial backers.
"There can be no doubt," the governor wrote, "that the prestige of the
Ministry and its supporters has been greatly increased by the passage of
the agrarian legislation."[20] More than three hundred local associations
urged early implementation of the legislation. In spite of strong nonagriculturalist opposition, the government organized an All-Punjab Zamindar Conference at Lyallpur in September 1938 to rally public support for the bills. As Sir Sikander told the conference, the agrarian bills
passed by the assembly represented the true fruits of Punjab's "democ-

pts. 6 and 7. Provisions of the Punjab Alienation of Land (Second Amendment) Act (1938),
which barred *benami* transactions, are in Shadi Lal, *Commentaries on the Punjab Alienation of Land Act XIII of 1900*, rev. C. L. Anand (Lahore: University Book Agency, 1939),
205–8. On *benami* transactions, see also Board of Revenue, file 442/1/100/16 A&B.

18. The text of the Punjab Alienation of Land (Third Amendment) Act (1938) is in
Lal, *Commentaries on the Punjab Alienation of Land Act*, 208–10. For the act's lack of
impact on agriculturalist landlords, see Chowdhry, *Punjab Politics*, 274–77.

19. On the Agricultural Markets Act, never fully implemented, see Chowdhry, *Punjab
Politics*, 277–79. Implementation of several acts was delayed by court challenges. A 1942
government review concluded that the 1938 acts, combined with those passed earlier in
the 1930s, had "amounted to the introduction of a new economic order in the life of the
agriculturalist. It meant that he could no longer be compelled to pay his debts." According
to the review, moneylenders' paper assets were wiped out; it was "reported from all quar-
ters that the moneylender is winding up his business to the best of his ability and migrating
to the towns." The acts gave more leverage to wealthy agriculturalists but also "brought
about a revolutionary change for the better in the economy of the zamindar on whom the
province depends" (Lyallpur Deputy Commissioner's files, file S-724-65 [Review of the
Working of the Agrarian Acts in the Punjab—April 1942]). For a different assessment, see
Chowdhry, *Punjab Politics*, chap. 9.

20. H. D. Craik to Linlithgow, 8 July 1938, H. D. Craik to Brabourne, 24 August
1938 (IOL, L/P&J/5/240).

racy." "This historic gathering prominently brings into relief that main
characteristic of the Punjab," he said, "viz., that it is primarily a land of
peasant proprietors and that the interests of the few bigger zamindars
are inextricably linked with those of the smaller zamindars and the
peasants by ties of blood and of community of interests."[21]

Whatever the economic position, the appeal to kinship and "class"
remained at the heart of the Unionists' position. Whereas the Congress
talked of *inqilab* (revolution), Sikander said, it was the Unionist government that had begun a real revolution in Punjab with its agrarian legislation—a revolution that would secure for Punjabi villagers their rightful
place in Punjab's political and economic life. To continue this transformation, he urged those present to spread a network of Zamindara
League branches "in every corner of the province."[22] But the measure of
the political success of the agrarian legislation did not lie in the spread
of Zamindara League organization; even after the elections Unionist organization remained very weak. The significance of the bills lay in their
effect on the prestige of the Unionist ministry which had successfully
cast itself, at least for the moment, as the upholder of the structure of
local, "tribal" political power in rural Punjab. Indeed, if the ministry
had brought a revolution to Punjab, it was a revolution that sought to
uphold this structure in a language consistent with Punjab's increasingly
"democratic" system.

THE POLITICAL CHALLENGE OF
RELIGIOUS SYMBOLISM

The political strategy behind the bills nevertheless highlighted also
the Unionists' ambiguous cultural position. Though Sir Sikander had
tried initially to establish a ministry encompassing representatives of all
the major divisions in Punjab—agriculturalists and nonagriculturalists;
Hindus, Muslims, and Sikhs—he had been forced to appeal ultimately
to the symbolism of the Land Alienation Act simply in order to hold
together the factions within the Unionist party. Use of what the governor called "spectacular" legislative measures,[23] was itself one measure of
the ministry's weakness. It lacked a transcendent cultural justification

21. Punjab, Information Bureau, *Full Text of the Presidential Address Delivered by
the Hon'ble Sir Sikander Hyat-Khan, Premier of the Punjab, at the All-Punjab Zamindar
Conference, Lyallpur, on September 4, 1938* (Lahore: Director, Information Bureau,
1938), 1–2.
22. Ibid., 20.
23. Emerson to Linlithgow, 27 December 1937 (IOL, file L/P&J/5/238).

for its power. For all their success in mobilizing an outpouring of rural support, the "golden bills" highlighted the continuing reliance by the Unionist ministry on the ideological structure of the colonial regime. Unionist ideology justified the party's position not as the protector of a broad Punjabi "community" of individuals but as the protector of innumerable local "communities"—communities politically defined and structured by the state itself. The languages of "tribe" and "class," whatever their popular appeal, had been transformed into a language of rule only by their incorporation into the structure of the colonial political system.

Considerable ferment in Punjab, marked by rapidly rising political expectations, followed the introduction of provincial autonomy. In the cities, communal leaders sought to define symbolic religious ideologies transcending their localized political bonds. The press and the public platform offered them arenas independent of the structure of colonial government. Urban competition between religious "communities" injected an intensity into public debate that the Unionists found hard to ignore. As the governor noted in the fall of 1937, communal acrimony in the press reached levels that few could remember. Communal violence erupted in a number of Punjab's cities.[24]

Such controversy offered no immediate political threat to the Unionists so long as it remained confined to urban areas. But Sikander was not oblivious to the symbolic challenge it posed to the legitimacy of his ministry. He attempted to dampen controversy in mid-1937 by launching a Unity conference to resolve symbolic religious issues. Under Sikander's guidance, leaders including Master Tara Singh of the Akali Sikhs and Maulana Zafar Ali Khan took up a number of issues dividing the communities, such as the playing of music before mosques and the use of *jhatka* and *halal* procedures for slaughtering animals.[25] The discussions produced few concrete results. But in the attempt to mediate, Sir Sikander sought to cast his government as a guardian of public order, above the contention of such communal controversy.

Nevertheless, this controversy seriously threatened the Unionist ministry's position. However strong the Unionist base among Punjabi agriculturalists, the legitimacy of the Unionists' right to rule could be easily

24. Emerson to Linlithgow, 8 October 1937 (ibid.). The first four months of the new ministry's regime produced eight serious communal riots in Punjab (Punjab, Information Bureau, *Eighteen Months of Provincial Autonomy*, 31).

25. Punjab, Information Bureau, *Eighteen Months of Provincial Autonomy*, 36–37; *Report on Newspapers and Periodicals in the Punjab*, 1937, 347–48, 384–85, 476.

called into question by the spread of rural communal controversy, which would explode the idea that society was structured only by local "communities," bound together by cultural and political intermediaries. The political implications of such a "communal" transformation of rural politics had in fact been illustrated graphically for the Unionists by political developments in the 1920s and 1930s among Punjab's Sikhs—a model that Sikander and other leaders could not afford to ignore. The Sikhs of the Punjab were, like the Muslims, an overwhelmingly rural population. But Sikh politics had been transformed by the political aftershocks of the gurdwara reform movement of the early 1920s. Though the structure of rural hierarchy had long provided a powerful defense for the Unionists against the spread of communal organization outside the cities, developments in Sikh politics suggested the potential difficulties facing the Unionists in the late 1930s in trying to control the structure of rural hierarchy in an era of increasingly "democratic" politics.

The history of political change among the Sikhs was closely bound in the 1920s and 1930s to the history of the Akali party. Before the emergence of the Akalis, the structure of rural authority among the Sikhs, as among the Muslims, had been shaped by the hierarchical ideology of the British administration. Control of Sikh gurdwaras had been dominated by hereditary gurdwara custodians (*mahants*), who were, in general, strong supporters of the British, and whose power fit generally into the political contours of the British administration. But in the period after World War I, the Shiromani Akali Dal had emerged as a party of religious reform, agitating for "community" control of the gurdwara endowments. It focused dissatisfaction on the religious behavior of the *mahants*, who were perceived as failing generally to meet correct standards of Sikh religious practice. But perhaps most important, the gurdwara reform movement also showed how such questions of religious reform were closely tied to reform in the Punjab's rural political structure. In attacking hereditary control of the gurdwaras, the Akalis attacked the structure of hierarchical colonial political authority that supported, as they saw it, a corrupt system of control over Sikh religious places.[26]

For the Akalis, the reform of religious organization and political structure were all of a piece, aspects of an attack on established hierarchies of mediation. As the movement developed, the Akalis came to see the voice of the Sikh community as legitimately embodied only in

26. For an account of the Akali agitation, see Mohinder Singh, *The Akali Movement* (Delhi: Macmillan, 1978).

popularly elected local gurdwara committees and in a Central Gurd-wara Managing Committee (S.G.P.C.) for the community as a whole. The Akalis "began to look upon themselves," Khushwant Singh writes, "as the sole representatives of the community. A decision of the S.G.P.C. became like a proclamation of the guru." [27] With the passage of the Sikh Gurdwaras and Shrines Act of 1925, the S.G.P.C. gained official recognition as the legal center of gurdwara management, an independent source of funding and patronage for the Sikh community. It embodied a new, provincewide community identity.

Akali politics thus challenged the colonial regime's cultural foundations in Punjab. At the heart of the Akali movement lay a vision of Sikh community shaped by the direct loyalties of individual Sikhs to a provincewide community whose political organization depended on popular, collective action, not on mediation. To this degree, it was a vision of community similar to the one that spread among urban reformist Muslims in the nineteenth and twentieth centuries—a vision that rejected hierarchy and stressed the individual's direct commitment to religious symbols as the key to political mobilization. Unlike the reformist movement among the Muslims, the Akali movement found its support not only in the cities but also in the countryside. Though its antecedents lay in part in the Singh Sabhas, social reform organizations of the late nineteenth and early twentieth centuries, the gurdwara reform movement had from the very beginning a strong rural following, particularly among Jat Sikhs. [28] The movement thus made possible the institutionalization of a Sikh "communal" identity independent of communal urban politics and colonial rural authority. It transcended both the cultural boundaries between countryside and city and the political contours of the colonial regime.

By its very existence, the Akali movement posed a significant threat to the ideology of Unionist power, one that Sir Sikander perceived clearly in the early 1930s. In assessing Sikh politics after the communal award in 1932, Sikander rationalized the dilemma that the rise of Akali

27. Khushwant Singh, *A History of the Sikhs* (Princeton: Princeton University Press, 1966), 2:207.
28. Though comparisons between the Akali movement and nineteenth- and twentieth-century reform movements in Islam are striking, the lack in Sikhism of a touchstone of "community" such as the *shari'at*, and of a religious elite defined by commitment to religious law—a group comparable to the *'ulama*—makes sweeping comparisons dangerous. The Singh Sabha movement was in some ways analogous to urban reform movements in Punjabi Islam and made extensive use of printing and the press. But the Sikhs lacked so clear an urban-rural division; many early Singh Sabhas were led by landowning Sikhs (Khushwant Singh, *A History of the Sikhs*, 2:141–46).

power presented to the Unionists. Since rural society continued to rest
on local loyalties, the spread of Akali influence, he argued, reflected not
the expression of an authentic rural voice but rather the successful manipulation of Sikh agriculturalists by an urban, nonagriculturalist Sikh
elite—an urban elite whose ideology owed little to the structure of rural
life. "Being intellectually superior and financially better off as compared
with the genuine agricultural Sikhs," Sikander wrote, "they [the urban
Sikhs] forced their way to the forefront and managed to consolidate
their position during the Akali agitation." Later, Sikander argued, it was
in the interests of urban Sikhs, largely Khatris and Aroras, that the Akali
party operated. With "the financial resources and the subtle machinations of the Arora," Sikander wrote, the urban Sikhs had won the rural
Jats to their side. The movement thus reflected, in this view, only a variant on an old pattern in Punjabi politics, the attempted domination of
Punjabi agriculturalists by wealthy and educated nonagriculturalist
Hindus.[29] To oppose the Akalis was thus fully in keeping with Unionist
opposition to other nonagriculturalist interests, who had tried to exploit
Punjab's true "agriculturalists"—Sikhs, Muslims, and Hindus alike—
for their own political and financial gain.

But such a view, however coherent and satisfying for the Unionists,
was too self-serving to contain more than a fraction of the truth. The
division between urban and rural Sikhs—Jats on one side and Khatris
and Aroras on the other—had at times played an important role in Sikh
politics;[30] still, it was wishful thinking on Sikander's part to suggest that
Khatris and Aroras were pulling the strings of the Akali movement. If
the Akalis represented attitudes that seemed to contradict Unionist assumptions about the nature of community identity in rural society, there
were in fact other, more telling explanations. The important economic
and geographical position occupied by Sikh Jats in central Punjab
proved a critical factor. Unlike Muslim Jats, Sikh Jats were concentrated
in the most highly commercialized parts of the Punjab. They were far
more active generally in collective agrarian agitation than were Muslim
Jats. On one level, Jat Sikh politics reflected the ambiguities in colonial
rule, which had supported a class of commercialized producers in central Punjab even as it relied on a structure of rural hierarchy to maintain
imperial power. Akali politics thus highlighted contradictions inherent in

29. Confidential report of Sir Sikander on reactions to the communal award, 12 April
1932 (Sardar Shaukat Hyat Khan collection, Islamabad).
30. See Khushwant Singh, *A History of the Sikhs*, 2:155–56, 225.

British administration, which had encouraged commercialization while trying to control Punjab within a hierarchical political structure.[31]

But perhaps even more important, the Akali movement reflected long-standing cultural patterns in rural Sikh society, exposed by the twentieth-century transformation of the political system. Unlike the classical urban tradition of political community in Islam, the tradition of militant Khalsa solidarity in Sikhism initiated in the eighteenth century, had from its origins been deeply rooted in the cultural values and social organization of agrarian Jat society. Despite the fact that the Sikh gurus were Khatris, "there can be little doubt," W. H. McLeod writes, "that the Five K's," the outward symbols of Sikh political identity and solidarity, reflected in their eighteenth-century development "the complex of Jat cultural patterns and contemporary historical events which produced so many of the features now associated exclusively with the Khalsa brotherhood." When the symbols of Khalsa solidarity were used to rally the Jats behind the gurdwara reform movement, therefore, their use signified more than manipulation of the Jats, as Sir Sikander had wishfully suggested, by wealthy and well-educated urban Khatris and Aroras. Instead, it represented a concept of religious community, increasing in popular appeal as arenas of political participation expanded in the twentieth century, a concept embedded in village society and Jat culture, and antagonistic to the hierarchies of colonial society.[32]

The Akali movement thus embodied a cultural structure in fundamental conflict with the structure of Unionist power. Still, in the 1930s the Akalis represented only a limited threat to Unionist political power. Sikhs were not Muslims; and in the past the Unionists had depended very little on the Sikhs for basic political support. Nor did the Akalis control Sikh politics entirely. In the late 1920s the British administration of Sir Malcolm Hailey had sought to shore up the position of Sikh *zaildars* and other landed intermediaries to keep an effective rural counter to the Akali challenge.[33] This countervailing political base in the Sikh community was one the Unionists took full advantage of. At the provin-

31. Fox, *Lions of the Punjab*, 27–51. Fox stresses the contradictory position of central Punjab's "petty commodity producers" in developing radical Sikh politics.

32. W. H. McLeod, *The Evolution of the Sikh Community* (Oxford: Clarendon Press, 1976), 51–52. Identification of the Akali movement with Jat culture overstates the case. But the coincidence of growing political power among rural Jat "communities," the triumph of the *keshdhari* tradition in defining Sikh identity, and the rise of the Akali movement is significant.

33. Rajiv A. Kapur, *Sikh Separatism: The Politics of Faith* (London: Allen & Unwin, 1986), 182–84.

cial level, the Unionists allied themselves in 1937 with the Khalsa National party, a party dominated by Sikh landlords that emerged from the 1937 elections with a substantial bloc of rural Sikh seats. By appointing the party's leader, Sir Sunder Singh Majithia, to represent the Sikhs in his cabinet, Sir Sikander sought to undercut Akali influence and secure a foundation of ideological support for Unionist rule even within the Sikh community itself.

But as Sikander eventually discovered, the Khalsa National party was a weak reed for the Unionists to rely on. The Khalsa National party's strong 1937 election showing owed as much to scandal and divisions among the Akalis as it did to the persistence of mediatory hierarchies in rural Sikh politics.[34] Despite their relatively disappointing 1937 election showing and internal conflict, the Akalis had established control of the S.G.P.C. and a network of gurdwara committees, a position of power that had transformed the character of Sikh politics fundamentally. Though divided in the 1930s along numerous internal lines, the Akalis had become a force in Punjabi politics to be reckoned with—a force whose importance could only increase as power was transferred increasingly into Punjabi hands. And in the days after the 1937 elections, the potential significance of this challenge for the Unionists became increasingly clear.

Stung by the challenge to their influence in the elections, the Akalis deliberately provoked conflict with the Unionist ministry to regain lost prestige. Focusing on religious symbols in public ritual, they stridently asserted their rights as Sikhs. "It now seems clear," the government observed in mid-1937, "that this party is determined to embarrass Government as much as possible, by insisting on what it looks upon as Sikh rights in the matter of music before mosques, processions and jhatka." For Sir Sunder Singh Majithia, Akali protests made life extremely uncomfortable.[35] But for the Unionists the political seriousness of the situation went beyond Sir Sunder Singh's embarrassment, for such actions were calculated to challenge Unionist power. Direct Akali action was evident, in fact, in a number of Sikh-Muslim clashes in widely scattered areas of rural Punjab in 1937 and 1938—at Kot Fateh Khan in

34. The Akalis won ten seats, the Khalsa National party thirteen. The Akalis lost support in the 1937 elections when the Central Akali Dal group of Giani Sher Singh defected to the Khalsa National party and were hurt when a scandal over use of gurdwara funds led to a court case against the Akali leader, Master Tara Singh (File 78 [Sikh Gurdwaras Judicial Commission], Sardar Sir Sunder Singh Majithia papers, Nehru Library, New Delhi).
35. Punjab fortnightly report for the first half of September 1937 (NAI, Home Politi-

Attock district, where a gurdwara surrounded by the property of a major Unionist landlord became the focus of an extended and bitter dispute; at the village of Jandiala Sher Khan in Sheikhupura district, where the holding of a Sikh public meeting to rally support on the *jhatka* issue provoked a sharp reaction from local Muslims;[36] and perhaps most important, at the Gujrat village of Ala, where in mid-1937 the most serious rural communal clash of the decade took place. In all these cases, public meetings, speeches, and direct communal organizing sought to focus political attention on religious symbols.

The Ala riot was particularly unsettling for the Unionists because it illustrated the danger that aggressive Akali organizing posed for the entire political system. In an atmosphere of heightened tension following the murder of a local Sikh, Sikh leaders organized a meeting near Ala in June 1937 to assert the political solidarity of Sikhs in a predominantly Muslim tract. Muslims responded by attacking the Sikhs, precipitating a riot in an area encompassing some 30 villages in Phalia tehsil. Of particular significance for the Unionists was the widespread report that Muslim reaction had been orchestrated by Pir Fazl Shah of Jalalpur, whose shrine was located immediately across the Jhelum River and whose Hizbullah organization claimed an important following in the area.[37] Though this organization was hardly analogous to that of the Akalis, its role in the Ala riot nevertheless indicated that rural Muslim leaders could respond in kind to Akali organizational efforts, galvanizing rural Muslim organization around a communal cause. The inherent political danger for the Unionists in the adoption of such a role by a prominent Chishti *pir* so alarmed Sir Sikander that he made a special trip to the *'urs* at Jalalpur two months after the riot in order to defuse the situation. Though allowing that the Sikhs had provoked local Mus-

---

cal, file 18/9/37). Sir Sunder Singh Majithia's problems on the *jhatka* issue are discussed in file 74 (Note on jhatka meat) (Sir Sunder Singh Majithia papers).

36. For Kot Fateh Khan, see Punjab fortnightly reports for the first half of April 1937 and of August 1937 (NAI, Home Political, files 18/4/37 and 18/8/37); also, *Report on Newspapers and Periodicals in the Punjab*, 1937, 143–44, 317–18, 350–51. For Jandiala Sher Khan, see Punjab fortnightly report for the second half of August 1937 (NAI, Home Political, file 18/8/37); *Report on Newspapers and Periodicals in the Punjab*, 1937, 359–60.

37. Emerson to Linlithgow, 18 July 1937 (IOL, L/P&J/5/238). The *Akali Patrika* (Lahore), 19 June 1937, held Pir Fazl Shah responsible for the rioting; *Report on Newspapers and Periodicals in the Punjab*, 1937, 244. Master Tara Singh called the *pir* "the soul of the Muslim aggressive movement in that Ilaqa" (Master Tara Singh to Sir Sikander, 10 September 1937, enclosure in Emerson to Linlithgow, 28 September 1937 [IOL, L/P&J/5/238]).

lims, Sikander urged local leaders to follow Islamic teachings of toler-
ance and put their trust in his government.[38] He also tried to enlist local
hierarchies of rural control, applying pressure through the *pir*'s influential landed relatives.

But however much he tried to manipulate the local political structure, the Ala riot represented at a deeper level a potential disaster for Sir
Sikander's system of control. The strength of the Unionist party depended on the maintenance of a mediatory structure of rural authority
that was religiously legitimized by the position of rural Muslim *pir*s.
Whatever the problems faced by the Unionists at the provincial level in
defining an indigenous cultural foundation for their authority, they relied in the localities on the influence of Muslim religious leaders whose
influence was embedded in a structure of authority based on mediation.
It was at this level that the Unionists had sought to reconcile their own
ideological appeal with the indigenous structure of Punjabi Islam. The
real challenge of Akali organizing lay, in the end, not in a direct political
attack on the Unionists, but in a challenge to the structure of rural mediation. Rural "communal" conflict threatened to undercut the "cultural system" on which imperial power was based.

SIKANDER AND ISLAM:
MOSQUES AND SHRINES

To meet such a challenge was no easy task. With the support of rural
intermediaries, the Unionists' immediate political position was secure.
But while rural *pir*s were intermediaries whose power fit generally into
the structure of Unionist influence, they were also Islamic religious leaders sensitive to the symbolism of Islam. Sikander had cast his ministry as
the protector of local power; it was far more difficult to cast his government as the protector of Islam. Nevertheless, to legitimize his authority
Sikander sought to identify his government with symbols that would
underscore, even in religious terms, his right to rule. His proposal in
January 1938 for the upkeep of Lahore's Badshahi mosque provides a
good example. Built in the time of the Mughal emperor Aurangzeb, the
Badshahi mosque was Punjab's largest and most important mosque—a
symbol derived from the history of imperial Muslim power in the Punjab. As a legacy of the Mughals, the mosque recalled, as Malik Barkat
Ali put it, "all that is noble and grand in the Muslim history of this

38. The speech was reported and commented on by a number of newspapers (*Report
on Newspapers and Periodicals in the Punjab*, 1937, 334–35).

country."[39] Sir Sikander tried to identify himself with this legacy. Though he could not officially patronize the mosque, he nevertheless proposed a resolution in the assembly calling for a voluntary and temporary cess on all Muslims in Punjab of one *paisa* per rupee on the land revenue for the mosque's repair and refurbishing. By proposing such a plan, he sought to establish himself as protector of the mosque and thus as protector of the Muslim "community"—even while maintaining in his collection of funds for the mosque the structure of the imperial administrative system.[40]

But in the British imperial context, this symbolic identity was extremely hard for Sir Sikander to maintain. A more dramatic demonstration of his difficulty was provided by the continuing controversy focusing on the Shahidganj mosque, a powerful public symbol in the 1930s of Islamic communal identity. When a legal appeal on the Shahidganj mosque case produced a High Court decision in January 1938 confirming Sikh control of the site, Sikander came under strong pressure from urban Muslims to support legislation in the assembly overturning the decision. To identify his government publicly with protection of the Shahidganj mosque would establish Sikander as a spokesman for the Muslim community far more securely than his patronage of the Badshahi mosque, in the eyes of both urban Muslims and rural *pirs* alike. But to support the bill would also identify Sikander with a concept of "community" separated from the structure of rural mediation and shaped by popular action in urban politics. Further, to overturn the court's decision in the name of Muslim community would alienate Sikander's non-Muslim colleagues and disrupt the coalition supporting the Land Alienation Act. In the end, Sikander opposed the Shahidganj bill. Far from underscoring his authority, the issue forced Sir Sikander to use all his political skills to prevent legislation restoring the mosque to the Muslims from becoming law.[41]

The issue prompted Sikander to seek other means to legitimize his government's position and its control over the structure of rural Punjabi

39. M. Rafique Afzal, ed., *Malik Barkat Ali: His Life and Writings* (Lahore: Research Society of Pakistan, 1969), 85.
40. For press comments, see *Report on Newspapers and Periodicals in the Punjab,* 1938, 38–39.
41. On the High Court decision and the Muslim Mosques Protection Bill introduced by Malik Barkat Ali, see *Report on Newspapers and Periodicals in the Punjab,* 1938, 44–46, 53–58, 62–64, 71–72, 83–85, 90–92, 107–12, 117–21. The bill's supporters lobbied Unionists to support the bill, "one device being for a small party to appear before them with a Quran," the governor wrote, "and to ask them to sign the bill, or to be considered unbelievers" (Emerson to Linlithgow, 4 March 1938 [Linlithgow papers, vol. 86]).

Islam. In 1937, Mir Maqbul Mahmud, Sir Sikander's shrewdest political advisor, introduced in the assembly a bill to regulate Muslim religious *auqaf*, the endowments supporting most of Punjab's mosques and shrines. Their regulation was not, in fact, a new issue.[42] But by taking it up the government responded to the broader political challenge raised in the 1930s by communal politics and by the establishment of the S.G.P.C. as a structure for communal organization among Punjab's Sikhs. The bill represented a Muslim effort to establish a counterpart to the Sikh gurdwaras committees, but one controlled by the hierarchies of Unionist politics.

The Muslim Auqaf Bill's political intent was reflected in its key provisions. In general outline it followed the Sikh Gurdwaras and Shrines Act of 1925. Like the endowments of the Sikh gurdwaras, Muslim *auqaf* were to be controlled by district Auqaf committees, which in turn were to be supervised by a provincial Auqaf board. An Auqaf tribunal was to rule on disputes over *waqf* status. These specific proposals, however, were quite different from the popularly elected committees established by the gurdwaras act. Elections to the district Auqaf boards were to be on an extremely limited franchise, with special provisions for the continuing association of *sajjada nishin*s with the administration of shrines. Further, the government itself was to nominate several members.[43] Though Mir Maqbul Mahmud, with perhaps unconscious irony, attempted to represent Muslim "communal" opinion on the provincial board through the appointment by occupation of one scholar, one lawyer, one editor, and one poet, this provision only highlighted the existing, amorphous character of "communal" leadership in twentieth-century Punjab. In spite of its similarities to the gurdwaras act, the spirit of the *auqaf* bill differed significantly from that of the gurdwaras act. Though the official regulation of *auqaf* was supported in principle by a wide range of Punjabi Muslims, Mir Maqbul Mahmud's bill reflected, in large part, the Unionists' concern to establish a more uniform structure of religious organization and control in the province. If they could not establish a clear, symbolic religious foundation for their authority,

42. Earlier all-India legislation to regulate *auqaf*, the Mussalman Wakf Act of 1923, relied heavily on the courts for its implementation, and its impact was limited (S. Khalid Rashid, *Wakf Administration in India* [New Delhi: Vikas, 1978], 26–28; see also Gregory C. Kozlowski, *Muslim Endowments and Society in British India* [Cambridge: Cambridge University Press, 1985]).
43. A copy of the Punjab Muslim Auqaf Bill (#5 of 1937) is in the Abdul Aziz collection.

they could at least define a more manageable institutional framework to organize local religious support.

But the fate of the *auqaf* bill demonstrated the dilemma the Unionists were facing. Politically attractive to provincial leaders because it offered greater institutional control over religious organization, the *auqaf* bill undercut that element of Punjabi Islam perhaps most essential to the Unionist party's political strength—its diffuse organizational character. The diffuse, mediatory structure of rural Islam had long helped to legitimize the political hierarchies supporting Unionist power. To attempt to bring that structure under direct government control through the control of *auqaf* struck in some ways at the underlying conceptual foundation of Unionist power. As Raja Ghazanfar Ali Khan noted, backers of the *auqaf* bill, in contrast with those who had passed the Sikh gurdwaras act, occupied a strange position. The gurdwaras act had been passed, he said, because the Sikhs had already "organized themselves and they had proved to the world that at any cost they were prepared to take possession of their religious places."[44] The Unionists, however, had made no effort to foster the popular Muslim communal consciousness that alone would justify community control of the shrines; they, in fact, had consistently opposed the development of such a popular communal ideology. Operation of the *auqaf* bill in such circumstances would, as the deputy commissioner of Jhang pointed out, be strange indeed. "Some of the shrines wield tremendous influence," he wrote, "and any local committee is bound to be influenced by the Mutawallis [that is, *sajjada nishin*s] with the result of either yielding to them or creating further factions and consequently adding more confusion to the present chaos of Dharabandi [factionalism] in rural areas."[45]

The Muslim Auqaf Bill ran into widespread religious opposition. Many rural *sajjada nishin*s opposed it to protect their local interests; many *'ulama* opposed it on the broader grounds that it violated the mandates of the *shari'at*. Some *sajjada nishin*s supported the bill.[46] Few could openly object to the principle that, in the interests of "modern,"

44. Punjab, *Legislative Assembly Debates*, vol. 4 (1938): 665.
45. Opinion of deputy commissioner, Jhang, 26 May 1938; second supplemental list of opinions on the Punjab Muslim Auqaf Bill (Press Branch, unnumbered file).
46. Major Mubarak Ali Shah, a close relative of the *sajjada nishin* at Shah Jiwana, spoke for it in the assembly (Punjab, *Legislative Assembly Debates*, vol. 4 (1938): 660–63). Another important supporter was Pir Jamaat Ali Shah (see pamphlet published by Muhammad Din, "Auqaf bil ke muta'llaq hazrat qibla-yi 'alam amir al-millat haji hafiz Saiyid Jamaat Ali Shah sahib muhaddis Alipuri ka irshad-i girami" [Abdul Aziz collection]).

effective management, *auqaf* should be subject to some regulation. But many important *sajjada nishin*s, on whom the Unionists relied for political support, registered their strong opposition to the bill's provisions. In Multan, the Gilani and Qureshi *sajjada nishin*s displayed a rare unity, publicly joining other religious leaders to oppose Mir Maqbul Mahmud's bill.[47] At Lahore, the central Anjuman Hizb al-Ahnaf voiced the belief of the Barelvi *'ulama* that the bill violated the *shari'at* and urged that no Muslim MLA should support it without reference to the Sunni *'ulama*.[48] Faced with such opposition, the Unionist leaders hesitated, unwilling to alienate local religious support and lacking assurance that the bill provided the institutional levers of religious control they desired. The deliberations of Sir Sikander and his advisors remain obscure, but in 1938 the bill was allowed to die without reaching a division.

The Muslim Auqaf Bill demonstrated the dilemma that the Unionists faced in meeting the challenge of increasing communal activity after 1937. It was essentially the same dilemma that faced them in trying to build an effective provincial political organization. Their strength lay in the diffuse, localized character of political and religious authority in the Punjab countryside. As they attempted to establish a more "modern" system of centralized control, the Unionists only underscored the weakness of their cultural position and threatened to undermine the diffuse political and religious base on which their power had been built.

THE EMERGENCE OF
THE MUSLIM LEAGUE

As new political patterns developed under provincial autonomy, the Unionists were thus caught in a contradictory position. They commanded a large majority in the assembly but lacked clearly defined cultural foundations for their power. They had inherited this position from the British. Continued commitment to the "agricultural tribes" offered the Unionists a platform for unifying local leaders to support them; it did not define a broad Punjabi community transcending local divisions. When challenged in an increasingly "democratic" system by communal leaders who sought broader cultural foundations for the state, the Unionists could offer little effective response.

Yet Unionist control in Punjabi politics limited the options open

47. Proceedings of a meeting held 2 June 1938 at Multan ("Karrawa'i jalsa—Auqaf Bil" [Abdul Aziz collection]).
48. *Ihsan* (Lahore) 3 November 1938 (Press Branch, file no. 7766).

to other Muslim political movements, as perhaps nothing indicated more clearly than the development of the Punjab Muslim League. The League, more than any other organization, claimed after 1937 to represent politically the larger Muslim "community" in India. It thus embodied the concern among many Muslims to define a broader political community within the structure of the British colonial system. But its position in Punjab, and its relationship to the Unionist party, had long been uncertain. Organized in 1907, the Punjab Muslim League had served as a public forum for the expression of Muslim identity by many leading Muslim politicians, including many Unionists. But after Sir Fazli Husain's rejection of alliance with Jinnah in 1936, the All-India Muslim League broke with the Unionists and in Punjab entered a phase of political eclipse. Although Jinnah reorganized the League as an all-India Muslim force, it was slow to establish an independent electoral base in Punjab, particularly in the rural areas. At the elections of 1937 the League captured only two seats in the Punjab assembly and soon lost one of those when Raja Ghazanfar Ali Khan defected to the Unionist party. With only one (urban) seat in the assembly, the Punjab Muslim League became a largely urban clique, centered on the admirers and associates of Sir Muhammad Iqbal.

But in the years after the 1937 elections, the League nevertheless began to play an increasingly important role in Punjab politics—a role that illustrated graphically the cultural contradictions in the position of the Unionist party itself. In fact, the League's increasingly strategic cultural position in the Punjab derived both from the important political position gained by Jinnah in all-India affairs, and, equally important, from the special character of the communal ideology championed by Iqbal. As a leader of increasing all-India influence, Jinnah fought after the 1937 elections to establish his position as spokesman for a Muslim "community" that subsumed Unionists and urban communalists alike. Even more important, Iqbal offered the cultural foundations for redefining the political meaning of Muslim identity within the structure of Punjabi and Indian politics. Indeed, Iqbal's thinking provides the key to an understanding of the League's growing significance in Punjab in the years after 1937.

Iqbal was not primarily a political philosopher, but in rethinking the meaning of Muslim community, his works came to have profound implications for the legitimate cultural definition of Muslim political power in the Punjab. Iqbal came from the urban Muslim communal tradition in Punjab, which defined Muslim community increasingly in the twentieth century as an alternative to colonial authority. Like many urban leaders, Iqbal refused to acknowledge the political legitimacy of an ideology of state power derived from the state's protection of local kinbased identities. Nor did he have much sympathy with the attempts of the British—and the Unionists—to establish religious foundations for their position through association with landed *pirs*. Iqbal denounced these *pirs* in one of his poems as merely pale reflections of the great medieval *sufi* saints, "crows" occupying the "eagles' nests" of Punjab's greatest religious men.[49] He rejected on idealist grounds a political order built on mediation—an order in which the state based its cultural authority, through structures of mediation, on local "tribal" identities. "Blood-relationship is earth-rootedness," he wrote.[50] Punjab's peasants should "break all the idols of tribe and caste," he advised, and search for meaning in life beyond their role as agriculturalist cultivators of the land.[51] Though Iqbal did not deny the importance of descent in local organization, the authority of the state required a broader conception of individual identity. For Iqbal the true realization of Islam—and of a broader Muslim "community"—meant the ultimate rejection of "bloodrelationship as a basis of human unity," and in its place the search "for a purely psychological foundation of human unity."[52]

This suggested a cultural definition of the state's authority that departed markedly from that of the British or the Unionists. But Iqbal's view of the state's authority also differed from that of many Punjabi urban communal leaders in the 1930s. Though Iqbal stressed communal identity as the "living operative factor in my present consciousness," he did not see the public articulation of communal identity as incompatible with the exercise of power within the structure of Punjabi politics. Iqbal had in fact served as a representative in the Punjab Legislative Council and had close personal relations with many Unionist leaders. His career thus contrasted with those of many urban leaders who, in their search for a public "community" identity, had sought to dramatize Islamic identity by attacking other communities in the arenas of urban public life. Though Iqbal often supported a public emphasis on religious symbols, he criticized an exclusively oppositional communalism that isolated its proponents politically and undermined the unifying power of

49. Muhammad Iqbal, "Disciples in Revolt," in *Poems from Iqbal,* trans. V. G. Kiernan (London: John Murray, 1955), 60.
50. Muhammad Iqbal, *The Reconstruction of Religious Thought in Islam* (Lahore: Sh. Muhammad Ashraf, 1971), 146.
51. Iqbal, "To the Punjab Peasant," *Poems from Iqbal,* 56.
52. Iqbal, *The Reconstruction of Religious Thought in Islam,* 146.

Islamic symbols. "There are communalisms and communalisms," Iqbal wrote, and "a community which is inspired by a feeling of ill-will towards other communities is low and ignoble."[53] The key to the political definition of the Muslim community for Iqbal did not lie in competing with others; it lay in expressing the positive heritage shared by all Muslims. The public power of Islamic symbols lay in their ability to direct each individual Muslim to realize his own "ideal nature," as Iqbal put it. Islamic community thus arose not as a marker of the boundaries between Muslims and other groups or as a rejection of local identities but as a critical part of the personal transformation of each individual Muslim. The Muslim community itself, and the ideal Muslim state, served for Iqbal as a symbolic cultural expression of the common striving of Muslims for Islamic fulfillment—a political manifestation of a common heritage and a common mission.

The concern for the Islamic transformation of the individual thus lay at the heart of Iqbal's concerns, shaping his conception of the political meaning of Muslim community as well. In some respects, this concern linked Iqbal's ideas to those of the reformist *'ulama*, a link that Iqbal acknowledged. But the political implications of Iqbal's ideas nevertheless differed significantly from those of the reformist *'ulama*. In a society without a Muslim state, the leading *'ulama* had stressed the importance of individual adherence to the *shari'at* in defining an Islamic community's political existence. But although Iqbal believed strongly in the importance of personal adherence to *shari'at,* he could not accept the political solutions to India's problems that the reformist *'ulama* offered. Faced with an alien colonial state, many *'ulama* had sought to create a society in which, in Iqbal's view, a passive acceptance of the dictates of *shari'at* by the common people, under the *'ulama*'s guidance, would define an Islamic "community." But this view missed, for Iqbal, the significant role of Islam as a transformer of individual Muslims into active instruments of change capable of creating their own political order. "Our modern Ulama do not see," Iqbal wrote, "that the ultimate fate of a people does not depend so much on organization as on the worth of individual men."[54] To rely on the organization of the *'ulama* while shutting off the community from public politics and state authority not only

53. Presidential Address of Dr. Muhammad Iqbal to the Twenty-first Session of the All-India Muslim League, Allahabad, 29–30 December 1930 (Syed Sharifuddin Pirzada, ed., *Foundations of Pakistan: All-India Muslim League Documents, 1906–1947* [Karachi: National Publishing House, 1970], 2:158).
54. Iqbal, *The Reconstruction of Religious Thought in Islam,* 151.

denied the community its full expression but also denied individuals the opportunity to reach their full potential.

The political answer for Muslims thus lay elsewhere, in a political system that would direct people's attention away from the everyday conflicts of the colonial system, based on "earth-bound" local identities, and toward the search for Muslim unity. Iqbal did not deny the importance of local politics or of local factions in the everyday operation of the political system. But the cultural definition of the state's authority depended on the definition of a Muslim community grounded in the Islamic self-awareness and active commitment of each individual. It depended on symbols; but it depended also on political leaders able to step outside the bounds of everyday political conflicts. In Jinnah, who headed the Muslim League, Iqbal saw a leader whose single-minded commitment to the political interests of the community seemed to point Muslims in the right direction. "The only effective power . . . that counteracts the forces of decay in a people is the rearing of self-concentrated individuals," Iqbal declared.[55] Jinnah was certainly not the self-aware Muslim of Iqbal's imagination. But his leadership of the All-India Muslim League focused Muslim politics toward the larger issue of Muslim political survival in India as a whole.

In 1936 Iqbal thus threw his support behind Jinnah's political leadership. This did not mean that Jinnah's leadership completely fulfilled Iqbal's religious vision. Disputes between the two leaders were numerous, particularly in the last year before Iqbal's death in April 1938. Nevertheless, Jinnah proved extraordinarily effective in establishing the League after 1937 as a symbol of Islamic unity; and this won Iqbal's strong backing. In the months after the 1937 election, Jinnah stressed Muslim unity above all else, rallying Muslims of all types in his struggles to maintain a significant Muslim presence in the face of growing Congress domination of all-India politics. Despite the Muslim League's loss to the Unionists in the elections of 1937, Jinnah was able to win the support after the elections even of leading Punjabi Unionists who recognized Jinnah as a spokesman for the interests of the Muslim "community" in all-India affairs. Such support came from Sir Sikander's closest lieutenants. As Ahmad Yar Khan Daultana wrote to Jinnah in May 1937, "Despite our party commitments you may well regard all Unionist Muslims as Muslim Leaguers for purposes of your all-India policy. The Punjab Muslims will unanimously support you in your brave fight

55. Ibid.

against the Congress onslaught on Muslim safeguards."[56] Whatever his religious shortcomings, Jinnah seemed to translate Iqbal's conception of an active, "self-concentrated" commitment to Muslim unity and Muslim interests into political terms, transcending even the political divisions of the Punjab.

But the implications of Jinnah's commitment for concrete political organization remained uncertain. The Unionists still firmly controlled the politics of rural Punjab. Even as he tried to keep the League above local political divisions, Jinnah thus sought to link the League at the all-India level with the protection of Muslim symbols, in order to underscore the League's identification with the interests of a broader Muslim community. Perhaps no issue indicated this more clearly in 1937 than Jinnah's championing the implementation of *shari'at*, an issue long of central concern to religious reformers, and a central symbol of Muslim "community" identity. For even Iqbal, the implementation of *shari'at* had occupied a central place in the definition of Islamic unity, for it symbolized the link between individual Islamic transformation and the definition of an Islamic foundation for the state's authority.[57] But the issue was also one of deep potential political division in Punjab. Supremacy of the *shari'at* meant in practice the supersession of the customary law and thus the undermining of the social and political basis of the Land Alienation Act. The issue in fact illustrated how difficult it was to separate the symbolic definition of the principles defining the state from the local organization of Unionist political power.

The political controversy surrounding the introduction of *shari'at* in Punjab first crystallized in the early 1930s with the introduction in the Punjab Council of a bill to replace customary law by the *shari'at* in all matters involving succession, family law, etc. This measure, introduced by a Lahore Arain, Malik Muhammad Din, was strongly supported by the *'ulama* and by much of the urban population of Punjab as well.[58] But as the government discovered, reactions in the rural areas differed. Though several local officers noted an increasing tendency with education for rural families to give up their adherence to customary law in favor of the *shari'at*, particularly with regard to inheritance by daugh-

---

56. Ahmad Yar Khan Daultana to Jinnah, 8 May 1937 (Quaid-i-Azam [Muhammad Ali Jinnah] papers, Islamabad, file 255).

57. Iqbal discusses the *shari'at* and Muslim unity (and ending Muslim poverty) in his letter to Jinnah, 28 May 1937 (Muhammad Ali Jinnah, ed., *Letters of Iqbal to Jinnah* [Lahore: Sh. Muhammad Ashraf, 1968], 17–19).

58. Malik Muhammad Din claimed that *'ulama* of all persuasions supported it (Punjab Archives, Home Judicial, October 1936, file 20).

ters,[59] Muslim agriculturalists still generally opposed the measure. Many feared that the rules of the *shari'at* in regard to female succession would fragment landholdings and undermine the protection offered by the Land Alienation Act. "By the Customary Law the property acquired by a common ancestor remains intact in the family or tribe," the deputy commissioner of Gurdaspur noted in explaining rural Muslim opposition, "and is protected by the Land Alienation Act. To this the Muslim agriculturalists attach very great importance."[60] If the *shari'at* were introduced, however, their situation would be undermined. As Sardar Muhammad Shahbaz Khan of Kasur noted warily, "Strangers will freely intermix, and their presence would lead to the disruption of tribes."[61]

Such concerns set the terms of the debate on the *shari'at* in Punjab well before Jinnah took up the issue. Few rural Muslims were willing to oppose the *shari'at* openly, for "nobody would stand the stigma of opposing the introduction of law sanctioned and sanctified by the Holy Quran."[62] But this did not prevent widespread yet quiet support for custom. As Nawab Fazl Ali of Gujrat argued in justifying his support, the zamindars of Punjab, had, by their widespread acceptance of tribal custom, already given it "the sanctity of the will according to the Shariat." Chaudhri Bahawal Bakhsh, a prominent Jat leader of Gujrat, declared in supporting custom that "most Muslim religious leaders being themselves zamindars have been following . . . custom."[63] This was doubtless an exaggeration; even among rural religious leaders there had been many, particularly among the revival *pir*s, who had long emphasized the importance of adherence to the *shari'at*. But that many religious leaders did support custom was indicated by opinions on Malik Muhammad Din's bill from Multan, where the deputy commissioner re-

59. Statement of Edward Sheepshanks, commissioner, Multan (ibid.).
60. Note by the deputy commissioner, Gurdaspur (ibid.).
61. Note by Khan Bahadur Sardar Muhammad Shahbaz Khan, honorary magistrate, Kasur. His remarks concerned the effects of the *shari'at* on Muslim marriage patterns (discussed in chapter 1). Where Muslims married their cousins, the social effect of succession by daughters would have been relatively small. But where Muslims married outside the family, the introduction of *shari'at* inheritance rules would have been far more disruptive. "The bill for such people is impracticable," a Lahore *zaildar* suggested, adding that education and propaganda might lead to more intrafamily Muslim marriages (ibid.). For further discussion of these issues, see David Gilmartin, "Women, Kinship, and Politics in Twentieth-Century Punjab," in Gail Minault, ed., *The Extended Family: Women and Political Participation in India and Pakistan* (Columbia, Mo.: South Asia Books, 1981), 251–73.
62. Statement of M. Sultan Bakhsh, *tehsildar,* Gujrat (Punjab Archives, Home Judicial, October 1936, file 20).
63. Views of Khan Bahadur Chaudhri Fazal Ali, OBE, MLC, and views of Chaudhri Bahawal Bakhsh, *zaildar,* Mangowal and president, Zamindara League, Gujrat (ibid.).

ported several important *pirs* in opposition.[64] Perhaps most important, however, direct opposition came also from many leaders of the Unionist party itself, who feared that the Islamic law would undermine the structure of rural authority on which the rural administration—and their own power—rested. As the secretary to the governor wrote in summing up such objections: "The Governor in Council considers that the bill is dangerous to the general economic structure of the province as a whole."[65] And, he might well have added, to the ideological structure of the colonial system as well.

Positions in Punjab were thus clearly drawn when a Shariat Application Bill was introduced into the Central Legislative Assembly in 1936, and Jinnah took up the issue.[66] The central Shariat Application Bill produced many of the concerns that had been expressed earlier in the Punjab. In submitting its views to the government of India, the Punjab government admitted that a majority of the Punjabi Muslims consulted in 1936 and 1937 had actually expressed support for the bill; but, they argued, if allowances were made for Muslims' uneasiness at openly opposing the *shari'at,* then the sense of rural Punjabi opinion was definitely against it. As Lahore High Court Justice Din Muhammad, who privately favored the bill, put it, the rural leaders of Punjab remained wary of the *shari'at* because "they thought that it would cut at the root of the system under which they were living."[67]

In fact, the character of the 1937 bill as it finally emerged for debate differed in some critical respects from the Punjab bill that had failed in the early 1930s. The 1937 bill excluded succession to agricultural land, as that subject was reserved under the 1935 Government of India Act for provincial legislation. This limitation alone undercut many of the most serious rural Punjabi objections. The central government nevertheless remained wary of the bill and, probably with the situation in the Punjab in mind, pressed unsuccessfully in select committee for a statement that Muslim law would not, under the bill, be allowed to override provincial statutes.[68] Despite the exclusion of agricultural property, the government feared that the bill would force the hands of provincial governments on local legislation dealing with agricultural property. When the

64. Note by the deputy commissioner, Multan (ibid.).
65. S. L. Sale, secretary to Government of Punjab, Legislative Department (ibid.).
66. Mohammad Jafar, I. A. Rahman, and Ghani Jafar, eds., *Jinnah as a Parliamentarian* (Islamabad: Azfar Associates, 1977), 299.
67. Views of Justice Din Muhammad (NAI, Home Judicial, file 36/17/35).
68. Summary of government attitude to Shariat Application bill, R. F. Mudie, 2 September 1937 (ibid.).

bill emerged for debate in late 1937, the position of its supporters remained a difficult one. It was in this atmosphere that "a meeting of the Muslim members of the Assembly was held and it was decided that Mr. Jinnah should be asked to pilot the Bill" through the house.[69]

As a master of legislative maneuver, Jinnah was at his best in such circumstances. His essential strategy was to compromise wherever necessary to broaden the bill's support. But underlying his compromises was a concern to maintain the symbolic significance of the bill as it affected all of India's Muslims. Indeed, the key to Jinnah's ultimate success in leading the bill through the assembly was his realization that, given the state of Muslim politics and his own concern for Muslim political unity, the details of the bill and the controversies surrounding them were less important than the symbolic value of the bill as an expression of the common "communal" identity of all of India's Muslims. To forestall objections to the bill, he thus pushed through several amendments that went even beyond the exclusion of agricultural land in limiting the measure's scope.[70] But at the same time he fought hard against another amendment that threatened to compromise the symbolic significance of the bill by striking the term *shari'at* itself from the bill on the grounds that the term was interpreted differently by different groups of Muslims. Though removal of *shari'at* and reliance on the words "Muslim personal law," would have made little practical difference in the working of the bill, Jinnah realized that "if the word '*shari'at*' was not there, the great sentimental appeal of the bill to the Muslims of India would be missed."[71]

In fact, Jinnah's political strategy on the *shari'at* bill hardly pleased everyone; some religious leaders objected strenuously to his compromises. But despite their misgivings, Jinnah was able to bring with him the great majority of Muslim political leaders, who saw in the passage of a *shari'at* bill a commitment to Islam that transcended the divisive political debates previously clouding the issue of commitment to the *shari'at*.[72] Among even Unionist Muslims, few felt comfortable about opposing the *shari'at* in public debate; Jinnah's strategy offered a welcome opportunity to express commitment to Islam and to the Muslim

69. Jafar, Rahman, and Jafar, *Jinnah as a Parliamentarian*, 301.
70. The most important compromise made the use of *shari'at* optional in adoptions, wills, and legacies for Muslims who had not previously followed it (Note by R. F. Mudie, 11 September 1937 [NAI, Home Judicial, file 36/17/35]).
71. Jafar, Rahman, and Jafar, *Jinnah as a Parliamentarian*, 303.
72. This point of view was articulated by Shaikh Fazl-i-Haq Piracha of Bhera (ibid., 308).

community in the public arena, whatever the local problems with implementing *shari'at*. The passage of the Shariat Application Act of 1937 thus underscored the growing political importance of Jinnah's position. Despite all the compromises and limitations, the result of his efforts was the first *shari'at* act in history that in principle covered all of India's Muslims.

The *shari'at* act's political implications were thus considerable, however limited its practical significance.[73] In pushing the measure through, Jinnah had bridged on a symbolic level the divide that had long separated those urban Punjabis who were concerned with the definition of an ideology of Muslim political solidarity from those rural leaders who controlled the political allegiances of the great majority of Punjabi Muslims. By emphasizing the significance of the *shari'at* as a symbol of solidarity, Jinnah took a concern that was at the center of radical communal thinking and detached it from the specific content that had long made urban communal ideology anathema to many rural leaders. Although not directly challenging the local roots of rural power, Jinnah suggested that there was, even for rural Muslims, a higher "communal" loyalty connected to their individual identities as Muslims.

Not surprisingly, the sharpest and most emotional critics of Jinnah's stand were those to whom the content of the *shari'at* was everything—the reformist *'ulama*. As religious leaders, they saw in the achievement of Muslim unity at the expense of the religious content of Muslim ideology a mockery of the ideals they stood for. Jinnah and the Muslim League had, for them, betrayed the *shari'at;* as Maulana Husain Ahmad Madani later wrote, they had "caused the failure of the *shari'at* bill which in its importance and necessity for the Muslim religion and the Muslims needs no arguments."[74] Among the reformist *'ulama* of the Jami'at-i 'Ulama-yi Hind the *shari'at* act's passage heightened a long-growing distrust of Jinnah. But although Jinnah's position alienated many leaders of the reformist *'ulama,* it hardly isolated him completely from the urban reformist tradition. He was still involved, despite his compromises, in defining a base for Muslim solidarity independent of the ideological foundations of the administration and the colonial state. Many Muslims took exception to the specifics of Jinnah's strategy, yet

73. After 1937, efforts failed to extend its practical scope in the Punjab; Baji Rashida Latif and K. L. Gauba introduced bills in the Punjab Legislative Assembly to apply the *shari'at* to the inheritance of agricultural land but gained little support (Punjab Archives, Home Judicial, B procs., 1939, file 499).

74. Maulana Husain Ahmad Madani, *An Open Letter to the Moslem League* (Lahore: Dewan's Publications, 1946), 62.

his identification with the *shari'at* act's passage left him at the center of the struggle for Muslim communal unity and identity, a man identified with no side in Punjab politics, but with the "community" itself.

The results of Jinnah's compromises for the evolution of Punjabi politics were nevertheless ambiguous. Though Jinnah's compromise on the *shari'at* pointed the way toward the definition of a symbolic commitment to Muslim unity, Jinnah's growing importance in Punjab politics led in practice to heightened controversy over the structure of Muslim League organization in the province—and over its relationship to the Unionist party. As the League gained increasing importance in Punjab after 1937, League politics produced a series of conflicts that focused on Jinnah, Sir Sikander, and Iqbal, who held differing views as to precisely how the Muslim League should function. Such controversies reflected the fact that the League had begun to achieve a position in Punjab as a touchstone of Muslim community, even for Sir Sikander and the Unionist party.

THE SIKANDER-JINNAH PACT

In a startling move in late 1937 shortly after the Shariat act's passage, Jinnah steered the League in Punjab onto a new organizational tack. To bring the League new organizational strength, he announced, at the annual Lucknow session of the Muslim League in October, the signing of a pact with Sir Sikander, which was intended to unite the Unionist party and the Muslim League into a single organization. Though this move caught many Punjab Leaguers unprepared, the alliance was in keeping with Jinnah's intent to make the League a symbol of Muslim unity and grew naturally from his policies in the previous year. For Sir Sikander as well, the pact grew from a long search to strengthen Unionist power; by linking himself directly to Jinnah and the League, he sought to tie the Unionist party to a political symbol of Muslim community that would legitimize Unionist authority.

In spite of its common significance for Jinnah and Sikander, however, the pact produced almost immediate confusion and controversy. Whatever the pact's cultural implications, Sikander's first political concern was to maintain the mediatory structure of Unionist power. In the promised amalgamation of Unionist and League organizations, Sikander saw an opportunity to bolster the Unionists' position. But for many of Jinnah's supporters in Punjab, including Iqbal and his urban followers, the incorporation of the Unionists into the Muslim League was part of an expected transformation of the politics of the province. Their conception of the ultimate aim of the pact was thus far different from that of Sir Sikander.

Whether either Jinnah or Sikander in fact realized the implications of the pact when they signed it is doubtful.[75] But conflicting interpretations arose almost immediately. Some urban League leaders initially welcomed the pact as the Unionists' acknowledgment of the League's organizational supremacy.[76] But they soon voiced concern about the practical impact of an influx of Unionist leaders into the League organization. To many it appeared that Sikander had signed the pact to immobilize the provincial Muslim League and shore up the Unionists' position. Iqbal wrote to Jinnah in mid-November, "After having several talks with Sir Sikander and his friends, I am now definitely of the opinion that Sir Sikander wants nothing less than the complete control of the League and provincial Parliamentary Board."[77] That Sir Sikander and his Unionist supporters should now be given some role in the affairs of the Punjab League was accepted by all. Jinnah, in fact, wrote to the sole original Muslim League representative in the Punjab assembly, Malik Barkat Ali, pointing out that new members of the League were as good as old. But Barkat Ali objected that the Unionists were not really interested in contributing to the League organization; they wanted to control the League to make it "a subordinate body to the Unionist Party."[78] "I see no harm in giving him [Sir Sikander] the majority that he wants," Iqbal wrote to Jinnah of the Unionists' demand for control of the Punjab Muslim League parliamentary board, "but he goes beyond the pact when he wants a complete change in the office-holders. . . . He also wishes that the finances of the League should be controlled by his men. All this to my mind amounts to capturing of the League and then killing it."[79]

Such conflicts, as they developed in the wake of the Sikander-Jinnah pact, put Jinnah in an extremely difficult position. His concern in forging the pact had been to develop a broad-based Muslim front, with support in both urban and rural areas, that would give substance to his

75. The governor, Sir Herbert Emerson, noted immediately afterward: "I am not sure at the moment whether the views of Sikander and Jinnah coincide as to what was or was not agreed upon" (Emerson to Linlithgow, 21 October 1937 [IOL, L/P&J/5/238]).
76. Afzal, *Malik Barkat Ali*, 41–42.
77. Iqbal to Jinnah, 10 November 1937 (Jinnah, *Letters of Iqbal to Jinnah*, 31).
78. Malik Barkat Ali to Jinnah, 3 December 1937 (Quaid-i-Azam papers, file 215).
79. Iqbal to Jinnah, 10 November 1937 (Jinnah, *Letters of Iqbal to Jinnah*, 31–32). The conflict over the Sikander-Jinnah pact is detailed in Ashiq Husain Batalvi, *Iqbal ke Akhiri Do Sal* (Karachi: Iqbal Akademi, 1969), 497–590.

claim that the League was a fully representative Muslim organization. In no way, however, could he eliminate overnight the deep-seated differences between urban and rural Muslim ideas concerning the nature of Muslim political organization. Though it was an exaggeration to say, as Iqbal had, that Sir Sikander and his supporters wanted to kill the local League organization, their conception of the political role of the League was completely different from that of urban League supporters like Iqbal. Sir Sikander was interested in the League as an organized expression of Muslim political solidarity; but he envisioned it as operating solidly within the confines of rural political authority. The League was not, for him, a primary focus of political loyalty for Muslims, but rather a secondary focus for those whose primary political loyalties were determined by their position as agriculturalists in the localities. As in Unionist efforts to control Muslim *auqaf,* Sikander wanted to control the League in order to defuse a threat to Unionist power from those who defined a direct political commitment to Islamic symbols.

To leaders like Iqbal, however, Sikander's actions after his return from Lucknow only confirmed their worst fears about Unionist plans to turn the League to Unionist ends. Sikander's first move after sealing his pact with Jinnah was not to form local branches of the League, as Jinnah had requested, but rather to use the pact to resurrect the Zamindara League, an organization whose primary aim, in the words of a resolution passed at an October 1937 meeting of zamindars, was to protect the "legitimate interests" of "the owners of land."[80] Local Unionist supporters were instructed to form Muslim League branches only after local Zamindara League branches had been successfully launched. As the Unionist resident secretary wrote in late October 1937 in explaining this policy to one local Unionist leader:

> After the Zamindara League is founded . . . in your ilaqa, you will then proceed at once to constitute the local Muslim League consisting of the Muslim members of the local Zamindara League. I hope I have been able to make myself clear that we have to constitute and then run side by side
>
> (a) Zamindara League, consisting of Zamindars of all communities
> (b) Muslim League, of course consisting of Muslims only.[81]

80. Proceedings of a meeting of two hundred zamindars held at Mamdot Villa, Lahore, 24 October 1937 (Nawab Muhammad Ahmad Khan Qasuri papers, Lahore). The proceedings, and a list of sixty-nine Zamindara League contributors, are also in Unionist party papers, file Z-1.
81. Afzal Ali Hasnie, resident secretary, Unionist party, to Mohammad Ahmad Khan Qasuri, 27 October 1937 (M. A. Khan Qasuri papers).

This was hardly the Muslim League organization that urban leaders had envisioned; they viewed these tactics as almost wholly obstructive. In reporting to Jinnah in November on the Punjabi situation, Iqbal castigated the Unionists for failure to sign the League creed and to hold a League session in the province, observing that "my impression is that they want to gain time for their own Zamindara League to function."[82]

The emphasis on the Zamindara League was only one part, however, of the Unionists' strategy to use the League to solidify their position, channeling Muslim communal concerns through the League organization without upsetting the structure of their rural political control. In organizing League branches, for example, Unionist leaders were particularly concerned that a hierarchy of authority be developed in which urban and rural League branches would be kept strictly separate. As Mir Maqbul Mahmud wrote to Jinnah in December 1937, "We are agreed on the desirability of creating solidarity and unity among Muslims." But this could be done only if the organizational relationship of district and city Leagues were clearly defined. Our workers "demand and with reason," he wrote, "the right of local tehsil organization with subsidiary branches in the rural areas working side by side with but not under the control of the city branches or urban membership."[83] Unionists intended to isolate local rural branches of the League from urban Muslim influence, to keep the League from spreading urban reformist ideas of Muslim solidarity into the countryside. At the same time, by controlling the provincial League leadership at the top of a hierarchy of both urban and rural branches, Unionist leaders hoped to use the League organization as an institutional lever to bolster their political control and cultural authority.

The consummation of this scheme by the Unionists was facilitated, to the chagrin of Iqbal and his supporters, by Jinnah's attitude in the months after the signing of the pact. Jinnah may not have approved of the Unionists' plan for League organization, but he apparently did nothing to stop the Unionists' efforts to implement it. Malik Barkat Ali objected strenuously and, right up to his death in April 1938, so did Iqbal. In November 1937 the secretary of the old Punjab Muslim League, Mian Ghulam Rasul Khan, writing on the instructions of Iqbal, objected to the very idea of reorganizing the League in Punjab since "already the Provincial League exists and we are forming District, Tehsil

82. Iqbal to Jinnah, 10 November 1937 (Jinnah, *Letters of Iqbal to Jinnah*, 32).
83. Mir Maqbul Mahmud to Jinnah, 29 December 1937 (Quaid-i-Azam papers, file 1091).

and village branches." When Jinnah insisted that all provincial Leagues reorganize and reapply for affiliation with the central League,[84] the old Punjab League complied, applying for new affiliation and submitting a list of officeholders, with Iqbal as official "patron." Its application for affiliation was rejected, however, on the grounds of technical violations of the All-India Muslim League constitution. According to Mian Ghulam Rasul Khan, the rejection caused "bitter resentment in the province."[85] When Barkat Ali and his associates took a revised application for affiliation to the April 1938 special session of the League at Calcutta, it too was rebuffed. Jinnah subsequently illustrated his intent by appointing a new Punjab Muslim League organizing committee, dominated not by the urban supporters of Iqbal, but by the nominees of Sir Sikander. Mian Ghulam Rasul Khan objected: Sikander and his supporters had not yet signed official Muslim League membership forms; they belonged to no local League branches and had no standing to take over the organization of the League. Jinnah was unimpressed.[86] For Jinnah, technicalities of League organization were less important than the overall pattern of broad-based League support. In 1938 he made whatever compromises were necessary to achieve this pattern.

Jinnah's support opened the door, however, for the Unionists to use the League organization to bolster their local political control. The leverage the Unionists had gained in communal affairs after the Sikander-Jinnah pact emerged most dramatically in urban politics, where the Unionists had traditionally exercised limited control. New Unionist leverage was in fact evident almost immediately after the Calcutta League session in a by-election for what had always been a center of reformist religious influence in the Punjab, the volatile Amritsar urban Muslim assembly constituency. This seat had been left vacant in 1938 by the voiding, on an election petition, of the 1937 election of Saif-ud-din Kitchlew, a Kashmiri radical and Unionist critic. The contest in the by-election was between Kitchlew, who stood on the Congress ticket;

84. Ghulam Rasul Khan to Jinnah, November 1937, in Ghulam Rasul Khan, *The Punjab Provincial Muslim League: Its Past and Present Position* (Lahore: Punjab Provincial Muslim League?, 1939?), 8. The new All-India Muslim League constitution adopted at Lucknow set out terms of affiliation (Jinnah to provincial Muslim Leagues, 12 February 1938, in ibid., 33–34).

85. Ghulam Rasul Khan to honorary secretary, All-India Muslim League, 12 March 1938 (Muslim League papers, Karachi University, vol. 131); Ghulam Rasul Khan to honorary secretary, All-India Muslim League, 15 April 1938 (ibid.).

86. For a list of the members of the new organizing committee, and the objections of Ghulam Rasul Khan, see Ghulam Rasul Khan, *The Punjab Provincial Muslim League*, 15–16.

Chaudhri Afzal Haq, a leader of the Ahrar party; and Shaikh Muhammad Sadiq, the Kashmiri *ra'is* defeated on the Unionist ticket by Kitchlew in 1937. His defeat had shown the Unionist party's weakness in Amritsar; his Unionist ties had made him a target for Kitchlew's supporters, who pictured him as a traitor to the cause of Muslim unity.[87] In the 1938 by-election, the situation was reversed. As conflict between the Muslim League and the Congress rose at the all-India level, it was now Kitchlew who was attacked for his failure to support Muslim unity at the center.[88]

In the election the Unionists threw their support behind Shaikh Muhammad Sadiq, but they were now able to back this support with an endorsement in the name of the Muslim League. The Unionist ministry's right to issue a Muslim League endorsement was hotly disputed by the urban Muslim League group led by Malik Barkat Ali. Though their claims for recognition as the official Punjab Muslim League had been rejected by Jinnah at Calcutta, they contested strongly the basis for Sir Sikander's offering such an endorsement. Since "there is no affiliated branch of the All-India Muslim League in this province," they argued, no League endorsement at all could be made.[89] But this protest did not stop Unionist leaders from using their position on the new Muslim League organizing committee to endorse Shaikh Muhammad Sadiq or stop Jinnah from wiring his support in response to a request from Muhammad Sadiq.[90] With such help, Shaikh Muhammad Sadiq reversed the 1937 election results, capturing the seat for the Unionists and leaving the old Muslim Leaguers around Malik Barkat Ali completely isolated.

Subsequent by-elections reinforced the value of association with the Muslim League in giving the Unionists influence in urban Muslim affairs.[91] The Unionists could not dictate the election of urban candidates, for commitment to the interests of the Muslim "community" remained a central criterion for urban election. But since they controlled the

87. Election petition case, Sheikh Muhammad Sadiq vs. Dr. Saif-ud-Din Kitchlew (Punjab, *Gazette,* pt. 1 [18 March 1938], 357).

88. Election petition case, Mohammad Zakria Kitchlew vs. Sheikh Mohammad Sadiq (ibid., [21 July 1939], 998–1034).

89. Resolution of Punjab Muslim League parliamentary board, 11 May 1938 (ibid., 1001).

90. Jinnah initially wired his endorsement by mistake to Shaikh Sadiq Hasan, Muhammad Sadiq's brother, but soon corrected his error (ibid., 1002).

91. For example, the Unionist–Muslim League candidate, Shaikh Muhammad Amin, won a Multan Division Towns (Muhammadan) by-election in October 1938 despite the opposition of Malik Barkat Ali and the urban Muslim League group.

provincial Muslim League and had Jinnah's support, Unionist leaders
exerted influence to see that candidates acceptable to them, urban *ra'is*
like Shaikh Muhammad Sadiq, were elected. Unionist control so galled
Malik Barkat Ali and his supporters that they pleaded with Jinnah:
"The Muslims of the city are anti-Unionist," Barkat Ali wrote to Jinnah
in regard to a 1941 Lahore city by-election; but "in order to silence their
opposition the name of the League will be used. . . . Please," he im-
plored, "see that the name of the League is not used in future by Sir
Sikander for getting his nominee returned from the urban areas."[92] In
this instance Jinnah was not unsympathetic to Malik Barkat Ali's pleas;
he refused to give his open approval to the Unionist nominee, the
wealthy Lahore Kashmiri *biradari* leader, Mian Amiruddin.[93] But he
also refused to block the selection, which would have meant overturning
the decision of the officially constituted, Unionist-dominated provincial
Muslim League organization. In these circumstances, Mian Amiruddin's electoral victory only marked the political leverage that the Unionists had gained.

SIR SIKANDER AND PAKISTAN

In the wake of the Sikander-Jinnah pact, Sir Sikander had thus scored
a remarkable political coup. Indeed, with Jinnah's help he was able to
use the Muslim League to secure symbolic legitimacy of the sort he had
long sought. But if the Punjab League had paid a high price for the pact,
so had Sikander. As the conflict between Sikander and urban Punjabis
intensified, Jinnah firmly established his own position—and that of the
All-India Muslim League—as a moral presence in Muslim politics that
Sir Sikander could not challenge. As the expression of Muslim "community" became the touchstone of political legitimacy for state power, the
pact made clear that Jinnah, not Sikander, was power's final cultural
arbiter.

In fact, nothing symbolized Jinnah's growing power more clearly
than the emergence in the late 1930s of the League's demand for "Pakistan," a state that would embody a Muslim "communal" identity. The
concept of a separate Muslim state in northwestern India had first been
enunciated by Iqbal in his presidential address to the League's annual

92. Malik Barkat Ali to Jinnah, 8 August 1941 (Rizwan Ahmad, comp., *The Quaid-e-
Azam Papers, 1941–42* [Karachi: East & West Publishing Company, 1976], 91–93).
93. On this incident, see Ashiq Husain Batalvi, *Hamari Qaumi Jadd-o-Jahd* vol. 3:
Janwari 1940 se Disambar 1942 tak (Model Town: Major Altaf Husain, 1975), 81–93.

session in December 1930—well before Jinnah's pact with Sir Sikander. "The life of Islam as a cultural force in this living country," Iqbal had stated, "very largely depends on its centralization in a specified territory."[94] This concept was further elaborated by a Muslim student in England, Chaudhri Rehmat Ali, who coined the term *Pakistan* itself. But for Jinnah the demand for Pakistan took on in the late 1930s an important symbolic meaning, which grew directly from his efforts to define a cultural foundation for Muslim power during the years of the Sikander-Jinnah pact. His commitment to Pakistan followed logically from the principles on which the pact with Sikander was based.

Pakistan signified for Jinnah the concept of a community that transcended the political structure of society. Jinnah remained of course much concerned with manipulating local political structures in Punjab to build support for the League, as his pact with Sikander made clear. But his symbolic political identification of the community with "Pakistan" revealed his view of the Muslim community not as an organized competitor for power within the colonial system but rather as a political entity standing above the organization of society. The definition of the community in such a conception did not depend on the precise organization of society—or on the structure of power—but on the significance of the state as a symbolic political expression of Muslims' common Islamic identity. As one of Jinnah's supporters said, the true "Pakistan" would be one "whose citizens would have the right to declare: 'We are the State.'"[95] By supporting such a conception of Muslim "community," Jinnah underscored his position as a political spokesman for the community transcending local divisions, even as he maneuvered to build up local support for the Muslim League's political position.

Though this carried obvious implications for the Unionists' position, such implications were not all immediately clear—largely because the Pakistan concept was vague. In fact, the conception of community embodied by "Pakistan" initially attracted the Unionists. Identification with Pakistan promised on one level to underscore Sir Sikander's political identification with the Muslim "community" without at the same time threatening the party's local structure. Using his substantial influence within the Muslim League organization, Sikander tried to guaran-

94. Presidential Address of Dr. Muhammad Iqbal to the Twenty-first Session of the All-India Muslim League, Allahabad, 29–30 December 1930 (Pirzada, *Foundations of Pakistan*, 2:159).
95. F. K. Khan Durrani, *The Meaning of Pakistan* (1944; reprint, Lahore: Islamic Book Service, 1983), 118.

tee that any official definition of Pakistan in the late 1930s would be
consistent with Unionist interests and with the structure of Unionist
power. When Jinnah appointed a Muslim League committee in March
1939 to examine potential separatist schemes,[96] Sir Sikander—himself a
member of the committee—was among the first to submit a plan.
Though it did not specifically mention the term "Pakistan," Sikander's
scheme called for a loose federation of India's provinces and states into
seven zones, to be combined in turn into a loose all-India federal system.
The plan was intended to safeguard Muslim interests at the center and
maintain Muslim power in the northwestern zone where Punjabi Muslims (and the Unionists) would predominate.[97] Nor was this the only
plan that suggested Unionist influence. Nawab Sir Muhammad Shah
Nawaz Khan of Mamdot, the president of the (Unionist-controlled)
Punjab Muslim League and a large landlord of Ferozepore district, financed the publication of another scheme calling for a confederacy of
zones in India—a scheme that stressed far more strongly the cultural
justification for a separate Muslim zone in northwest India (called "In-
dusstan"), with its own distinctive national identity.[98] Both schemes illustrated the Unionists' desire to legitimize their position by association
with Pakistan and at the same time to maintain the local foundations of
their power.

But Pakistan's long-range implications for the Unionist position were
in some respects far more disturbing. Articulating the concept challenged the ideology of integration on which the Unionists had built their
provincial control in the Punjab. It implied a theoretically different relationship between the state and society—one that promised to undercut
Sikander's relationship with the local rural magnates on whom the
Unionists relied for support.

Nothing indicated this more clearly than the debate over the Muslim
League's 1940 Lahore resolution, which transformed the call for a separate Muslim state (or states) into official League policy. As premier of
the Punjab, Sir Sikander played an important role in organizing the
1940 League session and joined with Jinnah in initially drafting the
resolution that articulated the Pakistan demand.[99] But as discussion pro-

96. Pirzada, *Foundations of Pakistan*, 2:xx–xxi.
97. Sir Sikander's scheme, published in July 1939, is reprinted in Rezaul Karim, *Pakisthan Examined* (Calcutta: Book Company, 1941), 131–47.
98. "A Punjabi," *Confederacy of India* (Lahore: Nawab Sir Muhammad Shah Nawaz
Khan of Mamdot, 1939), attributed to Mian Kifayat Ali.
99. Later, Sikander argued that he had little impact on the final resolution (Syed
Sharifuddin Pirzada, *The Pakistan Resolution and the Historic Lahore Session* [Karachi:
Pakistan Publications, 1968], 13).

gressed, Jinnah laid out a concept of individual Muslim "nationality" that seemed to clash with the principles of state authority underlying the Unionist position. Jinnah now grounded his demand for Pakistan on the "two-nation theory," the idea that all Muslims of India shared a common history and culture that defined them as members of a separate "nation." Though his actions showed the continuing significance of local loyalties in the actual working of Muslim politics, his language repudiated any other than Muslim identity in defining the state. Drawing on the thinking of urban Muslims, Jinnah in fact rejected outright the idea that political unity could be created by a hierarchy of mediation that linked local "communities" through an imposed political structure. The state, Jinnah said, could not create a nation merely by subjecting the people "to a democratic constitution and holding them forcibly together by the unnatural and artificial methods of British Parliamentary Statutes." [100]

Couched in these terms, Jinnah's championing of Pakistan put Sikander increasingly on the defensive, for it crystallized the dilemma Sikander and the Unionists faced in reconciling a claim to speak for the Muslim "community" with a structure of state authority that was a product of the colonial regime. Indeed, in the years after 1940 Sir Sikander faced a growing challenge in maintaining simultaneously a place of influence within the League and the authority of the Unionist party within Punjab. Responding to the Lahore resolution, Sikander attempted in early 1941 to convince the Muslim League working committee to abandon the term "Pakistan," which was not in the resolution's original language, to free himself to interpret the League's policy consistently with Unionist interests. [101] But his efforts failed; he found himself in an increasingly difficult position. To show his support for Pakistan, he accepted an invitation to preside over a "Pakistan Conference" organized by Muslim students at Lyallpur in May 1941. There, he emphasized only the vagueness of the Pakistan idea; the term, he noted, could be applied to a large number of widely different schemes, including, presumably, his own. "Which Pakistan [do] you mean or want?" he asked the students. [102] What the students wanted was an unambiguous state-

100. Jinnah's speech is published in Pirzada, *Foundations of Pakistan*, 2:327–39. For an analysis of Jinnah's language, derived in part from Mian Bashir Ahmad, see R. J. Moore, "Jinnah and the Pakistan Demand," *Modern Asian Studies* 17, no. 4 (1983): 544–46.
101. H. D. Craik to Linlithgow, 4 March 1941 (Linlithgow papers, vol. 90).
102. According to Malik Barkat Ali, Sikander attacked Jinnah strongly: "'I, Sir Sikander, may be a sinner but I say my prayers regularly. Your Qaid-i-Azam does not say even a single prayer in the day'"; it was, Barkat Ali concluded, "simply an unspeakable

ment of commitment to the concept. Sikander's public speeches on Pakistan were, as one local League supporter put it, "half-way in and half-way out."[103] Occasionally Sikander and his colleagues reacted to the political threat of pro-Pakistan propaganda by actively discouraging public discussion of Pakistan, particularly in rural Punjab.[104] But for political reasons, they did not dare to repudiate the concept. Sikander's defense of his position in the Punjab Assembly in March 1941 provides clear evidence of this ambivalence. "If Pakistan means unalloyed Muslim raj in the Punjab then I will have nothing to do with it," he said. "Punjab is Punjab and will always remain Punjab whatever anybody may say." To say otherwise would be to undermine the foundations of Unionist power. But having said this, he reaffirmed his support of the Lahore resolution. When Barkat Ali declared, "The Lahore resolution says the same thing," Sikander's reply was quick and telling: "Exactly; then why misinterpret it and try to mislead the masses?"[105]

Such vacillation on the subject of Pakistan led to increasing tension in Sikander's position within the Muslim League itself. With uncertain control over the symbolism of Muslim power in the Punjab, Sir Sikander found his relations with Jinnah strained in the years after the Lahore resolution. In his concern to maintain Unionist control in the Punjab, Sikander chafed at Jinnah's single-handed domination of All-India Muslim League politics and at his refusal to support the British war effort; with Punjab's large share in the army, full support was critical, in Sikander's eyes, both to maintain Unionist power in the Punjab and to maintain Punjabi Muslim power in Indian politics. "Even the 'Qaid-i-Azam' is after all a human being," he wrote in frustration to Jinnah in July 1940, "and it would do no harm . . . to do a little heart-searching to

speech" (Malik Barkat Ali to Jinnah, 21 July 1941 [Rizwan Ahmad, comp., *The Quaid-e-Azam Papers*, 63–64]).
    103. Khan Rabb Navaz Khan to Jinnah, 16 July 1941 (ibid., 41).
    104. In February 1942 the government halted a proposed rural Pakistan conference in Jullundur district. Ashiq Husain Batalvi, the conference president, protested that Sikander had no cause to stop the conference, since Sikander himself had been involved in the passage of the Lahore resolution (Batalvi, *Hamari Qaumi Jadd-o-Jahd*, 3:89). In a telegram to Jinnah (presumably referring to this incident) Sikander responded that district magistrates could stop any meetings likely to disrupt communal peace, and that in Jullundur "GRAVE PROVOKATION [*sic*] WAS GIVEN TO NONMUSLIMS BY PROMOTERS WHO STENCILED PAKISTAN ON NONMUSLIM HOUSES CATTLES [*sic*] AND EVEN IT IS ALLEGED ON CLOTHES OF SOME NONMUSLIM BOYS STOP," Sikander to Jinnah, 28 May 1942 (S. Qaim Hussain Jafri, ed., *Quaid-i-Azam's Correspondence with Punjab Muslim Leaders* [Lahore: Aziz Publishers, 1977], 377).
    105. The speech (11 March 1941) is published as an appendix in Menon, *The Transfer of Power in India*, 454–55.

see whether there is room for self-correction or self-improvement." [106] But well aware of Jinnah's important symbolic role in Muslim politics as the champion of Pakistan, Sikander dared not repudiate Jinnah. While joining Fazlul Haq of Bengal, for example, in calling the League's opposition to war cooperation "suicidal to the interests of the Musalmans," Sikander confessed himself "anxious to avoid anything at this juncture which may weaken the solidarity of the Musalmans or damage the prestige of the League." [107] And, despite serious misgivings, he resigned from the viceroy's National Defence Council in August 1941 rather than force an open rupture with Jinnah. [108]

Growing discussion of Pakistan thus put Sikander into an awkward position. But the most serious effects of the Pakistan demand were upon the structure of the Unionist party itself. The League's championing of Pakistan produced no mass movement to challenge the local power of Unionist leaders; Sikander had neutralized the League's organization through his pact with Jinnah. But his increasingly ambivalent position on Pakistan threatened to undermine the party's control of the diffuse rural factions that made up its base. The distribution of patronage, a perennial source of friction in the party, acquired a new and disturbing significance in the context of conflict and uncertainty precipitated by the Pakistan issue. Unionist vacillation over Pakistan led some groups to doubt its continuing ability to exercise central provincial power; others began to see in the All-India Muslim League and in the Pakistan idea symbols for a legitimate alternative central authority.

Indeed, the Pakistan issue dramatized weaknesses that had always been present in the Unionist system of rule. Even before the passage of the Lahore resolution, long-standing dissatisfaction with the distribution of patronage had combined with personal and policy grievances to produce important defections from the party. Most noteworthy were the departures of Mian Nurullah of Lyallpur and other leading rural Arains in January 1939, and the Gilanis of Multan in July of the same year. [109] With powerful local bases in the districts and connections to ur-

---

106. Sir Sikander to Jinnah, 8 July 1940 (S. Qaim Hussain Jafri, *Quaid-i-Azam's Correspondence*, 369).

107. Sir Sikander and Fazlul Haq to Jinnah, 5 July 1940 (Quaid-i-Azam papers, file 97).

108. Sir Bertrand Glancy to Linlithgow, 10 September 1941 (IOL, L/P&J/5/244).

109. Arains were concerned with government revenue policy and patronage. The defectors included Sardar Muhammad Husain of Ganja Kalan, MLA for Chunian, and Mian Abdur Rab of Jullundur (Unionist party papers, file 6-45: Arain affairs). Conflict between the Unionists and the Gilanis came to a head over Sir Sikander's appointments favoring the Qureshi faction on the Multan district board. "This was one of the greatest political blunders," Ahmad Yar Khan Daultana reported. After losing the board's chair-

ban politics, and with influential rivals inside the Unionist camp, these
groups had long been uneasy with the provincial Unionist leadership.
But following the Lahore resolution, their dissatisfaction became an
ideological challenge to the legitimacy of Sir Sikander's position. This
was evident, for example, in the defection of Sir Jamal Khan Leghari of
Dera Ghazi Khan, whose local power was rooted in the Biloch "tribal"
tradition, and who attacked Sir Sikander for his failure to adhere to the
discipline of the Muslim League.[110] And Sikander's failure to either repudiate or fully support the Pakistan position only compounded Unionist difficulties. As the governor observed in 1941, "The more intelligent
amongst the Muslims are obviously doubtful as to whether the Unionist
Party can remain indefinitely in the ascendent if it is tied to the wheels of
the Muslim League chariot."[111]

Such failings revealed their most serious consequences when Sir
Sikander died suddenly in December 1942 at a family wedding in Lahore.
Whatever his difficulties, Sikander had been a master at factional manipulation and personal politics, able through his political skill to prevent a serious disruption of the party. But when Sikander died, the political consequences of his policies began to emerge. Long-simmering
factional discontent in the Unionist party boiled to the surface. Though
the premiership and leadership of the Unionist party passed logically to
the senior rural Muslim in the cabinet, Malik Khizr Hyat Khan Tiwana,
his succession nevertheless marked a major shift in factional power. Sir
Sikander had originally brought Khizr into the cabinet to appease the
powerful Tiwana-Noon faction of Shahpur. But with Khizr's appointment as premier, Sikander's personal factional supporters found their
position in the party increasingly under challenge. Trying in turn to
pacify this group, Khizr appointed Sikander's son, Shaukat Hyat Khan,
to his own former position as the second rural Muslim minister. The
transition was outwardly smooth but only thinly concealed the strong
factional rivalries within the party. These rivalries now intensified Unionist uncertainties with respect to Pakistan. Indeed, in 1943 many of Sir
Sikander's old supporters began to criticize Malik Khizr Hyat—and
now they used the Muslim League and the Pakistan concept as an ideo-

---

manship, the Gilanis left the Unionist benches in the assembly to become independents
(Ahmad Yar Khan Daultana to Afzal Ali Hasnie, 16 July 1939 [ibid., unnumbered file
marked "Daultana's Correspondence"]).

110. Sir Mohammad Jamal's statement (S. Qaim Hussain Jafri, *Quaid-i-Azam's Correspondence*, 363–64).

111. Sir Bertrand Glancy to Linlithgow, 10 September 1941 (IOL, L/P&J/5/244).

logical platform for their attacks. In the summer of 1943, Shaukat Hyat strongly attacked Khizr's failure to take an effective stand in support of Pakistan. It soon became clear that Shaukat's criticism had the full support of Mumtaz Daultana, the son of Sikander's late ally, Ahmad Yar Khan Daultana, and the support of Mir Maqbul Mahmud, Shaukat's father-in-law. Shaukat could also claim the support of the young Nawab Iftikhar Husain Khan Mamdot, who had succeeded his late father as president of the Punjab provincial Muslim League. Mamdot now declared that the Sikander-Jinnah pact had lapsed with the death of Sir Sikander; the allegiance of Punjab's Muslims to Jinnah and the Muslim League was completely unfettered.

Jinnah initially tried to maintain his position of neutrality in Punjab affairs, a position he had cultivated assiduously since 1937.[112] As premier, Khizr also tried to continue Sikander's position of nominal support for Pakistan and at the same time to keep his own independence from Jinnah. But when an influential rural Muslim group emerged to oppose Khizr, Jinnah began to strengthen his own hold on the Punjab Muslim League organization. He began in 1943 to pressure Khizr to reinvigorate the League organization in the province and to dispel all ambiguity in Unionist support for Pakistan. When Khizr could not meet his expectations, Jinnah felt strong enough to order Khizr expelled from the League. Supported by prominent rural leaders, Jinnah asserted his direct control over a provincial Muslim League committed directly to Pakistan and to him.

But the expulsion of Khizr from the League in May 1944 did not bring the expected crumbling of the Unionist party. However significant the desertions from the Unionists, the split in the Unionist party had not signaled a groundswell of rural Punjabi support for Pakistan. Increased rural touring and Pakistan propaganda after passage of the Lahore resolution, particularly by Muslim students, had produced, by early 1944, only a very limited impact.[113] In spite of Malik Khizr Hyat's expulsion from the League, the great majority of rural Muslim assembly members remained loyal to the Unionist party, for they continued to see the Unionist government as the best protector of their local interests. The

112. Jinnah resisted pressure from urban Punjabi Muslim League supporters to abandon his alliance with the Unionists in the year after Sikander's death; he refused in early 1943 to sanction an attempted Muslim League workers board in Lahore separate from the Unionist-dominated provincial League (*Eastern Times* [Lahore] 12 February 1943).
113. Sarfaraz Hussain Mirza, *The Punjab Muslim Students Federation: An Annotated Documentary Survey, 1937–1947* (Lahore: Research Society of Pakistan, 1978), lxv–lxix.

structure of the colonial system remained intact. But the assertion of indigenous cultural foundations for its authority emerged now in a contest between the Unionists and the Muslim League. As the two parties squared off after 1944, the split between them shaped an explicit struggle to define both the cultural foundations of the state and the state's relationship to the society it ruled.

The struggle was in fact prefigured by the dilemmas the Unionists had faced ever since their assumption of power in 1937. Resting on the political and ideological structure of the colonial regime, Unionist rule in Punjab had hinged on the state's role as the protector of local power, and on the local influence of rural magnates. But as an indigenous ruler in an increasingly "democratic" political order, Sikander also required an indigenous cultural foundation for the state's power. It was this which had pushed him initially toward close association with Jinnah and made him sympathize, initially, with the concept of Pakistan. But as the final results of Sikander's flirtations with Jinnah indicated, these efforts were built on contradictions; Sikander was bound, in the end, by the structure and ideology of the colonial system.

As Jinnah embarked on an independent challenge of the Unionists, however, his position was marked by contradictions as well. Influenced by Iqbal, Pakistan signified for the Muslim League a broad "community" shaped by the common personal identities of individual Muslims. But as Jinnah mobilized Punjabi Muslims to make such an ideal a reality, he too faced problems. Despite long tension between urban Muslim Leaguers and Unionist Muslims, Jinnah first forged a pact with the Unionist party, and then broke with them only when he had secured the direct support of a group of rural magnates. Now Jinnah also had to reconcile the symbolism of urban "communalism" with the power structure of rural Punjab. As the movement for Pakistan began in earnest in 1944, the League's campaign reflected many of the same tensions that had faced the Unionists.

CHAPTER VI

Din and *Dunya:* The Campaign for Pakistan

Muslims! The Time of Testing Has Come!

Din [the Faith]	*Dunya* [the World]
On one side is *zamir* [conscience]	On the other is *jagir*
On one side is *haqq-koshi* [righteousness]	On the other is *sufedposhi* [rural office]
On one side is *diyanatdari* [honesty] and *imandari* [faith]	On the other is *zaildari* and *nambardari* [village headship]
On one side is Pakistan	On the other is Hindustan

—From a 1945 Punjab Muslim League election poem[1]

As the Punjab moved toward new elections in the mid-1940s and the Muslim League's campaign heated up, League leaders launched a direct ideological assault on the position of the Unionist party. The Unionist party, Jinnah and his supporters declared, was a creation of the British. Unionist power was rooted, they argued, in the colonial administration. It was a product of the world (*dunya*)—of the political hierarchies of the rural administration. But it provided no symbolic link with the promises of the faith (*din*)—or with the higher purposes of their presence in the world. It provided no link with the Prophet's original Muslim community. Though Jinnah himself, and many other Pakistan supporters, were men of no deep religious conviction, they presented in stark terms the symbolic contrast between the colonial system and Pakistan. Commitment to Pakistan came to symbolize commitment to the fulfillment of Islam—and to the fulfillment of each individual Muslim. A Muslim state was a symbol and a validator of the Muslim community's political presence in India and its claim to rule.

1. Poster published by district Muslim League, Lyallpur, n.d. (Punjab, *Gazette*, pt. 3 [13 September 1946], 853).

189

Yet the distinction between the Unionists and the Muslim League was not, in reality, so sharp; Jinnah himself had made sure of this. He had long courted Unionist support for the League and had rejected the Unionists only when he had secured his rural base. The very process by which the movement for Pakistan expanded and gained political support dramatized the tension in colonial India between *din* and *dunya,* between the cultural definition of the state and the structure of the society it ruled.

PAKISTAN AND THE CONCEPT OF COMMUNITY

Sensitivity to this tension was nowhere stronger in the mid-1940s than among the reformist *'ulama.* As the colonial state had failed to assert a symbolic Islamic foundation for central authority, many *'ulama* defined commitment to *shari'at* as an independent touchstone of commitment to Muslim community, and many opposed the idea of Pakistan altogether. Opposition to Jinnah had grown among these *'ulama* ever since his compromises on the *shari'at* in the late 1930s. They saw Jinnah as a man with no qualifications as a religious leader, a man who himself had, as Mazhar Ali Azhar of the Ahrar declared, foresworn religion when he married a Parsi in a civil ceremony in 1918.[2] More important, they saw Jinnah's attempts to build support for the Muslim League within the structures of colonial politics as a betrayal of the guiding principles defining the community's legitimate moral foundations. To highlight the bankruptcy of Pakistan as a symbol of community, some even offered their own vision of an alternative religious state, a "Hukumat-i Ilahi," or divine government.[3] As Maulana Husain Ahmad Madani of Deoband charged, in his 1945 presidential address to the Jami'at-i 'Ulama-yi Hind, Jinnah had sacrificed the idea of a true religious community to the urge for political power. "[The principles of the League] were yesterday shut off from the light of the holy Shariat," Madani declared. And with the League's support for Pakistan, they were "today also a thing apart."[4]

Other urban Muslims also were uneasy with Jinnah's compromises in

2. For example, *Tribune,* 1 April 1943; 11 April 1944. Also, Smith, *Modern Islam in India,* 274–75.
3. *Tribune,* 16 September 1945.
4. Maulana Husain Ahmad Madani, *Khutba-yi Sadarat* (Jami'at-i 'Ulama-yi Hind Conference, Saharanpur, May 1945), 48.

his quest for Pakistan's achievement. Although many supported Jinnah's rhetorical claim to all-India leadership within the Muslim community, they had developed their own conceptions of the political meaning of community during the symbolic communal agitations of the 1920s and 1930s. In the press and popular agitations, they had defined a Muslim community in Punjab that was, like that of the 'ulama, politically independent of the colonial administrative structure. Yet this community was shaped not just by adherence to shari'at but by the public, collective activity of the people. Having witnessed the compromise of their principles during the days of the Sikander-Jinnah pact, many now distrusted Jinnah's efforts to broaden the Pakistan movement by compromising with rural Muslims. They questioned whether any rural political base was consistent with the ideals of community they had defined. As the pro-League Eastern Times put it, the power of many rural leaders whom Jinnah had brought into the League was rooted in a political milieu largely divorced from Islamic principle—a milieu in which power hinged on the votes of "the rural illiterates." [5] The moral foundations of Pakistan would thus be easily compromised if the movement were adapted to the mediatory political "world" of rural Punjab. As Pir Tajuddin, an old associate of Iqbal, warned, the League's reliance on rural support, whatever its practical value, could well perpetuate the Unionists' cultural regime—a regime that had nearly destroyed the political power of "the urban intelligentsia," the guardians of an ideology of Muslim community. "If the same policy is continued," he noted warily, "it is bound to recoil with greater speed over the heads of the present authors." [6]

In the wake of Jinnah's split with the Unionists in 1944, much depended on the new generation of rural leaders who had assumed increasing power in the League as it began to develop an independent rural base. These young rural leaders—the sons of many old Unionists— had now assumed the task, as Malik Khizr Hyat Tiwana remarked ironically, of undoing the work their fathers, "the great builders of the Unionist Party," had done. [7] Few were bound by exactly the same concerns as their fathers. Mian Ahmad Yar Khan Daultana, for example, had been specifically trained by the British to take his place within

5. *Eastern Times*, 2 August 1945. The paper cited the "rural illiterate portion of western Punjab," mired in "landlordism" and "tribalism," which dominated politics; its "tribalism" indicated its "pagan" state (ibid., 25 March 1944).
6. Ibid., 10 August 1944.
7. *Tribune*, 6 July 1944.

the structure of colonial politics;[8] his son, Mian Mumtaz Daultana, the League's new general secretary, was educated at Oxford during the 1930s and could as well claim a place among the Muslim intelligentsia of the province as among the landed gentry. Less well educated, the young Nawab Mamdot, the League's president, could also claim a far greater degree of independence from the colonial administration than his father, who had been installed in the Mamdot estate by the British.[9] While president of the League, the elder Mamdot had been sternly lectured by the governor on at least one occasion for "placing his obligation to a political caucus above his loyalty to the King Emperor."[10] Far more independent in position and attitudes, the generation entering politics in the 1940s rejected a subordinate place within the Unionist party. Following the factional realignments after Sir Sikander's death, they had turned to the Pakistan idea as a new focus for their politics, and a new cultural foundation for their claim to provincial influence.

But in justifying their claim to political power, these leaders were also caught in the ambiguous cultural relationship between the structure of rural power and the state. Their power remained firmly fixed in the countryside and in the rural hierarchies through which it was ruled; their families, as landlords, had claimed a traditional place among the provincial elite—not simply as representatives of rural interests but as intermediaries within the British imperial system. Their power was tied to the protection of the local "communities" that provided the building blocks of the political system.

How, then, were they to speak for the Muslim community in the movement for Pakistan? Leaders such as Daultana and Mamdot attempted to differentiate their influence from that of their fathers, by rhetorically rejecting the ideology that had tied rural society to the structure of British rule. The power of the Unionist party, they argued, was a product of the bureaucratic system developed by the British to maintain their own power. They had imposed, Daultana said, "a leadership of

8. John Maynard wrote of Ahmad Yar Khan Daultana in 1919: "He is at a critical stage with brains, energy, and is ambitious. The fear is that he will never take up his position as a territorial magnate, but will live in Lahore and try to take a shortcut to fame by becoming a town politician. As such he will never come to the top as he is an outsider in that class in which he will be competing. I want him first to take up his position as 'squire', help the district and, 'qua' the representative of the local agriculturalists come forward as politician" (Demi-official note, John Maynard [financial commissioner], 5 April 1919 [Board of Revenue, file 601/?]). Thanks to Emily Hodges for this quotation.

9. Griffin and Massy, *Chiefs and Families of Note,* 1:232–33.

10. H. D. Craik to Linlithgow, 24 September 1940 (IOL, L/P&J/5/243).

large owners who have been given almost autocratic powers, and who in their turn, have been completely subjected to the bureaucracy by a subtle distribution of patronage and privilege."[11] To establish their independence of colonial ideology, the League's leaders sought to distinguish their position from those whose power had been encapsulated within this bureaucratic structure.

To secure their position, League leaders thus attacked primarily the ideology of mediation on which Unionist power was based. As inheritors of the structure of colonial authority, the Unionists had claimed to protect Punjab's local "tribal" structure. But the "communities" they claimed to protect, rural Leaguers charged, were wholly artificial. Unionist institutions of "popular," rural solidarity like the Zamindara League, and "tribal" associations like the Jat Mahasabha of Chhotu Ram, were in reality only instruments by which the colonial state had manipulated local loyalties for its own purposes. The Zamindara League provided a clear example. Though defended by the Unionists as an organization of agriculturalist "class" solidarity and revived in 1944 for Unionist political organizing, it was, said League leaders, nothing more than a government-supported front for collecting funds for the Unionist party. As Raja Ghazanfar Ali Khan charged in the Legislative Assembly, the collection of funds for the Zamindara League reflected simply "the Government selling their patronage by auction."[12]

The case was similar with respect to the "tribal" associations supported by the Unionist party. As the League saw it, the Unionists had encouraged the formation of a range of provincewide "tribal" associations in the mid-1940s, including the Jat Mahasabha and the Muslim Rajput conference, only in order to bolster the ideological foundations of their own position.[13] These had little connections with the authentic expression of local "community." In truth, asked the *Eastern Times,* what did Sir Chhotu Ram's Hindu Jats of Rohtak and the Muslim Jats of western Punjab actually have in common? "What social relations do

11. Address by Mumtaz Muhammad Daultana, chairman of the reception committee, to the fourth annual session, Punjab Muslim Students Federation, Lahore, 18 March 1944 (Abdul Aziz collection).

12. Punjab, *Legislative Assembly Debates,* vol. 23 (December 1944): 415.

13. Muslim League leaders attacked Punjabi tribal associations that ignored the differences between Hindus, Muslims, and Sikhs. Thus, Sir Chhotu Ram's Jat Mahasabha was attacked for trying to create Jat "consciousness" among Muslim Jats, simply to undermine the Muslim League and serve the Unionist party (*Eastern Times,* 31 March 1944, 11 April 1944). Muslim Leaguers also attacked Malik Khizr Hyat's efforts to include non-Muslims in the Muslim Rajput *anjuman* (*Dawn,* 8 April 1945).

they have? Do they interdine? Do they intermarry? Do they participate
in the domestic festivals of one another?"[14] Indeed, what local "communities" did these organizations actually serve? For all the talk "of Jat interests, of Rajput interests, of Gujjar and God knows what interests,"
Daultana declared, the appeal to "tribal" interests reflected at root the
political imperatives of colonial domination—and the need to define
cultural foundations for the power of the intermediaries who served the
colonial bureaucracy.[15]

On a broader scale, such contradictions were reflected also in the
economic ideology of the Unionist party and in its claims to speak for a
"class" of Punjabi agriculturalists. In League eyes, the contradictions in
the party's so-called "ideology" were dramatized nowhere more clearly
than in Unionist food policy during World War II.

Food supply problems gained public attention in the early 1940s
when the government of India established a price ceiling for wheat, Punjab's most important surplus foodgrain commodity. Intended to control
inflation and facilitate procurement for imperial war needs, this move
caused deep resentment among rural producers and led to their widespread withholding of grain stocks from the market. Political pressure—and a flourishing black market—led for a time to the lifting of
price ceilings in early 1943. But conflicts between Unionist policy and
imperial war needs became clear when the Punjab government was
forced in 1943 to assume a central role in foodgrain marketing; it li-
censed exports from the province and appointed purchasing agents
"who alone could act as middlemen between the Punjab and the outside."[16] This role gave the Unionist ministry added patronage, but it
pushed the party into close cooperation with the nonagriculturalist
Hindu interests who had long dominated the Punjabi grain trade. And it
illustrated for many League leaders the contradictions in Unionist claims
to speak for the local interests of a "class" of Punjabi agriculturalists.[17]

Such issues provided ready-made fuel for League attacks on the hol-
lowness of the Unionists' ideology. League leaders attacked the opera-

14. *Eastern Times*, 26 March 1944.
15. Address by Mumtaz Daultana, 18 March 1944 (Abdul Aziz collection).
16. Statement of Sardar Baldev Singh to the Fourth Food Conference, October 1943
(Abdul Aziz collection).
17. On broad problems of food administration, see Henry Knight, *Food Administration in India, 1939–47* (Stanford: Stanford University Press, 1954). On the political
ramifications of the food policy, see Ian Talbot, "Deserted Collaborators: The Political
Background to the Rise and Fall of the Punjab Unionist Party, 1923–1947," *Journal of
Imperial and Commonwealth History* 11, no. 1 (October 1982): 82–85.

tion of government rationing, for example, as benefiting only the non-Muslim population[18] and criticized the Unionists for excluding rural Muslims from the economic opportunities the war created. As Raja Ghazanfar Ali Khan charged in the Assembly, government regulations tying the ministry to Hindu grain traders had only succeeded in excluding rural Muslims from the government's bounty, consigning Muslim agriculturalists to a permanently backward position. "Agriculturalists are already very backward in trade and commerce," he said, "and in the presence of these regulations it becomes totally impossible for them to better their lot in these fields."[19] Nothing could have illustrated more graphically, he implied, the inherent contradictions in the Unionists' position.

Unionist leaders in the mid-1940s did not, of course, accept such charges quietly. Sir Chhotu Ram fought vigorously to reclaim the Unionists' ideological position as champion of the agricultural producers. In the face of mounting Unionist difficulties, he launched a frontal assault in late 1943 on all aspects of British food policy, bitterly denouncing a new government of India proposal to reintroduce price ceilings. Calling the government's policy unfair to Punjab's agriculturalists, Chhotu Ram urged producers once again to withhold stocks from the market—a move that incensed central food planners whose resources were already stretched to the breaking point with the famine in Bengal.[20] As tension over the issue escalated, in November 1943 the Unionists staked the life of their ministry on a motion of confidence against the reimposition of wheat price ceilings; the motion led to a full-scale assembly debate not only on food policy but also on the government's basic commitment to the interests of the agricultural population. This debate gave the Unionists the opportunity to restate their ideology of agriculturalist solidarity and to win a solid vote of confidence in the assembly.[21] But the vote only delayed the practical assertion of imperial supremacy on the food ques-

---

18. Ian Talbot, "The Growth of the Muslim League in the Punjab, 1937–1946," *Journal of Commonwealth and Comparative Politics* 20, no. 1 (March 1982): 17–18.

19. Punjab, *Legislative Assembly Debates*, vol. 23 (December 1944): 261.

20. The government took Chhotu Ram's criticism of its food policy seriously; in June 1943 Lord Linlithgow wrote: "Sir Chhotu Ram's attitude—if persisted in, is likely to lead in the not too distant future to a Section 93 position [direct Governor's rule] in the Punjab. Such ruthless political opportunism is impossible to reconcile with the general food position in India and the overriding calls of war" (note by Linlithgow, 18 June 1943 [Linlithgow papers, vol. 92]).

21. Punjab, *Legislative Assembly Debates*, vol. 22 (November 1943): 80–118, 133–62.

tion, for in the end the Unionists were forced to yield to a food policy determined largely in Delhi.

Contradictions in food policy thus fed directly into League attempts to expose the artificiality of Unionist ideology. Rural League leaders such as Daultana and Mamdot rejected the whole ideological structure of Unionist influence, with its ties to the British. But in the period following the League's break with the Unionists, they also asserted new theoretical foundations for their claims, as rural leaders, to provincial power. They suggested, in fact, a new theoretical relationship between the rural areas and the power of the state. And ironically, though they remained landlords, Daultana and Mamdot turned for help in developing such a position to Muslims in the Punjab Communist party.

An alliance between Muslim League leaders and Communists was an unlikely one in the Punjab, for despite considerable influence among a section of the Sikhs, Communists had never claimed much support among Punjabi Muslims.[22] But the door to Communist–Muslim League cooperation had been opened in 1944 by the official decision of the Communist party to recognize the legitimacy of the Muslim demand for Pakistan as a "just, progressive and national demand."[23] For Punjab's Communists, alliance with the League promised a much-needed increase in political influence among rural Muslims. As Sajjad Zaheer, the chief Communist theorist of League cooperation, put it, rural League leaders could play a critical role in stimulating popular rural consciousness in Punjab, in spite of their largely landlord backgrounds.[24] But for rural League leaders, alliance with the Communists served a different purpose. For them, cooperation with the Communists helped to legitimize their position as rural leaders, independent of the ideology of the Unionist party.

The foundations of this position were laid out most clearly in the Punjab Muslim League Manifesto of November 1944. Reportedly drafted by Daniyal Latifi, the office secretary of the provincial Muslim League headquarters in 1944,[25] the manifesto was, in the words of the Lahore

22. A few Muslims were prominent in the Punjab Communist party but its base in rural western Punjab was very weak; discussed in Bhagwan Josh, *Communist Movement in the Punjab* (Lahore: Book Traders, 1979–80?), 121–24.

23. Sajjad Zaheer, quoted in Gene D. Overstreet and Marshall Windmiller, *Communism in India* (Berkeley: University of California Press, 1959), 215. Sajjad Zaheer's Punjabi strategy is discussed in Punjab fortnightly report for the second half of May 1944 (NAI, Home Political, file 18/5/44).

24. Sajjad Zaheer, *Muslim Lig aur Yunyunist Parti: Punjab men Haqq o Batil ki Kashmakash* (Bombay: Qaumi Darul Isha'at, 1944?), 55.

25. Punjab fortnightly report for the second half of July 1944 (NAI, Home Political, file 18/7/44). Interview with Chaudhri Rehmatullah, Lahore, 27 December 1975.

Tribune, "wrapped up in phraseology which is popular among the professed adherents of Communism." [26] It was nevertheless unanimously adopted by the provincial League working committee in October 1944 and circulated over the signatures of Mamdot and Daultana. Though it dealt with a wide range of issues, the manifesto provided at its heart a comprehensive plan for redefining the structural and cultural relation between the state and rural society. And in doing so it sought to define a place for rural Muslims at the heart of Muslim communal life.

The key to the manifesto was its definition of an alternative to the ideology of mediation. What it proposed was a transformation of Punjab's economy. To bring this about the manifesto proposed a "radical national reconstruction" that would transform the contours of the colonial system with a sweeping series of state-sponsored economic and administrative reforms, ranging from the acceleration of rural road construction to the development of a system of state-planned industrialization. [27] Shaped by Communist influence, such reforms would also transform the position of Punjab's peasantry. If the peasants needed protection from the vicissitudes of capitalism and world markets, then such protection would come not from local intermediaries, the manifesto implied, but directly from the state. The state would take a direct role in marketing the peasants' produce, and it would also guarantee to the peasants "a fair return" on their labors. [28] Indeed, a unity of interest between the state and the mass of the peasants would provide, predicted the manifesto's authors, the basic foundation on which a new order would be built.

Such a transformation would also provide a blueprint for reconciling rural power with the League's communal ideology. By undercutting the structure of mediation on which the colonial system had rested, it not only undermined the raison d'être of the Unionist party but also suggested the possibility of a new, central place for the rural majority within the Muslim community—a community defined by the direct, unmediated commitment of rural Muslims to symbols of Islam. The connection between the manifesto's structural reforms and its vision of a state defined by such a community was clearest in its call for a new system of popular Muslim education. The British, Daultana argued, had deliberately "stood against all political education" for peasants, largely to prevent any challenge to the mediatory political structure of the colo-

---

26. *Tribune,* 8 November 1944.
27. Punjab Provincial Muslim League, *Manifesto of the Punjab Provincial Muslim League* (Lahore: Daniyal Latifi, 1944), 30.
28. Ibid., 18.

nial system.[29] But the result had been a system of education that had, in the manifesto's words, "destroyed our national morality and established an ethical system based on worldly greed, selfishness and cowardice." In Pakistan, however, all this would be changed. "The Muslims must be trained," the manifesto declared, "in the spirit of Islamic brotherhood and in the traditions of their religion so as to recreate a moral basis for their conduct." Practical skills were to be joined with the message of Islam. "We wish to make Quranic religious education a compulsory subject for all Muslims in the primary and secondary school standards," the manifesto's authors stated, "and a study of Islamic history and culture a compulsory subject for all Muslims in secondary and higher education." To guarantee that such instruction would permeate the lives of all Punjabi Muslims, this religious education was also for women. "The moral regeneration of our people," the manifesto declared, "must start at the cradle with the spiritual influence of the mother." [30]

Educational reform and "moral regeneration" thus went hand in hand with a structural transformation of rural Punjab's place in the state system. In fact the details of Punjab's cultural transformation were less clearly formulated in the League manifesto than the fundamental economic and administrative measures that were to transform the British colonial system. But the manifesto's cultural implications were nevertheless clear. With the rural areas directly integrated into a national system, the cultural and ideological divisions in Punjabi society on which colonial control and Unionist ideology had been predicated—divisions between agriculturalist and nonagriculturalist, Jat and non-Jat, country and town—would all disappear to make way for a single, unifying Islamic identity. These divisions were, the manifesto declared, "in direct contradiction of the time-vindicated message of Islam." [31] By directly linking individual Muslims to the state, the manifesto sought to reconcile the traditional conflicts between urban and rural politics in Punjab and to lay the foundations for a fully Islamic, and yet politically viable, Pakistan. By offering a new vision of the state, landlords such as Daultana and Mamdot thus offered, with Communist assistance, a theoretical perspective in which the tension between *din* and *dunya* would disappear. And with its disappearance, the political power of the rural majority in Punjab—and the place of rural leaders in the Pakistan movement— would be legitimized and secured.

29. Address by Mumtaz Daultana, 18 March 1944 (Abdul Aziz collection).
30. *Manifesto*, 11–12.
31. Ibid., 9.

THE LEAGUE ORGANIZATION AND
RURAL POLITICS

But the manifesto's contribution was far more theoretical than prac- *Important*
tical. In its call for a radical transformation, it served, ironically, more to
highlight than to resolve the immediate political dilemmas the League
faced as it organized to defeat the Unionist party. In keeping with the
manifesto's tone, rural League leaders sought publicly in 1944 and 1945
to build a rural organization for the League based on the practical rejection of localized "tribal" loyalties and mediatory hierarchies. "Our
basic strength," Daultana declared in mid-1944, outlining plans for provincial Muslim League organization, "must come not from the landlords of the zaildar-lambardar class but from the broad masses of the
Muslim people."[32] Beginning in the summer of 1944, they launched a
campaign of rural touring, forming League branches and recruiting by
May 1945 a reported one hundred fifty thousand League members. But
their organization fell far short of seriously transforming the structure
of rural power.[33] In fact, most League leaders showed little interest in
making this transformation an immediate reality. At the local level, the
power of most continued to depend on the mediatory structures that
had long served the Unionists. Though Communist ideas had proved
useful in differentiating their goals from those of the Unionists, few took
the manifesto very seriously. For most, support of the manifesto was
possible only because, in practice, Communist organization was so
weak in western Punjab that landlords had little to fear from it.

As League influence spread in rural Punjab after Jinnah's break with
the Unionists, it thus came to depend largely on patterns of rural influence similar to those underlying the Unionist party. The provincial
League working committee had warned that if the rural Muslims "remain disorganised or become the camp followers of local juntas and
cliques they will have lost a great future";[34] yet it was precisely in those

32. Mumtaz Daultana, Report of work [of the Punjab Provincial Muslim League]
for June and July 1944, submitted to the All-India Muslim League committee of action,
28 July 1944 (Shamsul Hasan collection, Karachi [Punjab, vol. 1]).
33. As League leaders admitted; in February 1945 a report on the provincial League
found membership lists incomplete and financial accounts inadequate. It concluded that
"the total amount of work done in the Provincial League . . . falls considerably short of
the proposed scheme" (Inspection report #10 of Punjab Provincial Muslim League,
26 February 1945 [Muslim League papers, vol. 201: Committee of Action Inspection Reports, 1945, 2]).
34. Resolution of the working committee of the Punjab Provincial Muslim League,
Montgomery, 16 July 1944 (ibid., vol. 162).

areas that, in practical terms, the League began to mount its most effective rural challenge to Unionist influence after 1944. As the Zamindara
League noted, the early centers of rural League strength were in districts
such as Jhelum, Ferozepore, and Multan, where traditionally powerful
rural magnates had thrown their support early to the League cause.[35] In
Ferozepore district, for example, the home of the Nawab of Mamdot,
the radical communal ideology expressed in the Muslim League manifesto counted for little. It was largely the Nawab's local influence that
guaranteed the League a strong local position. As a local Zamindara
League organizer wrote in August 1944, "there is no Muslim League
spirit here in the district, but," he added pointedly, "Nawab Mamdot's
personal influence counts."[36] Significantly, Mamdot himself showed
little interest in establishing a formal alternative structure for League influence that might undermine his local power.[37]

In other districts also, the development of League influence in 1944
and 1945 generally followed, not the League's propaganda campaign
but the shifting pattern of district-level factions, which, in turn, reflected
the persistence of the underlying "tribal" and mediatory structure of
the "democratic," colonial political system. In Shahpur district, where
Tiwana-Qureshi rivalry had already led to rival district Muslim Leagues
after Malik Khizr Hyat Tiwana had succeeded Sir Sikander as premier;[38]
it was the Qureshi group that provided the backbone of Muslim League
support after Malik Khizr Hyat's expulsion from the League. Likewise
in Muzaffargarh district, factional jockeying after the Unionist–Muslim
League split sent the group headed by Abdul Hamid Khan Dasti into
the Muslim League en masse after Dasti's factional rival, Malik Qadir
Bakhsh, appeared to have gained the special favor of the new Unionist
ministry.[39] As Malik Qadir Bakhsh described the Muzaffargarh Mus-

35. For Jhelum, see note on tour of northwest Punjab, 21 August 1944 (Unionist party
papers, file E-194); and for Ferozepore, see Ghazanfar Ali (divisional organizer, Jullundur
division) to organizing secretary, Zamindara League, 28 August 1944 (Unionist party
papers, file D-30). Multan, where the Gilani family had powerful support, received a
larger total allotment of Zamindara League funds than any other district (Note by Sultan
Ali Ranjha, 9 November 1945 [Unionist party papers, file marked "Financial Aid to Zamindara Leagues"]).
36. Ibid.
37. The secretary of the Ferozepore Muslim League wrote to Jinnah that Mamdot refused to help establish League branches on his estate. "By this time there is no league at
Jallalabad, Mamdot or any other place within the precincts of his estate" (Khan Rabb
Nawaz Khan to Jinnah, 25 March 1943 [Quaid-i-Azam papers, file 579]).
38. Hameed Ahmad (secretary, district Muslim League, Sargodha) to Jinnah, 14 August 1943 (Quaid-i-Azam papers, file 1101).
39. Interviews, Abdul Hamid Khan Dasti, Muzaffargarh, 26 January 1975; and Malik
Qadir Bakhsh, Lahore, 22 February 1975.

lim League in 1945, all "are under the influence of Khan Sahib Abdul Hamid Khan, Public Prosecutor and Vice-Chairman District Board and belong to his Party."[40] Similar patterns were repeated in many other districts.

These patterns reflected the emergence in 1944 of the provincial Muslim League not as the backbone of a structural challenge to Unionist power, but rather as a structurally similar provincial alternative to the Unionist party. Indeed, as the political conflict between the parties increased, both built their rural support primarily within the same local factional structures that had characterized rural politics since 1937, each seeking provincial alliances to protect its local position. Even where patterns of factional opposition differed from those of 1937, the social roots of local factions were similar. The common local roots of the League and the Unionists were in fact illustrated clearly in Gujranwala district, where local Zamindara League workers reported in 1945 that as the provincial conflict between the Unionists and the League intensified, most of the leading zamindar families of the district had split their allegiances between the two parties. "From the western coast of the district, i.e. Jalalpur Bhattian, down to its border adjoining Sialkot District," wrote the Zamindara League's organizing secretary, "nearly every important Zamindar family is practically divided so far as the so-called political conviction is concerned." Another local Zamindara League worker pinpointed the reason for this: "It is a common practice these days," he said, "that father and son intentionally join different parties in order to gain advantage from the party in power."[41] This produced a factional pattern different from that in many other districts, but it demonstrated the common local political bases that the two parties enjoyed. Indeed, the Zamindara League's organizing secretary, Mian Sultan Ali Ranjha, summed up the practical political options facing both parties in 1945. "There are," he observed, "two parties [that is, factions] generally in each of the districts." When a faction attached itself to one party, then the rival political party sought support from the opposing local group. This was the case for either party. "They are, I suppose, the right men to give us a ready response in the beginning in addition to those who are connected with the party otherwise."[42]

40. Malik Qadir Bakhsh (secretary, Zamindara League, Muzaffargarh) to headquarters, 13 October 1945 (Unionist party papers, file marked "Muslim League Office Bearers").
41. Sultan Ali Ranjha to Sardar Aminullah, 26 June 1945; and Sardar Aminullah to Sultan Ali Ranjha, 8 July 1945 (ibid., file E-99).
42. Sultan Ali Ranjha to Ghazanfar Ali, 29 August 1944 (ibid., file D-30).

In the months after the League-Unionist break, the two parties thus developed similar patterns of local backing. However important as a theoretical blueprint for resolving contradictions within the League, the manifesto had played little role in the League's development of a viable rural political base. Tensions within the League thus continued. Indeed, the influx of rural leaders into the League reminded many League supporters of the close connection that had long existed between the structure of rural power and the principles on which the state was based. Such connections became an increasingly important issue.

In spite of the rural Leaguers' repudiation of Unionist ideology, continuing ties bound them to the colonial power structure, and the tensions that these ties produced were evident in League ambivalent attitudes toward the Land Alienation Act. As the pivot in the entire "cultural system" of colonial control in Punjab, the Land Alienation Act was perhaps the most logical target for those who wanted to establish a new Pakistan state—and a new relationship between the state and rural society. But in spite of its strong association with the colonial state system, rural League leaders were hesitant to attack the act, largely because it was equally associated with the practical maintenance of local power. Indeed, few dared to repudiate the act openly.

The ideological complexities in this situation were illustrated by a bill that an urban Muslim League member introduced in the assembly in 1945, to give practical form to the classic Muslim ideal of *musawat*, the equality of believers. The bill asked the administration to recognize the centrality of the principle of *musawat* in Muslim political organization by ending the recording of Muslim caste or "tribal" names in the revenue records and by refusing to take cognizance of such distinctions in the future conduct of the administration.[43] The ideal of *musawat* was in fact one most rural League leaders had already symbolically espoused— and had articulated in their public attacks on the large pro-Unionist Jat and Rajput tribal associations. As Mumtaz Daultana had declared in 1943, echoing urban communal rhetoric, "Thirteen hundred years ago our Prophet taught us that all Muslims are one, that they have one culture, one organization, one interest, that Islam which is based on the brotherhood of religious culture is the exact opposite and the most determined enemy of 'tribal' factionalism."[44] The appeal to *musawat*

---

43. Punjab, *Legislative Assembly Debates*, vol. 24 (February 1945): 131–36. Introduced by Khwaja Ghulam Samad, this bill had appeared in earlier assembly sessions as well.

44. Address by Mumtaz Daultana, 18 March 1944 (Abdul Aziz collection).

would thus transform the political system into one in which direct individual Muslim loyalty superseded the mediated local loyalties prominent in the British imperial system.

But Unionist criticism of the Muslim Musawat Bill made evident that
the issues were far more complex. Unlike the attack on provincial tribal
associations, the focus of the attack of the Musawat bill was not just
"tribal" politics but the concrete working of the Land Alienation Act
itself. The two were intimately related; to end the recording of "tribal"
names in the revenue records was to undermine the foundation on
which the Land Alienation Act was based. Even the League manifesto
had avoided a direct attack on the Land Alienation Act, the Unionists
noted, because the League had not dared to challenge the act's importance as protection for Muslims against monied Hindu interests. The
act served as a symbol of the political levers long used by Muslim intermediaries to protect rural Punjabi Muslims' vital interests—a symbol of the state's role as a protector against the power of capital. For the
Unionists, the primary significance of the bill thus lay in its relevance to
the protection of Muslim land. "Is the object of the Islamic Musawat
Bill only this," a Unionist pamphlet asked, "that Muslim zamindars
should be deprived of their land?" Though they cloaked their interests
in religious terms, the Unionists charged, the Muslim League was in fact
threatening just that. "If the zamindars and especially the Muslim zamindars do not form a united front and oppose the attackers of the
Land Alienation Act, then they and their descendants will find themselves living in the end only as [landless] menials."[45] In the face of such
criticism, rural Muslim League leaders naturally proved wary of pushing their opposition to the Land Alienation Act—or support of *musawat*—very far. Indeed, nothing could have highlighted the ambiguities
in the positions of the League's rural leaders more clearly.

Ambivalence on the Land Alienation Act thus summarized the Muslim League's position. Urban Leaguers might criticize the Land Alienation Act as little more than an appeal to Muslims to "abandon the
brotherhood of Islam for your acres," as the *Eastern Times* put it;[46] but
the Muslim League could not afford to attack the act without putting "a
handle in the hands of the Muslim League's enemies." In spite of the
manifesto's vision of an Islamic state system, the Land Alienation Act

45. Punjab Zamindara League, *Punjab Muslim Lig ki Zamindar Dushmani Muslim
Musawat Bil* (Lahore: Punjab Zamindara League, 1945), 13.
46. *Eastern Times*, 4 April 1945.

must stand, the paper said, so long as "the present agrarian economy is there."[47] At the heart of the dilemma was the idiom of "tribe." The rejection of "tribe" as a constitutive element in the state system was central to the entire ideology of the Pakistan movement, for it symbolized the League's rejection of the British system of colonial domination. But the idiom of *biradari* nevertheless continued to play an important role in the construction of the local influence of many rural League supporters; it was linked both to the economic welfare of the population and to the system of landholding that had developed within the colonial state system.

biradari

Such paradox in the League's position ultimately told on the local positions of many individual League supporters, like Raja Khair Mehdi Khan, Janjua, of Darapur, a prominent landlord and League leader of Jhelum district. As president of the Jhelum district Muslim League, Raja Khair Mehdi came under heavy criticism in June 1945 for his efforts to emphasize his local "tribal" political leadership while at the same time publicly supporting the "communal" ideology of the Muslim League. To settle a disruptive inheritance dispute in his *biradari* involving the rights of sons of a mother from outside the *biradari* to inherit equally with those of a mother within it, Khair Mehdi put *biradari* solidarity uppermost and argued strongly for the maintenance of *biradari* distinctions in inheritance. But his position clashed not only with the *shari'at* but also with his public support of the Muslim League's communal ideology. As a local Zamindara League worker noted, in spite of his place within his *biradari,* "he is very loud in saying to the city public, that the Muslim League stands for equality in the Muslim ranks."[48] But this now seemed to clash with the system of power under which his own local influence had grown. In spite of the League's efforts to usher in a new political era with its campaign for Pakistan, such incidents highlighted the League's continuing dilemmas as it sought to build a base of rural influence.

A full year after the League's break with the Unionists, many urban Muslim Leaguers thus continued to be skeptical of the "communal" leadership provided by the League's new rural leaders. By early 1945 a solid core of rural leaders had come to support the League. Yet neither their enthusiastic support for Pakistan nor their ideological rejection of

47. Ibid., 7 March 1945.
48. Bashir Husain (Zamindara League district organizer, Jhelum) to Sultan Ali Ranjha, 30 June 1945 (Unionist party papers, file D-44).

the colonial administrative system had effected much change in rural politics. Echoing a common disillusionment, the *Eastern Times* observed in June 1945 that "so far as the masses are concerned," the League's accession to power under such leadership "would mean nothing more than a change of masters."[49] The underlying tension in the Pakistan campaign between *din* and *dunya* remained to be resolved.

PAKISTAN AS A RELIGIOUS IDEAL

Jinnah's policies themselves were responsible for many of the contradictions in the Muslim League position. For political purposes, he had encouraged the rural takeover of the Punjab Muslim League, and he had deliberately encouraged as well the manipulation by League leaders of the local factions that were needed in building political support. The development of a solid political base had always been Jinnah's top priority. But Jinnah nevertheless maintained his rhetorical commitment to an ideal Pakistan, a vision expressed publicly in the "two-nation" theory. Even as he had worked to build a solid rural political base in alliance with the Unionists, Jinnah had encouraged the outspoken commitment of a wide range of Muslim Leaguers to this "communal" ideal.

Jinnah's greatest strength never lay in resolving tension—it lay in his ability to transcend tensions, to direct Muslim politics toward symbolic goals, even as he compromised to build political support. Even with his policies marked by tension, Jinnah went out of his way to identify himself with those groups in Punjab politics who stood structurally outside the pattern of urban-rural conflict. Within Punjab, no group filled this role better than Lahore's Muslim college students. Even as they played an increasingly important part in Punjab's Muslim League politics, Muslim students, like Jinnah, had a position outside Punjab's political hierarchies. They came from a variety of rural and urban backgrounds and were identified with no political faction. But as they studied to enter the bureaucracy, the law, teaching, and other professions, most Muslim students developed a deep and direct concern with the cultural definition of central authority in the Punjab. The concern to define an Islamic identity that could justify Muslim control of power had in fact long been self-consciously inculcated in Muslim students at schools such as Lahore's Islamia College, run by the Anjuman Himayat-i Islam. It was

49. *Eastern Times*, 1 June 1945.

no accident that, as they became interested in politics, Lahore's Muslim students were among the first to support the concept of Pakistan. And it was equally no surprise that, for Jinnah, their support proved critical in helping to dramatize the Pakistan movement's central "communal" ideal.

Though their immediate practical influence on Punjab politics was limited, their strategic role in the evolution of the Pakistan movement proved substantial. In the late 1930s Muslim students in Punjab were among the first to organize independently to support the Pakistan cause. With Jinnah's blessing, the Punjab Muslim Students Federation was organized in 1937, largely among students from Islamia College, Lahore; in late 1937 it adopted the demand for a Muslim state as part of its constitution.[50] Subsequently, leaders of the federation played an active role in campaigning for Pakistan, while the regular League organization in Punjab remained largely inactive. During the years of the Sikander-Jinnah pact, the Punjab Muslim Students Federation provided an organized corps of Pakistan supporters who arranged a series of pro-Pakistan conferences during the early 1940s.[51] Despite its limitations, their support proved very important for Jinnah. It helped him to dramatize the Muslim League's public commitment to a communal ideal, even as the League sought to develop a solid rural base through compromise with the Unionists. As S. M. Ikram has written, the value for Jinnah of this organization, "free from the handicaps of the Unionists and more broad based than the small urban group was obvious."[52] Jinnah did not, of course, allow such student activity to interfere with the structure of rural politics. Aware that student organizing, intermittent at best, was no substitute for the political influence of rural politicians, Jinnah was careful not to let student activities go too far.[53] But the Punjab Muslim Students Federation played a critically important symbolic role in Punjab, embodying the disinterested personal commitment to Muslim community that morally justified the Pakistan demand.

50. On the founding of this federation, see Sarfaraz Hussain Mirza, *The Punjab Muslim Students Federation*, fiii–lii.

51. Ibid., pp. liv–r.

52. Ikram, *Modern Muslim India*, 263.

53. Jinnah wrote to Abdus Sattar Khan Niazi in August 1941, "I do not wish to be misunderstood that I am a party to stirring up opinion against Sir Sikandar Hayat Khan" (Jinnah to Niazi, 17 August 1941, in Sarfaraz Hussain Mirza, *The Punjab Muslim Students Federation*, 48). Jinnah cautioned Muslim students against using the name, "Pakistan Conference," for a conference in February 1941; he suggested simply supporting the Lahore resolution, "popularly known as 'Pakistan'" (Jinnah to Mirza Abdul Hamid, 20 January 1941, ibid., 15–16).

Perhaps even more important, student organization kept alive a particular conception of community identity that proved essential, in the end, to the triumph of the Pakistan campaign—a conception that owed its origins largely to Iqbal. Though Iqbal died in 1938, he too had taken an important personal part in encouraging the organization of Muslim students in the 1930s. The leaders of the Punjab Muslim Students Federation looked to Iqbal—sometimes more than to Jinnah—as the special ideological patron of their movement.[54] But the greatest significance of the students' connection with Iqbal lay in their propagation of his particular view of Pakistan. In his poetry and his philosophical writings Iqbal stressed the active, individualistic, and intensely personal—indeed, almost mystical—commitment to Islam that defined the Muslim "community" in India. Shaped by this commitment, the idea of the Muslim community transcended, for Iqbal as for Jinnah, the contours of political structure; it even transcended the 'ulama's preoccupation with the shari'at. Iqbal was certainly not oblivious to the importance of political structures in organizing the community's interests; his support for Jinnah had reflected his awareness of the political realities India's Muslims faced. But as an expression of the community, the only legitimate political foundation for the Pakistan movement lay, in Iqbal's view, in the common, yet personal commitment to Islam held by individual Muslims. The organization of Punjab's students embodied the essence of this commitment. More than any other organized body, the Punjab Muslim Students Federation linked Pakistan symbolically to Iqbal's political conception of the community.

As tension increased in the Muslim League organization, student organizers helped to maintain a central place in the Pakistan movement for Iqbal's conception of community. One of the most powerful voices in Punjabi Muslim politics after 1944, committed to the propagation of Iqbal's message, was the daily Nawa-i-Waqt, a newspaper edited by a former president of the Punjab Muslim Students Federation, Hamid Nizami. Strongly influenced by his background in the student movement, Nizami helped to start the Nawa-i-Waqt in 1940 as a fortnightly for the "promotion of Urdu and the popularisation of the message of Iqbal."[55] Though its influence was at first minimal, it was converted to a

54. Sir Abdullah Haroon addressed the Punjab Muslim Students Educational Conference at Lyallpur on 16 February 1941: "The Moslems of the Punjab owe [a] duty to the rest of the Islamic world, for if they had no great functions to perform, surely Iqbal would not have cared to cover and carry his soul in a coat of the Punjab clay" (ibid., 270–71).

55. Ikram, Modern Muslim India, 266.

daily at Jinnah's urging in July 1944 to serve as an Urdu mouthpiece for the Muslim League in Punjab. Its influence expanded rapidly, and it brought commitment to Iqbal's message to the center of the League movement. Ultimately, the newspaper became not only the most popular Urdu vehicle for Jinnah and the League in the Punjab, but also a voice for "the younger generation which had been inspired by Iqbal." [56] Even while building a rural base, Jinnah used his connections with the newspaper to identify the League with—and to popularize—an individualistic commitment to Pakistan drawn largely from Iqbal's thinking. The paper in fact played an important role in molding Muslim League opinion in Punjab as a whole.

Other Muslim student leaders brought into the Pakistan movement a religious perspective on Pakistan that helped, in the long run, to transcend many of the movement's tensions. Another president of the Punjab Muslim Students Federation, Abdus Sattar Khan Niazi, led a group within the students' movement that came to be known in the late 1930s as the "Khilafat-i-Pakistan" group, so named because of a proposal for a Muslim state (a caliphate) that they submitted to Jinnah and the Muslim League in the late 1930s. Though their proposal produced little immediate impact on Jinnah or the provincial Muslim League leadership, it nevertheless exerted a powerful influence on a section of Muslim students, who attempted to popularize the "Khilafat-i-Pakistan" idea in the early 1940s.[57] The proposal, which called for the formation of a Pakistan caliphate including much of northern India, was in fact important not so much because its specifics won at any time a wide popular following, but because it envisaged a Muslim society—a Pakistan—integrated as a religious community not by the structural transformation of society, or even, simply, by popular adherence to the *shari'at,* but by the active, yet intensely personal, religious commitment of its best men to the ideal of Islam. Indeed, the spirit of Iqbal's philosophy would thus define and guide the state, as the powerful example of "self-concentrated" men set the direction of the community and linked society—whatever its local political organization—to the Pakistan state.

Such ideas were loosely argued in the Punjab Muslim Students Federation's 1939 pamphlet on the "Khilafat-i-Pakistan" idea, and were restated, with increasingly clear implications for the development of the

56. Ibid., 266–67.
57. On the Pakistan caliphate scheme, see Sarfaraz Hussain Mirza, *The Punjab Muslim Students Federation,* lii–liii, 461–85.

Pakistan movement, in a book that Niazi published in 1945 with Muhammad Shafi, a journalist and former student leader, entitled *Pakistan Kya he aur Kaise Banega?* (What is Pakistan and how will it be created?). This book stressed first and foremost the essentially religious principles necessarily underlying the Pakistan movement, principles derived from classical Islam. The *ummat-i Islamiya,* or Muslim "community," was originally established, they wrote, on the realization of *tauhid,* the unity of God, and the foundation for Pakistan could only be the same.[58] In its ultimate social implications, therefore, the idea of Pakistan involved for them, as it did for most of its urban supporters, a classical religious foundation that transcended society's local divisions and local "communities." Whatever the League's practical appeal for support from "tribal" leaders in rural Punjab, there could be, in theory, no compromise with non-Islamic principles in the political organization of the community or in the formation of the state. But for Niazi and Shafi, as for Iqbal, questions of political structure were in practice far less important than the transformation of individual Muslims through *taqat-i imani,* the power of faith. This was the key to defining an Islamic community's presence in the Punjab. Islamic social organization was also, of course, of considerable concern; but it was, by implication, of secondary importance in Niazi and Shafi's view of the world. Individual religious transformation came first; social change would follow. In laying the foundations for Pakistan, the central requirement was not the reform of the religious or administrative structure of society so much as the transformation of individual Muslim lives through the power of Islam.

In translating this stress on individual transformation into a political movement, Niazi and Shafi found their key figure in the person of the *mard-i khuda,* the true man of God. Whatever the practical role of politics in the movement's organization, it was religiously inspired leaders who, by their saintly example and impassioned commitment to Islam, would provide the bridge between the common people and the classical Islamic ideals that defined the culture of the new state. As models, such men harked back, of course, to the time of the Prophet himself. But although the spread of religious learning—knowledge of *Qor'an* and *hadis*—was important, the power of these men did not derive from their expertise in the law or their intimate knowledge of the life of the Prophet.

58. Abdus Sattar Khan Niazi and Mian Muhammad Shafi, *Pakistan Kya he aur Kaise Banega?* (Lahore: Muhammad Shafi?, 1945), 87.

It came from their example. The ultimate example, the life of the Prophet, could in fact be carried into the world, in such a view, only by the active, personal commitment of individual men. No "extensive scholarship [*kitabi 'ilmiyat*] or long training" was essential, Niazi and Shafi wrote, to incorporate the illiterate masses into a new, Pakistan state system.[59] Instead, all that was required was to increase awareness of *taqat-i imani* among the *qaum* through committed religious men. And here were implications critical to incorporating Punjab's rural hierarchies into a new state system. This conception of Pakistan with the *mard-i khuda* at its symbolic center harked back to a long tradition of religious leadership in Punjab—a tradition largely responsible for rural Punjab's original conversion to Islam. It was a tradition in which the example of great *sufi* saints had linked rural society to the broader Islamic "community" even as it linked rural society to a culturally Muslim state. No matter how important as a vehicle for the transformation of Muslim society, a successful Pakistan movement would thus represent, in its essence, only the completion of the conversion of Punjab that had been begun centuries earlier by the medieval *sufi* masters who brought Islam to the Punjab.

> The flag of Islam [Niazi and Shafi wrote], which Hazrat Data Ganj Bakhsh planted in Lahore in the eleventh century, with which Khwaja Muinuddin Chishti encompassed the corners of India, and which Khwaja Qutubuddin Bakhtiyar Kaki, Baba Farid Shakarganj, Hazrat Nizamuddin Auliya, and Khwaja Nasiruddin Mahmud Chiragh-i Delhi had in their own times raised high, has by the misfortune of India for the last two hundred and fifty years awaited a standard bearer.

Now it was time for such a standard to be raised once again. "Oh today soften your stony hearts," Niazi and Shafi asked in conclusion, "and entreat in the court of God that He might remove the veil of our misery. Give us guidance that once again we may be worthy of the Khilafat of Muhammad."[60]

These views should hardly be counted as the definitive expression of a well-delineated and widely held theological conception of Pakistan or be taken as a practical political blueprint for Pakistan. But their stress on moral exemplars suggested an answer to the political dilemma of the Pakistan movement—one in which the role of Punjab's rural *pirs* was symbolically central. Punjab's *pirs* were not, of course, all "men of God" in Niazi and Shafi's sense or even, for that matter, in terms of the active Islamic commitment laid out by Iqbal. Indeed, Iqbal denounced

59. Ibid., 89.
60. Ibid., 172.

many of them as men who had lost the active, personal commitment to Islam held by their great forebears. But by their very position—and by their ancestry—the *pirs* of Punjab linked the province to the example of the saints and the Prophet himself. They were, by their structural position, the most immediate reminders in rural society of the role of the saints who, in their own persons had carried the example of the Prophet through time. For those who sought to define religious foundations for Pakistan, the position of Punjab's *pirs* thus assumed central importance.

Indeed, as the arguments of men like Niazi and Shafi suggested, the critical importance of the *pirs* derived from the fact that, like Punjab's Muslim students, they were men, in a sense, outside the normal concerns of society. Their special position was defined by their moral separation from everyday Punjabi politics—and by their links to a source of authority outside Punjabi society altogether. But unlike Muslim students or Jinnah and the All-India Muslim League, they had influence embedded in the political structures of the localities. Their strategic cultural and political position was similar to that described by Peter Brown for the Christian saints of late Roman times—saints who were not only patrons and mediators in local society, but also, at the same time, exemplars of the larger values of a civilization. In an empire with a "permanent ache of 'center' and 'periphery,'" a gulf between the core cultural values of a civilization and the political organization of everyday life, the Christian saints had exemplified in their persons, Brown wrote, the central values embodied by Christ.[61] Though the *pirs* of Punjab often embodied the central values of Islam at a more considerable remove, linked as they were to the Prophet and the saints by chains of descent, they also carried within their persons the *barakat* of the Prophet, the saints, and the early community. And they linked this tradition of community, as "men of God," to the mediatory political structure of rural Punjab itself.

There was thus a turning away from previous structural contradictions. Increasingly, Muslim students rejected the structural solution to the League's dilemmas offered by the Punjab Muslim League manifesto. They underscored their position by attacks on the position of Communists within the League and moved to exclude Communists from the All-India Muslim Students Federation's membership.[62] In Punjab Abdus

61. Peter Brown, "The Saint as Exemplar in Late Antiquity," *Representations* 1, no. 2 (Spring 1983): 9.

62. Mukhtar Zaman, *Students' Role in the Pakistan Movement* (Karachi: Quaid-i-Azam Academy, 1978), 47.

Sattar Khan Niazi pressed home this effort by organizing against Communists within the League in early 1945,[63] a strategy Jinnah had tacitly endorsed in an earlier critique of the League's Communists in a speech to the Punjab Muslim Students Federation.[64]

Their criticism in fact signaled a growing intensity in the Pakistan movement that transcended the contradictions between effective manipulation of local power structures on the one hand, and commitment to the community on the other. Some Leaguers continued to concern themselves with changing the rural power structure, particularly urban radicals and rural Communists who remained in the League's provincial organization. But rural factional leaders, like Sir Sikander's son, Shaukat Hyat, began to fill their speeches with increasingly powerful appeals for Pakistan in personal religious terms, as a state defined simply by the Islamic identity and commitment of individual Muslims. Pakistan would be based, Shaukat declared, on "a government of the *Qor'an*";[65] by this he meant not a state structured politically by the *shari'at* but a state that would, by its very existence, embody the Muslim community. The tension between *din* and *dunya* was transformed. The conflict was not between two irreconcilable political structures but between a world shaped by colonialism and one shaped by the exemplary personal qualities of the good Muslim. Thus, the demand for Pakistan was a demand less for the transformation of Punjabi society than for a new moral and ideological foundation for the state. Symbolically embodied in the state, Muslim personal ideals would be supreme in the definition of community.

This stress on personal ideals and individual commitment was underscored by an increasingly active role in rural touring now undertaken by Muslim students as the elections of 1946 approached. In a wave of rural touring in late 1945 and early 1946, batches of students from the Punjab Muslim Students Federation (particularly from Islamia College) and from Aligarh visited hundreds of Punjabi villages, urging individual rural Muslims to register, by their votes for Pakistan, their personal inclusion in such a community.[66] Entering each village in groups of twenty to twenty five, students were instructed by a pamphlet of the Punjab Muslim Students Federation to avoid all involvement in local disputes and to stress instead, with Qor'anic verses, the importance of Islamic

63. Noted by Obaidullah Biloch on 11 March 1945 (Biloch to Unionist headquarters, 4 June 1945 [Unionist party papers, file E-96]).
64. Sarfaraz Hussain Mirza, *The Punjab Muslim Students Federation*, riii.
65. *Saadat* (Lyallpur), 14 January 1946; reproduced in Punjab, *Gazette*, pt. 3 (13 September 1946): 867–68.
66. Report of Abdul Razzaq, general secretary, Muslim Students Federation, Islamia College, Lahore, 25 December 1945 (Shamsul Hasan collection [Students, vol. 2]).

unity and Islamic government. With verses from Iqbal, the students were to explicate for rural villagers the political importance and the religious meaning of such an Islamic commitment.[67] The practical political impact of such touring is hard to assess.[68] But it clearly marked a growing effort within the League, an effort encouraged by Jinnah himself, to ground the call for Pakistan in the individual Islamic identity of each Muslim—identities that were themselves at the heart of the identity of a Muslim "nation."

THE *PIR*S AND THE 1946 ELECTIONS

A closer look at the role of Punjab's *pir*s is essential to understand how such commitments and concerns were actually played out in the politics of rural Punjab. The activities of Muslim students cannot, of course, explain the Muslim League's growing influence in rural Punjab—nor can the support of a large number of *pir*s. It was Punjab's rural magnates who supported the League's growing political base in rural Punjab; its success depended heavily on powerful factional leaders and landlords who had shifted to the League camp. Yet it is precisely in these circumstances that the *pir*s took on vital significance, integrating into the structure of rural politics the ideal of Islamic community that had become so central to the Pakistan movement.

The political role of Punjab's *pir*s at this time was hardly monolithic. Many *pir*s had long been allied with other landed families in rural Punjab, and during the Pakistan campaign many continued to respond to local factional pressures. The first major religious family, for example, to repudiate the Unionists in favor of the League was the Gilani family of Multan, whose leaders had turned against the Unionists as early as 1939, partly for religious reasons but largely through factional rivalry in Multan district politics. In 1944 and 1945, leaders of other rural religious families, such as the Saiyids of Shergarh in Montgomery district, long prominent in local and provincial politics, took much the same course.[69]

67. Punjab Muslim Students Federation pamphlet "Tahrik-i Tabligh," 1945 (Muslim League papers, vol. 230).

68. *Dawn* estimated that Muslim students talked to 700,000 Punjabis on rural tours before the elections (*Dawn*, 20 January 1946). Malik Khizr Hyat Tiwana disparaged student touring; it was "an insult to the intelligence of Muslim stalwarts in the Punjab," he said, "that young students with no knowledge or experience of life should come and preach to us" (*Tribune*, 5 January 1946).

69. In early January 1945, the Saiyids offered the League sizeable donations (*Eastern Times*, 5 January 1945). Later that month, a local League organizer informed Jinnah the

But these considerations did not by themselves guarantee the League support. In Multan, for example, the Gilanis' district-level rivals, the Qureshi *pirs*, became increasingly strong supporters of the Unionist party as the Gilanis moved toward the Muslim League. And both sides used religious influence to bolster their local political positions. While the Muslim League attempted to use the religious shrines in Multan to spread propaganda for Pakistan, the Qureshis encouraged the dissemination of pro-Unionist propaganda at their own shrine, the *darbar* of Bahawal Haq.[70] A religious ally of the Qureshis, the *sajjada nishin* of the shrine at Sher Shah, not only appealed to his own *murid*s to vote for Major Ashiq Husain Qureshi, the Unionist candidate for the Legislative Assembly in Multan tehsil, but did so on the grounds that he was both a friend of the zamindars and "a descendant [*chashm o chiragh*] of Hazrat Ghaus Bahawal Haq."[71] In a reflection of an old political pattern, both sides appealed to the saints as they squared off in local conflict.

But the significance of rural *pirs*' support for Pakistan transcended local conflict. As the meaning of Pakistan itself was transformed in the months before the elections, a large number of pro-Pakistan *pirs* developed a special ideological stake in the Pakistan campaign—a stake illustrated most clearly by the concerns of the *sajjada nishin*s of the post-Mughal *sufi* revival. Though also influential locally, many of these *pirs* had long combined a concern for local mediation with a religious interest in the overall cultural definition of the state itself. With their intellectual antecedents in the reform movements of the eighteenth and nineteenth centuries, men such as Fazl Shah of Jalalpur and Pir Jamaat Ali Shah of Alipur took active parts in many of the largely urban communal agitations of the 1930s, demonstrating their direct concern with maintaining a public, symbolic center for the larger Islamic community. But with their local influence embedded in structures of rural mediation, the effective political expression of their religious views had long been circumscribed by their place in the colonial political structure. Now, join-

League would hold a Multan division conference at Shergarh to coincide with the saint's *'urs*. "Already," he wrote, "Syed Mohammad Husain, sajjadanashin, who has lacs of followers in the Central and Southern Punjab has started making suitable arrangements to get his followers to attend the conference in their thousands" (Nasim Hasan to Jinnah, 31 January 1945, in Shamsul Hasan collection [Punjab, vol. 1]).

70. Both Unionist and Muslim League workers tried to spread propaganda at the Qureshi shrines in Multan fort (activities diary of Obaidullah Biloch, 12 November and 17 November 1945 [Unionist party papers, file E-96]).

71. Circular letter of Makhdum Ghulam Akbar Shah, *sajjada nishin*, Sher Shah, 6 January 1946 (used as scratch paper in Unionist party papers, file E-96).

ing the League's appeal for Pakistan, they used their local influence in "democratic" politics to demand a new Islamic definition of the state. Indeed, their ideological commitment to Pakistan made politically explicit what was implicit in the position of all the rural *pir*s—that is, their concern to link the structure of local politics with the broader concept of Islamic community that the Pakistan idea embodied.

The active support of such *pir*s thus held special significance for the League. On one level, their support helped to neutralize religious opposition to Pakistan from many *'ulama* and thus underscored the religious foundation of the Pakistan demand. In fact, Jinnah had attempted in late 1945 to counter opposition from the leading reformist *'ulama*, by organizing a group of pro-Pakistan *'ulama* under the leadership of Maulana Shabbir Ahmad Usmani of Deoband, a group called the Jami'at-i 'Ulama-yi Islam.[72] But in spite of the enthusiasm generated by a big Jami'at-i 'Ulama-yi Islam conference at Lahore in January 1946— a conference at which Deobandi, Barelvi, and Ahl-i Hadis *'ulama* appeared on the same platform—Jinnah never succeeded in winning the support of the majority of Punjab's reformist *'ulama*.[73] The support from a large group of *pir*s thus proved a critical counter to these *'ulama*, particularly in the countryside where the influence of the reformist *'ulama* was weak. Few *pir*s were in fact incorporated directly into the official League organization. But as the election campaign developed many spoke frequently from League platforms.[74] Moreover, the League coordinated the support of these *pir*s by publishing and circulating large numbers of their public religious appeals, *fatwa*s, as the newspapers called them, in the *Nawa-i-Waqt* and in other Lahore newspapers.[75] Their support highlighted the religious foundations of the League's position.

More important, their support also validated the particular political style and strategy Jinnah had used to build a practical base for the

72. Hardy, *The Muslims of British India*, 242.

73. An account of this conference in *Ihsan* (Lahore), 29 January 1946, is reproduced in Punjab, *Gazette*, pt. 3 (13 September 1946): 861. In an interview on 22 January 1976, Maulana Ghulam Murshid, *khatib* of the Badshahi mosque and a principal organizer of the Jami'at-i 'Ulama-yi Islam, gave his opinion that the majority of Punjab's most prestigious *'ulama* continued to support the Jami'at-i 'Ulama-yi Hind.

74. The Pir of Sial spoke at a Sargodha district Muslim League conference (*Eastern Times*, 6 June 1945). Other Muslim League meetings were held at other shrines in Punjab; one at Sharaqpur, presided over by Mian Ghulam Ahmad, *sajjada nishin* (ibid., 17 February 1945). As the campaign progressed, some *pir*s took positions within the League, but more did so after the 1946 elections.

75. Some of these voluminous appeals appeared in election petitions; for one such collection, see Punjab, *Gazette*, pt. 3 (13 September 1946): 839–78.

League in rural Punjab. Opposition to Jinnah among the *'ulama* had long reflected personal animosity mixed with the common belief that Jinnah had subordinated commitment to the *shari'at* to his practical need to gain a political base among Punjab's rural majority. But for most leading *pirs*, Jinnah's concern to gain rural support had taken on a far different color. For them, commitment to the expansion and political success of the community was as important as commitment to the *shari'at;* indeed, their own positions reflected historical compromises that had been necessary to bring Punjab's rural Muslims effectively within the boundaries of the Muslim community. Pir Jamaat Ali Shah, for example, who had himself been designated as Amir-i Millat during the Shahidganj agitation, congratulated Jinnah in early 1946 for taking up this mantle for the community.[76] In Jamaat Ali Shah's view, Jinnah's ability to manipulate the world of colonial politics and to build a broad rural base, even among rural landlords, in no way undermined the legitimacy of his leadership—no more than did a rural *pir*'s ability to mediate the power of Islam to the local cultures of rural Punjab. When Jinnah was criticized at a Sunni religious conference in early 1946 by reformist *'ulama*, Jamaat Ali Shah defended him in language drawn from sufism itself. "Think of Jinnah Sahib whatever you like," he said, "but I say that Jinnah Sahib is 'Wali Allah.'"[77] Like the *pirs* themselves—and like Punjab's influential League landlords—Jinnah's bona fides as an Islamic leader included outward adherence to *shari'at* and inner commitment to the cause of the community. And this commitment found expression in his single-minded pursuit of Pakistan.

Such support was not, of course, without its contradictions. In dramatizing their own commitment to Pakistan, many *pirs* themselves borrowed the rhetoric of urban communalism. In spite of their own rural roots, many urged their followers to commit themselves wholly to Pakistan, ignoring if necessary the loyalties of *biradari* and "tribe" that normally figured so prominently in rural politics. In calling for votes for Pakistan, the *sajjada nishin* of the prestigious shrine at Ajmer, for example, warned Punjabis in a poster published by the Punjab Muslim League, that "Your vote is a trust of the community [*qaum*]. No question of someone's caste [*zat*] or conflicts of *biradari*s should at this time

---

76. *Nawa-i-Waqt*, 30 January 1946.
77. Hamid Hasan Qadri to Jinnah, 22 July 1946 (Shamsul Hasan collection [Punjab, vol. 2]).

come before you." [78] Raja Ghazanfar Ali Khan, uncle of Pir Fazl Shah, echoed these sentiments. It is "our duty," he said, "to erase the disputes of families and *biradari*s," and to keep before us at this time "only the honor of Islam." [79] Others made similar appeals. In calling for a new ideological foundation for the authority of the state, many *pir*s emphasized the direct public commitment by each individual to the Muslim community alone. And simultaneously illustrated their own commitment to the ideal of community that Pakistan represented.

But such rhetoric did not touch the source of their local influence, embedded in the structure of rural society. Whether products of *sufi* revival movements or not, rural *pir*s had long provided a symbolic link between the appeal to descent, which symbolically underlay the structure of rural power, and the idea of the broad Muslim community. But what gave their support its greatest significance was their willingness now to step into the political arena in 1945 and 1946 to exemplify direct commitment to the community, even in a world where hierarchy and "tribe" shaped local social and political organization. The importance of such action was emphasized in a poem of Iqbal's, cited by the *Nawa-i-Waqt* after a *pir* in Montgomery district risked prison in early 1946 by defying local officials with his public support for Pakistan.

> Nikal kar khanaqahon se ada kar rasm-i shabbiri
> Ki faqr-i khanaqahi he faqat andoh o dilgiri
> (Come out of the *khanaqah*s and enact the tradition of Husain,
> For the life of the *khanaqah* is only suffering and pain)

By stepping into the public political arena, *pir*s linked themselves to the paradigmatic struggles of the early Muslim community, even as their local position and influence remained grounded in a world in which descent defined local status. [80]

The direct political power of this example and of these appeals was illustrated as many *pir*s toured western Punjab in late 1945 and early 1946. In the days before the 1946 elections, local Unionist party workers watched in almost helpless dismay as rural Muslims responded. The son of Pir Jamaat Ali Shah toured Jhelum district in December 1945,

78. Muslim League poster, "Shaikh al-masha'ikh Hazrat Diwan Saiyid Al-i Rasul Ali Khan [*sajjada nishin*, Ajmer] ka paigham Musalmanan-i Punjab aur Suba Sarhad ke nam," n.d. (collection of Muslim League election posters, 3, in Abdul Aziz collection).

79. Poster issued by Raja Ghazanfar Ali Khan, titled "Bakhidmat Musalmanan-i Zila' Jhelum," pencilled date, 5 November 1945 (Unionist party papers, file D-44).

80. *Nawa-i-Waqt*, 1 February 1946.

bringing an anguished response from local Unionist organizers: "Pir M. Husain Shah, son of Pir Jamaat Ali Shah, is making a tour of the Jhelum Tehsil," a Zamindara League worker wrote, "and issuing *Fatwas* that Muslim League is the only Islamic community and that all the rest are Kafirs [unbelievers]." This, he went on, has "created great obstacles in the way of our workers. . . . No amount of individual propaganda can convert the blind adherents of the Pirs."[81] In Gujar Khan tehsil of Rawalpindi district, the situation was much the same. The touring of the brother and the son of Pir Fazl Shah of Jalalpur had, as the Unionists reported it, undermined their previously strong position, influencing "the illiterate voters to vote for the Muslim League. We have nothing," the Unionists reported helplessly, "to set off against this attack of the so-called spiritual Peers."[82] Unionist workers repeated these laments in many other areas. In the opinion of many Unionist supporters, these appeals threw all political calculations into confusion; for many, a vote for Pakistan had come to be synonymous with an assertion of a personal Muslim identity. As one Zamindara League worker reported, "Wherever I went everyone kept saying, bhai, if we did not vote for the League we would have become kafir. . . . We did not vote for individuals; if we did so, it was only to vote for the Quran."[83]

Such a formulation raised personal identification with Pakistan to a level that transcended politics. But it was the position of the *pirs* themselves that tied this identification to the structure of local conflict. Most local electoral contests continued in 1946 to revolve around the factions that had long influenced rural politics, and which remained at the heart of the Muslim League's power. But the presence of the *pirs* within this milieu gave special meaning in 1946 to the election process. A brief look at two key districts, Shahpur and Lyallpur, illustrates the important role *pirs* played, injecting a public concern for identification with the community into the heart of rural politics.

The case of Shahpur, where the Unionists managed to hold on to win the majority of rural Muslim seats in the district, shows clearly the important role of the *pirs*—even in the context of continuing local fac-

81. Bashir Husain to Sultan Ali Ranjha, 13 December 1945 (Unionist party papers, file d-44); Jhelum district organization (Zamindara League) monthly report for December 1945, 2 January 1946 (ibid.).

82. Murid Ahmad, Zamindara League Rawalpindi divisional organizer, to Sultan Ali Ranjha, 3 February 1946 (ibid., file E-105).

83. Report by Ch. Shahwali of Ghumman, Zamindara League worker, Jhelum, 20 February 1946 (ibid., file D-44).

tionalism among rural magnates. As in many other districts, the basic political structure of the 1946 elections in Shahpur hinged on the factional rivalries that had shaped the 1937 elections—here, on the rivalry between the Tiwanas and Noons on one side, and Nawab Muhammad Hyat Qureshi on the other. But the character of the League's campaign for a Muslim state—and the public position of the *pirs*—subjected Tiwana and Noon leaders to extraordinary political and religious pressures. The political participation of several important *pirs* in fact injected a religious intensity into the campaign that differentiated it sharply from the election campaign of 1937 and put Shahpur's "tribal" *maliks* under extreme public pressure. In the last months of the campaign the Pir of Sial and the Pir of Golra appealed openly to their followers, among whom were many leading Tiwanas, to throw their support to the Muslim League. At a meeting in December 1945 held at Jhavarian, near Khizr Hyat Khan Tiwana's Kalra estate, the Pir of Sial instructed Nawab Allah Bakhsh Tiwana, his *murid* and the Unionist candidate for Shahpur tehsil, to remain with the Muslim community at this critical time. This was not a matter of politics, he said, but of individual commitment to Islam. The Pir of Golra, he noted, had warned his own *murid*, Malik Khizr Hyat, not to separate himself from this Islamic movement lest he become "fuel for the fires of Hell." [84]

Such pressure was hard for any Muslim leader to resist. Yet the Shahpur contest showed that religious appeals did not sweep away factional alignments. To the degree that Malik Khizr Hyat and other landlords were themselves able to resist such religious pressure, they were also able to maintain much of their local political following. Though the defection of Sir Firoz Khan Noon and several other leading Tiwanas dramatically weakened the Unionist position in Shahpur, Malik Khizr Hyat was able to use government influence and his own local connections to counter the League's campaign; as the Unionist premier, he controlled a wide network of patronage and could manipulate local allegiances to shore up his support. Even in the face of such pressure, Khizr Hyat was able to secure for the Unionists three of their four Muslim seats in the district.

But few districts provided the League so formidable an opponent as Malik Khizr Hyat Tiwana. Few Unionist candidates could draw on the same degree of government influence. In Lyallpur, as in most districts,

84. *Nawa-i-Waqt,* 5 January 1946.

the final election results were therefore quite different. As in Shahpur, the underlying factional structure mirrored that of the 1937 elections. The most hotly contested race in the district (in Toba Tek Singh tehsil) opposed the district's two most serious factional rivals: Mian Nurullah, standing on the Muslim League ticket; and Pir Nasiruddin Shah, standing for the Unionists. But in Lyallpur district, the pressure of the League's religious message and of touring by rural *pir*s exerted a more critical influence on the campaign's outcome.

Both Mian Nurullah and Pir Nasiruddin Shah were men with strong, long-standing political bases in the constituency, Nasiruddin Shah among the settled pastoralist population, and Nurullah among the canal colony *abadkar*s, particularly Arains. In 1937 they had split the Lyallpur and Toba Tek Singh constituencies. But as in Shahpur, the nature of the League's religious appeal in 1945 and 1946 put Nasiruddin under difficult new pressures. He did not lack local religious influence; he was himself an influential landlord and *pir*. But Muslim League workers toured the district, disseminating the "*fatwas*" of prominent *pir*s and increasing pressure on Nasiruddin's local supporters.[85] Such pressure was increased by the touring of the young *sajjada nishin* of the Sandilianwali Darbar, who, according to Nasiruddin's own complaint, was "carried in a Doki" to "polling stations and other important places in the constituency before and during [the] election," urging support for the Muslim League on pain of becoming *kafir*. This religious influence did not succeed, it should be emphasized, in undermining the base of Nasiruddin Shah's support, which he bolstered before the election by increasing use of government influence.[86] But its political result strikingly illustrated the general reason for the Muslim League's success. It produced no revolution in the structure of local politics, where the basic division between *abadkar*s and *jangli*s remained clearly visible in the election returns. But it tipped the factional balance in the constituency toward Mian Nurullah. Though Nasiruddin Shah won the majority of

85. Nasiruddin also faced religious opposition from his step-brother, Pir Nazar Husain Shah; see petition of Pir Nazar Husain Shah to government, n. d. (Shamsul Hasan collection [Punjab, vol. 2]).

86. Punjab, *Gazette*, pt. 3 (5 July 1946): 406–17; election petition of Nasir-ud-Din Shah versus Mian Nurullah and others (Toba Tek Singh tehsil). Complaints are in Abdul Bari (president, Lyallpur district Muslim League) to Jinnah, 23 January 1946, with enclosed report on "Official Interference in Lyallpur District," by Ghulam Hussain, in charge, vigilant committee, Muslim League, Lyallpur (Shamsul Hasan collection [Punjab, vol. 1]). Similar complaints are contained in a petition of Makhdum Pir Nazar Husain Shah, n. d. (ibid., vol. 2).

votes at most *jangli* polling stations, he was unable to win majorities as large as those won by Mian Nurullah among the *abadkar*s.[87] And the result brought a clear Muslim League victory in Toba Tek Singh tehsil. In the end the League carried all four of Lyallpur's rural Muslim constituencies.

Such examples suggest clearly the sources of the Muslim League's electoral victory. In few other western Punjab constituencies were the League's triumphs even so narrow as in Toba Tek Singh. The pattern in Lyallpur was repeated throughout the province. The Unionists won a handful of Muslim seats while the Muslim League captured 73 of the 86 Punjab Muslim seats up for election. In areas like Jhelum and Rawalpindi districts, where touring by *pir*s was intense, the League won over 70 percent of the rural Muslim vote. And this combined, not surprisingly, with the League's clean sweep of Muslim urban constituencies. Its victory in the elections was decisive. Taken together, the League won over 65 percent of the total Muslim vote.[88]

As the role of the *pir*s illustrated, the League's political success thus rested on its ability to challenge the Unionist party for local control within the political structures of rural Punjab. This was Jinnah's strategy from the beginning. In building its base for Pakistan in rural Punjab, the League dramatized its claim to speak for a self-conscious Muslim community that transcended the local identities around which rural politics had been built. The *pir*s played a vital role in this process. Religious intermediaries, they remained embedded in a world of local identities and influence yet stressed their commitment to community symbols that bound them (and all Muslims) to the concept of the perfect community led by the Prophet. Many rural Muslims looked to the *pir*s for religious leadership and found also a powerful political model. Casting their individual votes for Pakistan came to signify, for many, identification with the broader Islamic community. But these votes were still cast within the structure of a political system largely shaped by local "tribal" idioms. Within this context, the colonial system established by the British, the battle for Pakistan was contested. The triumph of the Muslim League in the 1946 elections thus signified no rejection

87. Partial polling station results for this constituency were published in the *Nawa-i-Waqt*, 6 February 1946.

88. The 1946 election results for the Muslim constituencies are in Kirpal C. Yadav, *Elections in Panjab, 1920–1947* (Tokyo: Institute for the Study of Languages and Cultures of Asia and Africa, 1981), 109–17. The Muslim League percentage comes from a calculation in the *Eastern Times*, 13 April 1946.

of the old structure of rural society, but rather a new public expression of Muslim community—an expression that justified a cultural redefinition of the state. With *pirs* and rural magnates in critical roles, the elections offered a new arena where, at least for the moment, *din*—exemplary personal ideals—and *dunya*—the world of rural politics—publicly joined.

The elections of 1946 were a watershed in Punjabi Muslim politics. Rejecting the ideological foundations of the colonial system, Punjabi Muslims defined a new, communal foundation for the state. Yet the process was filled with ironies. Muslim League leaders committed to the Pakistan idea used the old colonial order, and local identities, to make that idea a reality. The political position of the pro-Pakistan *pirs* epitomized this ambiguity. To clarify their—and society's—commitment to the ideal of "community," many rhetorically condemned the politics of *biradari*. But the local structure for the elections guaranteed a continuing political place for *biradari* loyalties. Moreover, these loyalties had shaped the positions and influence even of most rural *pirs* themselves. One *pir* from Jullundur, for example, who condemned the politics of *biradari* during the election campaign as a distraction from the "life and death" struggle of the Muslim "community," went on to suggest that "if religion remains alive, then afterwards *biradari*s can be kept up and supported."[89] In fact, the continuing structure of local authority inherited from the colonial regime—and the system of "democracy" itself—guaranteed the persistence of such local political loyalties, even as the Muslim League swept to triumph. And they guaranteed, ironically, the persistence of critical elements in the ideological structure of the colonial system itself, even as a new, communal foundation for the state was defined.

Nevertheless, the election triumph of the Muslim League proved critical in 1946 because it made the ultimate establishment of Pakistan inevitable. With the stunning defeat of the Unionist party, the old system of state authority could never be fully reestablished. The change did not happen overnight. After the elections, Malik Khizr Hyat and the remaining rump of the Unionist party formed a coalition with the Akali party and the Congress to salvage the foundations of the old system and

89. Statement of Pir Saiyid Ali Hassan Shah of Pratapura, Jullundur (*Nawa-i-Waqt*, 9 January 1946).

to keep the Muslim League out of power. Initially, Muslim League leaders responded with outrage to this effort. But with little rural organization, there was no possibility of an immediate seizure of power. Though
they continued to talk of rural membership and propaganda drives, the
League's effort to form an official Masha'ikh Committee of leading *pirs*
in late 1946 highlighted its continuing dependence on rural intermediaries.[90] The League's renewed debates over the role of Communists in
the provincial organization confirmed the leadership's continuing drift.[91]

But the cultural and political implications of the 1946 election results
could not, ultimately, be denied. As the British departure from India
neared, the Muslim League established a Punjab committee of action in
October 1946 to coordinate provincial League activities with those of
the all-India body. Following the collapse of all-India negotiations on
the transfer of power, Jinnah used this committee in late 1946 to try to
mobilize Punjabi Muslims in active support for Pakistan.[92] When Malik
Khizr Hyat Khan shut down the headquarters of a newly expanded
corps of Muslim League national guards at Lahore in January 1947,
Muslim League leaders responded by launching an active movement of
civil disobedience aimed at overthrowing the Unionist-led provincial
government. Though spearheaded by the Muslims of Lahore and largely
confined to urban areas, the movement had a dramatic effect. Student
processions and meetings in defiance of government bans convinced
Malik Khizr Hyat that he could no longer rule with the majority of
Muslim opinion against him.[93] On 3 March 1946 Khizr's ministry resigned, marking the end of an era in Punjab politics. The structure of
ideological integration on which Punjab politics had been constructed
collapsed with the end of central Unionist authority. The growing com-

90. See, for example, *Eastern Times,* 6 April 1946, 31 May 1946, and 22 November
1946. The committee secretary, Ibrahim Ali Chishti, had belonged to the Punjab Muslim
Students Federation and supported the Khilafat-i Pakistan proposal; he was appointed to
train the masses in the spirit of Islam. Justice Munir noted the committee's problems: it
included not only *pirs* he charged, but Muslim League landlords who passed themselves
off as religious figures for greater influence with "the masses" (Punjab, *Report of the
Court of Inquiry* [Munir Report], 255).
91. Conflicts over appointments of Communist organizers led to a debate over "divided allegiances" in the League council (*Eastern Times,* 21 May 1946).
92. Khwaja Nazimuddin, chairman, All-India Muslim League committee of action to
Punjab Provincial Muslim League, 14 October 1946 (Muslim League papers, vol. 182
[Committee of Action, 1946–47, vol 2]).
93. On the early 1947 League civil disobedience campaign, see Penderel Moon, *Divide
and Quit* (London: Chatto & Windus, 1962), 75–76; and, for Muslim students' role in
particular, Sarfaraz Hussain Mirza, *The Punjab Muslim Students Federation,* pp. nvii–ciii.

munal violence that followed was but one piece of evidence of this, and partition was its inevitable outgrowth. But the system that was to replace it was by no means clear. The 1946 elections had signaled the emergence of a new communal foundation for state authority in the Punjab. But the political structure of a new state system, linking the state to Punjabi society, remained to be constructed in an independent Pakistan.

Conclusion

The successful demand for Pakistan destroyed the old Punjab. The partition of India split the province along a line passing between Lahore and Amritsar. Punjabis themselves were not wholly responsible for this outcome. Many of the political pressures that produced Pakistan—and led to Punjab's partition—originated outside the province. The events of 1947 in Punjab owed much to the broader currents that brought the decline of the British empire, the rise of the Congress, and the growth of Muslim separatism in other parts of India. Indeed, Jinnah's rise to all-India power in the League, which in its beginnings owed little to the Punjab, ultimately shaped events there deeply. But in the end it was the Muslims of Punjab who decided their own future, for after the elections of 1946 the creation of Pakistan could not be denied.

The Pakistan movement destroyed the ideological foundations on which the British colonial government had linked its authority to Punjabi society. With the collapse of the Unionist party, the state could no longer claim legitimacy as merely the organizer and protector of a system of local power in the Punjab. The Pakistan movement held out the vision of a popular Muslim community that could claim legitimate state authority. With its roots in the "communal" rhetoric of the press and urban politics, this ideal community found broad public expression in the League's successful election campaign of 1946. But the elections by no means transformed the structure of local politics. In the years after Pakistan's creation, the structure of local power in the Punjab continued to exert a powerful influence on the politics of the new Pakistan state.

And it molded the political tensions that continued to shape Pakistani politics.

Nothing crystallized these tensions more clearly than the workings of Punjabi "democracy." Popular elections had provided the public arena in 1946 for the demonstration of the existence of a popular Muslim "community" in the Punjab, encompassing both urban and rural areas. But the electoral system of Punjab was itself a product of colonial rule; its structure reflected the primacy of local intermediaries in the state system. The triumph of the Muslim League thus simultaneously defined a new symbolic foundation for the state and affirmed the same structure of mediation on which the power of the colonial state had rested.

The history of the Pakistan movement in fact highlighted many of the underlying contradictions in the development of colonial nationalism. Early supporters of Muslim communalism had defined the concept of a Muslim "community," and a Muslim "nation," as one in which individual Muslims identified directly with common Islamic symbols; it was very largely an urban phenomenon. But the idea of a "nation" was, by its very nature, inclusive, incorporating the large rural majority as well. To give it political reality, champions of a Muslim nation like Jinnah were forced from the beginning to appeal to rural intermediaries in a national cause, maneuvering within the structure of imperial power even as they proclaimed the primacy of individual commitment and culture as the foundation of "national" identity.

But if Muslim nationalists developed few popular institutions that structurally embodied a national community, they drew support, finally, from an appeal to the personal values shared by all Muslims as inheritors of an exemplary past. This provided the foundation for a demonstration of a national identity through the electoral process. But it also brought personal religion, with its emphasis on exemplary models, to a central place in the definition of "national" identity. Indeed, the Muslim League's campaign suggested why religion assumed such an important place generally in the shaping of "national" identity in the British imperial context. Only an appeal to personal religious models could link individuals to the concept of a Muslim nation independently of the structures of local community that shaped the formal imperial political system.

 It was in these circumstances that Punjab's rural *pirs* assumed a pivotal role in Punjab's politics. *Pirs* had long connected local cultures and local "communities" on the one hand, to Muslim values and Muslim

"community" on the other. Yet they occupied an equivocal position in
the structure of colonial politics and colonial "democracy." Though
they fit easily into the British state structure as intermediaries, their ritual ties to the broader Islamic community made this relationship ambiguous. Linked by ancestry to the saints and to the Prophet, *pirs* embodied society's continuing bond to the Prophet's "community" and to
its exemplary values, even as they exercised influence, like most rural
landlords, in a structure shaped by local political hierarchies and tribal
identities. When the movement for Pakistan emerged, they thus occupied a strategic political position. Drawing on a tradition of active devotion to Islam, persuasively articulated by Iqbal, their active involvement seemed to bring the saints themselves into the battle for Pakistan.
    But the tensions within the movement remained. Contradictions be-
tween the politics of *biradari* and the language of personal commitment
to Pakistan remained to be resolved, even as the Muslim League swept
to victory in the elections with a broad base of urban and rural support.
The rhetorical opposition of "Islam" and "tribalism" that developed
during the Pakistan movement was only one sign of this. The state's
symbolic cultural base underwent a revolution when the British left—a
new flag, a new anthem, and a new ideology of state power affirming the
new state's claim upon the loyalties of every Muslim. But the mediatory
structure of political authority in Pakistan—on which "representation"
was based—departed little from the imperial power structure of British
Punjab. For all its outward political trappings and public, ideological
identification with Pakistani "nationalism," the power of the Muslim
League rested largely on the same base as had the Unionist party.
    The subsequent history of Pakistan thus reflected contradictions that
had been inherent in the Pakistan movement. After independence, contradictory pressures erupted in the protracted debates over Pakistan's
constitution. Some debates focused on the role of the *shari'at*. For most
of Pakistan's *'ulama,* many of whom had opposed the creation of Pakistan, the *shari'at* was the touchstone of Muslim "community," and thus
central to the new state's legitimacy. Leading Pakistani *'ulama* argued
strongly for a state that was defined by its public commitment to Islamic
law. But leading politicians fought equally hard for a constitution that
would preserve the foundations of their local authority. Through long
debates in the late 1940s and early 1950s, politicians, *'ulama,* and others struggled to define a constitution for Pakistan that would preserve
the structure of authority on which the Muslim League's authority

rested, and yet define the state effectively as a cultural embodiment of the Muslim "community." At times they made significant progress.[1] But the tension inherent in combining an Islamic cultural definition of the state with a mediatory, "democratic" structure of authority simmered through the early 1950s and boiled into popular disturbances in Punjab in the anti-Ahmadi riots of 1953.

At the heart of the anti-Ahmadi riots lay a powerful reassertion of the construction of community identity that had carried the Pakistan movement to success—a reassertion of an ideal, drawn from the vision of Iqbal, that defined the Islamic identity of Pakistani society by the direct, active commitment of individual Muslims to symbols of Islam. The agitation focused on two issues: opposition to the Ahmadiyah, who were labelled non-Muslims for refusing to accept the finality of the Prophethood; and criticism of the government itself, which had failed to uphold the Islamic identity of the state and the community. In a period of conflict over the state's cultural foundations, the agitation recalled the urban communal agitations of the 1930s. Nothing more clearly dramatized the principles on which Pakistan had been founded than the emotional, public commitment to the Prophet exemplified by opposition to the Ahmadiyah.[2]

But at the same time, the agitation called into question the legitimacy of the government, with its political roots in the rural hierarchies that had supported the colonial regime. The Punjab riots were finally controlled in 1953 only by the intervention of the military and the implementation of martial law in the Punjab. But this marked more than just a practical response to growing unrest—it pointed the way toward another answer to Pakistan's dilemma. At the heart of the issue lay the problems of establishing an effective cultural relationship between the state and society, between the principles on which the state had been founded and those on which power was organized in Pakistani society. Continuing difficulties in the politicians' efforts to reconcile Pakistan's ideological foundations with a structure of state authority inherited from the colonial tradition led many bureaucrats and military leaders in the mid-1950s to fear for the stability of the state itself. It was in this

---

1. Leonard Binder, *Religion and Politics in Pakistan* (Berkeley: University of California Press, 1963).
2. The ideological implications of the anti-Ahmadiyah agitation find a prominent place in Justice Munir's report on the disturbances (Punjab, *Report of the Court of Inquiry* [Munir Report]).

context that the military came to assume a larger role in the politics of
Pakistan, seizing power finally in General Ayub Khan's 1958 coup.

Though Ayub's assumption of power had many causes, none was
more important from a long-term perspective than the concern of Pakistan's leaders to isolate the state apparatus from the popular, cultural
pressures to which Pakistan's creation had given rise. Indeed, Ayub's
chief concern under military rule was to protect the state from the pressure of popular politics. But at the same time he attempted to reorder
the political system to establish a new base for the state's authority in
Pakistani society. With the army in control, he began to reconstruct the
political system from above in order to try to reconcile the religious and
political forces that had brought Pakistan into being. Such policies had
many sides. He encouraged industrial growth, weakening the old landed
elites and creating alternative elites dependent on the government. At
the same time, he attempted to bring the mediatory hierarchies of local
politics more firmly under state control, by curtailing the power of many
of the old political families while setting up structures of local mediation
through so-called "basic democracies." Perhaps most important, he also
used the state to try to manipulate the structure of religious organization in Pakistani society in order to establish cultural foundations for
the state's authority in the structure of Pakistani society itself. By redefining the relationship between the state, the individual, and Pakistan's religious institutions, he sought to reconcile the state's exercise of
authority with the ideal of individual commitment that had justified Pakistan's creation.[3]

Central to this effort was the government's assumption of control
over Pakistan's religious *auqaf,* the endowments supporting mosques
and shrines. Using the control of *auqaf* to gain religious support for the
government was not a new idea; in the 1930s the Unionist party saw it
as an avenue for linking Punjab's diffuse system of rural religious authority firmly to its own regime. But Ayub's attempts to control *auqaf*
differed significantly from those of the Unionists. To reconcile rural Islam with the ideology of Pakistan and to stress the direct connection of
individual Pakistanis to the Muslim "community" and the Muslim state,
Ayub sought to change the ideology of mediation that underlay the *pirs'*
local authority. Some Unionist campaign workers had in fact noted dur-

3. For a general discussion of Pakistani politics, see Khalid B. Sayeed, *Politics in
Pakistan: The Nature and Direction of Change* (New York: Praeger, 1980).

ing the 1946 campaign that such a change was implicit in the ideology of the Pakistan movement itself. The creation of Pakistan inevitably implied, they argued, the emergence of a government that would seek—in the name of the community—to extend its influence over the shrines. As one Unionist worker described such dangers to the Pir of Taunsa: "When the Muslim League will come in power the first Act which will be passed will be [an] Auqaf Bill, which will take away all their properties and leave them almost destitute like Mahants under the Gurdwaras Bill." [4]

In fact, Ayub's efforts to gain control of Muslim religious institutions bore only a slight resemblance to those embodied in the Sikh Gurdwaras Act of 1925. Having inherited a political system tied to the authority of intermediaries in the localities, Ayub Khan could not have destroyed the *pir*s of Pakistan even if he had wanted to, which he clearly did not. But having taken over administration of many shrines, the government now drew on the thinking of Iqbal and the ideology of the Pakistan movement to redefine a popular religious devotion to shrines that would support the Pakistan state. As Katherine Ewing argues, the government sought to stress the importance of Punjab's shrines not primarily as gates of intercession but as monuments to Pakistan's great *sufi* exemplars. Iqbal had identified example as the key to mobilizing Pakistan's individual Muslims into active members of the community. The example of the great saints buried at the shrines was thus intended now to direct Muslims toward a personal awareness of their role in a community that transcended the local loyalties of kinship and faction—the Pakistani "nation" itself. Though this was a message carried to the people through their own local shrines—and one which was thus rooted in distinctive local traditions and power structures—it suggested the accessibility of a *sufi* ideal, and of access to God, for all Pakistanis. In redefining the meaning of the shrines, the government thus intended to institutionalize the critical role the *pir*s played in the 1946 elections. It attempted to define through the shrines an ideology that would legitimize both the Pakistan state and a system of political authority built on the power of local leaders. [5]

In important respects Ayub's *auqaf* policy was thus part of a general concern to relink the state culturally to Pakistani society. While main-

4. Murid Ahmad to Malik Khuda Bakhsh, 1 October 1945 (Unionist party papers, file E-105).

5. Katherine Ewing, "The Politics of Sufism: Redefining the Saints of Pakistan," *Journal of Asian Studies* 42, no. 2 (February 1983), 263.

taining firm control of the state through the army and the bureaucracy, Ayub attempted to gradually reestablish "democratic" institutions in Pakistan, firmly maintaining a structure of rural mediation (of "basic democracy") even as he recognized the state's need to turn, eventually, to a popular "community" of Pakistanis to legitimize its special authority. Policies such as that concerned with *auqaf* were intended to provide cultural foundations for such efforts. But the collapse of Ayub's own authority amid urban rioting in the late 1960s, and the secession of Bangladesh after the 1970 elections, demonstrated the continuing difficulties in this effort.

The continuing problems of Zulfiqar Ali Bhutto's democratically elected government, which came to power in 1970, illustrated this dilemma once again. Since his electoral base challenged the structure of mediation in rural Punjab, Bhutto appealed initially to the language of "Islamic socialism" to legitimize his regime in terms consistent with Pakistan's Islamic origins. Although his government continued the outlines of Ayub's policies with respect to *auqaf* and to the *pir*s, Bhutto used the language of economic reform and egalitarianism—much as the Punjab Muslim League had done in its radical manifesto of 1944—to transcend local hierarchies of mediation with an appeal to the concept of an egalitarian national community.[6] Pressing land reform and nationalization, he sought to transform the structure of Pakistani society, to make this community a reality. But in spite of successes in some areas, the government proved unable (and in many respects unwilling) to press ahead in the mid-1970s with the radical social changes that would have broken the mediatory structure of power in rural Punjab and fundamentally changed Pakistan's political structure. Ironically, Bhutto's government thus came to depend more and more on the same hierarchies of rural power that had supported the structure of "representative" politics under the colonial regime. In one of the great turns of his political career, Bhutto tied his fortunes in the 1977 elections to the same rural elites that had provided the backbone of support for the Muslim League in 1946. Even as he swept to victory, the results of the 1977 elections illustrated the continuing difficulties of the Pakistani state in finding a cultural base in Pakistani society.

Indeed, the significantly rigged elections of 1977 symbolized Bhutto's

6. For an analysis of Bhutto's "populism," see Sayeed, *Politics in Pakistan*, 84–112, Ewing discusses Bhutto's use of religious ideology and shrines (Ewing, "The Politics of Sufism," 263).

failure to define a cultural base for his government consistent with
Pakistan's original cultural meaning. It was no accident that the demon-
strations that brought him down focused largely on the romantic demand for a "Nizam-i Mustafa," a state system built on the model of
the Prophet's early community. Just as the supporters of Pakistan had
turned to an idealist definition of Pakistan in the wake of the Punjab
Muslim League's inability to implement its 1944 manifesto, Bhutto's
critics, largely urban, again harked back to Pakistan's original, idealist
promise.

But it offered little practical solution to Pakistan's difficulties. Indeed,
the response to this agitation was a second seizure of power by the military, a move reflecting the renewed concern of the military and the bureaucracy to protect the state by isolating it altogether from the cultural
and political pressures of Pakistani society. Like Ayub, General Zia ul-
Haq attempted eventually to link the state to popular political and cultural organization. But General Zia offered ultimately even less of an
answer to Pakistan's cultural dilemmas than Ayub had. Though not re-
versing the *auqaf* policies of previous governments, Zia turned to a program of symbolic "Islamization" in order to legitimize the authority of
the state, appealing to the *'ulama* and the Islamic textual tradition. By
stressing symbolic measures of commitment to *shari'at,* Zia sought Islamic legitimation for the state largely from sources outside Pakistani
society altogether. Though Zia's program won the support of many
'ulama and of the Jama'at-i Islami, it did not define a cultural identity
for the state consistent with the values of most rural Pakistanis. It lacked
connection and support, as the ambiguous impact of Zia's Islamization
in the countryside bears witness.[7]

Since its creation in 1947, Pakistan has faced no problem that is
more central than the definition of the cultural relationship between the
state and its people. But it is a problem whose contours continue to be
shaped deeply by the legacies of colonial rule. The reconciliation of mediatory "democracy" with the public assertion of Islamic "community"

7. Rural "Islamization" is discussed in Richard Kurin, "Islamization: A View from the
Countryside," in Anita M. Weiss, ed., *Islamic Reassertion in Pakistan: The Application of
Islamic Laws in a Modern State* (Syracuse: Syracuse University Press, 1986), 115–28. In
discussing the impact of General Zia's Islamization, one cannot, however, assume a static,
long-term rural religious structure; the number of religious schools, *madrasas*, in rural
Punjab has grown dramatically since 1960. But the extent of such change in transforming
the religion of the rural areas requires considerably more research. See comments of
Fazlur Rahman, *Islam and Modernity: Transformation of an Intellectual Tradition* (Chicago: University of Chicago Press, 1982), 115.

continues to preoccupy many Pakistanis. For many, Iqbal's concept of active commitment to the "community" as a foundation for political action continues to exercise a powerful appeal. Transcending the structure of local politics, this personal commitment has provided a foundation for the Islamic identity of society as a whole. But embodying this concept in the political structure of state authority has proved problematic. The role of the *pirs*—and the saints—as links to the structure of local society and as exemplars of personal commitment to the Prophet and to Islam, was a powerful one; it played a central role in Pakistan's creation. But the position of *pirs* since independence has proved ambiguous. Though the models of the saints exert for individual Pakistanis a great appeal, Pakistanis continue to struggle to define Islamic cultural foundations for the state consistent with the political and ideological legacies of colonial rule. The legacies of both empire and Islam continue to shape the history of Pakistani state and society.

Glossary

ābādkār—settler (term applied to central and eastern Punjabi settlers in the Punjab canal colonies)

ahl—people, as in Ahl-i Hadis (people of the Hadis)

ʿālim (pl. *ʿulamā*)—man trained in religious sciences

amīr—commander, chief

anjuman—society, committee, association

auqāf (see *waqf*)

baiʿat—act of swearing allegiance as the disciple of a *pīr*

bania (*baniyā*)—Hindu trader or moneylender

barakat—blessing; spiritual charisma of a saint, transferred to his tomb and descendants

baṭāʾī—division of the crop between landholder and tenant; rent paid in kind

birādarī—brotherhood, a community based on the model of common descent

dacoit—robber who acts as part of a gang, usually in rural areas

dār al-ʿulūm—institution for higher learning in Islamic religious sciences

darbār—court of a king or great saint

darvesh—religious mendicant

dastārbandī—turban-tying (ceremony signifying succession to authority)

dīn—faith, the Islamic religion

dunyā—world

fatwā—ruling of religious law issued by an *ʿālim*

fidāʾī (pl. *fidāʾiyān*)—devotee, one willing to sacrifice himself

gaddī—throne, seat of authority

ḥadīṣ—traditions of the Prophet

ḥajj—pilgrimage to Mecca

ḥalāl—lawful, with religious sanction; (an animal) slaughtered as prescribed by Islamic law

ḥimāyat—support, protection, defense

ḥukūmat-i ilāhī—divine government
ʿilāqa—locality
ʿilmīyat—learning, scholarship
imām—leader in prayers
īmān—faith (also *īmāndār*—having faith)
inʿām—tax-free land grant
inqilāb—revolution (also *Inquilab*, the name of a Lahore newspaper)
ittěḥād—unity, unionist (as in Unionist party)
jāgīr—land assignment, held by a *jāgīrdār*
jamāʿat—congregation, collective body
jāměʿ masjid—congregational mosque, the central mosque of a town or city
jamīʿat—congregation, concourse (see *jamāʿat*)
janglī—uncivilized (term applied to pastoralists settling in the canal colonies)
jathā—band of people
jhaṭkā—(an animal) slaughtered by having the head cut off, in the Hindu manner
jihād—striving; an Islamic war against unbelief, whether external or internal
jinn—ghost, spirit
kāfir—unbeliever, non-Muslim
kamīn—village menial, artisan
khādim (pl. *khuddām*)—servant of a shrine or of a saint
khalīfa—successor to the authority of a saint, or religious leader
Khālsa—the pure, the Sikh community
khānaqāh—ṣūfī hospice
khaṭīb—reciter of the *khuṭbā*, preacher
khilāfat—(1) succession to spiritual authority; (2) succession to the leadership of the Muslim community as a whole, claimed in the late nineteenth and early twentieth centuries by the Ottoman sultan; (3) movement among Indian Muslims before, during, and after World War I to preserve the Ottoman Khilafat
khudā—God
khuṭbā—sermon delivered in a mosque, address
kotwālī—headquarters of the city police
lambardār—village headman
langar—public kitchen to distribute food, often operated at ṣūfī shrines or by tribal chiefs
madrasa (pl. *madāris*)—school of higher learning
mahant—head of a Hindu religious order; custodian of a Sikh shrine (*gurdwārā*)
majlis—meeting, assembly, party
malik—property owner (also a title of respect used by certain Punjabi communities, for example, the Tiwanas and Noons)
mashāʾikh (see *shaikh*)
maslak—path, religious perspective
maulvi (*maulawī*)—learned Muslim, ʿālim
mīlād al-nabī—Prophet's birthday celebration (also *maulūd*)
millat—religious community

muftī—expounder of Islamic law
muḥalla—urban neighborhood
murīd—disciple of a *pīr*
musāwāt—principle of the equality of believers
mutawallī—manager of an endowment, custodian of a shrine or mosque
nambardār (see *lambardār*)
panchāyat—small council, committee of arbitration
pīr—*ṣūfī* guide
qarza—debts
qaṣba—small town (Muslim in cultural style)
qaum—community based on religion, descent or nationality
qazi—Islamic judge
ra'īs—urban notable, man of substance
Ramazān—Islamic month of fasting
sāhūkār—moneylender
Saiyid—title signifying a claim to descent from the Prophet
sajjāda nishīn—literally, 'one who sits on the prayer carpet'; successor to the authority of a *ṣūfī* saint at his shrine, usually a lineal descendant of the saint
shaikh (pl. *mashā'ikh*)—title of respect given to *ṣūfī*s (caste title for some Punjabi Muslim nonagriculturalists; also used in some Punjabi communities as a general title of respect)
sharī'at—Islamic Law, derived from the *Qŏr'ān* and *ḥadīṣ*
sufedposh—rural semi-official, usually subordinate to a *zaildār*
ṣūfī—Muslim mystic, or one connected to the *ṣūfī* orders
sunnat—way of the Prophet
tablīgh—proselytization
tafsīr—Qor'anic exegesis
taḥṣīl (also tehsil, in the most common British spelling)—major administrative subdivision of a Punjabi district (most districts were divided into three to six tehsils)
tanẓīm—organizing, organization
tauḥīd—unity of God
tumāndār—title given to the leading Biloch chiefs of Dera Ghazi Khan district
'ulamā (s. *'ālim*)—class of Muslims learned in religious sciences
ummat—Islamic people
'urs—celebration of the death-day of a *ṣūfī* saint; major annual festival at many *ṣūfī* shrines
walī (pl. *auliyā*)—saint, friend of God
waqf (pl. *auqāf*)—pious endowment
zail—administrative subdivision in the Punjab, each in the charge of a semi-official *zaildār*
zakāt—compulsory Islamic charity
zamindar (*zamīndār*)—holder of land (term used in Punjab for large and small landholders alike)
zāt—caste; endogamous marriage group
zirā'at pesha—agriculturalist

Bibliography

OFFICIAL RECORDS

ENGLAND

London. India Office Library and Records.

INDIA

New Delhi. National Archives of India.

PAKISTAN

Lahore. Punjab Archives, Anarkali's Tomb, Civil Secretariat.
Lahore. Punjab Archives, Press Branch, Civil Secretariat.
Lahore. Punjab Board of Revenue.
Jhang. Jhang Deputy Commissioner's Files.
Lahore. Lahore Deputy Commissioner's Files.
Lahore. Lahore Divisional Commissioner's Files.
Faisalabad. Lyallpur Deputy Commissioner's Files.
Sargodha. Shahpur Deputy Commissioner's Files.

PERSONAL PAPERS AND PRIVATE COLLECTIONS

Mian Abdul Aziz collection, Lahore.
Quaid-i-Azam (Muhammad Ali Jinnah) papers, National Archives of Pakistan, Islamabad.
Muslim League papers, Archives of the Freedom Movement, Karachi University, Karachi.
Nawabzada Khurshid Ali Khan papers, Lahore.

Lord Linlithgow papers, India Office Library and Records, London.
Sardar Sir Sunder Singh Majithia papers, Nehru Library, New Delhi.
Nawab Muhammad Ahmad Khan Qasuri papers, Lahore.
Shamsul Hasan collection, Karachi.
Sardar Shaukat Hyat Khan collection, Islamabad.
Unionist party (Zamindara League) papers, Kalra, Sargodha district.

NEWSPAPERS

Dawn (Delhi), 1944–1946.
Eastern Times (Lahore), 1942–1947.
Inquilab (Lahore), 1945–1946.
Nawa-i-Waqt (Lahore), 1945–1946.
The Tribune (Lahore), 1936–1938, 1942–1947.

JUDICIAL CASES

Mumtaz Mohammad Khan Daultana vs. Bulaqi Mal and Sons, Ltd., Revenue
    Revision no. 57 of 1941–42. *Lahore Law Times,* vol. 22 (1943), Revenue
    Rulings, pp. 1–2.
Khwaja Mohammad Hamid vs. Mian Mahmud and others, Privy Council Ap-
    peal no. 118 of 1921. Record of Proceedings, 3 vols. Lincoln's Inn Library,
    case no. 88 of 1922.
Khwaja Mohammad Hamid vs. Mian Mahmud and others, Privy Council Ap-
    peal no. 118 of 1921. *Indian Appeals,* vol. 50 (1922) pp. 92–107.

GOVERNMENT PUBLICATIONS

Griffin, Lepel, and Charles Massy. *Chiefs and Families of Note in the Punjab.*
    Rev. ed. 2 vols. Lahore: Civil and Military Gazette Press, 1910.
Ibbetson, Denzil. *Punjab Castes.* 1916. Reprint. Lahore: Sh. Mubarik Ali, 1974.
India. *Census of India, 1921.* Vol. 15 (Punjab and Delhi), pt. 2. Lahore: Civil
    and Military Gazette Press, 1923.
India. *Census of India, 1931.* Vol. 17 (Punjab), pt. 2. Lahore: Civil and Military
    Gazette Press, 1933.
India. *Report of the Committee Appointed in Connection with the Delimitation
    of Constituencies and Connected Matters.* Parliamentary Papers, Reports,
    1935–36, vol. 9.
Khan, Nawab Muzaffar. *Note on the Delimitation of Constituencies.* Lahore:
    Government Printing, 1934.
Kirpalani, S. K. *Final Settlement Report of the Lyallpur District and the Rakh
    Branch Colony Circle of Sheikhupura District.* Lahore: Government Print-
    ing, 1940.
Kitchin, A. J. W. *Final Report of the Revision of the Settlement of the Attock
    District.* Lahore: Government Printing, 1909.

Madan, B. K., and E. D. Lucas. *Note on the Sales of Gold and Ornaments in 120 Punjab Villages*. Lahore: Punjab Board of Economic Inquiry, 1936.

Punjab. *District Gazetteers*. Various districts. Various dates.

———. *Gazette*, 1937–1939, 1946–1947.

———. *Legislative Assembly Debates*, 1937–1945.

———. *Legislative Council Debates*, 1924–1936.

———. *Provincial Banking Enquiry Committee Report*. Lahore: Government Printing, 1930.

———. *Report of the Court of Inquiry Constituted under Punjab Act II of 1954 to Enquire into the Punjab Disturbances of 1953* [Munir Report]. Lahore: Government Printing, 1954.

———. *Report of the Industrial Survey of the Ludhiana District*. Lahore: Government Printing, 1942.

———. *Report of the Land Revenue Committee, 1938*. Lahore: Government Printing, 1938.

———. *Report of the Punjab Reforms Committee, 1929*. Lahore: Government Printing, 1929.

———. *Report of the Punjab Unemployment Committee, 1937–38*. Lahore: Superintendent, Government Printing, 1938.

———. *Report on Newspapers and Periodicals in the Punjab*, 1915, 1937–1938.

———. *Report on the Punjab Disturbances, April 1919*. Simla: Government Printing, 1919.

———. Financial Commissioner. *Report on the Administration of Estates under the Court of Wards in the Punjab*. Lahore: Government Printing, 1936.

———. Information Bureau. *Eighteen Months of Provincial Autonomy in the Punjab*. Lahore: Director, Information Bureau, 1939.

———. Information Bureau. *Full Text of the Presidential Address Delivered by the Hon'ble Sir Sikander Hyat-Khan, Premier of the Punjab, at the All-Punjab Zamindar Conference, Lyallpur, on September 4, 1938*. Lahore: Director, Information Bureau, 1938.

Rose, H. A. *A Glossary of the Tribes and Castes of the Punjab and North-West Frontier Province*. 3 vols. Reprint. Patiala: Punjab Languages Department, 1970.

Seth, R. K., and Faiz Ilahi. *An Economic Survey of Durrana Langana: A Village in the Multan District of the Punjab*. Lahore: Punjab Board of Economic Inquiry, 1938.

Singh, Labh, and Ajaib Singh. *Farm Accounts in the Punjab, 1937–38*. Lahore: Punjab Board of Economic Inquiry, 1940.

Tupper, C. L. *Punjab Customary Law*. 3 vols. Calcutta: Government Printing, 1881.

BOOKS AND ARTICLES

Abbas, Y. "A Tussle for Punjab Leadership." In *Proceedings of the Pakistan History Conference*, 9th session. Karachi: Pakistan Historical Society, 1959.

Afzal, M. Rafique, ed. *Malik Barkat Ali: His Life and Writings.* Lahore: Research Society of Pakistan, 1969.

Agnihotri, H. L., and Shiva N. Malik. *A Profile in Courage: A Biography of Ch. Chhotu Ram.* New Delhi: Light and Life Publishers, 1978.

Ahmad, Hafiz Nazar. *Ja'iza-yi Madaris-i 'Arabiya Maghribi Pakistan.* Vol. 2. Lahore: Muslim Akademi, 1972.

Ahmad, Jamil-ud-din, ed. *Speeches and Writings of Mr. Jinnah.* 2 vols. Lahore: Sh. Muhammad Ashraf, 1964.

Ahmad, Mian Bashir. *Justice Shah Din: His Life and Writings.* Lahore: author, 1962.

Ahmad, Muhammad Basheer. *The Judicial System of the Mughal Empire.* Karachi: Pakistan Historical Society, 1978.

Ahmad, Rizwan, comp. *The Quaid-e-Azam Papers, 1941–42.* Karachi: East & West Publishing Company, 1976.

Ahmad, Waheed, ed. *Letters of Mian Fazl-i-Husain.* Lahore: Research Society of Pakistan, 1976.

Alavi, Hamza. "Kinship in West Punjab Villages." *Contributions to Indian Sociology,* new ser., 6 (December 1972).

Algar, Hamid. "The Naqshbandi Order: A Preliminary Survey of its History and Significance." *Studia Islamica* 44 (1977).

Anderson, Benedict. *Imagined Communities: Reflections on the Origin and Spread of Nationalism.* London: Verso, 1983.

Appadurai, Arjun. *Worship and Conflict under Colonial Rule: A South Indian Case.* Cambridge: Cambridge University Press, 1981.

Aziz, Mian Abdul. *Reply to the Dobson Committee Report on the Affairs of the Municipal Committee of Lahore.* Lahore: Maclagan Press, 1932.

Baden-Powell, B. H. *Land Systems of British India.* 2 vols. London: Oxford University Press, 1892.

Baker, Christopher John. *The Politics of South India, 1920–1937.* Cambridge: Cambridge University Press, 1976.

Bakhsh, Khuda, and Abdul Haque. *Relief Legislation in the Punjab.* Lahore: authors, 1939.

Banerjee, Himadri. *Agrarian Society of the Punjab, 1849–1901.* New Delhi: Manohar, 1982.

Barrier, N. G. *The Punjab Alienation of Land Bill of 1900.* Durham: Duke University, 1966.

———. "The Punjab Government and Communal Politics, 1870–1908." *Journal of Asian Studies* 27, no. 3 (May 1968).

Barrier, N. G., and Paul Wallace. *The Punjab Press, 1880–1905.* East Lansing: Asian Studies Center, Michigan State University, 1970.

Batalvi, Ashiq Husain. *Hamari Qaumi Jadd-o-Jahd.* 3 vols. Lahore: various publishers, 1966–1975.

———. *Iqbal ke Akhiri Do Sal.* Karachi: Iqbal Akademi, 1969.

Baxter, Craig. "Union or Partition: Some Aspects of Politics in the Punjab, 1936–1945." In *Pakistan: The Long View,* ed. Lawrence Ziring, Ralph Braibanti, and W. Howard Wriggins. Durham: Duke University Press, 1977.

Bayly, C. A. "Local Control in Indian Towns—the case of Allahabad 1880–1920." *Modern Asian Studies* 5, no. 4 (1971).

———. "The Pre-history of 'Communalism'? Religious Conflict in India, 1700–1860." *Modern Asian Studies* 19, no. 2 (1985).

———. *Rulers, Townsmen, and Bazaars: North Indian Society in the Age of British Expansion, 1770–1870.* Cambridge: Cambridge University Press, 1983.

Binder, Leonard. *Religion and Politics in Pakistan.* Berkeley: University of California Press, 1963.

Brass, Paul. "Elite Groups, Symbol Manipulation, and Ethnic Identity among the Muslims of South Asia." In *Political Identity in South Asia,* ed. David Taylor and Malcolm Yapp. London: Curzon Press, 1979.

———. *Language, Religion, and Politics in North India.* London: Cambridge University Press, 1974.

Brown, Peter. *The Cult of the Saints.* Chicago: University of Chicago Press, 1981.

———. "The Rise and Function of the Holy Man in Late Antiquity." *Journal of Roman Studies* 61 (1971).

———. "The Saint as Exemplar in Late Antiquity." *Representations* 1, no. 2 (Spring 1983).

Chaudhri, Ali Asghar. *Tarikh-i Ara'iyan.* Lahore: 'Ilmi Kutubkhana, 1963.

Chowdhry, Prem. *Punjab Politics: The Role of Sir Chhotu Ram.* New Delhi: Vikas, 1984.

Churchill, Edward D., Jr. "Muslim Societies of the Punjab, 1860–1890." *The Punjab Past and Present* 8, no. 1 (April 1974).

Cohn, Bernard S. "Representing Authority in Victorian India." In *The Invention of Tradition,* ed. Eric Hobsbawm and Terence Ranger. Cambridge: Cambridge University Press, 1983.

Coupland, Reginald. *The Constitutional Problem in India.* London: Oxford University Press, 1944.

Darling, Malcolm. *The Punjab Peasant in Prosperity and Debt.* 1947. Reprint. Columbia, Mo.: South Asia Books, 1978.

———. *Wisdom and Waste in the Punjab Village.* Lahore: Oxford University Press, 1934.

Doyle, Michael W. *Empires.* Ithaca: Cornell University Press, 1986.

Durrani, F. K. Khan. *The Meaning of Pakistan.* 1944. Reprint. Lahore: Islamic Book Service, 1983.

Eaton, Richard M. "The Political and Religious Authority of the Shrine of Baba Farid." In *Moral Conduct and Authority: The Place of Adab in South Asia Islam,* ed. Barbara Daly Metcalf. Berkeley: University of California Press, 1984.

———. *The Sufis of Bijapur.* Princeton: Princeton University Press, 1978.

Ewing, Katherine. "The Pir or Sufi Saint in Pakistani Islam." Ph.D. diss., University of Chicago, 1980.

———. "The Politics of Sufism: Redefining the Saints of Pakistan." *Journal of Asian Studies* 42, no. 2 (February 1983).

Faiz, Maulana Faiz Ahmad. *Mihr-i Munir.* Golra: Saiyid Ghulam Mohyuddin, 1973?.

Faruqi, Iqbal Ahmad. *Tazkira-yi 'Ulama-yi Ahl-i Sunnat o Jama'at, Lahore.* Lahore: Maktaba-yi Nabviya, 1975.

Fazl Shah, Saiyid Muhammad. *Hizbullah.* Lahore: the author?, 1928–29.

Feroze, S. M. A. *Press in Pakistan.* Lahore: National Publications, 1957.

Fox, Richard G. "British Colonialism and Punjabi Labor." In *Labor in the Capitalist World-Economy,* ed. Charles Bergquist. Beverly Hills: Sage Publications, 1984.

———. *Kin, Clan, Raja, and Rule.* Berkeley: University of California Press, 1971.

———. *Lions of the Punjab: Culture in the Making.* Berkeley: University of California Press, 1985.

———. "*Varna* Schemes and Ideological Integration in Indian Society." *Comparative Studies in Society and History* 11 (1969).

Freitag, Sandria B. "'Natural Leaders,' Administrators and Social Control: Communal Riots in the United Provinces." *South Asia* 1, no. 2 (1978).

Gallagher, John, Gordon Johnson, and Anil Seal, eds., *Locality, Province, and Nation.* Cambridge: Cambridge University Press, 1973.

Gauba, K. L. *Friends and Foes.* New Delhi: Indian Book Company, 1974.

Geertz, Clifford. *Islam Observed.* Chicago: University of Chicago Press, 1968.

———. "Religion as a Cultural System." In *The Interpretation of Cultures.* New York: Basic Books, 1973.

Gellner, Ernest. *Nations and Nationalism.* Ithaca: Cornell University Press, 1983.

Ghani, Abdul. *Amir Hizbullah.* Jalalpur Sharif: Idara-yi Hizbullah, 1965.

Gilani, Saiyid Aulad Ali. *Muraqqa'-yi Multan.* Multan: author, 1938.

Gilmartin, David. "Women, Kinship, and Politics in Twentieth-Century Punjab." In *The Extended Family: Women and Political Participation in India and Pakistan,* ed. Gail Minault. Columbia, Mo.: South Asia Books, 1981.

Gilsenan, Michael. *Recognizing Islam.* New York: Pantheon Books, 1982.

Gopal, Madan. *Sir Chhotu Ram: A Political Biography.* Delhi: B. R. Publishing, 1977.

Habib, Irfan. *The Agrarian System of Mughal India.* Bombay: Asia Publishing House, 1963.

Haq, Mushir U. *Muslim Politics in Modern India, 1857–1947.* Meerut: Meenakshi Prakashan, 1970.

Hardiman, David. "The Indian 'Faction': A Political Theory Examined." In *Subaltern Studies I: Writings on South Asian History and Society,* ed. Ranajit Guha. Delhi: Oxford University Press, 1982.

Hardy, Peter. *The Muslims of British India.* Cambridge: Cambridge University Press, 1972.

———. *Partners in Freedom—and True Muslims: The Political Thought of Some Muslim Scholars in British India.* Lund: Scandinavian Institute of Asian Studies, 1971.

Hasan, Mushirul. *Nationalism and Communal Politics in India.* Columbia, Mo.: South Asia Books, 1979.

Ikram, S. M. *Modern Muslim India and the Birth of Pakistan.* Lahore: Sh. Muhammad Ashraf, 1970.

Iqbal, Muhammad. *Poems from Iqbal*. Translated by V. G. Kiernan. London: John Murray, 1955.

——. *The Reconstruction of Religious Thought in Islam*. Lahore: Sh. Muhammad Ashraf. 1971.

Irving, Miles. "The Shrine of Baba Farid Shakarganj at Pakpattan." *Journal of the Panjab Historical Society* 1 (1911–12).

Jafar, Mohammad, I. A. Rahman, and Ghani Jafar, eds. *Jinnah as a Parliamentarian*. Islamabad: Azfar Associates, 1977.

Jafri, S. Qaim Hussain, ed. *Quaid-i-Azam's Correspondence with Punjab Muslim Leaders*. Lahore: Aziz Publishers, 1977.

Jafri, Syed Rais Ahmad, ed. *Rare Documents*. Lahore: Muhammad Ali Academy, 1967.

Jalal, Ayesha. *The Sole Spokesman: Jinnah, the Muslim League and the Demand for Pakistan*. Cambridge: Cambridge University Press, 1985.

Jalal, Ayesha, and Anil Seal. "Alternative to Partition: Muslim Politics Between the Wars." *Modern Asian Studies* 15, no. 3 (1981).

Jinnah, Muhammad Ali, ed. *Letters of Iqbal to Jinnah*. Lahore: Sh. Muhammad Ashraf, 1968.

Jones, Kenneth. *Arya Dharm*. Berkeley: University of California Press, 1976.

——. "Religious Identity and the Indian Census." In *The Census in British India: New Perspectives*, N. G. Barrier, ed. New Delhi: Manohar, 1981.

Josh, Bhagwan. *Communist Movement in the Punjab*. Lahore: Book Traders, 1979–80?.

Kalim, Muhammad Din. *Lahore ke Auliya-yi Chisht*. Lahore: Maktaba-yi Nabviya, 1967.

Kapur, Rajiv A. *Sikh Separatism: The Politics of Faith*. London: Allen & Unwin, 1986.

Karim, Rezaul. *Pakisthan Examined*. Calcutta: Book Company, 1941.

Kashmiri, Shorish. *Tahrik-i Khatm-i Nubuwat*. Lahore: Matbu'at Chatan, 1980.

Kerr, Ian. "The British and the Administration of the Golden Temple in 1859." *The Panjab Past and Present* 10, no. 2 (October 1976).

——. "Urbanization and Colonial Rule in 19th-Century India: Lahore and Amritsar, 1849–1881." *The Panjab Past and Present* 14, no. 1 (April 1980).

Kessinger, Tom G. *Vilyatpur, 1848–1968: Social and Economic Change in a North Indian Village*. Berkeley: University of California Press, 1974.

Kessler, Clive. *Islam and Politics in a Malay State: Kelantan 1838–1969*. Ithaca: Cornell University Press, 1978.

Khan, Ghulam Rasul. *The Punjab Provincial Muslim League: Its Past and Present Position*. Lahore: Punjab Provincial Muslim League?, 1939?.

Khan, Munshi Abdurrahman. *A'ina-yi Multan*. Multan: Maktaba-yi Ashraf al-Ma'araf, 1972.

Knight, Henry. *Food Administration in India, 1939–47*. Stanford: Stanford University Press, 1954.

Kozlowski, Gregory C. *Muslim Endowments and Society in British India*. Cambridge: Cambridge University Press, 1985.

Kumar, Ravinder. "The Rowlatt Satyagraha in Lahore." In *Essays on Gandhian Politics*, ed. R. Kumar. Oxford: The Clarendon Press, 1971.

Kurin, Richard. "Islamization: A View from the Countryside." In *Islamic Re-assertion in Pakistan: The Application of Islamic Laws in a Modern State*, ed. Anita M. Weiss. Syracuse: Syracuse University Press, 1986.

Lal, Shadi. *Commentaries on the Punjab Alienation of Land Act XIII of 1900*, rev. C. L. Anand. Lahore: University Book Agency, 1939.

Latif, Syed Muhammad. *Lahore: Its History, Architectural Remains, and Antiquities*, rev. ed. Lahore: Syed Muhammad Minhaj-ud-Din, 1955?.

Lavan, Spencer. *The Ahmadiyah Movement*. Delhi: Manohar Book Service, 1974.

Lelyveld, David. *Aligarh's First Generation: Muslim Solidarity in British India*. Princeton: Princeton University Press, 1977.

McLeod, W. H. *The Evolution of the Sikh Community*. Oxford: Clarendon Press, 1976.

Madani, Maulana Husain Ahmad. *An Open Letter to the Moslem League*. Lahore: Dewan's Publications, 1946.

———. *Khutba-yi Sadarat*. Jami'at-i 'Ulama-yi Hind Conference, Saharanpur, May 1945.

Malik, Hafeez. "The Man of Thought and Action." In *Iqbal: Poet-Philosopher of Pakistan*, ed. Hafeez Malik. New York: Columbia University Press, 1971.

Malik, Hafeez, and Lynda P. Malik. "The Life of the Poet-Philosopher." In *Iqbal: Poet-Philosopher of Pakistan*, ed. Hafeez Malik. New York: Columbia University Press, 1971.

Malik, Iftikhar Haider. *Sikandar Hayat Khan (1892–1942): A Political Biography*. Islamabad: National Institute of Cultural Research, 1985.

Marriott, McKim. "Village Structure and the Punjab Government: A Restatement." *American Anthropologist 55* (1953).

Mayer, Adrian C. "*Pir* and *Murshid*: An Aspect of Religious Leadership in West Pakistan." *Middle Eastern Studies* 3, no. 2 (January 1967).

Mayne, Peter. *Saints of Sind*. London: John Murray, 1956.

Meherally, Yusuf. *A Trip to Pakistan*. Bombay: Padma Publications, 1943.

Menon, V. P. *The Transfer of Power in India*. Princeton: Princeton University Press, 1957.

Metcalf, Barbara Daly. "Islam and Custom in Nineteenth-Century India." *Contributions to Asian Studies* 17 (1982).

———. *Islamic Revival in British India: Deoband, 1860–1900*. Princeton: Princeton University Press, 1982.

———. "The Madrasa at Deoband: A Model for Religious Education in Modern India." *Modern Asian Studies* 12, no. 1 (1978).

———. "The Reformist 'Ulama: Muslim Religious Leadership in India, 1860–1900." Ph.D. diss., University of California, Berkeley, 1974.

———, ed. *Moral Conduct and Authority: The Place of Adab in South Asian Islam*. Berkeley: University of California Press, 1984.

Mirza, Janbaz. *Karwan-i Ahrar*. 5 vols. Lahore: Maktaba-yi Tabassura, 1975–81.

Mirza, Sarfaraz Hussain. *The Punjab Muslim Students Federation: An Annotated Documentary Survey, 1937–1947*. Lahore: Research Society of Pakistan, 1978.

Moon, Penderel. *Divide and Quit*. London: Chatto & Windus, 1962.

Moore, R. J. "Jinnah and the Pakistan Demand." *Modern Asian Studies* 17, no. 4 (1983).

Muhammad, Shan. *Khaksar Movement in India*. Meerut: Meenakshi Prakashan, 1973.

Murray, W. "On the Manners, Rules, and Customs of the Sikhs." In *Origin of the Sikh Power in the Punjab*, H. T. Prinsep. Patiala: Punjab Languages Department, 1970.

Nath, Amar. *The Development of Local Self-Government in the Punjab, 1849–1900*. Lahore: Punjab Government Record Office, 1929.

Naushervi, Maulana Abu Yahya Imam Khan. *Hindustan men Ahl-i Hadis ki 'Ilmi Khidmat*. Chichawatni: Maktaba-yi Naziriya, 1970.

Niazi, Abdus Sattar Khan, and Mian Muhammad Shafi. *Pakistan Kya he aur Kaise Banega?* Lahore: Muhammad Shafi?: 1945.

Nizami, Khaliq Ahmad. *The Life and Times of Shaikh Farid-u'd-din Ganj-i-Shakar*. Lahore: Universal Books, 1976.

———. *Tarikh-i Masha'ikh-i Chisht*. Karachi: Maktaba-yi Arifin, 1975.

Noon, Firoz Khan. *From Memory*. Lahore: Ferozsons, 1969.

O'Brien, Aubrey. "The Mohammadan Saints of the Western Punjab." *Journal of the Royal Anthropological Institute* 41 (1911).

Oldenburg, Veena Talwar. *The Making of Colonial Lucknow, 1856–1877*. Princeton: Princeton University Press, 1984.

Overstreet, Gene D., and Marshall Windmiller. *Communism in India*. Berkeley: University of California Press, 1959.

Owen, Roger. "Anthropology and Imperial Administration: Sir Alfred Lyall and the Official Use of Theories of Social Change Developed in India after 1857." In *Anthropology and the Colonial Encounter*, ed. Talal Asad. London: Ithaca Press, 1973.

Page, David. *Prelude to Partition: The Indian Muslims and the Imperial System of Control, 1920–1932*. Delhi: Oxford University Press, 1982.

Pirzada, Syed Sharifuddin. *The Pakistan Resolution and the Historic Lahore Session*. Karachi: Pakistan Publications, 1968.

———, ed. *Foundations of Pakistan: All-India Muslim League Documents, 1906–1947*. 2 vols. Karachi: National Publishing House, 1970.

A Punjabee [pseud.]. "Punjab Politics." *The Muslim Revival* 5, no. 1 (March 1936).

"A Punjabi" [pseud.]. *Confederacy of India*. Lahore: Nawab Sir Muhammad Shah Nawaz Khan of Mamdot, 1939.

Punjab Provincial Muslim League. *Manifesto of the Punjab Provincial Muslim League*. Lahore: Daniyal Latifi, 1944.

Punjab Unionist Party. *Rules and Regulations*. Lahore: Punjab Unionist Party, 1936.

Punjab Zamindara League. *Punjab Muslim Lig ki Zamindar Dushmani Muslim Musawat Bil*. Lahore: Punjab Zamindara Lig, 1945.

Qureshi, Ishtiaq Husain. *Ulema in Politics*. Karachi: Ma'aref, 1972.

Qureshi, Makhdum Murid Husain. *Khatra ka Alarm*. Lahore: author?, 1930–31?

Qureshi, Muhammad Hyat. *Zamindaron ki Barbadi ki Taiyariyan! Kangres kya Karna Chahti he?* Lahore: author?, 1930?

Rahman, Fazlur. *Islam and Modernity: Transformation of an Intellectual Tradition.* Chicago: University of Chicago Press, 1982.

Rai, Satya M. *Legislative Politics and the Freedom Struggle in the Punjab, 1897–1947.* New Delhi: Indian Council of Historical Research, 1984.

Ram, Chaudhri Chhotu. *Indebtedness in the Punjab.* Lahore: Punjab Unionist Party, 1936.

———. "A Speech of Sir Chhotu Ram, 1st March 1942." *Panjab Past and Present* 8, no. 1 (April 1974).

Ram, Chaudhri Tikka. *Sir Chhotu Ram: Apostle of Hindu-Muslim Unity.* N.p, n.d.

Ranger, T. O. "From Humanism to the Science of Man: Colonialism in Africa and the Understanding of Alien Societies." *Transactions of the Royal Historical Society* 26 (1976).

Rashid, S. Khalid. *Wakf Administration in India.* New Delhi: Vikas, 1978.

Robinson, Francis. "Islam and Muslim Separatism." In *Political Identity in South Asia,* ed. David Taylor and Malcolm Yapp. London: Curzon Press, 1979.

Sayeed, Khalid B. *Politics in Pakistan: The Nature and Direction of Change.* New York: Praeger, 1980.

Scott, James. *The Moral Economy of the Peasant.* New Haven: Yale University Press, 1976.

Seal, Anil. "Nationalism and Imperialism in India." In *Locality, Province, and Nation,* ed. John Gallagher, Gordon Johnson, and Anil Seal. Cambridge: Cambridge University Press, 1973.

Shafi, Sardar Muhammad. "Pahle edishan par chand tabassure." In *Tarikh-i Ara'iyan,* Ali Asghar Chaudhri. Lahore: 'Ilmi Kutubkhana, 1963.

Shah, Haider Husain. *Shah-yi Jama'at.* Lahore: Maktaba-yi Shah-yi Jama'at, 1973.

Shah, Saiyid Akhtar Husain. *Sirat-i Amir-i Millat.* Alipur Sayyedan: author, 1974.

Shahnawaz, Jahan Ara. *Father and Daughter.* Lahore: Nigarishat, 1971.

Siddiqi, M. Zameeruddin. "The Resurgence of the Chishti Silsilah in the Punjab During the Eighteenth Century." In *Proceedings of the Indian History Congress, 1970.* New Delhi: Indian History Congress, 1971.

Singh, Ganda. *History of the Gurdwara Shahidganj, Lahore.* Lahore?: author?, 1935.

Singh, Iqbal. *The Ardent Pilgrim.* London: Longmans, Green, 1951.

Singh, Khushwant. *A History of the Sikhs.* 2 vols. Princeton: Princeton University Press, 1966.

Singh, Mohinder. *The Akali Movement.* Delhi: Macmillan, 1978.

Smith, Wilfred Cantwell. *Modern Islam in India.* Lahore: Sh. Muhammad Ashraf, 1969.

———. "The 'Ulama' in Indian Politics." In *Politics and Society in India,* ed. C. H. Philips. London: George Allen & Unwin, 1963.

Talbot, Ian. "Deserted Collaborators: The Political Background to the Rise and Fall of the Punjab Unionist Party, 1923–1947." *Journal of Imperial and Commonwealth History* 11, no. 1 (October 1982).

———. "The Growth of the Muslim League in the Punjab, 1937–1946." *Journal of Commonwealth and Comparative Politics* 20, no. 1 (March 1982).

Thursby, G. R. *Hindu-Muslim Relations in British India.* Leiden: E. J. Brill, 1975.

Trimingham, J. Spencer. *The Sufi Orders in Islam.* Oxford: Oxford University Press, 1971.

Turner, Bryan. *Weber and Islam.* London: Routledge & Kegan Paul, 1974.

Uprety, Prem Raman. *Religion and Politics in Punjab in the 1920's.* New Delhi: Sterling Publishers, 1980.

van den Dungen, P. H. M. *The Punjab Tradition: Influence and Authority in Nineteenth-Century India.* London: George Allen & Unwin, 1972.

Washbrook, David. "Law, State, and Agrarian Society in Colonial India." *Modern Asian Studies* 15, no. 3 (1981).

Wolpert, Stanley. *Jinnah of Pakistan.* New York: Oxford University Press, 1984.

Yadav, Kirpal C. *Elections in Panjab, 1920–1947.* Tokyo: Institute for the Study of Languages and Cultures of Asia and Africa, 1981.

Zaheer, Sajjad. *Muslim Lig aur Yunyunist Parti: Punjab men Haqq o Batil ki Kashmakash.* Bombay: Qaumi Darul Isha'at, 1944?

Zaman, Mukhtar. *Students' Role in the Pakistan Movement.* Karachi: Quaid-i-Azam Academy, 1978.

Ziauddin, Shaikh. *Anjuman Himayat-i Islam Diamond Jubilee, 1967.* Lahore: Anjuman Himayat-i Islam, 1967.

Zulfiqar, Ghulam Hussain. *Zafar Ali Khan: Adib o Sha'ir.* Lahore: Maktaba-yi Khiyaban-i Adab, 1967.

INTERVIEWS. CONDUCTED IN PAKISTAN,
NOVEMBER 1974–MARCH 1976.

Saiyid Amjad Ali Shah. Lahore.
Sardar Shaukat Hyat Khan, Islamabad.
Mian Mushtaq Ahmad Gurmani, Lahore.
Abdul Hamid Khan Dasti, Muzaffargarh.
Malik Qadir Bakhsh, Lahore.
Pir Khurshid Ahmad Qureshi, Multan.
Saiyid Alamdar Husain Gilani, Multan.
Saiyid Ali Husain Shah Gardezi, Multan.
Begum Shah Nawaz, Lahore.
Muhammad Sarwar Bodla, Dera Ghazi Khan.
Mian Hayat Bakhsh, Rawalpindi.
Shaikh Muhammad Saeed, Jhang.
Shaikh Zafar Husain, Lahore.
Abu Saeed Enver, Lahore.
Chaudhri Rahmatullah, Lahore.
Chaudhri Nazir Ahmad Khan, Lahore.
Saiyid Fida Hassan, Lahore.
Chaudhri Faqir Husain, Lahore.
Maulana Ghulam Murshid, Lahore.

Index

Agricultural Markets Act (1939), 151
agricultural tribes, 28–37, 39, 108, 164;
as status category, 31–33, 86; as ar-
tificial state creation, 34, 37, 193; and
religious leaders, 50–51, 62; and
Kashmiris, 86–87; and Arains, 89,
91; as a "class," 116, 118; as debtors,
123, 127
Ahl-i Hadis, 55, 61, 215
Ahmad, Mian Bashir, 183 n
Ahmadiyah, 97, 228
Ahrar, 37, 113, 114, 179, 190; formation
of, 96; and Kashmir agitation, 96–
99; and Shahidganj agitation, 100,
102, 106
Ajmer, *sajjada nishin* of, 216–17
Akalis, 70, 154–160, 222–23
Alavi, Hamza, 83
Ali, Malik Barkat, 160, 175, 177–80,
183 n
Ali, Mirza Zafar, 82 n
Ali, Nawab Fazl, 170
Alienation of Land Act (1901), 27–38,
50, 62; and definition of status, 31–
32, 86–87; as pro-landlord, 33, 117;
and religion, 29–31, 32–33, 62, 170;
and Unionist ideology, 115–18, 120,
122–23, 125, 127–28, 149, 150, 152;
and Muslim Musawat Bill, 203–4
Aligarh, 78, 91, 146, 212
Amin, Shaikh Muhammad, 179 n
Amir-i Hind, 63
Amir-i Millat, 103–4, 216
Amiruddin, Mian, 84, 88, 180

Amritsar city, 23, 63, 79, 81, 149; Kashmiris in, 83–84, 85, 87, 97; Shahidganj conference in, 106; 1938 by-
election, 178–79
Amritsar district, 149
Anderson, Benedict, 4
*anjuman*s, 77, 80, 83, 95, 107; Anjuman
Fida'iyan-i Islam, 138; Anjuman
Himayat-i Islam, 77, 91, 205–6; An-
juman Hizb al-Ahnaf, 104, 164; An-
juman Islamia, 77; Anjuman Kash-
miri Musalmanan, 85–86; Anjuman
Khuddam al-Sufiya, 60; Anjuman-i
Tahaffuz-i Masjid Shahidganj, 100;
Arain *anjuman*, 91, 93, 94, 142
Arains, 29, 89–95, 169; in Lyallpur, 141,
142, 143; defection from Unionist
party, 185
army recruiting, 16, 69; of Arains, 91
Aroras, 30, 156, 157
Arya Samaj, 77
Attock district, 20, 23, 24, 51, 146, 159
auqaf legislation, 162–64, 230–31, 232
Awans, 51
Azhar, Mazhar Ali, 190
Aziz, Mian Abdul, 92–95, 100–101, 142

backward classes, 116–17
Baden-Powell, B. H., 19
Badshahi mosque, Lahore, 77, 101, 160–
61, 215 n
Baghbanpura, Mian family of, 75, 90–
92, 94. *See also* Ahmad, Mian Bashir;
Shafi, Mian Muhammad; Shah Din,

Baghbanpura (*continued*)
  Mian; Shah Nawaz, Begum Jahan
  Ara; Shah Nawaz, Mian Mu-
  hammad
Bahawalpur, 57, 58
bai'at, 104
Bakhsh, Chaudhri Bahawal, 170
Bakhsh, Haji Rahim, 87
Bakhsh, Malik Qadir, 200–201
Bakhsh, Mian Karim, 84
barakat, 42, 43, 66, 211
Barelvi *'ulama*, 60, 61, 82, 103–4, 164,
  215
bata'i, 121–22
Batalvi, Ashiq Husain, 184 n
Bayly, C. A., 75
Bhalwal tehsil, 134, 135
Bhutto, Zulfiqar Ali, 231–32
Biloch, 17, 48, 57, 186; *tumandars*, 26,
  66; of Sahiwal, 134
biradari, 18, 19, 26, 37, 75, 95, 100, 107;
  definition of, 83; Kashmiri, 83–88,
  98; Arain, 89–95; in Pakistan move-
  ment, 204, 216–17, 222, 227. *See
  also* "tribe"
Bokhari, Saiyid Ataullah Shah, 96–97
Bokhari, Saiyid Jalaluddin, of Uch, 40, 43
Bosan, Muhammad Akram Khan, 137 n
British colonial ideology, 5, 6, 11–13,
  17–18, 25, 26, 32, 37; and structure
  of religious organization, 46, 49, 50–
  52, 62, 63, 71
Brown, Peter, 211

canal irrigation, 8, 133, 140; colonies, 8,
  17, 72, 76, 89, 119–20, 123, 140,
  143; colony land grants, 25–26, 50,
  51; colony settlers (*abadkars*), 141,
  142, 143, 220, 221. *See also* pastoralists
capitalism, 117
Chishti, Ibrahim Ali, 223 n
Chishti order, 57–59, 65, 68, 113
Cohn, Bernard, 11–12
communal award (1932), 70, 155
communalism, 3–4, 111–12, 114, 141,
  153, 158–59, 161, 162–63; in cities,
  79–81; and *biradaris*, 83, 87; in public agitations, 95–107; of the Sikhs,
  154–60; in Iqbal's thought, 165,
  166–67; and Pakistan, 180–83
Communists, 196–98, 199, 211–12
Congress, 99, 107, 178–79; and the depression, 120, 126; opposition to
  Unionists, 37, 149, 151; coalition with
  Unionists, 222
Court of Wards, 48–49, 121

Craik, H. D., 36
"cultural system," 40, 41, 52, 56, 61, 62,
  71, 86, 160, 202
customary law, 13–18, 19, 86; and
  shari'at, 169–70

Darling, Malcolm, 117, 130, 150 n
dastarbandi, 48
Dasti, Abdul Hamid Khan, 200–201
Daultana, Ahmad Yar Khan, 121, 168,
  185 n, 187, 191–92
Daultana, Mumtaz Muhammad Khan, 1,
  187, 192–93, 194; and Communists,
  196; and Muslim League organization, 199; and Muslim League manifesto, 196–99; and "tribalism,"
  202–3
debt conciliation boards, 127
Debtors' Protection Act (1936), 127–28
debts and indebtedness, 28, 48, 120–21,
  122–25; legislation, 127–28, 129,
  133, 134. *See also* moneylenders
Delhi, 6, 40, 53, 57, 134, 196
"democracy," 9, 107, 108, 129, 151–52,
  154, 215, 231; and the colonial state,
  110, 200, 226, 227, 228; Unionist
  efforts to adapt to, 126, 128, 164, 188
Deobandi *'ulama*, 54, 55–56, 60–61,
  63, 92 n, 190, 215. *See also* Jami'at-i
  'Ulama-yi Hind
depression, 118–20; effects on landlords
  and tenants, 120–22; effects on credit
  relations, 122–25; in the canal colonies, 119–20, 140; and Unionist legislation, 125–28, 150–51
Dera Ghazi Khan district, 26, 57, 67
Din, Malik Muhammad, 169, 170
district boards, 27, 50, 109, 124, 131;
  Sheikhupura, 131; Multan, 136–37,
  139, 185 n; Lyallpur, 141

Eastern Times, Lahore, 191, 193, 203–4,
  205
Eaton, Richard M., 41, 43 n
elections, 4, 22, 67, 70, 87–88, 93–94,
  102, 162, 180; under Government of
  India Act (1935), 109–10; 1937 Legislative Assembly, 135–36, 139–40,
  141–43, 147; 1946 Legislative Assembly, 189, 212, 217–21
Emerson, Herbert, 100
Ewing, Katherine, 230

factions, 22; definition of, 129–30; and
  "tribal" idioms, 130, 133, 135, 141; in
  Unionist party, 130–32, 144–45,
  147–50, 185–87, 201; in Shahpur,

132–36; in Multan, 136–40; in
    Lyallpur, 141–43
Fagan, P. J., 35
Fakhruddin, Shah, of Delhi, 57
*fatwa*s, 59, 64, 215, 218, 220
Fazilka tehsil, 30
Ferozepore district, 89, 126 n, 131 n, 200
Fox, Richard, 17

Gauba, K. L., 87–88, 173 n
Geertz, Clifford, 40, 52
Gilani, Saiyid Muhammad Ghaus, of
    Uch, 45, 58
Gilani, Saiyid Muhammad Raza Shah,
    139
Gilani, Saiyid Sadruddin Shah, *sajjada
    nishin*, 138, 164
Gilani, Saiyid Sher Shah, 139
Gilani, Saiyid Zainulabedin Shah, 102,
    103, 138
Gilani, Saiyids of Multan, 113, 136–37,
    137–39, 185, 200 n, 213, 214; and
    shrine of Pir Musa Pak Shahid, 45,
    136
Girot, Saiyids of, 134
Golra, *pir*s of, 64, 113, 219; Saiyid Mehr
    Ali Shah, 58, 61 n; Saiyid Ghulam
    Mohyuddin, 103
Gondals, 135
Government of India Act (1935), 107,
    108
Grunebaum, G. E. von, 73
Gujar Khan tehsil, 218
Gujars, 20, 194
Gujranwala district, 20, 98, 201
Gujrat district, 8 n, 20, 70, 144 n, 170
Gurdaspur district, 8 n, 20, 30, 170
Gurmani, Mushtaq Ahmad, 121, 148 n

Habib, Irfan, 45
Habib, Syad, 80
Hailey, Malcolm, 37, 157
hajj, 68, 106
Haq, Chaudhri Afzal, 179
Haq, Fazlul, 185
Haroon, Abdullah, 207 n
Hasan, Shaikh Sadiq, 84 n, 179 n
Haye, Mian Abdul, 147 n
Hindu Sabha, 32, 37, 126
Hindus, 6, 8, 15, 34, 75, 77, 91, 96, 105,
    111, 123, 124, 141; and the Land
    Alienation Act, 30, 32–33; and the
    Unionist party, 35, 115; and the Con-
    gress, 107, 149
Hizbullah, 69–70, 159
Hoshiarpur district, 20, 92
Hukumat-i Ilahi, 190

Husain, Fazli, 34–35, 36, 38, 110, 132;
    and Islamic ideology, 111–14; as com-
    munalist, 80–81, 111–12; and Union-
    ist reorganization, 108–9, 116–17,
    132, 135; and Muslim League, 113–
    15, 165; death, 144
Husain, Sardar Muhammad, 185 n

Ibbetson, Denzil, 51, 84
Ikram, S. M., 206
iman (faith), 189, 209–10
*in'am*s, 23
Indus, 6, 43, 51, 57
Iqbal, Muhammad, 165–69, 217, 230,
    233; as Kashmiri, 85, 87 n, 88; views
    on *pir*s, 166, 211; views on *'ulama*
    and *shari'at*, 167–68; views on com-
    munalism, 166–67; and Jinnah,
    168–69; and Sikander-Jinnah pact,
    175–78; and Pakistan idea, 180–81;
    influence on Muslim students and
    evolution of Pakistan concept, 207–
    11, 213
Islamia College, Lahore, 77, 205, 206, 212
Islamic socialism, 231
Ittehad-i Millat, 101, 103, 106, 138

*jagir*s, 19, 48, 189
Jahanian Shah, Saiyids of, 48 n, 134
Jalalpur, *pir*s of, 68–71, 218; Saiyid
    Ghulam Haider Ali Shah, 68; Saiyid
    Muhammad Fazl Shah, 64 n, 68, 69,
    70, 98, 103, 113, 159, 214, 218; Na-
    wab Mehr Shah, 68–70
Jalalpur Bhattian, 201
Jalalpur Pirwala, *sajjada nishin* of,
    48–49
Jama'at-i Islami, 232
Jami'at-i 'Ulama-yi Hind, 64, 81, 82, 85,
    215 n; founding of, 63; and Ahrar,
    99; and Muslim League, 114, 190;
    and *shari'at* Act, 173
Jami'at-i 'Ulama-yi Islam, 215
Jandiala Sher Khan, 159
*jatha*s: in Tanzim movement, 81; in Kash-
    mir agitation, 97, 98
Jats, 17, 20, 21, 25, 29, 30, 91; Sikh, 30,
    155, 156, 157; and Sir Chhotu Ram,
    125–26, 193; associations of, and
    Muslim League ideology, 193–94,
    198, 202
Jhang district, 8 n, 47, 50 n, 124 n, 127 n,
    163
jhatka, 153, 158, 159
Jhavarian, 219
Jhelum district, 20, 68–70, 200, 204,
    218

jihad, 69
jinn, 42
Jinnah, Muhammad Ali, 1, 3, 93, 114,
    165, 168–69, 225, 226; and *shari'at*
    Act, 169, 171–74; Sikander-Jinnah
    pact, 174–80; and definition of Paki-
    stan, 180–83, 213; tensions with Sir
    Sikander, 183–85; break with Union-
    ists, 187–88, 199; and tension within
    Muslim League, 190, 191, 205; and
    students, 205–8; and Communists,
    212; and *pirs,* 216
Jullundur district, 89, 184 n, 222

kafir, 218, 220
Kalimullah, Shah, of Delhi, 57
kamins (village menials), 31, 91, 203
Kashmir, 83; agitation of 1931–32,
    96–99
Kashmiris, 83–88, 89, 95, 97–98
Khaksars, 105
Khakwani, Ghulam Qadir Khan, 65
Khalsa National party, 147, 158
Khan, Ayub, 229–31
Khan, Mian Ghulam Rasul, 177, 178
Khan, Nawab Liaqat Hyat, 137 n
Khan, Nawab Muzaffar, 109
Khan, Raja Ghazanfar Ali, 69, 70, 163,
    165, 193, 195, 217
Khan, Raja Khair Mehdi, Janjua, 204
Khan, Raja Saif Ali, Khokhar, 68
Khan, Shaukat Hyat, 186–87, 212
Khan, Sikander Hyat, 59, 70, 94, 106,
    110 n, 137, 144; early career of, 146;
    leadership of Unionist ministry, 147–
    48; and agrarian legislation, 148–52;
    and communalism, 153, 159–60;
    views on Sikhs, 155–56; and Islam,
    160–64; Sikander-Jinnah pact, 174–
    80; relations with Jinnah, 182, 183,
    184–85; and Pakistan, 180–86;
    death, 186
Khan, Zafar Ali, 78–79, 80, 100–101,
    103, 138, 146, 147, 153
Khatris, 33, 156, 157
Khattaks, 51
Khilafat movement, 37, 63, 64, 79, 81,
    84–85, 96
Khilafat-i Pakistan, 208–10
kisan committees, 149, 150
Kitchlew, Saif-ud-din, 81–82, 84–85,
    178–79
Kot Fateh Khan, 159

Lahore city, 8, 60, 63, 74, 75, 77, 78,
    109, 131, 139, 164, 169; 1927 riot,
    79–80; Kashmiris in, 84, 85, 87, 88;

Arains in, 89–94; Municipal Com-
    mittee, 84, 88, 93; Shahidganj
    mosque agitation in, 100–101, 102,
    103, 106; 1941 by-election, 180;
    Jami'at-i 'Ulama-yi Islam conference,
    215; 1947 anti-Khizr agitation, 223
Lahore district, 80, 89, 92 n, 126 n, 147
Lahore High Court (formerly Chief
    Court of Punjab), 11, 90, 93, 161
Lahore resolution (1940), 182–83, 184,
    186
Lal, Lala Harkishen, 87
lambardars (*nambardars*), 22, 67, 189,
    196
Land Alienation Act. *See* Alienation of
    Land Act (1901)
langar, 43–45, 138
Latif, Baji Rashida, 173 n
Latifi, Daniyal, 196
law. *See* customary law; *shari'at*
Lawrence, John, 23 n; statue of, 11, 93
Leghari, Jamal Khan, 186
Ludhiana city, 83, 84
Ludhiana district, 21, 36, 126 n
Ludhianvi, Habib-ur-Rahman, 92 n, 105
Lyallpur city, 76
Lyallpur district, 89, 119, 126 n, 149,
    150 n; Unionist party and 1937 elec-
    tions in, 140–43; 1946 elections in,
    220–21
Lyallpur tehsil, 143

Maclagan, Edward, 27 n, 51
McLeod, W. H., 157
Madani, Husain Ahmad, 173, 190
madrasas, 61, 232 n; Deoband, 54; Dar
    al-'Ulum Naumaniya, 60–61; Dar
    al-'Ulum Hizb al-Ahnaf, 60–61
Mahajan Samachar, 124
Maharvi, Nur Muhammad, 57
Mahmud, Mir Maqbul, 106, 148, 162,
    164, 177, 187
Majithia, Sunder Singh, 147, 158
Makhad, *pir* of, 51
Mamdot, Iftikhar Husain Khan, 187,
    192, 196–98, 200
Mamdot, Muhammad Shah Nawaz
    Khan, 182, 192
Mamdot family, 66 n
Manoharlal, Sir, 146–47
Manshervi, Muhammad Ishaq, 64
marriage, 15–16, 17, 134 n, 170 n; of *pirs,*
    63, 65, 68
martial law, 228
masha'ikh, 70; committee formed in late
    1946, 223. See also *pirs*
Maynard, H. J., 32, 34, 51, 66, 118, 192 n

mediation and intermediaries: in the
structure of British rule, 22, 24, 31–
32, 37, 45, 46, 48, 49, 63, 71, 115,
120; in Islamic organization and
leadership, 9, 42, 45, 52, 54–56, 58,
59, 60, 61–62, 71, 137, 139, 160, 211,
215; in urban politics, 74–75, 76, 79,
82, 88; the Akali challenge to, 154,
155, 158; Iqbal's views on, 166; Jinnah's views on, 183; the Muslim
League challenge to, 193, 197; in
Pakistan, 227–28, 231
Mianwali district, 8 n
milad al-nabi, 61
Mohammad, Justice Din, 171
moneylenders (banias), 28, 29, 30, 31,
34, 120–24, 125, 134, 141, 150–51.
See also debts and indebtedness
Montgomery district, 51, 62, 120, 150 n,
217; Unionist organization in,
131–32
Moon, Penderel, 148 n
mosques: as symbols of community, 81,
161; in Tanzim movement, 81–82; in
Kashmir agitation, 98–99. *See also*
Badshahi mosque; Shahidganj mosque; Wazir Khan mosque
Mughal Empire, 46, 47, 54, 160; and
shari'at, 13; and "tribal" leaders,
18–19; and religious leaders, 45, 47,
52–53, 57; land grants of, 45, 47,
90; as model for Unionists, 146–47
Multan city, 47, 67, 74, 102, 103, 113,
214; 1922 riot, 79; Gilanis and politics of, 138
Multan district, 8 n, 47, 48, 50 n, 51, 65,
124, 150 n, 185 n, 200; Unionist party
and 1937 elections in, 136–40
Munir, Justice Muhammad, 3, 223 n
*murid*s, 42, 58, 59, 106, 137–38, 219
Murshid, Ghulam, 215 n
Muslim Conference, 87 n, 111
Muslim League, 1, 70, 91, 93: reorgani-
zation, 114; development in Punjab,
164–65, 168, 169, 174; and Sikander-
Jinnah pact, 174–80; and Pakistan
idea, 180–81; 1940 Lahore resolution, 182–83; 1944 manifesto, 196–
98, 211, 231; rural organization,
199–201, 204–5; and *pir*s, 213, 215;
success in 1946 elections, 218–22;
1947 anti-Khizr agitation, 222–23
Muslim Musawat Bill, 202–3
*mutawalli*s, 82, 163
Muzaffargarh district, 25, 50 n, 51, 121,
124 n; shrines in, 42 n; Muslim
League in, 200–201

Naqshbandi order, 59, 92 n
nation: concept of Muslim, 4, 5, 213,
226–27; two-nation theory, 183, 205
"natural leaders," 74
Nawa-i-Waqt, Lahore, 207–8, 215, 217
Niazi, Abdus Sattar Khan, 206 n, 208–
11, 212
Nizami, Hamid, 207–8
Nizami, K. A., 57
Nizam-i Mustafa, 232
nonagriculturalists, 30, 31, 32, 33, 115,
120, 122, 123, 126, 127, 137, 141, 149,
150–51, 156
Noon, Malik Firoz Khan, 35 n, 81 n,
110–11, 132, 219
Noon, Malik Sardar Khan, 135
Noons. *See* Tiwanas and Noons
Nurpur, shrine of Bari Shah Latif at, 50
Nurullah, Mian, 94 n, 142, 143, 185, 220,
221

O'Dwyer, Michael, 25, 51, 86

Paisa Akhbar, Lahore, 78
Pakistan, 1, 2–3; first proposals for,
180–83; as embodiment of Muslim
community, 180–81, 183, 189–91,
197, 212; support of students for,
205–13; support of *pir*s for, 210–11,
213–22; ambivalence of Sikander toward, 183–86; as independent state,
226–32
party government, 109–10
pastoralists ("*jangli*s"), 8, 16, 19, 42, 47;
settlement of, 8, 17, 41; called *jangli*s,
141; in canal colonies, 141, 142, 143,
220–21
Pathans, 33, 51, 57, 65
*patwari*s, 135
Peasants Welfare Fund, 150 n
Pindigheb tehsil, 23
Piracha, Shaikh Fazl-i-Haq, 172 n
*pir*s: *sajjada nishin*s, 42, 43, 45, 46–51,
52–53, 58, 59; of Taunsa, 65–68; of
Jalalpur, 68–71; and Kashmir agitation, 98; and Shahidganj mosque agitation, 103, 104–5, 106; relations
with *'ulama*, 52–53, 55, 58, 59,
60–61, 63–64, 82, 104; Iqbal's views
on, 166, 211; relations with Unionists,
62, 113, 137–39; role in Pakistan
movement, 210–11, 213–22, 226–
27; role in Pakistan, 229–30, 231,
233
Prophet Muhammad, 2, 5, 56, 61, 73,
87, 97, 102, 202, 221, 227, 228, 232
provincial autonomy, 108, 109

Punjab Laws Act (1872), 14
Punjab Muslim League. *See* Muslim
  League
Punjab Muslim Students Federation, 206,
  207, 208, 212, 213
Punjab National Unionist party. *See*
  Unionist party

Qadri order, 58, 59, 62, 136
qaum, 18, 19, 26, 88, 217
Qor'an, 2, 55, 68, 96, 102, 170, 209, 218
Qureshi, Ashiq Husain, 137, 139, 214
Qureshi, Makhdum Murid Husain, *saj-
  jada nishin*, 123, 137, 139, 164
Qureshi, Makhdum Shah Mahmud, *saj-
  jada nishin*, 47–48
Qureshi, Nawab Muhammad Hyat, of
  Sabhowal, 124n, 134, 135, 136, 219
Qureshi family of Multan, 48, 75, 113,
  136–39, 214; and shrines of Bahawal
  Haq and Shah Rukn-i Alam, 45, 47,
  136, 214
Qureshi family of Shahpur, 135, 200

Rab, Mian Abdur, 185n
ra'is, 66, 76, 77, 78, 81, 103, 180; definition of, 75; Kashmiri, 84, 85, 86,
  179; Arain, 90, 91, 92
Rajoa, Saiyids of, 47
Rajputs, 29, 91, 194; associations of, 193,
  202
Ram, Chhotu, 35, 36, 37–38, 149, 195;
  and organization of Jats, 125, 193;
  and Zamindara League, 126; and
  agrarian legislation, 126–28; and the
  Unionist party, 35, 94, 108, 125, 129,
  147n, 195; definition of "zamindar,"
  115–16
Ranjha, Sultan Ali, 135, 201
Ranjhas, 135
Rawalpindi city, 79, 103, 105
Rawalpindi district, 50, 58
Relief of Indebtedness Act (1934), 127,
  128
riots: in Punjab's cities, 78, 79–80,
  153n; at Taunsa, 66–67; at Ala, 159;
  near riot at Sial, 64
Rohtak district, 125–26

Sadiq, Shaikh Ahmad
Sadiq, Shaikh Muhammad
Saiyids, 33, 50, 68. See also *individual
  Saiyid families*
*sajjada nishin*s. See *pir*s
Samad, Khwaja Ghulam, 202n
Sandilianwali, *sajjada nishin* of, 220
Sargodha, 76

Scott, James, 119
separate electorates, 4, 27, 39
Shafi, Mian Muhammad, of Baghban-
  pura, 90, 91, 94
Shafi, Mian Muhammad ("Meem
  sheen"), 209–11
Shah, Pir Jamaat Ali, 59–60, 61, 98, 113,
  163n, 214, 218; and Shahidganj
  mosque agitation, 103–7; and Jinnah,
  216
Shah, Pir M. Husain, 218
Shah, Pir Nasiruddin, of Kuranga, 143,
  220, 221
Shah, Saiyid Amjad Ali, 131n
Shah, Saiyid Mubarak Ali, of Shah Ji-
  wana, 163n
Shah Din, Mian, 90, 91
Shah Jiwana, Saiyids of, 48n, 163n
Shah Nawaz, Begum Jahan Ara, 94
Shah Nawaz, Mian Muhammad, 93n
Shahabuddin, Chaudhri, 88n, 144
Shahidganj mosque, 100; agitation, 70,
  100–107, 161, 216
Shahpur, Saiyids of, 135
Shahpur district, 8n, 24, 26, 130; Unionist party and 1937 elections in, 132–
  36; 1946 elections in, 218–19; and
  Muslim League organization, 200
Shahpur tehsil, 133n, 134, 135, 136
Shalimar Bagh, 90
Sharaqpur: Mian Sher Muhammad of,
  92n; Mian Ghulam Ahmad, *sajjada
  nishin* of, 215n
shari'at, 13, 63, 86, 92; inheritance and
  marriage patterns, 16, 170n; and re-
  vival *pir*s, 57, 59, 60; and Shahidganj
  mosque agitation, 102, 106; and *au-
  qaf* legislation, 163–64; and *shari'at*
  legislation, 169–74; and Pakistan,
  190, 212, 227, 232
Shariat Application Act (1937), 171–74, 190
Sheikhupura district, 131–32
Sher Shah, Saiyids of: estate, 48n, Makhdum Ghulam Akbar Shah, *sajjada
  nishin*, 214
Shergarh, Saiyids of, 213–14; Saiyid
  Muhammad Husain, *sajjada nishin*,
  62, 214n
Shujabad tehsil, 48
Sial, *pir*s of, 113, 215n, 219; Khwaja
  Shamsuddin, 59, 68; Pir Ziauddin, 64
Sialkot city, 8n, 84, 85, 87, 97
Sialkot district, 25, 59, 201
Sikander-Jinnah pact, 174–78, 180–81,
  185, 187, 188, 206
Sikh Gurdwaras and Shrines Act (1925),
  155, 162, 163, 230

Sikhs, 6, 8, 18–19, 23, 30, 35, 46–47, 57, 141, 153; and Shahidganj mosque agitation, 100, 102; and rural credit, 30, 123; and agrarian opposition to Unionists, 118, 150; gurdwara reform movement and Akalis, 154–60; Shiromani Gurdwara Prabandhak Committee (S.G.P.C.), 81n, 155, 158, 162
Singh, Giani Sher, 158n
Singh, Harnam, 33
Singh, Iqbal, 85
Singh, Jogendra, 38
Singh, Khushwant, 155
Singh, Master Tara, 153, 158n, 159n
Singh, Ranjit, 23
Singh, Sabhas, 155
Smith, Wilfred Cantwell, 2n, 53
students: in Pakistan movement, 187, 206–8, 212–13, 223. *See also* Punjab Muslim Students Federation
*sufedposhe*s, 67, 91, 131, 189
*sufi*s and sufism, 70; *khanaqah*s, 41, 57, 58, 59, 67; spread of shrines, 43, 57; shrines as foci of local identities, 41–42, 49–50, 58; links of shrines to the state, 45, 46, 47–52, 59, 62, 63, 67; *sufi* orders, 43, 55, 56, 57, 59; attacks on, 55, 60; revival movement, 56–62, 63–65, 69, 71; and Pakistan, 210–11, 216. See also *individual orders; pirs*

tabligh, 57, 60
Tahim, Mian Ghulam Rasul Khan, 127n
Tajuddin, Pir, 191
Tanzim movement, 81–82, 84
tauhid, 209
Taunsa, *pirs* of, 57–58, 65–68, 113, 280
Tiwana, Malik Khizr Hyat Khan, 147n, 148, 186, 187, 191, 201, 213n, 219, 222–23
Tiwana, Malik Umar Hyat Khan, 59, 132–35, 148
Tiwana, Nawab Allah Bakhsh, 135, 136, 219
Tiwanas and Noons, 24, 26, 133–34, 136, 186, 219. See also *individual Tiwanas and Noons*
Toba Tek Singh tehsil, 141, 143, 220, 221
"tribe," 5; British definition of, 14–15, 17–18; custom and "tribal" kinship, 15–16; contiguity of settlement, 18, 19–20; "tribal" leadership and the British, 18–24; in the Land Alienation Act, 28–31; and religious organization, 40–41, 48, 49–52, 57–58,

59, 62, 63, 65, 68; "tribal" idioms and politics, 19, 21, 22, 27, 71, 109–10, 116, 130, 204, 221; "tribal" associations, 193–94, 202. *See also* agricultural tribes, *biradari*
Tribune, Lahore, 34, 196–97
Tupper, C. L., 14–18, 19–20

'ulama, 45, 52–56, 72; in Punjab's cities, 75, 77, 78, 81, 85; in Kashmir and Shahidganj mosque agitations, 96, 98, 102–3; and *auqaf* legislation, 163–64; and *shari'at* legislation, 169, 173; and Pakistan, 190, 215, 216, 227. *See also* Deobandi *'ulama*; Barelvi *'ulama*; Ahl-i Hadis
Unionist party: formation of, 35; and agricultural tribes, 35, 36–37, 118, 127, 145, 164; "class" base, 115–18, 129, 130, 145, 152, 194, 195; and *pirs*, 59, 62, 68, 69–70, 113, 137, 213–14, 217–18, 219; and urban politics, 87–88, 93–94, 178–80; and Shahidganj mosque agitation, 110, 112; ideology as validation of local power, 120, 130, 132, 136, 145, 152, 188, 225; and political control over the market, 125, 128, 151; and mediation, 160, 163, 193, 199; party organization, 108–110, 126, 129–31, 144, 148–49; and Sikander-Jinnah pact, 174–80; and Sikhs, 155–160; World War II food policy of, 194–96; generational gap in, 191–92; internal factionalism in, 129–44, 147–48, 150, 185–87; attitude toward Jinnah, 168–69, 184–85; and Muslim Musawat Bill, 203; coalition with Congress and Akalis, 222–24
Unity conference (1937), 153
'urs, 43, 45, 56, 59; at Taunsa, 58; at Sial, 64; at Jalalpur, 69, 70, 159; at Pakpattan, 49, 64n; at Shergarh, 214n; at Ajmer, 105
Usmani, Shabbir Ahmad, 215

Waliullah, Shah, of Delhi, 53, 57
Washbrook, David, 13
Wazir Khan mosque, 82n
Wazirabad, 98
Wilson, James, 50

Young, Mackworth, 29

Zaheer, Sajjad, 196
*zail*s and *zaildar*s, 20–26, 27, 34, 50, 67, 90, 91, 93, 109, 157, 189, 199; in

Unionist organization, 109, 130, 131, 132, 134
Zakariyya, Shaikh Bahawal Haq, 40, 41, 138 n
zakat, 98
Zamindara Association, 135
Zamindara League, 125–26, 128; as organizing arm of Unionist party, 126, 152, 176–77, 193, 200–201, 218

zamindars, 21, 32, 34, 38, 108, 123, 128, 131, 170, 176, 203; as category in government recruitment, 35–36; includes large and small landholders, 152; as synonymous with agricultural tribes, 36, 116. *See also* agricultural tribes
zat, 18
Zia ul-Haq, 232

Compositor:	G & S Typesetters, Inc.
Text:	10/13 Sabon
Display:	Sabon
Printer:	Braun-Brumfield, Inc.
Binder:	Braun-Brumfield, Inc.